NOT BY A LONG SHOT

NOT BY A LONG SHOT

A Season at a
Hard-Luck Horse Track

T. D. THORNTON

PublicAffairs
New York

Copyright © 2007 by T. D. Thornton.

Published in the United States by PublicAffairs™, a member of the Perseus Books Group.

All rights reserved.

Printed in the United States of America.

No part of this book may be reproduced in any manner whatsoever without written permission except in the case of brief quotations embodied in critical articles and reviews. For information, address PublicAffairs, 250 West 57th Street, Suite 1321, New York, NY 10107. PublicAffairs books are available at special discounts for bulk purchases in the U.S. by corporations, institutions, and other organizations. For more information, please contact the Special Markets Department at the Perseus Books Group, 11 Cambridge Center, Cambridge, MA 02142, call (617) 252-5298, or e-mail special.markets@perseusbooks.com.

Book Design by Janet Tingey

Library of Congress Cataloging-in-Publication Data
Thornton, T. D.
Not by a long shot : a season at a hard luck horse track / T.D.
Thornton. —1st ed.
    p. cm.
ISBN–13: 978–1–58648–449–1 (hardcover)
ISBN–10: 1–58648–449–4 (hardcover)
1. Suffolk Downs (Boston, Mass.) 2. Horse racing—
    Massachusetts. I. Title.
SF324.35.M4T56 2006
798.4006'87446—dc22
2006030202

First Edition

10 9 8 7 6 5 4 3 2 1

CONTENTS

INTRODUCTION

SUFFOLK DOWNS is built on a dump.

In 1935, when the popularity of horse racing was just beginning to soar, the track was constructed on an oceanside landfill straddling the cities of East Boston and Revere. Quickly transformed into the showcase racecourse of the flourishing New England circuit, the onetime trash heap was nationally lauded as one of the finest horse facilities of its era. Champions such as Seabiscuit, War Admiral, Discovery, and Whirlaway graced the Massachusetts turf in its early years, and as racing prospered throughout the country in the 1940s, so did business at Suffolk Downs. During those glory days, horse racing was *the* hot Boston sports topic in regional newspapers and on city street corners. Local jockeys and trainers were worshipped as heroes. Million-dollar betting pools, or "handles," and weekday crowds upward of 20,000 were not uncommon at Suffolk Downs. The money was easy back then, and so were the smiles and handshakes.

Times changed, but racing, by and large, did not. By the late 1950s, the Thoroughbred industry's only overarching strategy was to attempt to entrench itself as a gambling monopoly, digging in its heels and remaining set in its ways. Nationally, the sport's fan base was dwindling across the country, in part because people now stayed at home to watch other sports on television—a form of broadcasting that the racing industry had emphatically decided against embracing, mistakenly fearing that the "fad" would usurp fans from its stands. In the 1960s, lotteries and sweepstakes became legal in New England, and Suffolk Downs began to feel the pinch of unprecedented competition for the public gambling dollar. Given increased entertainment options, people went elsewhere and so did their money.

The immediate geographic area surrounding Suffolk Downs was also in a constant and furious flux: By the 1970s, the famed amusement park mecca at nearby Revere Beach was razed to make way for a bland, generic condominium complex. The working-class Italian and Irish neighborhoods of adjacent Orient Heights and Beachmont were being infiltrated by outsiders, and the Puerto Ricans, Dominicans, and Cambodians who moved into the battered triple-deckers in the shadow of Logan International Airport were not exactly welcomed with open arms by longtime residents, who just a generation before had been immigrants themselves. Tensions were high. Resolve was low. Property values came down while barbed wire, vacant lots, and crime rates shot up.

The racetrack itself stumbled through a series of ownership changes, and every new operator seemed to focus more attention on the value of 190 acres of prime urban property than on the future and well-being of the sport of horse racing. By the mid-1980s, management indifference, frequent race-fixing scandals, and the overall poor quality of horseflesh had earned Suffolk Downs the well-deserved reputation as the worst-run Thoroughbred facility in the country. In 1989, the track was forced to close amid allegations of corruption and insolvency.

Shuttered for two years, Suffolk Downs was resurrected in 1992 by new owners. The local media trumpeted the rebirth of the racetrack as "the greatest comeback since Lazarus," and a new attitude was infused into the local racing scene, along with millions of dollars for much-needed infrastructural improvements. Slowly but surely, the quality of racing returned to a respectable level. The storied Massachusetts Handicap, the richest and most historic horse race in the region, was restored to its annual place of prominence on the national racing calendar. In just a few short seasons, Suffolk Downs had surprised even the most ardent of skeptics. Heading into a new century, it appeared as if the only way to go was up.

But just as meteorically as the track rose through the ranks, the reversal of fortunes came hard and fast in the late 1990s.

Too much of a good thing seemed to be to blame: With Suffolk Downs successful once again, the insiders' game known as Boston politics took over, and the track was thrust into a statutory straitjacket over regulatory issues. Just as racing had shunned emerging technology decades earlier with television, local leaders ignored the prospect of in-home wagering via telephone and the Internet to bolster business. At the same time, neighboring states adopted a progressive attitude toward other forms of wagering. Busloads of local fans flocked to Foxwoods, the newly opened casino just over the state border in Connecticut, which soon flourished into the highest-volume gaming operation on the continent. Track attendance and betting declined steadily. Portions of the property were put up for sale, razed, and rezoned for retail development.

By the turn of the twenty-first century, the Suffolk Downs racing product had atrophied to the point where a self-fulfilling cyclical degradation set in: The racing was lousy, meaning fewer people wanted to wager on it. With fewer fans betting, there was less money to put back into improving the racing. Thus, even fewer people bet. Profits were down, not to mention morale and attitude. A good number of longtime horse owners, trainers, grooms, backstretch workers, jockeys, and customers reluctantly jumped ship as long-term trouble became evident. Many packed up for greener pastures. A few escaped the racing industry entirely. Yet some defiant souls remained, holding out hope.

Those who stayed are my story.

This book is about one recent season at a single, struggling racetrack. But it also represents a crucial slice in time for a tradition-rich industry that overemphasizes its wealthy champions and flashy headline-grabbers. At low- and midlevel Thoroughbred venues all across the country, hard-luck humans and obscure horses toil in unheralded fashion so those at the pinnacle of the profession can bask in the spotlight. Without this strong foundation of minor-league support, the high end of the industry would topple under its own weight.

Suffolk Downs *is* horse racing, the real deal stripped of all pretense. Anonymous, behind-the-scenes characters at backwater tracks everywhere are the game's true stars. Only they don't realize it, and neither does their sport—yet.

CHAPTER ONE

OFF AND RUNNING

The racetrack empty, viewed from the grandstand, up the track, suggests every dream worth imagining, whether discredited, or still unknown.
　　　　　　—BRENDAN BOYD, *Racing Days*

NO OTHER SPORT is as profoundly affected by the start of a new year as Thoroughbred racing.

The impact of the date change is significant both symbolically and statistically for all horses and humans connected to the industry: January 1 is the universal birth date for every registered Thoroughbred in North America, meaning that regardless of their actual foaling date, all horses turn a year older every time the calendar year changes. For owners of both individual racehorses and the racetracks themselves, it's time to take stock of profit or loss from the previous year and formulate a plan of attack for the coming season. For bettors—the fans, the lifeblood of the sport—it's a chance to wipe the slate clean and start anew. Regardless of whether you won or lost last year, you start fresh on the first day of a new season.

New Year's Day dawns unseasonably mild and sunny, with temperatures in the balmy (for January in the Northeast) 50°F range. A rejuvenated crowd of 5,608—not high even by New England's modest standards, but decent nonetheless, considering most sporting folk are hung over at home or glued to televised bowl games, or both—is out in force to watch and wager on the nine-race program. The opener is a romp, with Ernie the King wiring the field by 13-3/4 lengths, and there are even a few cheers from the stoic diehards on the outdoors grandstand apron. In the back half of the daily double, Forest Frankie comes from way off the tailgate in a sprint to nip the speedsters in the final jump at 26 to 1. In general, the season-starting card (the race-day program) is competitive, with full fields and honest favorites, evenly split between sprints (short races less than a mile that require quick bursts of speed) and routes (at least an entire lap around the one-mile track where stamina is key). The atmosphere is upbeat, and the buzz in the plant is as close as Suffolk Downs ever comes in the dead of winter to exuding the electricity of a big racing day. The afternoon unfolds, satisfyingly filled with the perplexity of horse-race handicapping and the simple pleasures of socialization among Boston's uniquely diverse cast of racetrack characters. But just as the field reaches the starting gate for the featured eighth race, high above trackside directly overlooking the Suffolk Downs finish wire, a rumor makes its way into the press box. The news rivets the attention of everyone who hears it.

Unsubstantiated hearsay, gossip, innuendoes, and allusions buzz about Suffolk Downs as frequently as low-flying jumbo jets to and from Logan International Airport two miles south. But this is the best kind of racetrack rumor: a truly outlandish one with roots way down in the backstretch stable area. It makes its way through the grapevine of horse laborers, grooms, and hot-walkers; to exercise riders, pony girls, and part-time jockeys; to horse owners, trainers, and racing officials; over to the frontside, through the grandstand and clubhouse, up numerous stairs and across the catwalk to the rooftop judges' stands, and finally down press row from assorted hangers-on to chart-callers, camera operators, columnists, racing writers, publicists, part-time gamblers, full-time deadbeats, and finally, to me.

"You won't believe what Bobby Raymond has back in his barn," says a breathless someone who knows, or thinks he knows. "An *Aphrodite!*"

Although skeptical that the ancient Greek goddess of love, beauty, and sexual rapture is hiding out in Barn 17 at Suffolk Downs, I am acutely aware after more than a decade in this press box as a writer, and now, as the track's media relations director, that anything can happen at this joint. But in this case, I have absolutely no idea what the guy is talking about.

"You know, one of those Aphrodite things. They go both ways," the tale-teller says, raising his eyebrows. He struggles with the pronunciation of the word, sounding it out like *afro diet*.

"A *what?*" I reply, still fully without a clue.

"A horse with a female opening but also a cock and balls!" he finally blurts out. "They say Bobby couldn't figure out what sex the thing was so he took it to the medical center at Tufts and they still don't know if it's a filly or a colt!"

Of all things, a hermaphrodite horse.

Newcomers might mistake this for a sign of the impending millennial apocalypse on the first day of the new year, 2000.

Local railbirds know better: Business is indeed back to normal, and the racing season is most definitely in session at Suffolk Downs.

IN NEW ENGLAND, where racing is conducted at Suffolk Downs from January to June, the prospect of a fresh start is particularly appealing for the year 2000 because the previous year was an exceptionally tumultuous one for the regional horse-racing industry. Bad weather bombed the race meet right from the beginning, burying precious business opportunities under daunting snowdrifts and forcing the East Boston oval to play catch-up the entire rest of the year. In the spring, an upstart harness racetrack opened on the South Shore of Massachusetts some thirty-five miles away from Suffolk Downs, siphoning away a small but significant number of customers and igniting rounds of vicious infighting among the state's four competing pari-mutuel facility owners. In early August, a popular jockey was paralyzed from the chest down in a horrific racing accident at Rockingham Park in nearby New Hampshire. And while that single catastrophic incident sapped the strength and enthusiasm from everyone on the circuit, the racing season plodded along until its merciful conclusion under an entirely separate black cloud that threatened the existence of all forms of racing in Massachusetts: The House and

Senate had neglected to extend the necessary laws that permitted betting on horse and greyhound races in the Commonwealth before they adjourned in November, and the entire $622 million pari-mutuel racing industry was almost legislated out of business.

The holiday season wasn't a very festive one at Suffolk Downs, with 400 track employees, 1,600 hands-on horse workers, and thousands of others in peripheral businesses related to the racing industry holding their collective breath, not knowing if Santa was going to drop a pink slip or a legislative reprieve in their stockings in time for the new year. The Massachusetts legislature—notorious for its reputation as an insider-dominated political body; a kickback culture rife with backroom scheming and pay-for-play deal making—needlessly hemmed and hawed for weeks over the issue of whether the betting laws would be extended in a special voting session. It was only after an extremely tense eleventh-hour on-again, off-again closed-door bureaucratic rodeo that the necessary paperwork was passed into law to allow the existing framework of legislation to continue. Aside from immediate relief, the only good measure to come out of the fiasco was that a special "blue-ribbon panel" would be appointed to reexamine the state's archaic racing legislation during the coming session, with the hope that the inane year-to-year extension mandated in a framework of laws first drawn up in the 1970s would finally be laid to rest.

All across the country, racing used to have a distinct and definite season. Horses raced for six weeks here or two months there, then packed up and moved along to the next venue. Before the 1960s, winter racing was conducted almost exclusively in warm-weather climates on the West Coast and in the South. In the Northeast, fans couldn't wait for the season to start and greeted the return of racing each spring with zeal. In New England, more tracks besides Suffolk Downs and Rockingham ran back then—Lincoln Downs and Narragansett Park in Rhode Island, Green Mountain Park in Vermont, Scarborough Downs in Maine, and in the summer, up to nine other small county-fair racecourses on the "leaky roof" circuit in Massachusetts alone—but their race meets lasted for shorter durations, and the natural winter break in training served to keep horses, workers, and racing fans fit, fresh, and sound.

Inevitably, the succinct seasonal structure of horse racing began to unravel and erode. Thanks to avaricious track owners who pushed for more and more racing and revenue-hungry politicians who endorsed them by granting the dates, the bloated New England racing season was forced into year-round operation by 1970, and outfits no longer had to head south to race year-round. Over the next decade, the stress of nonstop racing forced the weaker links in the circuit out of business. Eventually, Rockingham Park (which closed when its grandstand burned in 1980 but reopened four years later) and Suffolk Downs (out of business because of overwhelming fiscal woes in 1990 and 1991) were the only two local Thoroughbred tracks left standing, and today they remain locked in a weary race against progress and each other, staggering toward an unseen finish line that could signify victory or might just mean the end of the road.

These days, a two-week break every season in late December constitutes the only scheduled respite in a mostly monotonous regional racing scene. But on this particular New Year's Day, from the backstretch shed rows and tack rooms to the depths of the cavernous grandstand, from the high flyers in the Turf Club to the shuffling old-timers squinting into their *Daily Racing Form*s in the mezzanine, the fourteen-day winter break seems surprisingly enough to have recharged everyone's batteries. The New England racing community is a curiously tight and sometimes strange family: Its ragtag members complain incessantly about each other and about the circuit's conditions. But once the racing and its people go away—whether for two weeks or two years—customers and participants alike ardently defend the local sport and can't wait for it to return to action. This is the prevailing attitude and atmosphere on opening weekend of the 2000 racing season at Suffolk Downs, exactly eight years since new owners and a fresh management team reopened and revitalized the decaying East Boston oval.

RITUAL AND ROUTINE are everything at the races. So to me, there is but one way to enter Suffolk Downs first thing in the morning—by a prescribed yet meandering route.

Although it would be difficult to mistake the 190-acre parcel of property for anything other than a horse track if viewed from above or seen on a map, Suffolk Downs at street level is perplexingly hidden from view by its own insular neighborhood along the heavily congested airport road three miles north of downtown Boston. Fenced off behind twists of barbed wire at an irregular corner where the reckless undulation of Revere Beach Parkway bisects trash-strewn Route 1A, the sixty-five-year-old facility hulks hard by the clatter of the Blue Line subway, just a few furlongs from the offshore blasts and roiling winter riptide of the Atlantic Ocean.

Approaching from the city, soon after the barrage of billboards gives way to the skinny side streets of tightly packed triple-decker apartment buildings that comprise Orient Heights, the first and most obvious racetrack landmark is the Madonna Queen National Shrine, a thirty-five-foot Virgin Mary standing unintentional but benevolent guard over Suffolk Downs and its surroundings. Erected in honor of an Italian apostle who once proclaimed, "Beside every work of charity shall stand a work of faith," the Catholic monolith stands on a lonely hillside overlooking a gargantuan industrial fuel farm. Three dozen squat, multistory tanks block any available frontage for a quarter mile along 1A, sprawling north past the border where East Boston (locally called "Eastie") meets Revere—the city that rhymes with *severe*, and the historical home of the nation's first public beach. In the domineering shadow of the oil yard, the highway landscape becomes a blurry hodgepodge of suspicious used car lots and auto body shops, surly gas stations, a greasy diner, and a smoke-filled bar called the Esquire Club that closely resembles a 1950s atomic bomb shelter.

Bending to the right onto the Route 145 parkway at the corner, where traffic lights are ruthlessly ignored and street signs have been rendered unreadable by graffiti, the beach road to the racetrack is lined on one side with functional blue-collar houses opposite a row of decaying, vacant buildings, a cramped and bare trailer park, and the occasional grocery cart from the nearby mega-mart, abandoned to rust in a culvert of thick brown reeds. Farther east but before the road meets the sea is the modest Beachmont neighborhood, dotted with storefront coffee and sandwich shops, small ethnic restaurants with names like "Luigi's," liquor stores that do brisk business in nips and individual cigarettes, and the VFW post abutting the spacious Belle Isle Marsh tidal flats, a popular hangout frequented by bird-watchers during the day and nefarious local hoodlums after nightfall.

When I turn into the track at its main stable gate, on the immediate left is the barn area, home to some 1,200 Thoroughbred racehorses and a hundred or so caretakers who live on site in subsidized dormitories and tack rooms. The shed rows—numbered, white, barracks-like one-story barns with porch-roof overhangs—are visible behind a red wooden fence topped by slanted blue chain-link, there to either keep people out or in; no one knows for sure. The access road opens into a huge windblown parking lot, a vast expanse of potholed, pock-marked asphalt so large and underused that Suffolk Downs rents parts of it to Logan Airport for overflow parking and to an offshore waste-water plant for use as a shuttle lot. Cast to one side are a handful of horse vans and hitch trailers parked at odd angles, salvaged either for parts, or, for the homeless, a place to sleep. Opposite the abandoned vehicles are steep mountains of sand, clay, and loam that will, by closing day in June, be part of the horse track itself, added to the one-mile oval in truckloaded increments to combat erosion, attrition, and runoff.

The press parking area, where I am headed, is immediately in front of the massive tan exterior of the Suffolk Downs grandstand, built for $2.4 million in 1935 and considered for years thereafter to be the largest, most modern concrete sports facility in the nation. The building is skirted with colorful flags and green-accented awnings with the sleek but simple logo of an elongated white horse in full stride, but some of the awnings show signs of neglect and hang tattered by punishing winter winds. A cleaning-crew worker, seemingly the same old Hispanic gentleman every single day, slowly pushes a wheeled garbage bin around a rectangle of pavement that decades ago used to be the fancy backyard paddock; he is herding and sweeping the refuse of yesterday's losing programs, *Racing Forms*, and discarded tickets amid a hovering flock of mournful, scavenging gulls.

Entering the unlit grandstand many hours before post time, I sense history in the shadows beneath the banks of silent television monitors and vacant, brick-walled betting stations on the sloping first-floor concourse. Unlike the close, claustrophobic layouts and generic food-court decor of newer venues, Suffolk Downs was designed to comfortably accommodate crowds upward of 40,000 on several simple, open levels in endless rows of tiered seating. Although average daily attendance has now dwindled to roughly one-tenth that figure, little has changed structurally. The impressive, exposed geometric framework makes the grandstand feel like an important public place in an old-fashioned kind of way. Boisterous, five-figure racetrack crowds turn out only once a year now, on Massachusetts Handicap Day just before the Suffolk Downs season ends in June, and as I walk toward the escalators humming obediently at the far end of the muted pavilion, I gaze up at the Hall of Champions banners high above the wagering floor, which honor MassCap winners from a bygone era: Top Row–1935; War Relic–1941; Market Wise–1943; Promised Land–1958. Names and years span the length of the grandstand ceiling, bright flags swaying gently in the darkened chamber, brief bits of racehorse glory and Suffolk Downs lore whose relevance is hazily recalled by a sadly diminishing few.

As I step off the escalator onto the second-floor mezzanine and take the first left up the racetrack ramp into section 207, I am initially blinded by the eastern sun. But as I climb the gradual concrete incline, Suffolk Downs is revealed in increments: First the black, skeletal, right-angled steelwork framing a sheer glass wall of windows; beyond that, the fallow, brown expanse of infield sprouting a bounty of scattered trees and shrubs, and within it, the hand-stenciled tote board fronting a small man-made pond fringed with a variety of winter birdlife; the perfect twin symmetry of the racecourse rails with the sleeping green turf course concentrically ensconced inside the larger and wider banked-dirt oval; the truism of the tall, striped wooden marker poles, each topped with a gold orb and solidly spaced a six-teenth of a mile apart. Then finally, the athletes themselves come into focus—scores of beautiful Thoroughbreds sweating, steaming, and prancing in the morning chill; running and gunning alone, in tandems, or in teams, flaring plumes of exhaled vapor as they skip over the rich brown racing surface. The more furious trainees hug the inside Fontana rail, cornering effortlessly, while way off on the back-stretch, nervous fillies and contented old geldings gallop parallel to the cacophonous subway rail that rattles through the salt marsh. An exer-cise girl on a patient pony schools a young, unraced prospect on a leather shank, while anonymous jockeys in blue jeans, flak jackets, and ski vests bear down astride steeds who whiz through the homestretch unencumbered by betting odds or past performances. Off in the dis-tance, the deep waters of Massachusetts Bay sparkle crisply in the early sun.

As I stand there alone in the Suffolk Downs morning amid rows of upturned orange grandstand seats, it is easy to understand why some people come to the track for a day at the races and never leave, choos-ing Thoroughbreds not so much as a way to make a living, but as a way of life.

JOSIAH HAMPSHIRE JR., consistently one of New England's lead-ing jockeys, was conspicuously absent from Suffolk Downs for the first two days of the season. While much of the racing community spent December fretting about the legislative extension that would allow the sport to continue operating in Massachusetts, Joe took off on vacation to Jamaica.

Although staying home and worrying definitely wouldn't have helped solve the situation, it is also true that Hampshire, unlike many Suffolk Downs riders, could certainly afford to enjoy some time away while waiting for the industry to correct itself. With the "purse" (or cash prize) earnings of his mounts averaging around $1.5 million over the previous few racing seasons (as a general rule, a rider's take-home pay is roughly 10 percent of those prize winnings), Hampshire was at the top of the totem pole financially compared to most New England jockeys. His riding talent was right up there among or above the best reinsmen in the region, and if Suffolk Downs went out of business tomorrow, it is a safe bet that Joe would soon be landing live entries at some other decent track elsewhere in the country. A guy with Hampshire's ability can afford to call his own shots instead of fearing unemployment when things get tough. Still, success did not always come easy for this thirty-six-year-old race-rider, and money was not the only thing that kept him in the Caribbean at the start of the season.

A native of working-class South Philadelphia and the son of a long-time paper-factory worker, Hampshire always wanted to be an athlete while growing up, but his size made it tough to compete in organized sports with bigger kids the same age. When Joe was fourteen, partly to keep him out of trouble and partly to pursue the dream he once had of being a jockey himself, his father randomly picked the name of a Thoroughbred farm out of a Kentucky phone book and called up trainer John Ward, who had stables near prestigious Keeneland Race Course. He wanted to find out how a young kid could learn to be a jockey. Ward explained that all riders work their way up from the bottom, shoveling manure and cleaning feed tubs while first learning the ins and outs of horses and the business. Shortly thereafter, the younger Hampshire found himself mowing the Lexington bluegrass, hot-walking horses (leading overheated horses in endless circles to cool them after exercise), and even, after a while, learning to ride them himself.

Hampshire liked the work and learned fast. At age eighteen, he began serving his mandatory year as an apprentice rider, winning his first lifetime race with just his third overall mount, a horse named Sir Pip at River Downs outside Cincinnati. Then at old Latonia in northern Kentucky, he won six stakes races right off the bat and was considered an up-and-coming prospect. Eager to return home to Philadelphia, Hampshire shifted his tack in late 1982 to Keystone, where he was among the leading young riders on a competitive Pennsylvania circuit. But accomplishment seemed to go to his head, and after a year back on his home turf, Hampshire hit a downslide.

Several on-the-record bouts with booze chased Joe from Philly in the mid-1980s, and he bounced around tracks on the East Coast for several seasons trying to fit in and make his mark. He ventured north to New England and was able to gain a foothold in 1988 when the local riding colony was split between simultaneous meetings at Suffolk Downs and Rockingham Park. He earned a reputation as a nervy, front-running rider who could hustle a mount out of the gate and calmly nurse a horse's speed all the way to the finish. Yet once again, fast horses and a fast lifestyle caught up with him, and Hampshire's social life began to interfere with business. After several seasons of falling in and out of favor in New England, he headed back to Philly, unsure whether this career move would boost him up back up or drop him back down to even lower professional and personal depths.

When he got home, Hampshire hooked up with Tony Black, a fellow rider and a longtime hard-partying friend. But in the time Hampshire had been away, Black had changed, trading a life on the edge for life as a leading jockey at Philadelphia Park—now he was living clean, driving a new Mercedes, and enjoying his hard-earned success. Black could not be coaxed back into his old ways. Although he saw the benefits of a sober lifestyle for his former drinking buddy, Hampshire still would not or could not accept that the same path might be right for him.

"It was a rough ten years," Joe would later recall in an August 23, 1998, *Lawrence Eagle-Tribune* interview. "Toward the end, I would basically drink all day. I'd get up. I'd drink a beer before I went to work. When I got done [exercising horses] in the morning, I'd go have a couple more, then go to the room, and get ready [to ride races]. I'd go home at night, I'd drink until I fell asleep. Some days two six-packs, some days a case. I never really remember riding drunk. But I can tell you this: I wasn't right. I wasn't 100 percent."

After six more months of uninspiring results both on and off the track, Hampshire realized he was caught in a rut. What bugged him most, he would later say, was that he *knew* he had the ability to be as good as his friend Tony if he wanted to be. Black even agreed and encouraged this line of reasoning. Something was missing, so

Hampshire finally decided to put his race-riding career on hold. The way Joe tells it, he checked himself into rehab at Riverside House, a Philadelphia detox center that specializes in alcohol abuse, figuring if he got his head back in order, his body and natural race-riding ability would follow. "I think I hit bottom more than once," he said in the *Tribune* piece. "The last bottom I can remember was, I was sitting outside of a bar, quarter 'til seven in the morning, waiting for the bar to open up, and I was actually shaking. Every time I think about picking up another drink, I think about that moment."

When he returned to the track, Hampshire acted like a new man both in the saddle and out of it. In 1993, he decided to give New England another try, now that Suffolk Downs had reopened and the racing in Boston had undergone its own rejuvenation. Joe was sharper mentally and physically, and his newfound focus showed. He started winning races, lots of them. His riding weight was steady at 114 pounds, and the throbbing, daily headaches were gone. At the time, Hampshire had a new wife and a young daughter, and credited his family for helping him hold it all together. In a 1994 Suffolk Downs press profile, he said, "Everybody all my life always told me I had talent, but that I was my own worst enemy." As for his ultimate goal in horse racing, Hampshire was quoted as saying that he'd "give his right arm" to be able to help someone the way Tony Black had helped him. Joe Hampshire rocketed up the standings, and this time he stayed there.

Hampshire has remained in New England ever since, with the brief exception of a foray to newly lucrative Delaware Park in 1997. In recent seasons, there was no question about Joe's status as a first-class rider at Suffolk Downs and Rockingham Park. The only thing in his way to undisputed top honors was local legend and perennial leading jockey Rudy Baez, a fan favorite and a deeply religious and inspirational spokesperson for the sport who had ruled the local colony for close to two decades. For six straight years since its inception, Baez had won the Outstanding Jockey Award as voted by the New England Turf Writers Association and was showing no signs of slowing down as he approached age fifty. By 1997, though, public perception and the voting shifted enough so that Joe and Rudy tied and shared the award, and many in the racing community speculated it was only a matter of time before Baez passed the torch to Hampshire as both top reinsman and inspirational leader for the region's forty or so other riders. No one suspected that Josiah Hampshire would be tested before his time the way he was in the torturous, nightmarish summer of 1999.

All season long, Hampshire and his family had been hurting from the impact of a devastating racing accident at Calder Race Course in Miami that nearly killed jockey Linda Hughes, the mother of Joe's daughter. Hughes, thirty-four, had been pitched face-first into the dirt when her mount clipped heels (a horse close behind another one can reach out and crack its front hoof against the rear hoof of the horse in front). She severely bruised her spinal cord, punctured a lung, broke ribs, and crushed her spleen. Doctors said Linda would never walk again, would be a wheelchair-bound paraplegic for life. Shortly there-after, Hampshire won the biggest race of his career, the $200,000 New Hampshire Sweepstakes at Rockingham Park, aboard a sleek New York import named Adcat. The victory was bittersweet.

Nearly two months later, on August 4, in an otherwise forgettable race for low-level horses at Rockingham Park, Hampshire was racing alongside Rudy Baez, his good friend and fierce competitor. As the field for the second race scrambled for position out of the starting gate in a six-furlong sprint (a furlong is one-eighth of a mile, and six furlongs is the most common race distance), there was the usual bumping and shouting, drifting and clipping down the backstretch, as there always is, day after day, year after year at racetracks all across the country. Hampshire, atop front-running favorite Dorato, had broken from the outside ninth post and was attempting to seize the lead while angling inward to gain a ground-saving position. Baez, aboard 11-to-1 long shot Gator Bait, was close behind the leader on the fence after breaking from the inside post but soon found himself boxed in when Newsflash and rookie jockey Dyn Panell were forced into his path by the chain-reaction jostling Hampshire had triggered. Gator Bait, a skittish and smallish horse, became intimidated by the pressure of the pack of horses to his right and the unforgiving inner rail to his left after leaving the narrow starting chute. Baez hollered out for racing room while bailing back slightly to third—a dicey situation for sure, but still, nothing too far removed from the norm in one of the few professions in the world where an ambulance is required to follow the workers during the course of their daily duties.

Fellow riders always give their brethren a break when it comes to safety, but such decisions are split-second, instinctive by nature, and far easier to scrutinize after the fact. Jockeys are schooled to be inherently protective of each other, but realistically, in the heat of battle, they also learn never to allow a top rider a racing edge if danger does not appear imminent. Neither Hampshire nor the other riders seeking the lead were going to give Baez a tactical advantage if they had him pinned down on the rail where the top jock would have to drop back to last and later circle the field. The speeding pack of horseflesh imperceptibly shifted and tightened around the nervous Gator Bait instead of affording a reasonable safety buffer. At the same time, the midgroup runners—Phosphorite, Trackataro Pete, and Your First—had all hit full stride, closing the gap on the heels of the cagey veteran rather than allowing Baez some sort of seam to maneuver or steady away from the close quarters. With the inside rail rushing by on his immediate left, an ever-threatening pair of horses leaning inward from the direct right, and a solid equine wall flush behind him, Rudy suddenly found himself in a predicament that had gone from perfunctory to perilous in the matter of a heartbeat, and something had to give.

Faster than anyone could react to it, Baez and his animal went down—hard, without warning, and in a tangle of legs. Rudy was catapulted forward, headfirst into the fertile black loam of the Rockingham Park backstretch, while the remainder of the fight-or-flight pack of Thoroughbreds scattered, veering wildly to the side or jumping to avoid the carnage. The impact was so vicious and clean that it snapped Baez's neck instantaneously, leaving the jockey's lithe, strong body crumpled and broken in the dirt. Hampshire, up close, an arm's length away and in full horror, could only watch. Racing at thirty-five miles per hour, there was nothing he could do to help. Joe sped away unobstructed, winning the race wire to wire. Another hollow victory.

Airlifted to Massachusetts General Hospital in Boston, Baez underwent immediate surgery to stabilize his spine. Two metal rods were inserted to support his severed T-5 vertebra. He remained in a coma for ten days while the New England racing community held vigil. When he awoke, doctors explained that he had a 1 percent chance of ever walking again. Paralyzed from the chest down, the champion race-rider was told he would spend the rest of his life in a wheelchair.

The Rockingham stewards reviewed the race tapes and publicly declared the tragedy an accident, a freakish occurrence with no obvious cause and no one to blame. Track management refused to release accident footage to the press and strongly suggested that other tracks such as Suffolk Downs destroy any videotaped copies of the race broadcast. But the official Equibase race chart, the industry-standard statistical document published on-line and in *Daily Racing Form* recording the particulars of each race, survived to list seventeen separate notations of horses in that ill-fated nine-horse race who *angled in, came over, bumped, steadied, clipped heels,* or were otherwise *in tight, forced in, squeezed back,* or *steadied sharply.* The comments, if nothing else, indicate that the contest was a very roughly ridden affair. Little mention of this fact was made by the judges in their non-ruling, but realistically, hanging the blame on any one jockey or even suspending a rider for a week or ten days would hardly undo the awful event or allow Rudy Baez ever to regain the use of his lower extremities.

Joe Hampshire, however, took this second tragedy of the season extremely personally. He cried openly on television cameras, organized moments of silence and racetrack prayer vigils for Rudy, and spoke very publicly on behalf of the riding colony, talking candidly about the inherent risks of the game, how the show must go on for the healing to begin. The remaining six weeks of the Rockingham racing season wound down in bleak, passionless fashion. There were perceptible changes in attitude and performance. Veteran jockeys—at least those who could afford to—began begging off horses they knew to be sore or unsound and would opt not to ride at all if it rained and the racetrack became wet and possibly unsafe. Thrilling finishes—the highlight-film type where a jockey guns a horse up the rail or weaves through an impenetrable pack of Thoroughbreds to win at the last jump—became fewer and farther between. The already sparse crowds in the Rockingham Park grandstand thinned, and even the two-dollar regulars who shouted from the same spots on the rail every day became a little less acerbic with their catcalls and post-race insults to the jockeys. The overall feeling was that everybody involved just wanted to leave the scene of the accident as soon as possible.

Articulate and earnest in a somber, blue-collar way, Hampshire often talked of the Rockingham accident in general terms, speaking up on behalf of all the jockeys, putting words to the feelings of helplessness and sorrow they all shared. But what Joe did *not* say in specifics about the incident was also revealing: His horse was in the clear and directly outside of the one ridden by Rudy Baez on that fateful August afternoon, and it is very likely that only those two riders know the exact and lucid circumstances of what happened in the microseconds before the spill. To date, Hampshire has never publicly offered a detailed, step-by-step account of the incident. Baez, tight-lipped and steely-eyed, says he recalls everything but will only refer to "the riders" or "the guys" when pressed for his version of who or what specifically caused the crowding leading up to his fall. This mutual silence leaves many questions: Were Joe Hampshire's tactics overly aggressive? Was he too concerned with carrying out the entirely legal but fine-lined strategy of intimidation to be aware of the danger of the situation? Should he have backed off? Or—just as fairly—should highly skilled but stubborn Rudy Baez have known better than to run up into such a tight pocket on the rail? In any case, when racing returned to Boston in late September, Joe by default had inherited the role of locker-room leader, although not in a manner he ever wanted.

Hampshire was not his usual easy-going self and seemed distracted through the autumn race meet. He was quick to comment, even quicker to criticize. His brow seemed permanently furrowed, and the corners of his handsome, usually smiling mouth now turned downward. From June to September, in a little less than twelve weeks since the last Suffolk Downs season, Joe's dark, wavy hair had begun to blanch noticeably gray.

On January 3, Hampshire breezes into the Suffolk Downs jockeys' room looking tanned, refreshed, and fit. He had become quite selective about his mounts over the past five months, insisting that his agent book horses of quality rather than quantity. Even after missing the first several days of the racing season, Hampshire could probably have had a mount in each of the nine races on today's program if he chose to. But instead he is opting for only three: A logical contender for Ardboe Stable, the well-connected racing outfit owned by Patricia Moseley, chairwoman of Suffolk Downs; and a pair of steeds from the power-house barn of leading trainer Ron Dandy, for whom Hampshire almost always rides first call. Joe finishes second in the sixth race with Perfect Storm and an off-the-board yet not badly beaten sixth with Ride 'em Rags in the eighth event. But in the nightcap he figures to make amends with Hitched, and so does the betting public, sending the horse postward as the even-money favorite for the final race of the day. Given his dominant reputation, it is the mere presence of the circuit's top jock in the saddle, and not the merits of his mount, that heavily swings the wagering in Hitched's direction.

Breaking from the disadvantageous outside post in a field of nine for a mile race, Hampshire gets off to a slow start in the two-turn race when Hitched breaks with her head turned sideways. Dead last leaving the starting gate and losing precious ground around the clubhouse turn, Joe guides the racemare along patiently, not panicking, picking off horses one by one down the backstretch, settling into stride. He makes his move on the far turn and lets his horse out a notch turning for home, then with a quick flick of his wrists he opens the equine throttle all the way, timing the acceleration perfectly. Under a full-out drive, Hitched blows by the pacesetters and pours it on late, winning by an easy 7-1/2 lengths at the finish wire.

The commanding margin of victory makes it seem as if Joe did nothing, as if he was simply a passenger along for the ride.

WITHIN THE CIRCUSLIKE CONFINES of the horse-betting world, to be known as a racetrack degenerate among one's press-box peers is a deferential badge of respect, only slightly tinged with sarcasm. It's a brusque, backhanded term of endearment that defies quantification, with absolutely nothing to do with how much one wagers or how often one wins. Degenerates stay up way too late at night poring over dog-eared *Daily Racing Forms*; can recite long-forgotten historical data about obscure horses and defunct tracks that even hard-core fans could care less about; mark the passage of time singularly by landmark racing events; and refuse to attend Saturday weddings and family functions that coincide with the sport's important dates like the Triple Crown series in the spring (the Kentucky Derby, Preakness Stakes, and Belmont Stakes) or the autumn Breeders' Cup Championships. Someone else at the racetrack has to call you a degenerate first before you can go about proclaiming yourself one, and I vividly recall the first time a crotchety old turf writer bestowed the title upon me during my rookie season in the press box: "You drove 150 miles in a fucking rainstorm on your day off to bet cheap speed at Great Barrington Fair? Kid, there's no turning back—you are one sick racetrack degenerate."

For me, the path to degeneracy was a product of both nature and nurture. My dad liked to gamble and dabbled in training horses, and my family happened to live in a racetrack town. When I was growing up in the 1970s, Salem, New Hampshire, had two claims to fame: the Yankee Cannonball roller coaster at Canobie Lake Park and the horse races at Rockingham Park. The action at the racetrack was the greater lure for me, even at a young age. I can remember being mesmerized by the flashing lights and hypnotic *click-click* of the massive, old-fashioned mechanical odds board; collecting fistfuls of distinctively printed, hand-cut betting tickets from the sea of losing slips on the grandstand floor, and being allowed two-buck bets on the sly from my grandmother, based solely on names I picked out of the program. But most of all I recall being about five or six years old and watching my father, Paul Thornton—tight-lipped with his serious face on—saddling racehorses from the other side of the fence at the Rockingham paddock (children were not permitted in the saddling enclosure) just before the visceral, throaty surge of the crowd during a wild, stampeding stretch drive. I didn't have it all figured out, but I *knew* I wanted to end up on the other side of that damn fence where the horses and jockeys were, the epicenter of action.

The summer I was twelve, I woke up one morning to ceaseless sirens and a haze of oily smoke. Rockingham Park had erupted into flames shortly after dawn, and although the devastating fire was contained to the racetrack, it might as well have been the entire soul of Salem set ablaze. The charred, twisted skeleton of the seventy-four-year-old grandstand symbolized the end of an era for many locals, including my dad, who decided to give up his modest stable rather than make the daily trek to East Boston to train and race at Suffolk Downs. There was talk of razing the entire chunk of property to build a grand hotel/sports arena/retail sales complex, but after a while the plans were abandoned and only the horse track returned. A modern, scaled-down version of the historic plant reopened in 1984, and the christening of the new Rock just happened to coincide with the year I got my first driver's license. You were supposed to be eighteen to bet, but as long as you walked to the windows with confidence and pretended to know what you were doing, no one ever checked.

Racetrackers are creatures of habit, and I soon had my own horse-playing rituals. On weekdays, high school would get out at 2:30 PM, and I'd sneak over to Rockingham in time for the seventh race, when the admission gates were left open for anyone who wanted to catch the last few races for free. The track had installed a new lighting system, so on Fridays and Saturdays the horses now ran at night, and just about every weekend was the same: Slam a few beers in my 1978 Granada in the dark of the parking lot, hop the side fence when the fat security guard wasn't paying attention, pick up a discarded program off the floor, then fish out the remains of someone else's *Racing Form* from the trash. The programs and *Form*s were covered in strange pen marks and hieroglyphics, remnants of another horseplayer's strategy gone bad. Aside from learning the basics about picking winners, I became intrigued by the nuances of turning a profit by playing against overbet favorites, immersing myself in the intricate challenge of hand-icapping not just horses but the betting public *itself* in order to discern how herd mentality affected the fluctuating odds. That summer

I bought my first handicapping book, Paul Ader's *How to Make a Million at the Track*. I didn't, but kept going anyway.

In 1986, I went off to college. I loved reading and writing, and soon began to harbor a wild fantasy about how great it would be if I could someday con some employer into actually paying me to attend the races and write about them. I majored in English, but my minor might as well have been exotic betting strategies. The University of New Hampshire was only forty-five miles north of the Rock, so I was endlessly borrowing cars or imploring fraternity brothers to cut classes to drive down to the races with me. After writing for the school newspaper, I landed a series of journalism internships and soon found myself reporting from the New Hampshire bureau of the *Boston Globe*. In the spring of 1990, two weeks before I graduated, I talked an editor into letting me do a feature piece about struggling low-level trainers at Rockingham Park, selling him on the juxtaposition of the high-profile notion of the horse industry versus what *really* goes on at a racetrack. The very same day that Unbridled won the prestigious Kentucky Derby at Churchill Downs in front of 128,257 fans and millions more on national television, I was sitting under a lonesome, leaky shed row on the muddy Rockingham Park backstretch, wearing a shiny new press pass around my neck, interviewing a down-on-his-luck horseman about his 45-to-1 no-hoper named More Fog. I might as well have been in heaven.

I stuck on through that summer as a freelancer with the *Globe* before landing my first full-time job as a reporter with the *Haverhill Gazette* in the northeast corner of Massachusetts. The hours were lousy, the pay worse, and my beat consisted of a steady diet of police-blotter roundups, school-board meetings and community ham-and-bean suppers—staples of small-town journalism, but assignments that were utterly mindless to a budding racetrack degenerate. But since the town meetings were mostly at night and I had to be in the newsroom by six each morning, that meant afternoons off, enabling me to become an everyday regular at Rockingham. One day at the track, barely four months into my job, an article in *American Turf Monthly* caught my eye: Noted racing writer Steven Crist was leaving the *New*

York Times to launch a brand-new daily racing newspaper, and the start-up was seeking staffers. I immediately fired off a letter of application, telling (or practically begging) the editors that I'd relocate to any track in the country just to break in. Yet it happened that the fledgling paper was looking for a New England columnist and handicapper, and within a month I began my dream job as a racetrack reporter in the Rock press box. At twenty-three, I was the youngest staffer on the industry's bold and brash new broadsheet, the *Racing Times*.

The country's racing journalism had been dominated for close to 100 years by a single entity, *Daily Racing Form*. By 1991, the paper had a monopoly on the industry's core statistical data, but its news section was a tired insiders' organ that rarely featured objective content or examined controversial issues. On the occasional instance that mildly critical commentary offended some racetrack management bigwig, all the executive had to do was pick up the phone and call one of the old-boy editors at the *Form* to have the writer transferred off the beat or fired. Yet the publication made a mint because fans bought it exclusively for its "past performances"—the statistical section of in-depth betting info on every horse. Rival racing papers had tried to dethrone the *Form* before, but had failed because they concentrated solely on trying to match the *Form*'s massive statistical resources. The *Racing Times* aimed to be different, though, and this was its competitive advantage: Crist was a Harvard-educated journalist and horseplayer. He had more than a hunch that racetrack customers would welcome modern, high-end data geared to sophisticated handicappers, and the founding editor envisioned delivering that data alongside an edgy, literate news presentation that gave a voice to the previously neglected concerns of the betting public. Backed by an eccentric British media magnate, Crist hired the most talented degenerates he could find and encouraged his *Times* staffers to be as creative and journalistically aggressive as possible. "Either you're a paper of substance," Crist openly challenged the rival publication in a series of slick television commercials promoting his new venture, "or you're just a *Form*."

Fresh out of journalism school and eager to make a mark, I fully embraced this us-versus-them mentality, and it really did feel like the

Times was breaking new ground. A wise old newsroom editor once told me that if everyone on your beat liked you as a reporter, then you probably weren't doing your job properly. So I dug deeply and hit hard in my stories, and sure enough, within a week of the paper's launch in New England, I had already been pulled aside by both the Rockingham racing secretary and the track's publicity director and told in no uncertain terms that assertive reporting wasn't the way the news was supposed to be covered in their little corner of the Thoroughbred universe. Yet the unflinching stance of the paper was a hit among local horseplayers, with the on-track editions of the *Times* often selling out and overall New England sales steadily eating into the *Form*'s dominant share of the market. Fans who recognized me from the photo alongside my byline began to stop me in the grandstand, praising the fresh perspectives of the paper, while veteran horsemen grabbed me as I made the rounds on the backstretch to tell me that the *Racing Times* was the first industry entity to stick up for the little guy in the game. Through it all, I churned out blunt, insightful betting analysis and provocative columns about racehorse welfare, jockeys' safety, and fraud in the horsemen's union elections. Yet it wasn't until my tenth month of writing that I finally had my big breakthrough—a long-shot journalistic windfall, thanks to a highly unlikely source.

December 2, 1991, was a Monday, and Mondays were the day my weekly column ran. Over the weekend I had penned a piece about Rockingham's remarkably inept inability to foresee the need for specialized legislation that would allow the track to "simulcast" (to broadcast simultaneously and take bets on) televised races from other tracks across the country. I had also filed a second article that detailed the arrest of the track president's son, who had been caught trafficking narcotics while employed as the Rock's director of valet parking (state police nailed him for operating a drive-though cocaine operation outside the main admissions gate). That particular weekend had been especially slow for news in the racing industry, so both pieces got prominent play in the *Times*, with the drug bust leading Monday's front page. Immediately upon arriving to work, I was summoned to the office of Rockingham general manager Ed Callahan, who, in a five-minute tirade, essentially threw three things: (1) a temper tantrum, (2) copies of that day's *Racing Times*, (3) me out of the Rockingham Park press box.

I played it cool but was a bit shaken. Callahan told me I could continue to work out of the track's grandstand as a paying customer, but that my access to the press box and stable area was cut off because of my "bullshit." The first thing I had to do was call Steve Crist, and I didn't really know how all of this was going to go over with my boss. The way I saw it, the *Times* was suddenly out of a reporter in one of its fastest-growing markets. But by the time I got to the press box to clear out my belongings, Crist had already called me, and it was a relief to hear him upbeat and jovial. Buy yourself the best seat in the house, he told me, continue to do what you've been doing, and keep up the good work. Steve was already crafting a press release to be sent out to the national news media about Rockingham's attempts to restrict freedom of speech and a reporter's right to fair and accurate commentary. Within an hour, working from a table in the clubhouse, I had already fielded interview requests from the Associated Press, both Boston dailies, a number of New York newspapers, the *Los Angeles Times*, and several Thoroughbred trade magazines. Then I expensed a big lunch, bet the daily double, ordered myself a cocktail, and settled in to savor my curious new role as flag-carrying martyr for the *Racing Times*'s journalistic cause.

The uproar was reported on sports pages nationwide the next day, and Rockingham management only succeeded in drawing more unwanted attention to the two articles it wished had never been published. Callahan, pressed to explain his side of the issue, simply quoted things he didn't like from my column. When pressed further in one interview for the reason he didn't agree with what was written, Ed could only sputter, "He has a sarcastic flair." The controversy simmered for several weeks, then died down over the holidays. In January, the New England circuit moved south to newly reopened Suffolk

Downs. The hard-hitting reporting continued and I enjoyed the change of scenery, blissfully unaware that the meteorically successful *Racing Times* had less than a month to live.

Shortly before the Rockingham brouhaha, Robert Maxwell, the oddball British media mogul who had bankrolled the *Times*, went missing at sea off the coast of Spain in what was at first believed to be a boating accident. But as investigators pored over his finances, they soon uncovered a trail of corporate malfeasance and missing pension funds, and speculation became rife that Maxwell had jumped—not fallen—from his yacht in an act of suicide. Forced to pay down the debts, authorities ordered the wholesale liquidation of his properties, including the subsidiary that owned the *Racing Times*. Rumors were flying around our New York newsroom about whether we'd be bought out by a savior or simply sold off to the highest bidder. Late on the afternoon of February 6, 1992, I was having trouble connecting remotely to the computer server to file my stories from East Boston. When I called down to the news desk to find out what the problem was, the copy chief was crying, and she told me not to bother: The *Times* had been the victim of a hostile takeover by the rival *Form*, which had paid big money to buy out our assets and shut down the paper.

For the second time in eight weeks, I set about the grim task of cleaning out my desk in a racetrack press box. *Party's over*, I thought, almost one year to the date from which I escaped the monotony of small-town journalism. Out of work and facing the bleak prospect of having to go back to reporting on school-board meetings, I said my good-byes to the assembled degenerates and headed out over the long, high catwalk that connects the Suffolk Downs press office to the grandstand. It was there that I ran into the track's recently hired executive vice president of racing, Lou Raffetto Jr., who listened to my story about the shutdown. Grasping at straws, I babbled something about how if the track ever needed media help, Lou should give me a call. Raffetto politely said he'd keep me in mind and we parted ways, he in the direction of the press box, me away from it, probably for good.

Much to my surprise, Raffetto did call me the very next afternoon. Suffolk Downs was embarking on a new era of simulcasting its races to betting outlets all around the country, and would I be interested in providing between-race handicapping commentary as the track's first-ever on-camera race reporter? Not bothering to contain my enthusiasm, I accepted at once, eager to get back on track after twenty-four hours of unemployment.

I had never appeared on television before, but the gig was fun, the in-house crew easy to work with. Over the course of the next several seasons, I gradually picked up additional duties—compiling the track's media guide, hosting and producing a weekly radio show, calling races as the backup play-by-play announcer—while becoming educated in the operations side of the industry the way executives do at minor-league tracks everywhere, by wearing many different hats. Because he now had a son involved in the sport, my dad even bought a few horses and returned to training after a fifteen-year hiatus. In 1998, after six years with Suffolk Downs, I was promoted to media relations director. My vantage point for this 2000 racing season is an office high above trackside, directly above the finish wire, and I still consider it a privilege to actually get paid to attend the races.

But from a purely nostalgic perspective, it's not quite the heady blast that hopping the fence was back in the formative years of my racetrack degeneracy, at least not in that mildly illicit, indulgently romantic, Runyonesque racetrack sort of way . . .

INCIDENTS OF ANIMALS—including humans—born with a combination of both sex organs are by no means common, but they do occur in many species. The reasons are not clear, but the prevailing theory cites genetic errors in cell division during early embryonic development. Anecdotal research has further shown that when the condition occurs in equines, the result is almost always overly aggressive and dangerously studdish behavior, presumably because the horse is sending mixed signals to itself about its sexuality and carnal urges.

I run into Bobby Raymond, the man with the alleged Aphrodite on

25

his hands, in the paddock before the second race, on yet another unseasonably warm January afternoon. A longtime New England trainer with a murky past and a short fuse, the fifty-two-year-old Raymond has a reputation for not being very receptive to members of the media. For example, Gator Bait, the horse Rudy Baez fell from, was one of Raymond's runners, and he was vehemently upset when his name as the trainer of record was mentioned as a matter of basic reporting in news accounts about the accident. Ten days ago, Raymond was the focus of an investigative newspaper article that chronicled the tragic death of one of his horses, who went from being a graded-stakes star to an overraced also-ran before suffering a very public and fatal injury in the Suffolk Downs homestretch. If Raymond could be considered reclusive before, he was downright unapproachable now, and it is with both great curiosity and trepidation that I stop to ask him about his supposed hermaphrodite horse.

"Oh yeah, you should see this thing," he says, surprisingly affable and obviously amused by the lecherous notoriety of his odd animal. "But you can't. Because I got rid of him. This fucking freak was going to hurt someone, real soon and real bad."

Raymond explains that the two-year-old Thoroughbred, named Casino Queen, was born with a vaginal opening, a pair of testicles just now starting to descend from its body, and a bulbous, elongated clitoral sheath that at first was thought to be a penis. The foal's mother died shortly after giving birth, and the woman who bred and owns the horse had bottle-fed the weanling until it was strong enough to eat on its own. The young Thoroughbred seemed normal until it began to go through equine adolescence, but once it began figuring out the nature of its body, the yearling began to go, in Raymond's words, berserk.

"I've seen three of 'em in my life," he tells me. "One was when I was a kid in Rhode Island on a farm. Another was up at Finger Lakes twenty years ago. The thing grabbed [jockey] Jill Jellison right off its back with its teeth, threw her to the ground and started attacking her with its hooves while spraying all over the place. And then this one here that I had. Believe me, this one was the worst."

The owner had sent Casino Queen to Raymond to be broken for training, hoping hostility could be channeled into the ability to win horse races. Right away he noticed obvious behavioral problems but was still able to school the juvenile into galloping a few times around the track during morning training sessions. But by late December, the very first day the hermaphrodite started feeling its sex and getting into heat, it launched into an unprecedented fit of ferocity and tried to crush its exercise rider, an experienced handler whom Raymond had specifically chosen for his work with troubled horses.

"She—he, whatever—didn't know what he or she was," Raymond tells me. "All I knew was that she was going to kill someone if I kept her around here. We took her—him—over to Tufts and the horse lasted fifteen minutes there. They didn't want anything to do with it. They gave me a letter saying they wouldn't be responsible for gelding it. I've got the letter out in my car. They typed up the letter before they typed out the bill."

Veterinarians at the noted Tufts University equine research clinic told Raymond that removing the horse's testicles by gelding the animal was its best chance to lead a more docile life. But at $5,000, the operation was prohibitively expensive, likely to be complicated, and the doctors would offer no guarantee for success. Their recommendation was to euthanize the animal for the sake of its own safety and the safety of others.

Instead, too attached to her odd animal, the owner took Casino Queen back home to her farm in rural Massachusetts, abandoning hopes of a racing career. When I ask, Raymond refuses to reveal the woman's name or the location of her farm. "She's got the thing out in a paddock in the middle of the woods somewhere is all I can tell you," he says. "I told the woman the horse would be okay alone out there."

Narrowing his eyes, Raymond then breaks into a disturbing grin. "But if some kid ever comes up alongside the fence to pet it, he's dead."

———

THERE IS A HIERARCHY of Thoroughbred racetracks, which currently number around 125 or so in North America. The premier race meets—Keeneland and Churchill Downs in the spring for the Kentucky Derby; historic Saratoga just south of the Adirondacks for the summer; the autumn championships at Belmont Park in New York City; and winters at Gulfstream Park in Florida—are the ones that lure the fastest and most competitive horses, not to mention the swanky high rollers who bankroll them. Then come the top-notch metropolitan tracks: Arlington Park in Chicago, Calder Race Course in Miami, and Hollywood and Santa Anita near Los Angeles are among fifteen or so that offer solid, quality racing. Next in the pecking order are the "minor leagues" of racing, although this line of demarcation is very much unofficial and arbitrary: Philadelphia Park, Tampa Bay Downs, Lone Star Park in Texas, Thistledown in Cleveland, Hoosier Park in Indiana, and yes, Suffolk Downs in East Boston all represent varying degrees of midlevel racing, and about sixty other tracks fit a similar description. Lowest and most laid back on the totem pole are the dozens of scattered county fairs and one- or two-day informal "mixed meet" races that accompany rodeos and Quarter horse trials out west.

Always, the focus of the sport is on the top-tier courses and highest-profile races. But the smaller, more modest tracks make up the bulk of all Thoroughbred racing on the continent, and these lower-caste tracks are the most crucial in the chain. They serve as a necessary proving ground for promising young jockeys and trainers on their way up and provide useful levels of competition for the tens of thousands of Thoroughbreds foaled every year who, no matter how hard they try, just can't keep pace with the most talented steeds at the apex of the game. Despite their importance, these low- and midlevel tracks also happen to be the ones disappearing fastest: Detroit Race Course, Hialeah Park in Florida, Sportsman's Park in Illinois, Garden State Park in New Jersey, and Longacres near Seattle are all examples of once-proud tracks that have recently closed because of increased competition for the gambling dollar or because their real estate is too valuable to be used for horse races. Today, many financially endangered horse tracks exist precariously on a season-to-season basis, and the two remaining Thoroughbred venues in New England in 2000—Suffolk Downs and Rockingham Park—are the unfortunate poster children for tracks with historic value that just might slide off the grid next.

New England has always been horse-centric, with steeds of all kinds supplying labor, transportation, and pleasure. In colonial times, Rhode Island was the equine center of the New World, home of the first legal racecourse in the region. Lawful or not, racing immediately flourished throughout the Puritan world, thanks to the proliferation of horses and the early settlers' inherent zeal for a good gamble. In 1674, the bayside village of Plymouth, where the pilgrims landed the *Mayflower*, banned the popular but dangerous pastime of racing on public streets, making it a crime punishable by a fine, a stint in the stockades, seizure of one's horse, or all three. Other Yankee towns followed with similar measures, but bans against racing only whetted the public's appetite for forbidden pleasure. In 1775, Paul Revere rode a Narragansett Pacer into history to warn Bostonians that the British were coming (the city where half of Suffolk Downs now stands is named in his honor), and by the early nineteenth century almost every local community boasted some sort of loosely organized race meet where bets would be exchanged between rival horse owners and small, mostly elite, circles of partisans. By the end of the 1800s, racing had gained popular acceptance and numerous small Thoroughbred and trotting grandstands become fixtures on the pastoral New England landscape. But the dawn of the new century brought a resurgence in social morality and a backlash against gambling that closed nearly 200 tracks nationwide. Boston, too, was swept up in the national trend toward temperance, and the "vice" of racing was stomped out by an ardent few in the alleged best interest of many.

After World War I, racing began to rebound. In Massachusetts, crowds numbering in the tens of thousands flocked to Raceland, a private estate twenty-five miles west of Boston that showcased steeplechase events and betting via on-track bookmakers. Technically, gambling was still illegal, but the Roaring Twenties crowd wasn't collectively caught up in rules, and bookies got around the laws by either crafting creative schemes to veil the true nature of their business (i.e., sweepstakes "drawings" that just so happened to reward those who bought chances on the winning horse) or by employing the time-honored and highly effective Boston tradition of unabashed bribery of public officials. But just when things were going well, the Great Depression rocked the country. Fashionable folks got bounced from betting lines straight into unemployment lines. By 1933, states were so desperate for revenue that even risking disrepute seemed alluring, and governments began examining ways to profit from such "sins" as liquor, tobacco, and gambling.

The method that gained acceptance in the United States was horse-race wagering through pari-mutuels, a French term that means "betting among ourselves." A mechanical system collects all bets and pools them centrally, allowing the volume of money wagered on each horse to dictate that horse's relative odds and payouts. Since the arbitrary practice of allowing bookmakers to set their own odds was broadly assumed by public officials to be criminally dangerous (not to mention financially unproductive for states), stepping forward to eradicate bookmakers in the name of virtue was a convenient way for government entities to appear to fight the good fight while getting an exclusive cut on the action. Cloaked in the name of morality, it was plain old government need and greed that spurned the most explosive period of legalized gambling growth in the United States.

Although pari-mutuel betting was—and still is—a fair practice, the added security and oversight comes at a cost to the public in the form of surcharges on the betting handle, and that "takeout" is how tracks and states make money. From its infancy to this very day, the pari-mutuel process has worked like this: The public puts up the gambling money. The track holds the wagers and puts on the racing show. The state hovers in the background, regulating the system to ensure everything is on the level. After each race, the track extracts the lawful takeout from the betting pool—sort of like a stockbroker's fee for facilitating the transaction—then divides it with the state and returns the remaining money to those who correctly wagered on the winning combinations. Because the odds are set strictly by the proportion of money that people wager on each horse, neither the track nor the state has a stake in the outcome of the race, earning instead a fixed commission on the overall volume (bookmakers, on the other hand, set their own odds and can either overextend themselves into insolvency or make a financial killing by how well they handicap both the horses and their customers).

A typical takeout structure calls for 80 cents on the dollar to be returned to bettors, with 17 percent reverting to the racetrack and 3 percent going to the state. Although it might seem as if track operators make out rather handsomely on this arrangement, it is important to note that a huge chunk of that money must first pay for purses, operational costs, upkeep, payroll, maintenance, licensing fees, and property taxes. What's left over for a racetrack, even in a good year, looks a lot closer to the state's single-digit slice.

For most of the twentieth century, Massachusetts has had a strange knee-jerk relationship with New Hampshire, its smaller but more politically powerful neighbor to the north. Fervently opposed to broad-based income or sales taxes, the Granite State has always had to scramble for funding, and in 1933 New Hampshire became one of the first four states (along with California, Michigan, and Ohio) to legalize pari-mutuel betting. After two seasons of watching trainloads of fans rush their money over the state line to bet at Rockingham Park in the tiny border town of Salem, the state of Massachusetts countered with legal horse racing of its own, granting a license to operate a Boston track to Eastern Racing Association. Two million dollars and two months later, a trendy, well-built racecourse rose from forsaken marshland that had been used as a garbage dump out by the train tracks north of city limits. On July 10, 1935, a horse named Eddie Wrack crossed the finish line first to the cheers of an estimated throng of 35,000, and Thoroughbred racing was born at Suffolk Downs.

If you were into sports, fashion, and a fast crowd during the late 1930s and 1940s, then Suffolk Downs was the place to see and be seen in Boston. Racing for no more than sixty dates at a stretch, mostly in the late spring and summer, the horses at the East Boston oval soon became the dominant local pastime. Newspapers devoted scores of columnists and handicappers to the racing beat, and afternoon editions were hawked on city sidewalks not on the strength of breaking news but by updated race results from Suffolk Downs. On-track betting was brisk, but playing the ponies was so popular that anyone—from grandmothers to big-shot gamblers—could get a bet down in any Boston neighborhood just by calling out to the street-corner bookie. Successful jockeys and horse trainers dressed to the nines, drove expensive automobiles, fought off groupies, and were treated to sumptuous dinners and nightclub cocktails by strangers who recognized them in a crowd. The quality of horseflesh rivaled the racing anywhere in the land, and almost every single sepia-toned photograph from this era shows the Suffolk Downs grandstand packed from end to end, tens of thousands of heads all topped with stylish ladies' hats, rakish fedoras, and servicemen's caps. Even during leaner years, when conflict flared in Europe, Suffolk Downs continued to be a major player, donating $635,864 to the National War Fund in August 1943, a sum the track touted as the single-largest contribution by any sports venue in support of the victory effort.

Suffolk Downs changed hands in 1944, when the Eastern stock was bought out by Boston broker Gordon Hanlon, then was sold again a year later to a group called Aldred Investment Trust. The 1945 meet was the first to generate an average daily handle of $1 million, and although that mark would be eclipsed in years to come, the season's staggering *average* daily attendance of 18,883 has yet to be equaled. Despite—or perhaps because of—its guaranteed profitability, the track would switch owners for the third time in as many years, with Judge John C. Pappas heading a group of successful bidders to purchase Suffolk Downs at a public auction in 1946.

In the 1950s, the popularity of racing began to backslide a bit, although the effects were not really noticed for years to come. The game had enjoyed enormous success for close to two decades straight, and the blessing of profits coming so easily was a hidden curse, because the industry had never really had to work hard to earn its niche. Television was the hot new technology, and when network executives reached out to the most popular sport in the country, the

Thoroughbred industry declined the invitation to broadcast races, fearing that widespread distribution of the product to the home would keep fans from coming out to the track. Repeatedly rebuffed, programmers turned to baseball, football, and basketball to see if those sports could benefit from added exposure. The leagues agreed wholeheartedly, investing in television as a long-term tool. Business hardly seemed to suffer immediately from this decision—for example, on Memorial Day of 1960, players pumped a whopping $2,175,836 through the Suffolk Downs mutuel windows, establishing an on-track betting record that still stands—but twenty years later, racing was limping back to broadcasters with late and lame offers to pay the sport's way back onto the airwaves, by that time impenetrably dominated by lucrative Major League Baseball, NFL, and NBA programming.

In 1964, two significant changes occurred on the New England gambling scene: On March 1, after eighteen years of continuous ownership by the Pappas group, Suffolk Downs was purchased by David Haber, a local businessman repeatedly described in archived press releases as "energetic." Lively or not, that news would be all but forgotten eleven days later when New Hampshire once again put its Live Free or Die state motto where its revenue-hungry mouth was, becoming the first state in the nation to begin selling lottery tickets. Average handle and attendance dipped at Suffolk Downs in each of the next three seasons, and although it is inconclusive to say the New Hampshire Sweepstakes was directly to blame for the tailspin, it was obvious by the middle of the decade that both the racetrack and the Commonwealth would have to begin giving serious thought to how to remain competitive in the rapidly escalating struggle for gambling dollars. Fighting the country's only legalized lottery thirty-five miles away was arduous enough. But because the political power in the Granite State was so heavily concentrated in a single, key New Hampshire citizen who also happened to own Rockingham Park, Massachusetts might as well have been battling an iconic pari-mutuel philanthropist named Lou Smith every time it attempted to keep pace with its nemesis neighboring state to the north.

"Uncle Lou" was the mastermind behind the Rock. A ruthlessly shrewd deal maker whose success coincided with the country's emergence from the depression, Smith was widely hailed as a foreign-born runaway who fought his way through the ranks before purchasing an abandoned New Hampshire racetrack that he transformed into a flourishing Thoroughbred showcase. An intensely private man who went to great pains to avoid public controversy, Smith is said to have enlisted the help of longtime tale-spinning pal Damon Runyon to hone his aura of benevolence so that his background as a boxing promoter, circus worker, saloonkeeper, whiskey runner, and operator of seven other racetracks in the United States, Canada, and Cuba never became an issue. Although at first reluctant to embrace "sin taxes" in the tenuous 1930s, New Hampshire Republicans warmed to the notion when betting on races at Smith's horse track soon supplied an incredible *one-fifth* of the general funds budget for the sparsely populated state.

Smith also donated vast sums to numerous worthy causes, and the annals are rife with publicity photos of Uncle Lou and his kindly wife, Lutza, handing oversized checks to orphans, churches, crippled children, war relief projects, and veterans' homes. Smith rubbed elbows with Hollywood stars, lunched in the Rockingham clubhouse with famous athletes, and routinely took calls from influential New England politicians and the region's highest-ranking religious leaders. And though almost every old-timer who knew Smith will attest to his avuncular aura and copious generosity, it is also relevant to note that such overt and, at times, outlandish endowments were simply the cost of doing business, fiscal lubricants to pave the way for gambling in one of the nation's most conservative states.

Uncle Lou made sure elected officials were well taken care of in the form of jobs, free passes, and numerous perks, some of which presumably arrived inside fat white envelopes. In turn, the gentlemanly racing boss from Salem almost always got what he wanted. When Smith said in 1958 that both he and the state needed night harness racing, the legislature not only signed his suggestion into law but also established a sixty-mile buffer zone around the Rock, effectively banishing competing license-seekers to the rural borderlands. When Suffolk Downs began to get on Uncle Lou's nerves and separate New Hampshire interests were clamoring for a greyhound track on the Granite State seacoast, Smith—just because he could—teamed with the well-connected operators of Wonderland dog track in Massachusetts to quell both fronts. And in what has to be the classic Uncle Lou coup of all time, when the Bay State was building Interstate 93 from Boston to the New Hampshire border in the early 1960s, Smith was somehow able to persuade leaders of *both* states to divert the project fifteen miles east to where his horse track sat, so that the first highway exit over the state line was abruptly switched from more densely populated Nashua to smaller Salem. As an added bonus, the high-speed roadway was further reconfigured to include Rockingham Park Boulevard, a brand-new access road that delivered thousands upon thousands of Massachusetts patrons right to Smith's front door.

Suffolk Downs countered as best it could against such clout, responding with night harness racing the year after the Rock first ran sulkies under the lights and trying to bring in additional revenue by renting its cavernous facility out for off-season conventions, traveling expositions, and flower shows. The Beatles played the racetrack in August 1966, drawing 25,000 for the only Boston date on their final U.S. tour. In 1969, maverick baseball-team owner Bill Veeck took over Suffolk Downs on behalf of Realty Equities Corporation, but his fresh ideas and flat-out refusal to do things "because they've always been done that way" rubbed the entire New England racing circuit the wrong way. His two-year tenure was dotted with popular—although unconventional—promotions such as chariot races, livestock giveaways, and mock Indian battles in the infield. But lost in the hoopla were several benchmark legal victories and important horse-racing precedents, such as one in which Veeck sued the state to allow children to attend the races and another that permitted female jockeys to ride for the first time in Massachusetts. Worn ragged by the grind, Veeck would retire from track management after only two seasons to write a book about his brief foray into the world of racing. He titled his memoir *Thirty Tons a Day*, referencing both the copious amount of manure generated by Suffolk Downs steeds and the amount of political dung Veeck felt he'd endured as an outsider fighting the insiderish Bay State political thicket.

Lou Smith died in April 1969, and the 1970s marked the true unraveling of New England racing. The entire circuit was in an uproar and everyone was blaming Veeck for causing a "dates war" that led to several tracks expanding their racing schedules, encroaching upon the territorial calendars of others. An unstable Suffolk Downs was unloaded onto Ogden Corporation in 1971, the same season racing exceeded 100 days and extended into December for the first time. Racing on Sundays debuted in 1972, and the East Boston oval further attempted to boost business by expanding exotic wagering. But the disquieting presence of organized crime began to simmer to the surface of the circuit more openly than ever before, and in 1973 a rash of betting scandals throughout New England led to the brief banishment of exacta (picking the first and second place finishers exactly on a single ticket) and trifecta (picking first, second, and third place) wagering in Massachusetts, New Hampshire, and Rhode Island. With Rockingham no longer a formidable political force, New Hampshire pushed through the legalization of dog racing in 1973, squeezing the gambling landscape even tighter. A year later, Massachusetts retaliated by becoming the first state to sell "instant" lottery tickets that did not depend on weekly drawings, uniquely setting up the Commonwealth as both regulator and competitor of Suffolk Downs. By the end of the decade, regional Thoroughbred racing was so unprofitable that it had ceased at Green Mountain Park in Vermont, Scarborough Downs in Maine, Lincoln Downs and Narragansett Park in Rhode Island, and at about half the county-fair courses in Massachusetts. The circuit was down to two major tracks, and on the otherwise blissfully serene summer dawn of July 29, 1980, Suffolk Downs became the winner by default when the Rockingham Park grandstand exploded in ferocious flames, gutted to the ground by a fast-moving fire of unknown origin that spread swiftly and horrifically as horses galloped around the track in the daily ritual of morning training.

With the marketplace to itself, Suffolk Downs should have flourished. But it didn't. Certainly, the logistics of being the only game in town allowed the track's betting handle and attendance to rise, but no real improvements were made to bolster business and any increases were mainly attributable to the advent of nonstop racing. By the early 1980s, the lagging quality of horseflesh and the prevailing public notion that the races were crooked fed the overall image that Eastie and Revere were towns rife with crime and that Suffolk Downs itself was now the major source of the seediness. Media archives from this era do nothing but reinforce that notion: Race-fixing scandals involving bribed jockeys and horses drugged by hoodlums hopping the stable-area fence with hypodermics topped the Boston headlines and led the six o'clock news. Narcotics transactions became an open secret in the bowels of the grandstand, and some corners of the plant were absolutely unapproachable because of the stench of urine and accumulated rubbish. Shortly after the Rockingham fire, Suffolk Downs itself was hit with a pair of suspicious barn blazes that killed twenty-five horses, and in 1982, a brazen daylight shoot-out between rival thugs in the track clubhouse sent hundreds of patrons scurrying for cover amid the spray of gunfire. By 1984, word was out that an afternoon at Suffolk Downs was more of a danger than a diversion, and by that time the Rock had completely rebuilt and reopened, siphoning horses, fans, and their money to its new facility thirty-five miles up the interstate in the decidedly safer confines of New Hampshire suburbia.

The salvation of the East Boston oval was supposed to come in the form of a man nicknamed Buddy, although in retrospect one would have difficulty finding a human being more vilified in the history of New England racing than the man who purchased the track for $22 million in 1986 and had the audacity to christen his venture "New Suffolk Downs." Edward G. LeRoux was the longtime athletic trainer for both the Celtics and Red Sox who reportedly made a killing in Florida real estate before setting his sights on the prized Boston baseball club in 1977. Immediately upon installing himself in the front office, the LeRoux tenure at the helm of the Red Sox was hallmarked by constant, roiling controversy, including the nullification of the original sale, a series of lawsuits, botched free-agency dealings, and—worst of all in sports-crazed Boston—the chronic inability to field a winning team. When his Sox partners attempted to dislodge him, LeRoux zeroed in on troubled Suffolk Downs, presumably with an eye on development. Because of his part-ownership in the team, Buddy was barred by Major League Baseball from being involved in the day-to-day operations of a gambling facility. So in 1986 he established Belle Isle Ltd. with a pair of investors to buy the property, then constructed a thinly veiled lease that rented the racing rights back to his own two cronies. Plans for the site were grand—a major sports arena to replace the aging Boston Garden, a first-rate convention center, top-notch hotels, parking garages, restaurants, the works—but while blueprints were being drawn up and searches for financial backing were floated, everyday business at the track went unattended, further deteriorating and souring the sport. After only one year of operation, nose-diving New Suffolk Downs was at the center of hostile debate, alternately pleading with and threatening the Massachusetts legislature for a financial bailout, with LeRoux vowing to derail the racing industry by closing the plant for good if Belle Isle didn't get its way.

The state came through for LeRoux in 1987, restructuring the racing laws to give Suffolk Downs a break. But the legislation was set to expire in two seasons, and by 1989, with the region rocketing toward a recession, political insiders on Beacon Hill finally had enough of Buddy's tantrums and decided to call his bluff. LeRoux made it emphatically clear that he would allow his racing license to expire and raze the property for other purposes without a new deal from the state, and the implication was strong that he didn't give a damn what happened to Thoroughbred racing. On December 30, shortly after Tuned For More skipped under the Suffolk Downs finish wire in the gloaming of the nightcap and the paltry crowd of 2,317 filed out of the grim, gray facility, LeRoux abruptly padlocked the plant and canceled the next day's season finale, fearful of vandalism, mayhem, and perhaps the sting of accountability from the angry, abandoned group of longtime workers and loyal horseplayers.

Suffolk Downs remained shuttered for two years, and behind-the-scenes battles erupted to acquire the racing license before Buddy could cut a development deal. After the pretenders were culled from the contenders, only restaurateur Charles Sarkis, operator of nearby Wonderland Park, and the general partnership led by wealthy Thoroughbred owner James B. Moseley and prominent real estate developer John L. Hall II, remained in the running. Over months, negotiations played out in typically tumultuous LeRoux fashion, with Sarkis thinking he had a handshake agreement on a long-term lease before Buddy awarded the racing rights to Moseley and Hall at the last minute for $8.5 million. After seven frenzied months and additional millions of dollars invested in renovations, capital improvements, and political wrangling, racing returned to Suffolk Downs on January 1, 1992, accompanied by an emotional crowd of 15,212 that greeted the return of the horses with unabashed appreciation, embracing the long-shot homecoming with such intensity that one wizened Boston sports columnist christened the rebirth of the racetrack as "the greatest comeback since Lazarus."

The new operators knew that more than fresh paint and flowers were required to erase the negative image that Suffolk Downs had jus-tifiably earned over several decades, and they worked diligently to overcome that stigma. At first, they even wanted to change the name of the track, but eventually dropped the idea for "Sterling Downs" in deference to history. Moseley, a former state representative and racing commissioner, was a stickler for credibility. He hired key racing exec-utives from outside New England and infused them with his passion for turning the track into a world-class racing organization, freeing up time for him to do what he did best—meeting and greeting fans and backstretch workers as he strolled the grandstand, accepting their heartfelt thanks for saving local racing, and putting a much-needed human face on the operation. Hall, a newcomer to the sport, preferred to function in the background as track president, using his savvy as a wheeler and dealer to pull strings and exert influence.

Suffolk Downs remained true to its word to reestablish a circuit arrangement with Rockingham Park, ending years of head-to-head competition. The track secured legislation that included rights to export and import simulcasts (races run at one location with bets taken elsewhere) and a more favorable takeout structure. Management implored customers to be patient, explaining that quality day-to-day racing was its first goal before establishing an ambitious big-money stakes program. Riding an upward spiral, Suffolk Downs bolstered its purses—the cash prizes awarded to the owners of horses that finish in the money—which in turn attracted more talented stables. As a result, more customers bet on the product, because the races were more competitive. Within three seasons, New England's richest race, the storied Massachusetts Handicap, was back to its place of prominence on the national calendar, highlighted by the sport's top horses, star jockeys, and a one-day festival of racing featuring more than $1 million in purses. Racing writers across the country featured Suffolk Downs as the comeback track, portraying its operation as a model for modern-day racing. The industry weekly *Blood-Horse* went so far as to proclaim that "Suffolk Downs has become one of racing's small tracks that thinks big," while even the historically stoic *Boston Globe* editorialized that the facility was "a green place with an eat-off-the-floor level of cleanliness . . . the best-kept entertainment secret in Boston."

But in the fickle way it sometimes does, quick success proved to be too much of a good thing for the rejuvenated racetrack. As Suffolk Downs regained respectability, management tried to make the case to the Massachusetts legislature that it needed additional tools—not subsidies—to compete with surrounding states such as Rhode Island, Connecticut, New York, New Hampshire, and Maine that allowed more progressive forms of phone and Internet wagering. But the pleas were largely ignored because business appeared so rosy, and Suffolk Downs's efforts to try to keep pace with technology were characterized as greedy. The track and its lobbyists pointed out the fiscal damage caused by Foxwoods, North America's highest-volume casino, which opened in 1992 only 100 miles away, and Mohegan Sun, another Connecticut tribal gaming palace that began operating four years later. Together, the two competing casinos contributed to a dozen-busload *daily* exodus of bettors from East Boston and Revere, but the increased tone of desperation went unanswered by the state.

In 1997, Sterling Suffolk Racecourse Limited Liability Company was able to wrest the property outright from Belle Isle for $40 million, escaping the crushing LeRoux lease but further constricting its cash flow with mortgage payments. Making a profit on the purchase hinged on the expected passage of casino legislation, but after months of positive buildup, the slot-machines bill was quixotically abandoned on Beacon Hill, and changes for the worse at defeated Suffolk Downs began to make themselves obvious in subtle ways: First, key employees began leaving the company and were not replaced. Then, small perks and extras were pared from the track's budget, followed by cuts in basic services like cleaning and maintenance. Morale and attitude slipped in tandem with day-to-day details and the foundering plant's general upkeep. But the crushing blow to the track's underdog spirit slammed home hard a few months later when a six-year battle with lymphoma claimed the life of ever-optimistic boss Jim Moseley. And when the well-liked Suffolk Downs chairman died in April 1998, the unspoken but obvious truth was that so too did his dream of making the scrappy little track on the Boston seashore one of the nation's finest showcases in Thoroughbred racing.

Although financial records are heavily guarded, the party line at Suffolk Downs going into the 2000 season is that the track has been marginally profitable, with any meager income plowed back into improving the business. But investors in the limited partnership are understandably getting antsy after eight years of struggle, and the most recent eighteen months at Suffolk Downs has been a lesson in the politics of split-decision ownership: Neither president John Hall nor Patricia Moseley (who inherited her husband's title as chairman) maintain an office at the racetrack, and while both are active at the legislative and planning levels, the company's top two officials remain dissociated from day-to-day operations. At board meetings, the ruling duo's divergent business beliefs underscore the glaring rift between the Moseley-loyal shareholders with a background in racing who want to continue toughing out an existence in the uncertain world of wagering, and the development-minded deal makers like Hall who believe that the best bet might be to cash out and sell the 190 acres of prime urban real estate, the last and largest undeveloped parcel of land in all of Greater Boston.

JIM BISHOP is the resident wiseguy at Suffolk Downs. A hulking, bespectacled horseplayer somewhere in his midforties (I have never known the man to reveal his true age), Bish has been a press-box degenerate since the late 1970s. A former lineman on an amateur Boston football team that used to play prison inmates and a lifelong Revere resident who knows every street tough, gangster, bookie, and wanna-be hood in the area, Bish is a master of understatement with the driest, blackest sense of humor on the racetrack. He has a zealous cult following as the ace program handicapper for Suffolk Downs, but because of his steadfast resistance to having a publicity head-shot photograph taken and his adamant stance against wearing a coat and tie to work like other media relations employees, Bish moves through the grandstand largely unrecognized by fans. Decades working the Eastie press box have fed Bish's unintentional but unparalleled repertoire of disquieting one-liners, his voracious nicotine habit, and a penchant for decisively ending conversations with an emphatic "Fuggedaboutit," but the hard-boiled, gruff exterior belies Bish's true nature. Polite, reliable, and patient, Bish is a true gentle giant, and the best thing about him is if you called him that to his face, he'd look you dead in the eye and offer ever so calmly and casually to rip your goddamned head off.

Of no relation to Jim Bishop is Regal Bishop, a frail-footed, small-ish Ohio-born Thoroughbred who just happens to be the second betting choice in the back half of today's daily double, a six-furlong sprint for low-level horses that have never won a race.

Through his first few tries, Regal Bishop has shown absolutely no ability or affinity for the game. In five races exclusively against other horses who have never won, the three-year-old colt has elicited the following official comments from the Equibase chart-caller (whose job is to describe the running pattern of each horse during a race) that epitomize his clumsiness as a racehorse: *Steadied into turn; steadied near stretch; slow start; trailed; lost jockey.* In his sixth career start, Regal Bishop finally rallied to come in third at 63 to 1. Today, in try number seven, taking a drop down the class ladder to race against even lesser competition for lower prize money, you can have him at the ridiculously low odds of 7 to 2. (Horse racing odds are traditionally fractional; in this case a winning ticket would return $7 for each $2 wagered.)

When Jim Bishop was an Equibase chart-caller himself several seasons back, he would sometimes stray from the preprogrammed database comments and get creative with his past-performance charts. For sorry horses such as Regal Bishop, he liked to utilize his favorite self-coined disparity: *Appeared to dislike racing.* Yet today, the timid colt—sporting an oversized set of blinkers cupping each eye to limit his field of vision to the task at hand—circles the field on the turn and makes a powerful move for the lead. Despite racing awkwardly with a choppy stride, Regal Bishop sails home while drawing off from the pack for his first career victory. After the race, the horse appears out of place in the winner's circle, as if he has no clue why here's there. His trainer, a scuff-along blue-collar backstretcher with a barnful of slow animals, is all smiles. He knows it might be a long time before he visits the charmed enclosure again.

Scrutinizing the race replay, Jim Bishop watches Regal Bishop struggle mightily with the rider for lateral movement. The horse appears to be running sideways, and jockey Antone Barreira does a good job just to keep his horse straight and hang on, let alone win the race. "He's lugging in and drifting out at the same time," says press-box Bish of his equine namesake, pointing out how the colt's head is cocked toward the infield while his ass juts out to the grandstand. "I've never seen that before."

Later in the day, the $25,000 featured Floyd Duncan Stakes is won in a romp by 3-to-5 fan favorite Kayla's A Gem, an eight-year-old racemare with twenty-three lifetime trips to the winner's circle and victories in six straight stakes tries at Suffolk Downs. Every time she races on her home court, the betting public backs her so prohibitively that the reward is hardly worth the risk of walking to the windows. Yet because of her dominant form, Kayla is tough to bet against. When she runs, it is often wise just to pass the race and watch her win.

The daily double bet involves picking the winners of consecutive races on a single ticket, and there are usually two of them each day, an early and a late double. This afternoon, Kayla's A Gem is so heavily favored that it is obvious many racegoers have simply "wheeled" her in the wagering, meaning they have plunked down big money dependent on Kayla's winning the first "leg" (race) of the late daily double with tickets that cover every possible winning outcome in the second leg. Thus, when 31-to-1 bomb Mischievous Sheikh—a stablemate from the same low-percentage barn as Regal Bishop—plods home in the nightcap, the daily double payout combining two separate winners on a single ticket ($58.60) comes back *less* than the win ticket on Mischievous Sheikh alone ($65.00), a pari-mutuel rarity.

"You think that price is remarkable?" says Bish at the end of the day, heading for a cigarette break after a tough afternoon at the windows. "Mischievous Sheikh's trainer won two races today. That guy didn't win two races all last season. Now *that's* remarkable."

EVEN THOUGH it sounds feminine, all Thoroughbreds—regardless of sex—start out as "maidens" in the odd vernacular of horse racing. At the bottom level of the sport's "class ladder," maiden races are the easiest level of competition, restricted to winless horses. Once a horse wins at this level ("breaks its maiden"), it must advance the next step up the ladder. At a midlevel joint like Suffolk Downs, there are usually quite a few maiden races, largely because the track's horse population contains no shortage of lifetime losers.

In theory, a horse who breaks its maiden will then race next at the "allowance" level, and there, too, is a complicated subsystem of classification: A first-level allowance is for horses who have never won two races, a second-level allowance is for horses who have never won three, and so on, with the goal being to group together horses of similar ability and accomplishment. In most cases, these races are further restricted by age and sex, with still-developing two-year-olds and three-year-olds segregated from their elders until roughly age four, when most Thoroughbreds are at or near maturity.

If a steed is highly gifted, it will *win through its allowance conditions* and be pointed for the highest classification level—stakes races, which feature the sport's richest prize money. Gala events like the Kentucky Derby or the Breeders' Cup Championships offer stakes purses measured in the millions of dollars. The Massachusetts Handicap, the most important two minutes of the year at Suffolk Downs, offers a $600,000 purse. By contrast, the regular Saturday afternoon stakes (sometimes called "handicap") races at the East Boston oval are contested for $25,000, a modest but respectable weekly feature for a midlevel racetrack. The more money a track offers in purses, the higher the caliber of racehorse it attracts. The higher the caliber of racehorse, the more money customers will bet, raising the handle, and thus profits, for the track.

In practice though, most Thoroughbreds don't waltz right through their allowance conditions to keep on facing better competition for bigger money. The majority simply aren't fast enough, and even the fastest of the fast get injured and deteriorate in productivity. Some, of course, are retired, but the others must fit into the pecking order somewhere, and although the industry does not usually trumpet this aspect of the sport because it lacks sexiness and star power, the industry has found a remarkably efficient solution: claiming races.

A claiming race is one in which all horses are entered for a fixed sales price, and any other licensed horseman can "claim" your horse away simply by putting up the cash and filling out an official slip. The claim must be made fifteen minutes prior to post time, when the race starts, and the claim is irrevocable: If the claimed horse wins by the length of the grandstand, the previous owner gets the purse check and the claiming money from the new owner but has to forfeit the horse. Conversely, if the animal gets hurt or suffers a fatal injury during the running of the race, the prospective owner who dropped the claim slip is out of luck and still has to hand over the cash and perhaps be stuck with a horse who might never race again.

Claiming races at Suffolk Downs are run for "tags" (claim prices) as low as $4,000 and as high as $20,000, and the intriguing pecking order that this economic system produces is very much a mishmash of horse trading, poker bluffing, and used-car salesmanship. Certainly, a horseman could take a Thoroughbred who is truly worth $20,000 and enter that horse at the $4,000 level to run roughshod over the weaker competition—he'd likely win the race, but he'd probably lose the horse via claim because other trainers would know that the steed is worth much more than the bargain-basement asking price. Or, there is nothing stopping a guy who wants to take a shot with his $4,000 steed against $20,000 claimers for a better purse (as the claiming prices rise, so too does the prize money), but this also would be a mismatch: The ambitiously entered $4,000 runner stands little chance against horses who are proven to be worth five times that amount, and Thoroughbreds who are consistently "outclassed" do not earn their keep.

What usually happens is that the horses on any given circuit rise or sink to the claiming plateau that reflects their actual abilities, so that animals worth $4,000 generally seek their own level and the ones worth $20,000 seek theirs. The claiming ranks help level the playing field so that even races for lower-quality horses can be competitive. Even though these contests lack the drawing power of the game's top names, claiming races are what keeps the industry humming along on a daily basis, providing a product on which patrons can wager and horsemen can earn purse checks: Of the 60,579 Thoroughbred races that will be run nationwide in 2000, two out of every three will be claiming races.

Suffolk Downs has always had a reputation as a track with a hard-trying, blue-collar core of claiming steeds. Thus, it is no coincidence that as I write here about the events of 2000, the winningest racing stable in New England is primarily a claiming outfit. Its owner is Michael Gill, a highly driven conundrum of a man, and his lofty goals, hefty checkbook, and abstruse but effective practices could serve as a case study supporting whether or not nice guys finish last. Or, more aptly, if ruthlessness does indeed breed success.

In one sense, Gill seems like just the type of person Thoroughbred publicists revel in promoting, and the leading local owner, who turns forty-four on this January afternoon, often repeats the amusing anecdote of how he literally fell into racing as a teenager: Growing up in Salem, New Hampshire, Gill accidentally stepped through thin ice on a stream behind Rockingham Park one winter afternoon, went into the track to get warm, made a score with his first bet ever, and was hooked for good on the rush of racing and winning. A self-made mortgage businessman who parlayed a one-horse hobby into a power-house outfit of more than 100 runners, Gill profitably supports local racing, speaks highly of it, and is an animated figure who forgoes the pompously refined pleasures of the Turf Club in favor of the gritty Suffolk Downs grandstand. He is known for giving inexperienced backstretch workers ample opportunity to rise through the ranks, even encouraging some of his help to learn an off-track trade in his real estate operation. When Gill wins, he reinvests his profits in the sport, asserting that he is in the game for the long haul, and it comes as no surprise that his ultimate dream is to win the Eclipse Award as the continent's top horse owner.

But there is a schizophrenic side to Gill's tale that is not so palatable: He is a cutthroat competitor with a brash attitude who comes across as a control freak, exuding an air of exasperated petulance and a mindset that seems locked on buying his way into the winner's circle. Large-framed and jowly, nearly always dressed in denim and sneakers, Gill can often be found shouting at a bank of Suffolk Downs television monitors by the first-floor beer stand, sometimes storming directly out to the paddock to publicly berate his riders after losing efforts. His record on file with the Association of Racing Commissioners International lists six separate infractions that resulted in the suspension or revocation of his license over the past two decades.

As an owner, Gill unearths and unloads new trainers for his horses at an astonishing clip and unconventionally juggles his stock between as many as five different conditioners at the same racetrack at the same time. Many of his new hires are unknowns or rank newcomers to training: grooms and assistants who have never before managed a stable of racehorses. The only aspect of the Gill operation that eclipses the rapidity of his revolving-door training wizardry is his penchant for claiming new racing stock. But instead of relying on the advice of a seasoned trainer like many owners do, Gill is emphatic about calling the shots when it comes to wheeling and dealing, making horse purchases based on statistical information in the *Racing Form* rather than relying on a knowledgeable horseman who needs only to glance at a Thoroughbred's legs to tell you if the animal has hurting ankles or a tendon that is about to bow. Because of this, Gill's common-sense horsemanship often comes under question, and on more than one occasion he has inadvertently claimed steeds that are so obviously unsound that the racing commission veterinarians assigned to pre-race safety checks have had to order them scratched when the time comes for their next start.

Regardless of his motives or methods, the undeniable truth is that there is strength in Gill's numbers, and financial clout on a midsized claiming circuit like New England routinely grinds down the opposition. At the recently concluded autumn meeting at Suffolk Downs, Gill's horses won forty-eight races, an impressive total greater than all the wins of the second, third, and fourth leading owners combined. Aided by prize money from twenty-nine second- and twenty-two third-place finishes, Gill grossed $352,262 in purses during the ten-week season, a figure that also eclipses the cumulative tallies of the owners left in his torrid wake. Yet to achieve such statistical prowess, the Gill stable had to start a mind-boggling 203 runners during the fall meet, a number that is also vastly disproportionate to all other local racing stables. Horses used to racing once every two or three weeks for other outfits were often entered on short rest with only a handful of days between starts for the Gill stable, and when these overworked steeds did not produce they were dropped down the claiming ladder to be unloaded with the hope that someone else would claim them, and Thoroughbreds who won for others were added to the Gill rotation by aggressive day-trading claim-box tactics. Money was no obstacle, and by all appearances neither was the unwritten backstretch code of larger stables not raiding smaller one- or two-horse outfits to the point where mom-and-pop trainers become victims of hostile equine takeovers.

My first personal encounter with Mike Gill is also my most enduring impression of the man: Back in 1994, when he burst onto the New England racing scene with a splash of superfluity and a renegade style, Gill visited the media relations office to purchase an advertisement in the track program for his real-estate banking business. The move seemed like a genuine effort to give something back to the racetrack in the form of a small contribution to the Suffolk Downs revenue stream, because entrenched Boston bettors were unlikely customers for his booming New Hampshire home-financing firm. Per custom, we offered to work up some ad copy, have it properly typeset, and allow Gill the option of proofreading the final version before the print run so he could be sure to catch any errors.

"No," said Gill, reaching into the front pocket of his blue jeans for a crumpled, creased piece of notebook paper with his own ad copy outlined in pencil. "Just use this."

As he walked out of the press box, I unfolded the advertisement and stared at its heading, where Gill had scrawled the name of his business: Morgage Specialists.

Christ! I thought. *Is this guy making so much money churning house loans in the obscenely lucrative real estate market that he doesn't have to attend to small stuff like knowing how to spell what he does for a living correctly?* Sure, anyone can make a mistake, but the lingering impression was one of inattention to detail, leaving me to wonder if such sloppiness was how Gill intended to build his dominant dream stable. He seemed innocuous at best, laughable at worst.

But that was before Gill hired and fired a head-spinning litany of trainers. That was before he began openly quarreling with rival horsemen on the backstretch, before he began floating conspiracy theories about the jockeys who worked for him. All that happened before Gill took out his own trainer's license and then on the very same day had one of his winning horses test positive for the highly controversial and federally banned drug clenbuterol. It was before a 1995 search of Gill's Rockingham Park barn turned up illegal horse medications, hypodermic needles, and syringes, and before Gill accused fellow trainers of planting the contraband even though some of the drugs were bagged and labeled with his name on them in a knapsack in his own locked tack room. It was before Gill was cited for illegally transferring ownership of his racing stable to his wife while under suspension, before the New Hampshire Pari-Mutuel Commission finally banned him indefinitely from participating in any form of Thoroughbred racing, and before the federal reciprocity rule took effect that would make him ineligible for licensing in any state in the nation for at least three years because of the extent of his wrongdoings.

Of course, Michael Gill denied all these charges. But by the time he decided to return to racing with a vengeance, his operation and its impact no longer seemed as harmless or humorous as it had during our first encounter.

BOSTON HAS GONE 303 days without any measurable snowfall, the longest recorded stretch since the compilation of local weather statistics started. But storms during the two consecutive off days in the Suffolk Downs schedule break the streak and leave five inches of white stuff in Greater Boston. An extreme cold snap follows into Saturday, and the racing week starts with −30°F wind-chill factors in the morning. In the backstretch stable area, grooms bust ice from water buckets in pre-dawn darkness and hand-walk horses under the cover of plastic-covered shed rows. No one wants to go out onto the windswept racetrack and gallop horses during morning training hours. By 10:00 AM the word is out that the jockeys don't want to ride the afternoon races, either.

The temperature has risen to 16°F by 12:15 PM, half an hour before post time. As the National Anthem plays, I see that three of the swans who live in the infield appear to be frozen in the small pond behind the tote board. I watch them through binoculars for ten minutes. The birds don't move.

Although they do not act as if they are in distress, the swans are firmly rooted in ice. An occasional head twitch is the only indication they are even alive. In the press box, we degenerates debate what to do. Someone suggests going down to chop them out of the ice, but anyone who has ever ventured close enough knows that the beautiful birds can get downright nasty and territorial when approached, and a swan bite can be horrifically vicious. Someone else suggests pouring hot water around the bottom of the birds to break the ice seal, but this might scald them, and it puts whoever goes out there in danger of falling in too if the ice gives way. Lacking a solution, I go down and ask the veterinarian assigned to the paddock what she would advise. As the doc examines the horses for the first race, she admits she isn't really sure what to do either, although she agrees that someone should probably go out there and manually free the swans from their predicament, considering how bracingly cold it is.

For the most part, horses don't mind the chilly weather. The average Thoroughbred weighs between 1,000 and 1,200 pounds and generates an acceptably proportionate amount of body heat, particularly during the course of a proper warm-up, race, and cool-down. Horses stabled at Suffolk Downs for the past few months have long since grown thick winter coats, and the animals are pretty well adapted to the regimen of training, racing, shed-row walking, and waiting that encompasses the winter racing months in New England. As far as actual winter danger, fresh snow that balls up underneath the horses' concave hooves is far more perilous, making footing like walking on ball bearings. Under such conditions, racing is almost always canceled in deference to safety.

The jockeys' attitude toward frigid conditions is another story entirely.

As a group, riders abhor bitterly cold weather. Because the jocks must weigh out and in for each race at a specific, assigned weight, they do not have the luxury of layering on extra clothes or bulking up on cold-climate outerwear. The vast expanse of a one-mile racing oval naturally makes the open terrain prone to violent wind gusts and exposure to the elements, and the fact that the track is but a few furlongs off the Atlantic Ocean only makes matters worse at Suffolk Downs.

Gunning from a standstill start to thirty-five miles an hour on horseback in a winter race, the onrushing wind sometimes makes it difficult or impossible for the jockeys to breathe. Riders frequently admit their hands are so numb on freezing days that they can't tell if they're even holding the reins, let alone using them correctly to control a speeding horse. If the temperature has changed during the day and there is moisture in the track, lethal clods of dirt and ice will form throughout the surface. "Death cookies" is the term coined in the Suffolk Downs press box for such frozen projectiles, and it is far easier to talk about them from the warmth of the grandstand than to ride with them flying through the air. When they occur, the advantage swings decidedly in favor of front-runners and the fastest horses out of the gate, because, like one old-time jockey once explained to me, racing in mid-pack behind horses in winter "is like trying to ride with somebody throwing baseballs at your skull." Split lips and bloody noses are the most common injuries at winter meets, even more routine than frostbite.

The races manage to start as scheduled, and on the way back from visiting with the vet in the paddock, I stop to watch the first event from the jockeys' locker room. Waits River, a lowly maiden claimer, barrels his way through the pack from post 11, checks (pauses briefly) behind traffic at the top of the lane, steadies again with jockey Efrain Saune standing straight up in the irons as the field banks for the stretch drive, then staggers down the lane and head-bobs known stopper Premier Crusade at the wire to score a 35-to-1 upset. On TV, the race appears to have been run without trouble, at least as far as contests for the slowest, most awkward animals on the grounds go.

The jockeys bring their horses back after a brief gallop around the clubhouse turn, dismount, and offer excuses to trainers. Then they rush back into the locker room hooting and hollering. The Suffolk Downs riding colony is a decidedly vocal bunch to begin with, but the curses and wails of protest about the conditions are particularly loud and foul on this frigid afternoon. Most of the jockeys wear ski masks and headbands under their helmets and goggles, and the chaos of the returning throng from the first race is peppered with so much rapid-fire Spanish shouting that the riders in their multicolored outfits and face coverings resemble a scaled-down version of a disorderly Sandinistan rebellion.

Bringing up the rear are a pair of jockeys lending support to one of the walking wounded, a hunched-over rider in blue and white silks whom they have to help into a chair, tell to relax and breathe normally, then again assist by removing the jockey's headgear and unwrapping the facial masking. When all the layers are finally cleared away, the dazed and bewildered jockey is revealed to be Christina Gray.

Gray, twenty-nine, has recently made the transition from rookie to journeyman status. Getting by more on her strong work ethic than raw race-riding ability, she has been mired in the depths of a 1-for-23 slump the past two weeks since winning her only race of the season back on Opening Day.

"She can't breathe!" shouts Winston Thompson, a wiry Jamaican who finished tenth and last in the first race aboard Give Em Your Best. "No one can breathe out there! She almost fell off at the three-sixteenths pole!"

Gray looks like she might be in shock after her fourth-place ride aboard 72-to-1 long shot Fames Case. She comes out of it slowly as the confusion continues around her. When finally able to speak, she quietly tells the clerk of scales to find a replacement rider for her remaining mounts of the afternoon.

Lou Raffetto Jr. is the executive vice president of racing for Suffolk Downs, and it is his job to face complaints and work out some sort of compromise plan for racing when conditions are questionable. In situations like this, the general manager must balance the safety of the horses and riders against the practicality and profitability of the track's balance sheet, and it is never an easy task. Usually, Raffetto is gregarious and approachable. But today he does not radiate friendliness and instead stands with his arms crossed across his chest as the riders file past him near the digital scale in the front of the locker room.

Although no one mentions past troubles, it is almost exactly four years to the date since Raffetto threw a number of jockeys off the property and told them never to return to Suffolk Downs after a much-publicized spat over winter safety issues. Tempers flare and accusations fly whenever it snows in Boston, and when weather arguments arise, everyone always seems to take things way too personally. The raging debates over whether to race have produced some prolific screaming matches and deeply rooted bad blood between key participants on all sides of the issue. Every season the fracas erupts anew come the first snowstorm or snap of cold weather, and the bickering is played out with varying dramatics but similar outcomes every time, every year. When Raffetto banned the vocal opponents back in 1996, a slew of overweight exercise riders and some guy from out of nowhere who claimed to be a champion jockey in Greece were instantly licensed to ride. The scabs ruled the racecourse, made some money, and got a brief taste of Thoroughbred glory for a couple of days. But once the sun came back out and the weather got warm, the regular riders returned, everyone kissed and made up, and peace reigned—at least until the next winter.

There are more factors involved than are evident on the surface when it comes to calling off an entire day's worth of races at any track. At Suffolk Downs, a written agreement jointly adopted years ago by track management, the horsemen's union, and the jockeys is supposed to be in effect, but the highly subjective guidelines are largely ignored because they are based on relative terms that are easier to implement in theory than in practice. For the most part, owners and trainers want their horses to race and earn purse money as long as conditions are safe, because if the races are called off it might be several weeks before a certain class of race is scheduled again. But a jockey's definition of what constitutes "safe" can be quite different from that of those who don't have to go out and actually put their life on the line astride a Thoroughbred. And even though an individual jockey always has the option of refusing to ride any or all of his mounts on a given day, if another rider replaces him in the saddle and wins, that mount could very well be business lost to a rival jockey, because trainers often allow winning pilots to ride the same horse again in future races. In addition, engagements from other conditioners could also be in jeopardy, because some hard-nosed trainers view a decision to opt off when everyone else rides as an act of cowardice.

Based on the my-loss-is-someone-else's gain mindset, it naturally follows that the top riders will almost always try to lobby all the other jockeys into a group boycott so the cancellation ends up being a zero-sum equation. But this idea of unification does not often go over well at Suffolk Downs. There is always the chance that some jockeys will think it's a risk to ride when others won't. Plus, at any track, there will be a handful of desperate riders at the bottom of the pecking order who barely make ends meet and welcome *any* sort of racetrack stipend, even in the form of the mandatory $35 "mount fee" all jockeys receive regardless of where their horse finishes.

At the same time, Suffolk Downs as a business hovers both above and smack dab in the middle of the situation when it comes to cancellations: If management orders the races to proceed in dire weather and there is an accident, it must bear the burden of responsibility and answer to whomever got hurt. Conversely, if track management pulls the trigger and calls off a program too soon and conditions turn out to be amenable as the afternoon progresses, it must answer not only to angry horsemen who are contractually entitled to purse money but to the Commonwealth of Massachusetts, which depends on the track as a source of revenue and stipulates that it must run each and every one of its assigned 150 dates for the year. Track executives must also consider customers, who have invested time and money to handicap the races beforehand and then attend them, and they rightfully expect a show to go on if they've made the effort to come out for the day. In addition, workers of all sorts are on the payroll; mutuel windows and concession stands are staffed, and the entire afternoon of racing is expected to be up and available on satellite for simulcast wagering at intertrack and off-track betting outlets all around the continent. Sometimes the weather is so lousy and on-track attendance is so poor that it is actually more profitable in the long run for the track to take a financial hit and eat the cancellation, but by and large Suffolk Downs wants all of its horses and riders to make it around the track without mayhem and for the money to flow swiftly through the mutuel machines without impediment.

Raffetto listens to the jockeys state their case: It's cold, but the temperature wouldn't be so bad if the wind gusts weren't like a fist to the throat. The riders can't get air. It's tough to breathe. And there are frozen rocks out there, unpredictable clods of ice and dirt. Almost everyone who rode in·the opener voices an opinion, but by far the most vocal opposition comes from two top jockeys, the affable Jose Caraballo and the more strained and serious Josiah Hampshire Jr. Although both are on everyone's short list as the best and most respected riders on the circuit, neither even rode in the first race.

Michel Lapensee, at fifty-three, is the oldest active jockey in New England. He was born in Quebec, is now riding into his fifth decade, and has always had trouble maintaining the low weight requirement of the sport. He rarely complains about anything. In 1994, Lapensee suffered a heart attack in the Suffolk Downs jockeys' room, didn't tell anyone, quietly left, and drove himself to a hospital some forty miles away near his home in Rhode Island. Switching silks to ride again in the second race, Lapensee seems the least bothered by the elements, even though he is also the least bundled up.

"It affects everyone differently, I guess," Lapensee says with a shrug, the edges of his speech thick with French Canadian accent. "Me, the heat at Rockingham in the summer—I don't like that."

Raffetto, who has grown weary of these battles over the past eight years, suggests to the jockeys that maybe they're just not used to the cold air because it's been so mild this winter. He urges them to go out and ride the back half of the daily double, to give it at least one more chance before calling off the important Saturday card. He does not mention to the jockeys—at least not as an announcement in front of the group—that just prior to coming down to the locker room, he was upstairs in the Terrace Dining Room visiting with Rudy Baez, the wheelchair-bound rider who was making his very first visit to a racetrack since his August accident. Legendary in the winter months, Baez was one jockey, despite star status on a small circuit, who always wanted to go out and compete, regardless of the rigors or conditions. But since his paralysis, the New England racing community has been walking on eggshells with regard to safety issues, and the collective mindset seems to be that erring on the side of conservative protection is far more important than running horse races.

"You guys remember, stick together," cautions Hampshire as the jockeys file out of the locker room and up the tunnel to the paddock stairway. Joe is again without a scheduled mount for the second race and can only sit and watch as his comrades reluctantly agree to ride again. He commiserates, "You leave on your own, and someone's going to take your mount."

Howard Lanci is a forty-year-old journeyman who has a spastic personality and a reputation for riding recklessly on the half-mile bullrings on the Western Massachusetts county-fair circuit, where the purses are low, the risks high, and two jockeys have been killed in the past four seasons. He also has an answer for everything, and counters Hampshire's caution by shouting at him derisively from across the room. With but one win from seventeen rides on the season, Lanci barely scrapes by at the bottom of the Suffolk Downs standings, gets few live mounts, and under no circumstances does he want to lose the opportunity to make whatever money he can.

"Don't be naive," yells Lanci, waving his hands. "You think [leading trainer Ron] Dandy is going to give me all your mounts for the rest of the year if you take off for a day?"

The assistant clerk of scales asks "The Howitzer" if he's willing to pick up Christina Gray's vacant mount in the second race aboard Big Lisa.

"Hell, I'll ride anything, all day," says Lanci. "But I'm not going to ride hard from the gate like these fucking guys are doing. Let's just gallop around 'til the eighth pole and ride hard from there."

In race two, Harry Vega stalks the pace aboard 9-to-10 favorite Jackie Fawcett—ironically, a filly named after Lou Raffetto's kindly administrative assistant—then opens up in the stretch to win by the length of the grandstand. No one is eager to follow in the winner's wake of frozen debris. The riders return to the locker room after unsaddling and so do their criticisms about the elements.

"I don't mind the cold," gasps Winston Thompson. "But I can't breathe!"

"I told you guys," Lanci chimes in, eager for action, a few dollars richer. "Fuck this riding hard all the way around the track! No wonder you can't breathe! Just gallop around like you do in the mornings!"

Someone raises the point that such a tactic isn't exactly fair to the betting public. It might also be a cause for concern to the stewards, who enforce the rules of racing and have jurisdiction over everything that goes on at the track. In theory, their job is to protect the fans who wager on the races by policing the riding colony and ensuring that every jockey rides to the best of his or her ability at every point in a race; otherwise, a jockey can be charged with throwing a race.

"Fuck the betting public!" roars Lanci, infamous for his outbursts. He wears thick Coke-bottle glasses that magnify his wild eyes, and although he is relatively harmless, Howard sometimes acts like a crazy person you might cross the road to avoid if you saw him walking alone on a city street. Fused with a mercurial personality, his erratic logic often produces quixotically complex, albeit entertaining, bits of conversation. But like a Shakespearean clown who speaks in riddles, Lanci's off-the-cuff remarks always seem to make sense when you think about them later. "You think the betting public gives a fuck about *us*?"

Over by the tack table in the center of the room, Dyn Panell, a twenty-three-year-old Puerto Rican who speaks little English and has a constant studious look on his determined face, silently readies himself for the third event. Everyone in the jockeys' room mispronounces his name as *Din* instead of *Dean* but he is too soft-spoken to correct anyone, let alone voice an opinion about canceling the races. Panell has already participated in the first two events of the day without comment or complaint. At the rear row of lockers next to the shower room sits recently imprisoned Vernon Bush, who despite—or more likely, because of—a lifetime of crime and punishment, comes across as the most genuine and humble jock in the colony.

"This ain't fair to the public," the thirty-eight-year-old says in a somber, level voice, shaking his head. But no one pays attention to Bush, and the call goes out over the loudspeaker for riders to report to the paddock for the third race.

Hampshire has a horse in this race, and almost as if riding in defiance of those who would not heed his recommendation to cancel, he muscles 5-to-1 shot Tiro A Segno to the lead as soon as the gates fly open and never looks back, winning by a solid three lengths. Jose Caraballo, also riding in his first race of the afternoon, chases the winner all the way around the track aboard 5-to-2 choice Proud Jimmie, necking jockey Tammi Piermarini and 21-to-1 long shot Tuff Number for the place. The $4,000 claimers zip the six furlongs in 1:10-4/5, a very fast time for such a lowly caliber of horse.

"Somebody will break a leg on that racetrack," shouts Piermarini after the race, referring to the quick clocking caused by frozen footing. "It's too hard."

"It's like this," says Hampshire, irritated despite the victory, stomping his foot to make a comparison with the cement tile floor after stepping off the scale.

"Watch the head-on," says a laughing Lanci, meaning the race replay angle that shows the horses running directly at the camera. "I'm in the one hole and I break slow and go all the way to the outside fence because I'm not gonna get in there and get hit." Sure enough, the replay shows Lanci deliberately leaving the gate tardily aboard 64-to-1 long shot Good Omen before taking a sudden right turn to avoid the frozen clods, veering almost off the TV screen. "I'm not stupid."

A number of riders and valets begin to rib Lanci for his lack of effort. Winston Thompson especially is needling him, and Lanci launches back.

"What the fuck do you care?" he screams at Thompson, who in 1997 received a severe ninety-day suspension from the Suffolk Downs stewards for repeated failure to try with his mounts. "That's the way you ride all the time anyway, you fucking ape!"

Lanci lunges at Thompson and a brief scuffle ensues. The state trooper on duty in the jocks' room looks around as if he doesn't know whether to break it up or burst out laughing. But before the cop can decide, the melee is over before it really starts. Thompson escapes by crawling under a table and Lanci backs off, cackling.

"One big happy family," Lanci shouts to no one in particular, throwing his arms wide open for an imaginary group embrace before gathering his well-worn tack to be weighed out for the next race. "One big fucking happy family!"

Once it becomes apparent that the program will proceed, however reluctant some of the jockeys may be, races four through eight unfold without incident. The Saturday afternoon progresses with Panell, Caraballo, and Piermarini each winning a race. Vega scores in two and so does Hampshire, who goes wire-to-wire in the feature, a $17,000 allowance event, aboard Corporate Runner at 9 to 2. The fans who blindly bet the top jockeys on the standings page—and there are a plenty who do—have fattened their wallets for the afternoon. When the field of ten takes to the track for the ninth and final race of the program, the sun has just hidden behind the massive Suffolk Downs grandstand.

But this afternoon the winter sunset is more than symbolic, because just as the horses reach the gate, it is apparent from the press box that something is wrong down on the track. First there is a slight delay to the start. Then the field circles behind the gate, with the horses idling in place instead of being loaded. The field circles some more. Then the veterinarian assigned to the starting gate radios to the stewards that upon his advice, the betting favorite should be scratched from the nightcap because Why Tell Bob is having difficulty standing up and keeping his balance on the track.

The scratch is announced, costing precious time in the cold for everyone on horseback and some $10,000 in refunded bets for Suffolk Downs.

After several more minutes, the horses have still not loaded and now there seems to be trouble with other runners, too. More frantic walkie-talkie discussion ricochets back and forth between the stewards, the starter, and the vet. It seems that with the ensuing loss of daylight, the temperature has dipped just enough so that the complexion of the entire racing surface has changed dramatically, becoming extremely hazardous in only twenty minutes since the previous race. The jockeys have reached their breaking point and refuse to continue, even though they are at the gate and less than two minutes away from the end of the racing day and an additional paycheck.

The last race is canceled, and track announcer Larry Collmus explains that all wagers will be refunded. The jockeys return to the paddock and dismount. The unraced horses are walked back to their barns. Some of the grandstand fans boo and curse the jockeys; many were banking on the nightcap to bail them out at the end of a losing day.

Beneath the stands in the jockeys' room, Joe Hampshire undresses in front of his locker, unburdened of protective equipment except for his safety vest, waterproof pants, and riding helmet. I ask him why the jockeys refused to try to get the last race in, considering they had already ridden in the first eight events and everyone was out there and set for the start.

"You want to know why?" says an exasperated Hampshire, slamming his headgear into the wooden bench in front of him. "Because the chunks of ice were as big as this fucking helmet, that's why!"

Back in the press box, I look out into the gloaming of the infield, beyond the still-lit tote board. Amid all the distraction and commotion, I have forgotten about the swans stuck in the ice. I get my binoculars and check the pond.

The ice is smooth, hard and cold. The birds are gone.

CHAPTER TWO

WINTER GRIND

You learn to beat the horses
by digging, digging below the frostline,
then digging in the cloudy sky,
by talking to the tygers of wrath
who do not talk back.
Steel shoes are nailed down to the quick.
If truth is a straight line,
a thoughtful man doesn't stand a chance.
—MAJ RAGAIN,
Always Eight Furlongs in a Mile

THE DAY AFTER the first cancellation of the racing season, temper-atures are still bitingly cold. But the wind isn't as bad, so the Sunday show goes on as scheduled at the East Boston oval, Thoroughbred racing in no-frills fashion with little fanfare.

The overnight sheet that lists the advance schedule of races is dis-tributed with a prominent plea printed in both English and Spanish: Please Do Not Clean Feed Tubs in the Showers. Apparently, instead of using the outdoor hot-water hoses provided free of charge in each barn, the arctic conditions are causing some of the less scrupulous sta-blehands to rinse buckets of uneaten oats inside the backstretch bath-room facilities, which clogs the drains.

In more promising plumbing news, someone from the maintenance department has gone out to the infield, chopped a hole in the iced-over pond behind the tote board, and installed a circulation pump so the water won't freeze. Two of the Suffolk Downs swans swim con-tentedly in the small opening, but the third is nowhere to be seen.

I mention to the press-box gang how ironic it was that Rudy Baez chose yesterday for his first visit to the races since his accident, considering the appearance coincided with the season's first full-tilt blowup between management and jockeys over safety issues. But one of the resident degenerates who is best friends with Baez's longtime jockey agent, Mike Szpuk, informs me that I am incorrect, that yesterday was not Rudy's first trip to the track this year.

No one really knew about it, but Baez stopped by Suffolk Downs several weeks ago in a very low-key and inconspicuous manner. Szpuk parked Rudy in his wheelchair outdoors on the clubhouse side of the paddock one warm afternoon, away from the crowd where no one would bother him.

"Rudy was okay until he saw the riders getting up on the horses," the wiseguy tells me, shaking his head. "Then he lost it. Said the sight of the post parade, the horses going out on the track, was too tough on him. He couldn't take it. Rudy told Szpuk to get him the hell out of there. The two of them had to go home."

TODAY IS Martin Luther King Jr. Day, a rare chance for the track to handle some serious betting money on an otherwise mundane winter Monday. But Mother Nature is not a racing fan, at least not today. At 8:00 AM the thermometer reads 0°F, and the brutal blasts ripping in off the ocean make the wind-chill factor −50°F. According to newscasts, it is the coldest day in Boston in six years and one of the chilliest overall since the advent of modern record keeping. A full five hours before first post, the lucrative holiday card is scrapped by track management, and by all accounts, the decision is a no-brainer because every track on the Eastern seaboard is similarly forced to call off live racing.

Usually, the warmest location in all of Suffolk Downs is the press box, simply by virtue of its location behind the huge rooftop blowers that heat the massive concrete and glass grandstand. Because our office is often likened to the sauna in the jockeys' locker room, the press-box windows have to stay open nearly every single day of the year so that working conditions are bearable, and even in the middle of massive snowstorms, staffers have been known to crank up the air conditioning just to ensure moderate ventilation. Yet as always, surprises abound at the racetrack, and this morning is markedly different when Bish and I arrive for work.

During the night, the fire-exit door onto the roof gusted open—blown literally off its hinges—and the entire media relations office feels just as cold as the great outdoors. In fact, it is so frigid inside the press box that decades-old paint on the ductwork has flaked off in huge chunks, thanks to the massive contraction of the tin reacting against the elements, and a cup of water left on my desk overnight even has a thin veneer of ice crystallizing across the top. We immediately spring into action to combat Siberia: Bish goes upstairs and lodges a cinder block against the open door to keep it from shearing open again, while I turn up the press-box heat for the first time in years and start the all-important process of making fresh, hot coffee.

Minor catastrophe averted, we sit in the office fielding phone calls, shooting the shit, reading the Boston papers and our *Racing Forms*. On days when live racing is canceled, the press-box atmosphere is much like those childhood New England school days when classes were called off because of a snowstorm. Those who do make it in to the office are laid back, not dressed in a suit or tie, and everyone's attention usually turns to hitting a simulcast daily double before calling it quits to head into town for beers and billiards by midafternoon.

At about 11:00 AM, with my head buried in the past performances for the first race at Gulfstream in sunny Florida, Bish pricks his ears like an alert watchdog. "Do you hear that?" he asks, and I do: A loud hissing noise, rapid and insistent, like an angry snake right around the corner in the press-box hallway.

Bish sticks his head out to see what's going on, then motions me over to the door. "I bet you didn't bring your bathing suit today," he quips.

The source of the pressurized noise is instantly obvious: A free-flowing avalanche of water is cascading down from above, pooling deeply on our linoleum walkway. We trace the source of the torrent and find that the water is gushing from a burst pipe outside the stewards' stand, adjacent to where the door had been left open all night. The wall of water first collapsed part of a hanging ceiling one flight up, then flooded the upstairs hallway, spilled over into the photo-finish and teletimer room, spread down through the wiring in the walls to the press-box entryway, and then let gravity do its thing, jetting downward in a spectacular forty-foot arc onto the clubhouse box seats reserved for Suffolk Downs bigwigs and the track's leading owners and trainers.

"Too bad nobody was down there," Bish wisecracks as we observe the chilly waterfall from the catwalk high above. "*That* would have been interesting."

We call the maintenance department to handle this fiasco. This is clearly a job for union plumbers, not racetrack degenerates. Bish and I turn our attention back to the Gulfstream daily double.

Later, with the flood fully under control, I sit hunched in front of a VCR trying to cull archived racing video for a cable news station that has requested footage for an upcoming feature. This is a good project for a day when racing has been canceled, because as a history zealot, making such tapes always ends up taking me three times longer than it should—I get lost and sidetracked, mesmerized by old races, familiar horses, blasts from the past.

I watch one Suffolk Downs race circa 1987 featuring a winner whose name is spelled "Wrecked 'Em." But it doesn't sound that way when former announcer Jim Hannon, the New England hoss-hollering legend with the gravelly bass voice, gives the steed a big call across the wire.

"We had a horse called 'Rectum' who used to race here?" an incredulous intern queries from the press box.

"I would have thought I'd remember that one," quips Bish from behind his newspaper.

Soon after, while dubbing a race off the 1989 MassCap Day tape, I come across another oddly named runner whose moniker also apparently slipped past the censors at the Jockey Club, the organizational body that regulates and registers Thoroughbred names: a long-shot maiden winner called Priapism.

Bish doesn't remember this horse either. Nor does the intern know the meaning of the name.

I explain that priapism describes a medical dysfunction that causes men to suffer from a constant, relentless penile erection. The condition sounds humorous in a locker-room sort of way, but doctors say you won't laugh if you actually suffer from it, because an untreated case of priapism is said to be excruciatingly painful. Apparently it is most common in males who have sickle-cell anemia.

"Why would you even want to know that?" Bish asks, wincing. He sidesteps out of the office to go light up a smoke.

We drop the talk about Thoroughbreds with ignoble names. For the rest of the afternoon, I watch more archived races from years gone by, absorbed by obscure bits of trivia while outside the wind rages and howls across the frozen, vast expanse of darkening racetrack.

I'M STANDING adjacent to the outer rail at the finish wire prior to an $8,000 claiming sprint for fillies and mares. One of the entrants, a six-year-old racemare named Huckster's Girl, becomes agitated while being loaded for the start and flips over backward within the confines of the narrow steel gate.

A blur of panic and flailing hooves, the frenzied Thoroughbred dislodges jockey Harry Vega and whipsaws the 112-pound veteran backward out of his irons and over the rear door of the starting gate before getting her own legs crossed underneath her. Thrashing violently on her back in the claustrophobic stall, the startled and stricken mare is freed several torturous moments later by four assistant starters, the guys on the ground floor of the game who not only help load horses into the gate in an orderly fashion, but are also paid to rush to the immediate aid of terrified animals in situations where backing off in the opposite direction would be a rational human being's instinctive reaction.

There are only a few patrons outdoors on the grandstand apron on this dreary Wednesday, but one of them, a harried-looking woman in tattered attire leaning on the winner's circle fence, begins spewing expletives and cursing both the gate workers and the horse. After being disentangled from her nightmarish entrapment, Huckster's Girl stands panting and pawing behind the starting stalls three-quarters of a mile away out by the Blue Line subway stop, her No. 6 black-and-gold saddle towel askew from her flank and smeared with dirt. An equine doctor is stationed at the starting gate as a precaution for every single race at Suffolk Downs in case of such incidents, which occur maybe a handful of times a season. When Larry Collmus announces that the animal has been scratched by the stewards on the advice of the attending veterinarian, the woman then directs her hostile profanity in the direction of the judges' stand atop the grandstand roof.

My best guess is that the lady is an irate but relatively ignorant fan who has no concept of the risks to humans and horses when high-strung animals are made to stand very still before exploding on cue. I write her off as a two-dollar bettor who is both oblivious and obnoxious, and mention this to one of the jockeys' valets standing next to me, who by now has also turned around to glare at the woman's unseemly—even by racetrack standards—fit of hysteria.

"Actually, that's Pearl Chain," the racetracker corrects me, gesturing to the woman, then pointing to the line in his program denoting her as both owner and trainer of Huckster's Girl. "Nice to see her so concerned for the welfare of her horse."

Chain, thirty-five, has trained or worked on New England backstretches for a number of seasons, but she is hardly a household horseracing name or a topper on the Suffolk Downs standings page. She has owned Huckster's Girl since July 1998, when she claimed the 1-for-23 racemare for $5,000 at Rockingham Park. The dark brown Florida-bred filly lost her initial nine starts for her new outfit, then snapped the streak by winning twice in a row in Boston after teaming up with jockey Joe Hampshire. Since stepping up to face more difficult company, Huckster's Girl has more than earned her oats, winning $17,790 in purses and accounting for three of her trainer's six total wins last year. Although a modest racehorse by most standards, Huckster's Girl is the star of a small stable, recouping more than triple the value of her original claiming price. During the past eighteen months, the daughter of unheralded stallion Huckster has also carved out a notable reputation as a mudlark, running best when the track comes up muddy or sloppy, boasting two lifetime wins and a solid 8-for-11 in-the-money record over wet racing surfaces.

But horse racing has always been a strict *What have you done for me lately?* sport. And recently, life at the track has been luckless for both owner Chain and her main mare. Huckster's Girl, at 4 for 48 lifetime, hardly figured as a world-beater today but might have brought home some sort of paycheck for finishing at least fifth in an eight-horse race. And it's a good bet that Chain was desperate for any piece of the purse, because nearly three weeks into the season, the $375 that Huckster's Girl earned for capturing fourth place eleven days ago has been the stable's only income from horse racing so far this year.

THE $25,000 HOLIDAY FEATURE wiped out by Monday's cancellation is carded back today. The Private Terms Stakes—named after the final MassCap winner before the track closed in 1989—comes up as a "loaded" race, meaning a betting affair of unusually good quality. The race includes a trio of venerable locals who ran in recent MassCaps themselves.

Prolanzier is a fan favorite, long known as the Old Man of New England racing. He's now a ten-year-old with twenty-seven lifetime wins and at least one stakes victory a year in six of the last seven seasons, and Boston horseplayers vividly recall the day he ran third with Rudy Baez in the saddle in the 1996 Massachusetts Handicap. Name recognition usually renders the consistent gelding overbet any time he pops up in the entries, but coming off an uncharacteristic seventh-place try in his most recent race, the general consensus seems to be that Prolanzier has lost a step or two in the twilight of his career and may be ripe for a beating today. After going off as the heavily hammered favorite in nearly every race showing in his past performance lines, Prolanzier tilts dramatically upward in the odds this afternoon, settling to an almost unfathomable 5 to 1 by post time.

"No respect," says Bish, grimacing. He has a thing for resilient old warhorses who won't quit.

The first jump out of the gate, Prolanzier bashes his foot against the side of the steel starting stall, goring out a nasty flesh wound. Breaking fourth behind speedsters Mister Jiggs and Favorable Regard, and just to the inside of graded-stakes sprinter King Roller, Prolanzier pulls jockey Winston Thompson right into the thick of the developing duel, surging past the leaders before the first quarter mile of the six-furlong race. The maneuver, however gutsy it appears, is often a recipe for failure at all levels of Thoroughbred racing: *Slow start, rushed up, then empty when it counts* is the usual outcome after an overly taxing, auspicious start.

Yet determined as ever, the oldest horse in the race blasts headlong into the far turn, setting a breakneck pace with the quickest local chasers hot on his heels. Prolanzier's lead of an open length is down to a head after a grueling half mile. With 220 yards to run, the tested veteran finally puts away the pesky Favorable Regard, but now Prolanzier must brace for the cavalry charge of King Roller, the richest racehorse on the grounds, and favored Galloping Gael, who dusted Prolanzier last time out. Thompson urges his mount on vigorously, crouching low and thrusting hard with both hands every time the bay gelding extends his muscular shoulders forward. King Roller has run past Galloping Gael but appears to be spinning his wheels while trying to gain on the leader, who kicks on with something akin to an extra equine gear in the shadow of the wire.

The Old Man grinds out a neck victory in a valiant performance, and the mutuels return a generous $13.40 to every two-dollar bettor who backed Prolanzier to victory. In the winner's circle, his rear legs are covered with so much blood, dirt, and sand that it's difficult to tell which limb Prolanzier injured in that first stride out of the starting gate. Although fistfuls of worthless tickets abound in the press box, no one really seems to mind losing when the beating is administered by such a classy contender.

"No respect," repeats Bish, condemning the fools who dared bet against Prolanzier.

———

THE GLACIAL WEATHER that has gripped the Northeast the entire week shows no signs of abating. If anything, the cold has intensified. The forecast is so dangerously frigid that management decides at noon on Friday to call off the Saturday card twenty-four hours in advance. Suffolk Downs will lose its second coveted day of holiday or weekend business within the same week, but the unusually early call makes life a lot easier for workers, fans, and horsemen who appreciate the advance planning. It ends up being a wise move because the temperature will only flirt with the positive side of zero for the next forty-eight hours while the winds rip in off the ocean, pummeling the bunkered stables and cavernous steel-and-concrete betting factory at gusts of up to fifty miles per hour.

In the morning, before the Friday simulcasts start, the track hosts a double-session customer-service seminar sponsored by the National Thoroughbred Racing Association, the industry organization that is gamely trying to affix a friendlier public face to the sport. Workers from the mutuels, food service, security, and admissions departments have been asked to attend one of two voluntary training sessions. The seminars are not mandatory, but as both an incentive and a way of saying thanks, the track offers a complimentary breakfast to all workers who show up.

The tellers who punch betting tickets and cash out the winners are the ground troops on the front lines at any racetrack. The clerks interact constantly with the betting public, and their appearance and attitude can make or break a wagering facility. A mixture of old-timers who have worked the windows for decades and relative newcomers who have landed a plum pari-mutuel position thanks to some political string-pulling, the bulk of tellers at Suffolk Downs are good-natured, honest, and efficient. As is the case in any monotonous job, they complain and kibitz a great deal of the time among themselves, but as a whole, the clerks are accurate, reliable, and loyal almost to the point of fault.

Boston is an organized labor stronghold, and like many track employee groups, the Suffolk Downs tellers benefit from the backing of an ironclad union contract that dictates even the most minute terms of their employment. The agreement covers everything from cigarette breaks to bathroom privileges and contains numerous stipulations based on seniority so that it is virtually impossible to fire even the most unproductive and incompetent of employees. Although the rank and file at Suffolk Downs have a reputation as a hardened lot who sometimes border on surliness, this perception is only partially true, and for the most part it is a product of immersion in a hardscrabble, urban environment. Bostonians in general can be correctly characterized as unabashedly blunt, but behind the chiseled street-smart exteriors of a good number of locals, you'll find a lot of honest people with rock-jaw work ethics, some of whom are so surprisingly trusting and good-hearted that they have been known to give rides home to customers—complete strangers—who have car trouble in the parking lot at night after the races. On more than one occasion, track cleaning-crew staffers have returned lost wallets to their rightful owners, fully intact, with more money inside than the employee might see in a month. Like members of a family that is constantly squalling, squabbling, and bickering, Suffolk Downs workers are quick to unite if the track or the local racing industry comes under criticism, and this fervent combination of blind allegiance coupled with raw self-preservation is at once the most damaging yet somehow most endearing collective quality of track employees at the Eastie oval.

As the workers assemble, the crowding for free breakfast at the steam tables is reminiscent of the first few jumps out of the gate for the Breeders' Cup Sprint, with a lot of bumping, colliding, and jockeying for best position as the masses enthusiastically avail themselves of the free food. One gentleman—obviously a buffet veteran—opts to forgo the serving tongs at the sausage tray and instead dips his entire plate into the greasy platter to maximize his portion of pork, fully embodying the spirit of the old racetrack adage: If it's free it's for me!

Julie Sarno, a marketing executive from the tony Del Mar track near San Diego ("Where the Surf Meets the Turf!"), leads the seminar. She moves along at a good pace, not just lecturing but really making an attempt to listen to what the workers have to say, encouraging the staffers for their input and praising them for their efforts. Racing has long suffered from an awful industry-wide reputation when it comes to customer service, and presentations such as this one are long overdue, not only in Boston but all across the country.

Much of the problem stems from the good ol' days, when Thoroughbred racing was the nation's number-one spectator sport and the only thing even close to a marketing or customer relations strategy was to (1) tell people when first post was, and (2) open the turnstiles so money could flow through the mutuel windows. It is safe to say that industry leaders, so used to basking in their own glory and profits, were caught flat-footed when other entertainment options and gaming venues were spawned in the 1960s, 1970s, 1980s, and 1990s. Even with a forty-year head start, tracks today still have no answer for casino tactics like free drinks, deep discounts on meals and lodging, or even the most basic of customer-service tenets, a pleasant attitude and a smile.

The turnout for the optional-attendance function is good on this frigid morning, and there appear to be a lot of heads nodding in agreement as Sarno tries to get the workers to view the often-confusing and sometimes-intimidating racetrack experience from the perspective of a newcomer. A small cluster of employees is really getting into the group discussion, and in all honesty, their enthusiasm probably stems from having the first opportunity in years to have their opinions heard in a public forum in front of track management. The only downside I notice, viewing the audience from the back of the room, is that the majority of those in attendance are the Suffolk Downs employees who are personable and presentable to begin with. The most grievous offenders of tact, common sense, and workplace etiquette are nowhere to be found.

Sarno explains that every employee should strive to achieve the Walt Disney model of trying to make each interaction with customers a "magic moment." This understandably inspires more than a few frontline veterans to roll their eyes. She encourages the workers to memorize the acronym WOMBAT: Word of Mouth Is the Best Advertising Technique.

She is right, of course. But Sarno has never worked a shift at Suffolk Downs, which is decidedly different from her home track, where barefoot Southern Cali beauties sip blue margaritas in the infield and surfers on the sparkling Pacific shores serve as the backdrop for Thoroughbred racing in all its casual splendor. A day at the races at resort-like Del Mar would never be confused with the "racing experience" in East Boston, where a raunchy reputation and tacit indifference to the betting public long ago earned the joint the hard-to-shake sobriquet of Sufferin' Downs.

Just before the final stage of the presentation, which is composed of role-playing games designed to end the session on a fun note, one mutuel teller interrupts Sarno to ask a question, which he prefaces by respectfully begging to differ with her frame of reference of what really happens at an urban racetrack. As she has encouraged her seminar attendees to do all morning long, Sarno listens intently as the persistent young man makes his point.

"I don't doubt the value of what you're saying, ma'am, but to be realistic, how can you relate in terms of what we do here every day?" the clerk implores politely but passionately. Then he goes on:

We have the ocean in the winter on one side of us and the huge oil tank farms on Route 1A on the other. We're not a Del Mar or a Saratoga where people come for a picnic in the sun. This is a fast-paced environment with twenty-five tracks and all simulcasting. The live racing grinds on almost all year long. People come here for the sole purpose of betting, and a lot of them are angry because they're losing by the end of the day and it just doesn't stop. I'm not trying to be a wiseguy, but I would venture to guess you aren't aware of what it's like at 1:00 AM on a Friday when there's still an hour and a half to go for the Hollywood simulcasts, and people are coming in off the streets just for a place to get warm and fall asleep. Some of us are even afraid to go into the bathrooms here at night. We appreciate what you're saying, but can you please give us something that relates to *our* day-to-day interactions here at Suffolk Downs?

There is a pause, a long one, before others in the crowd murmur their assent. The mutuel clerk is right on the money: Despite her experience in many facets of marketing the sport, an outsider like Sarno has immense difficulty relating to the Suffolk Downs environment, which is unique even among the other hard-core, urban Thoroughbred outposts all across the country.

Caught off guard, Sarno does her best to fluster an answer.

Then the seminar hostess rushes on to the role-playing games, and a few more employees get up to raid the buffet.

MIKE GILL, the highly driven leading horse owner, has been juggling his steed rotation among four local trainers while belting out seven wins, eight seconds, and nine thirds for $75,074 in purse earnings through the first three weeks of the season. His better stock seems to be cycling into the stable of conditioner Michael Catalano Jr., a third-generation Suffolk Downs horseman whose solid reputation is backed by a 22 percent win ratio and current second-place standing on the leading trainers list. The move seems logical—unless you're one of Gill's three other trainers—and is further validated by Catalano's background, which reads like a black-type pedigree for a New England kid born and bred to train Thoroughbred racehorses.

Catalano, thirty-one, follows in the racetrack footsteps of his trainer father, Michael Sr., and great-uncle P. T. Catalano, who raced horses at the very first Suffolk Downs meeting in 1935. As a street-tough teenager, Mike alternated learning the family business with a passion for fisticuffs. For a while he pursued a career as an amateur boxer before trading in his gloves for a Thoroughbred license at age nineteen. On his very first day as a professional conditioner, Catalano saddled three winners at Suffolk Downs, a quirky feat that is quite likely unprecedented in the difficult-to-document history of New England racing. It wasn't long before word spread that Catalano had a knack for coaxing victories out of once-classy horses who had fallen on hard times, with an attention to detail and a head for the game that rivaled most veteran hands-on horse workers. Emboldened with a self-confidence that bordered on boastfulness, Mike sold himself to clients looking to own a piece of the action, and it was not long before his

74

small stable grew to twenty head and Catalano and his owners became frequent and flamboyant visitors to the winner's circle.

Unfortunately, Catalano's early success peaked at about the same time Suffolk Downs bottomed out, and when the East Boston oval closed in 1989, he took his show on the road to the New York and New Jersey tracks. But the formidable out-of-state competition served as a humbling lesson that both deflated Mike's ego and depleted his client list, and when he no longer had the horsepower to back up his combativeness, Catalano's cockiness began to ring hollow. "I had an attitude problem," he admitted nearly a decade later in a *Boston Globe* interview. "I scared some people. I thought I knew it all. I was young, and to tell you the truth, I thought it was easy."

Difficulty proved only a temporary deterrent. Catalano returned to New England in 1991, intent on rebuilding his racing stable by concentrating on local ties. He still carried himself with an Italian wiseguy swagger, but the anger and edginess in his personality had slipped beneath the surface, softened by experience. The number of steeds under his shed row increased steadily and so did his winning percentage and purse earnings. Over time, Mike became a credible spokesperson for the sport, a throwback sort of guy who still donned a sharp sport coat to saddle his horses in the paddock and readily agreed to media requests, press interviews, and even barn tours for visiting schoolchildren. Always crediting his help when he won and never blaming them when he lost, Catalano evolved into the default Suffolk Downs trainer when the media relations office wanted to send reporters and camera crews to the backstretch for a good human interest story with a quotable up-and-comer who could talk in detail about the game while still coming across as genuine and enthusiastic. In 1994, with business on the upswing at Rockingham Park and Suffolk Downs, Mike married popular jockey Abigail Fuller, and with their exchange of vows, the blue-collar battler not only gained a winner of a wife but also entrance into what many consider to be the grand first family of New England racing.

In the often smarmy circles of the Boston elite, one would be hard pressed to find a gentrified New England family other than the Fullers whose humility and modesty ranks so closely proportionate to their social status and collective wealth. Patriarch Alvan Fuller, a working-class laborer, made his mark as a New England bicycling champ in the late 1800s before earning enough money to venture to Europe, where he became intrigued by a new invention called the horseless carriage. In 1900, he imported the very first motorcars into Boston, foresaw the future by landing stateside distribution contracts, and became widely acknowledged as the inventor of the automobile dealership. Flush with cash and drawn toward progressive politics, Fuller served as a state representative before his eventual election as two-term governor of Massachusetts, leading a reform movement against corruption by top-pling notoriously entrenched rival James "Rascal King" Curley in 1924. Legend has it that Alvan Fuller, noted for his philanthropy, refused to take a dime from the Commonwealth of Massachusetts dur-ing his decades as a public servant, retaining as family souvenirs—uncashed—every single one of the salary checks issued to him during his political life.

Although Alvan was responsible for the automobile replacing the horses on the streets of Boston, his son, Peter, reintroduced equines to the Fuller legacy half a century later. A Harvard wrestling captain, amateur boxer, U.S. marine, and Boston businessman with a penchant for all things sporting, Peter Fuller bought his first Thoroughbred in 1951 and immediately became infused with a passion for breeding and racing. The green-and-gold Fuller silks gained success on a local level, but Fuller's attempts as a Yankee newcomer branching into the Kentucky-dominated bloodstock scene were met with resistance from the good ol' boys. In fact, some bluegrass hardboots openly ridiculed Fuller when he claimed a $5,000 racemare in the mid-1960s with the intention of breeding her, unaware that word was out that Noors Image had no ovaries and would never be able to produce a foal.

Fuller had the last laugh when he bred his new mare to prolific stal-lion Native Dancer, and Noors Image proved to be quite fertile indeed. In 1965, she gave birth to a precocious gray colt named Dancer's Image, who proved talented enough to tangle with the best in the country. "Dancer" won the prestigious Governor's Gold Cup at

Bowie Race Course in April 1968, sparking at least one reported offer of $1 million. Not only did Peter Fuller decline to sell his steed, but he privately went a step further, quietly donating the winner's share of the $119,100 race to Coretta Scott King, whose husband had been assassinated several days prior to the race.

Fuller had met Dr. Martin Luther King Jr. at a Boston University trustees meeting in 1967, the same year the civil rights leader had organized a Kentucky Derby sit-in to protest housing conditions in Louisville. The gift had intentionally been made without fanfare, but when Dancer's Image won the Wood Memorial at Aqueduct two weeks later, the donation was made public by an announcer who needed to fill air time after a jockey had fallen. With his homebred horse heading to Churchill Downs as one of the favorites for the Kentucky Derby, Fuller found himself embroiled in a political firestorm during an extremely tense and dangerous time. Savage letters and racist threats concerned him to the extent that he thought of hiring his own security team for the Derby, and although he eventually did not bring his own guards, the very rumor that he was even planning to do something so unconventional further flamed his image as an anti-establishment Northerner. The only saving grace of the tumultuous Derby trip was the race itself, which unfolded as a masterful last-to-first performance by Dancer's Image, who circled the field even after jockey Bobby Ussery lost his whip and had to hand-slap the sleek colt home, gunning down favorite Forward Pass in the shadow of the wire for a hard-fought 1-1/2-length win.

Peter Fuller's glory lasted a mere forty-eight hours before unraveling into a nightmare of controversy. According to Kentucky State Racing Commission officials, the post-race urine test on Dancer's Image had returned positive for phenylbutazone, a drug likened to mild equine aspirin. Commonly known as "bute," the medication is now legally allowable in a Thoroughbred's system on race day all across the country, with a usage ratio that approaches 100 percent of all starters (bute was also permissible before, and after—but curiously, not during—1968 in the state of Kentucky). Dancer's Image, Fuller readily admitted, was stout of heart but frail of ankles and had been treated with bute by a licensed veterinarian a week prior to the race, but he argued that dosage records proved the drug had been administered well before the accepted clearance time to pass through the horse's system. Dancer's Image immediately became the first and only horse ever disqualified from a Kentucky Derby win, and stories circulated that Peter Fuller had gotten what he deserved for being a brash, Negro-sympathizing Yank in the back-slapping cradle of bluegrass country. The uproar made the cover of *Sports Illustrated,* and rumors proliferated about how the lax security conspired to create an opportunity for the horse's feed to be tampered with or how the urine sample was intentionally tainted. Fuller spent $150,000 and five years exhausting every single one of his legal appeals to regain the Kentucky Derby trophy and his own personal honor, but in the end all he succeeded in saving were memories.

One of Fuller's most cherished recollections is captured in the official winner's circle photograph of that race, which shows his young daughter, Abigail, standing awestruck amid the chaos of the Kentucky Derby, gaping adoringly at winning jockey Ussery. At the time, the nine-year-old thought she had a crush on Bobby, but it later turned out that Abby's love for the sport ran much deeper. As a bright and athletic teenager, she was adept at riding show and jumper horses, but became increasingly frustrated at the subjectivity of such contests. Her father suggested that the diminutive Abby try race-riding, where the difference between winning and losing is much more clearly defined. Both father and daughter wanted to avoid the obvious stereotype of Abby living out a rich girl's whim, so the twenty-three-year-old started from the bottom, walking hots and mucking stalls on the Suffolk Downs backstretch like any other aspiring rider, accepting little, if any, special treatment. She rode her first race in November 1982 but didn't hit the winner's circle until eight months later. In between, Abigail shoveled a lot of horseshit and enjoyed every single minute of it.

"When I first came around, people would look at me and say, 'What's this kid doing here?' And really, they had every right to ask that," Abby admitted in a *New England Sport* magazine interview during her third full season of race-riding. "It was really hard at first.

People were always making comments. I was so shy. When someone said something, it would make me feel terrible." Once it was clear that Abby Fuller had earned a spot in the saddle on her own merit, she began picking up mounts on better steeds, including those owned by her father. In 1985, the Peter Fuller homebred Mom's Command burst out of New England and onto the national racing scene with Abby in the irons, sweeping the prestigious Filly Triple Crown and a total of four Grade I stakes races against major-league competition (top stakes races are ranked by a national committee on three levels, with Grade I being the most prestigious). As the wins piled up and the popularity of "Mom" and her cute, intelligent jockey grew all across the country, some sportswriters suggested that the storybook series of events was analogous to *National Velvet*, the classic girl-becomes-jockey tearjerker film. "No," vowed a proud but emphatic Peter Fuller whenever the question was put to him. "It's better."

Nine days after Suffolk Downs reopened in 1992, Abby Fuller was thrown from a lowly bottom-level claimer who hadn't won in ages, landing face-first in the homestretch, fracturing her first thoracic vertebra and suffering cuts to the face while her five-year-old son watched from the grandstand. The unsettling circumstances of the injury, magnified by the pleading of her youngster to quit, made the difficult decision to temporarily retire an easy one for Fuller. She then split her time at the track exercising horses in the mornings while working as a television commentator for the Suffolk Downs broadcast team in the afternoons, and after her marriage to Mike and the subsequent birth of the couple's first child, she began riding again in 1996, almost exclusively on Team Catalano's soundest and fastest horses.

With a third child on the way, Abby recently announced another leave of absence from the saddle, but the stability of both track and family life seem to be working in favor of the couple during an otherwise unsettled time for New England racing. Success breeds success, and the recent infusion of horseflesh from power client Mike Gill has upped the ante significantly. Although it remains to be seen how the headstrong, wealthy horse owner will mesh with the tenacious but talented trainer, the potential of the arrangement is enough for Catalano to accept Gill's offer of becoming the exclusive conditioner of his top stock—but with the stipulation that Catalano split the stable and take the best horses south himself to Maryland and Delaware, where the competition is fierce but the purses and prestige are substantially higher.

On the surface, one wonders how this combo can lose: A guy with lots of money hooking up with a competent trainer whose family is immersed in the sport and whose individual career is just now starting to peak. There is no such thing as a sure thing in Thoroughbred racing, but in a business where every decision is a gamble, the Gill-Catalano entry certainly seems worth a wager.

RUDY BAEZ has shown an unbelievable amount of resilience, fortitude, and progress since his August accident. Recently returned from the Kessler Institute, the noted spinal-cord injury rehabilitation center in New Jersey, the seventeenth-winningest rider in the history of the sport has begun physical therapy at his home in nearby Wakefield and someday aspires to return to the racetrack in a different capacity. Rudy's upper body is still strong and his handshake remains a vise, the product of decades in the irons controlling, coercing, and cajoling half-ton animals bred to run their eyeballs out with only the flick of a wrist or the subtle pressure of his fingers. Baez vividly recalls the day in the hospital last summer when his wife, Judy, broke down in tears and confided that the odds were overwhelming against him ever walking again. Cool as ever in the heat of adversity, Rudy's first thought was to calm his spouse; his second was how he would combat the restlessness of a reduced lifestyle. "We'll live with it," he told her. "It will be all right. But I can't just sit around, you know."

Even up to age forty-nine, when his racing career came to an abrupt halt, it was not uncommon for Baez to ride every race on a nine-event program. Lithe and athletic, Baez was an off-track inspiration for many of his colleagues. He quietly studied his Bible between races, never turned down a public appearance or charity request, and had a competitive drive that endeared him to the two-dollar bettors, perhaps the hardest group of people to impress at any racetrack. Baez rode hard for downtrodden trainers who needed the difference between a fourth- and fifth-place purse check just to make ends meet, as well as the railbird regulars counting on his horse to round out some desperate trifecta. Many jockeys simply do not try their best for minor shares in cheap races once it becomes evident that they are not going to win. But not Rudy. His competitive spirit sometimes got Baez into trouble—like the day in 1991 he won seven races on a single afternoon at Rockingham Park, lost by a bob for the eighth, and then cracked his mount over the head with his whip in frustration, earning a fine from the stewards—but overall, Rudy's fire and spirit has been sorely missed in the locker room since his accident. Several weeks ago, the January 9 edition of the *Boston Globe Sunday Magazine* profiled the Dominican native, who spoke of growing up in Santo Domingo and the source of his faith, competitiveness, and optimism:

We lived two blocks from the racetrack. I started very young. You could start legally when you were 16, but a trainer got my license for me, got me in [at age fourteen]. I got a record, winning the most races in one year, even though I rode one day a week only. That was 1966. I won something like 200 races. It was tough because there wasn't too much money in those days, although I helped my family a little. I bought land, a bigger house . . .

We were a very poor family. There were four boys and two girls, and my father was driving a truck and was out of town most of the time. My mother was the one that did everything. She was a good mother, she believes in God, a lot of faith. She [recently] broke her hip and got a hip replacement; she's got to walk with a walker. She had two heart attacks. She's 73 and still doing good. She's a tough, tough, tough lady. I'm just like her, got the same kind of spirit . . .

Coming home, if I didn't win that day, that's a tough night for me. I think about what I did wrong. You didn't want to be around me. I didn't want to talk. I would just think about my business, what I did wrong. I'd go to bed thinking about it . . .

The Guy up There is the one who's going to get you through

every day, you know. He helped me a lot. You've got to work and do your own thing, but sometimes, I don't know how I did it, and I have to figure that it was Him who helped me.

HANG AROUND the racetrack long enough and you'll get attached to certain horses for reasons you can't even explain to yourself. Maybe you cashed a ticket on a particular runner early on in his career and have followed him ever since. Maybe you liked a Thoroughbred's name when it first appeared in the entries and never let it go. Or maybe something charismatic about an animal's personality or running style caught your eye for a brief instant and you never forgot. The rationale and motives don't really matter. Having a sentimental favorite is part of the fun, and even the game's most objective and rigid handicapping degenerates will admit to having a soft spot for at least one such steed on their local circuit.

Mine is Saratoga Ridge, and after being absent from the entries for nearly two months, he is back in action today, making his seasonal Suffolk Downs debut at age eleven.

I have no idea exactly when or why this workmanlike gelding first appeared on my equine radar screen, but hindsight can help explain part of the attraction: First and foremost, Saratoga Ridge is gray. Technically, his official foal papers list him as "roan," which means he was born with fine white hairs mixed into a base-colored coat of red, brown, or in his case, black, with a touch of red sparkle. But "roan" was abandoned as a distinct term by the Jockey Club in 1995, and the son of Saratoga Six with the sculpted, angular face and unruffled demeanor has long since aged to nearly all white anyway, which is what happens to wizened old racehorses with salt-and-pepper genetics.

Gray horses abound in racing lore, with both negative and positive connotations largely rooted in superstition. "They say a gray won't earn its hay" is one oft-repeated racetrack rhyme that lacks supporting documentation. "Never bet an unknown gray"—meaning a horse picked out of the program without first seeing its coat color—is another. On the flip side, some backstretch veterans are emphatic in their belief that grays run faster in the mud than their darker, mostly brownish contemporaries ("Gray horses for gray days"), although I've yet to meet anyone who can explain why. A separate scenario set forth by breeding aficionados argues that the process of natural selection has caused gray horses to evolve as faster Thoroughbreds overall, because for eons their distinctly lighter color made them more visible to predators in the wild, enabling surviving grays to pass along superior speed to their offspring. Although plausible, this conjecture similarly lacks solid proof.

Other bits and pieces of folk wisdom don't have anything to do with how swiftly the horses can run, and instead embrace grays for their alleged good fortune: The luckiest horseshoe of all is said to be off the hind leg of a gray mare, and if found by accident, it is supposedly doubly blessed. For those superstitious enough to make the effort, bad luck brought about by breaking a mirror or spilling salt is thought to be reversed by leading a gray horse through your house. The same goes for ill fate brought about by walking under a ladder, although in that instance the remedy is said to be to keep your fingers crossed until you have seen three grays (outdoors, one guesses) in succession.

Saratoga Ridge also tops my personal list of favorites because of his gutsy nobility. A Thoroughbred who races for nine straight seasons doesn't survive 122 lifetime starts on legs alone, and this ancient roan gelding with the ornery black eyes, flared nostrils, squat sprinter's hindquarters, and unpretentious attitude clearly knows and enjoys his job, embodying that elusive and difficult-to-define racetrack quality known as "heart."

After launching his career with promise in August 1992 at the prestigious and historic New York racecourse after which he was named, the Ridge toiled in anonymity at major tracks up and down the Eastern seaboard, managing but three wins from fifty-eight starts through his initial three years of racing. But his career took a turn for the better in May 1995 when Saratoga Ridge was purchased at auction for $10,200 and shipped to New England, where he rose through the ranks in rough-and-tumble fashion. Rarely overpowering but always consistent, the gritty gray finished no worse than fifth in his first thirty-three starts on the local circuit, bringing home a piece of the purse every single time he stepped out of his stall at Rockingham Park or Suffolk Downs from July 1995 through May 1997. It was only when his connections (which in racing parlance means his owner and trainer) ambitiously entered Saratoga Ridge against $200,000 stakes company on New England's Million Dollar Day of Racing that he faltered to sixth, tiring behind some of the best sprinters in the country on the 1997 MassCap undercard. The Ridge found the winner's circle in his next start against allowance foes, took one more unsuccessful shot against stakes company in a minor handicap at Rock five weeks later, then began *another* torrid oat-earning stretch that currently stands at thirty-six outings in which he has finished fifth or better. Sidelined by ouchy ankles and dropped back into the claiming class out of competitive necessity over the last two and a half seasons, Saratoga Ridge has been claimed away but always claimed back by his original and current New England connections, owner Manny Roos and trainer Arthur Duffy Jr. The pair seem to know how to keep the old gelding happy and productive after all these years, despite one distinct but endearing quirk that truly sets this gray grinder apart from all other horses at Suffolk Downs.

Throughout the course of his career, Saratoga Ridge has displayed an uncanny knack—almost an intentional preference, really—for finishing second. As strange as it seems, the eleven-year-old acts as if he willfully possesses the odd intelligence and ability to do anything and everything in his power to round out the back half of the exacta, which he has accomplished like an ultra-consistent white blur on thirty-three career occasions. Not only does he own more bridesmaid finishes than any other horse on the grounds, the Ridge often races against horses who haven't even made as many lifetime starts equal to his astounding number of seconds. If chasing the pace from the back of the pack, Saratoga Ridge will come wide and driving, flying from way off the tailgate to nail the place position. Left alone on the lead, the gelding will hesitate ever so slightly inside the final furlong, waiting for one of his friends to edge closer before turning on the jets to make it a race to the wire. It's almost as if the Florida-bred son of Saratoga Six gets bored, which does happen to some pack animals. But the difference in the Thoroughbred sport is that these so-called "hangers" are usually weeded out of the mix early on in their careers. The inclination to be polite to company isn't exactly a productive trait for a racehorse. In fairness, Saratoga Ridge has also made an impressive eighteen lifetime trips to the winner's circle. But still, every time he hits the track, the bulky gray looks most at home and pleased with himself when cantering back second best.

Approaching the starting gate, the Ridge knows what's coming and gets his game face on. Today he'll be plying his trade at the $10,000 claiming level, and the gray is champing at the bit, jerking his head up and down as if nodding "yes" while planting his front legs and blasting both hind hooves out, up and back in one final kick of aggression before being handed off to the assistant starter at the barrier. Through binoculars from the press box, the mottled, light coat of Saratoga Ridge is camouflaged against East Boston's backdrop of sooty snow, and even though jockey Harry Vega can't see from stall number four that the odds on the Ridge have dipped to 8 to 5, he is probably as aware as the betting public that even if not in top racing shape after a seven-week layoff, the reliable roan is as game to win this race as any of his six tensely coiled rivals awaiting the explosive cacophony of the start.

A field of veterans, the group of seven exits the gate on cue and in stride, and Vega immediately puts Saratoga Ridge into a tactically advantageous position just behind long-shot leader Imabucklite. The favored gray is "on the muscle"—meaning aggressive—and he toys with the 11-to-1 pacesetter through the turn until the top of the homestretch. When Vega asks the old roan for run, he reels in the leader, spurting to the top and dropping closer to the inside rail with eager, reaching strides. But soon after Saratoga Ridge sails to the lead, other riders make their moves, and company arrives first in the form of Rivalry, a 4-to-1 closer ridden by Winston Thompson. Sensing that Saratoga Ridge might not be able to combine his sharp early pace with the critical kick of stamina in his first race back from an extended vacation, Thompson guides Rivalry to the three path (three lanes out from the inner rail), engages the Ridge in a brief tussle approaching the eighth pole, then blows on by.

Either that, or the seasoned gray fully knows what he's doing and lets Rivalry pass him. The outcome is the same no matter how one reasons, and Saratoga Ridge is second once again. His whitish coat now mud-flecked, the gelding gallops out fluidly and full of run, basking in the afterglow like an aging athlete who knows he is no longer the fastest but is content to remain the most crafty.

When the horses jog back to the homestretch in front of the paddock to be unsaddled and untacked, Saratoga Ridge gets a not-entirely-unexpected visit from a Racing Commission employee who attaches a small red identifying tag to his bridle. For $10,000, he has been claimed by a new owner. Saratoga Ridge will make the long walk back to the barn area to eat supper under a new shed row and to sleep in a new stall, now the property of up-and-coming conditioner Mike Catalano Jr.

THE MASSACHUSETTS HANDICAP is the richest and most historic horse race in the region and the linchpin of Suffolk Downs. In fact, as far as most folks are concerned—be they international industry insiders or casual local fans—the MassCap *is* Suffolk Downs.

The showcase race at the gritty East Boston oval boasts a tradition touched by class and graced by champions. Since its inception from humble beginnings in 1935, the 1-1/8 mile event has featured nine equines who ascended to the sport's top honor, the Horse of the Year Eclipse Award. Four victors each of the Kentucky Derby, Preakness Stakes, and Belmont Stakes went on to race in the MassCap, and two subsequent MassCap winners emerged to score in the Breeders' Cup Classic, the 1-1/4 mile culmination for the year's best distance runners. Adding to the intrigue, the MassCap has also produced its share of underdog hometown hopefuls who have turned the tables on heavy favorites through the decades, earning the race a reputation for a consistently good story line—win, lose, or draw. Thanks to the glow of history fine-tuned by modern marketing, the $600,000 race now qualifies as the one day of the year each spring when Suffolk Downs enjoys unparalleled attention as the biggest show in Boston, and what has evolved into New England's Million Dollar Day of Racing ensures scrappy little Suffolk Downs a guaranteed annual position in the glare of the worldwide racing spotlight.

Sixty-five years ago, Top Row won the initial $25,000 edition of Boston's big race by a narrow nose, and the MassCap was off and running in the sport's first season at Suffolk Downs. In 1937, the raucously popular Seabiscuit, who began his career as a nondescript New England claimer, scored in the $50,000 MassCap en route to becoming the most famous racehorse of his era. One year later, Triple Crown winner War Admiral finished out of the money in the 1938 MassCap, losing at 2 to 5 to an unlikely lightweight named Menow before a stunned crowd of some 60,000, the track's largest recorded attendance. In 1942, Whirlaway romped as the first and only Triple Crown champ to tally in the MassCap, and the swift steed's winning share of the purse from that race established him as the game's all-time earnings leader. First Fiddle was the first of five horses to win the big Boston race twice, but his 1945 MassCap received more notoriety for the rioting race fans who toppled the stewards' stand and demolished the tote board after a controversial disqualification in that afternoon's final race. Shortly thereafter, the judges moved their booth from ground level at the finish wire to the grandstand rooftop, several stories above the crowd in a decidedly more isolated spot. Local wiseguys still quip that making that move was the only good call the track stewards ever made.

As track ownership changed hands, the role of the MassCap fluctuated with the times. The positioning of the race roved on the calendar, initially serving as an autumn centerpiece (back when the East Coast season ended in October or early November) before drifting backward through the summer months and as early as May before finding its current home on the first Saturday in June. It might strike modern racing enthusiasts as odd to learn that for decades, and as recently as 1971, the MassCap, much like other major races of the era, occupied a midweek time slot. The thinking back then was that Saturdays are always a big draw anyway, so why not reap another 30,000-plus crowd when you know every sports nut in town will cut work to attend the main event on a Wednesday? From 1948 through 1969, the MassCap was raced at what is widely referred to as the sport's "classic" distance of 1-1/4 miles. In 1970 and 1971, when a different form of experimenting with grass became popular throughout the nation, the MassCap was scheduled as a 1-1/2 mile turf race before reverting to its original distance of 1-1/8 miles on the main track.

The thirtieth edition of the MassCap in 1964 began a torrid aberration of losing favorites, with odds-on (meaning win odds of less than 1 to 1) choices tanking in three straight years, followed by the unfathomable ($115.20 to win) score by unlikely party crasher Good Knight in 1967. Heavily backed horses hit the board but did not win a MassCap from 1969 until 1973, when powerhouse Riva Ridge outclassed the competition at 2 to 5, equaling Whirlaway's thirty-one-year-old track record of 1:48-1/5. But the very next season the Suffolk Downs favoritism jinx returned in full force, and the betting choice would not win for another fifteen consecutive MassCaps. It is worth noting that the dearth of favorites coincided with the decade during which the region began to receive notorious attention for its underworld betting scandals. Although these MassCap results certainly seem unrelated to any chicanery, legend nevertheless spread that outsiders might want to think twice before shipping in to Suffolk Downs to try and take big money away from the sly Boston boys on their home court.

The season before the race turned fifty, the Massachusetts Handicap featured a beefed-up purse of $150,000 and was awarded coveted Grade II status. In 1987, the season that Buddy LeRoux first threatened to close the plant, fans embraced a massive gray workhorse named Waquoit, who emerged as the first top equine hero from New England in decades, and his all-out MassCap win by a nostril over even-money choice Broad Brush produced one of the most, if not *the* most, thrilling stretch drives in the history of Suffolk Downs. By the

late 1980s, when the quality of day-to-day racing was severely eroding, the track heavily leveraged its future on the annual draw of the
MassCap, boosting its purse even higher, to $250,000, and then
$300,000. While Suffolk Downs went all out to secure national tele-
vision coverage and lure well-known equine stars such as Lost Code,
Cryptoclearance, and Crème Fraiche for a single race, longtime local
outfits were vacating the Boston backstretch in droves because of meager overnight purses for year-round racing and a callous, antagonistic
attitude on the part of management. By the time Private Terms won
the fifty-fifth renewal, news was simmering behind the scenes that the
1989 MassCap would be the track's last. Six months later, Suffolk
Downs not only limped out of big-league racing but left the
Thoroughbred business altogether, beginning a doleful hibernation
that would last a bitter two years.

When the racetrack reopened in 1992, the relentless question from
fans and the media was whether the storied MassCap would be
brought back to life, too. In retrospect, the popularity of the race had
been underestimated by the new operations team, which in every way
possible was seeking to distance itself from anything related to the previous regime and the persistent stigma of old Sufferin' Downs. Opting
for the long view, the announced goal was to first solidify everyday racing before tossing a lot of money into a single showcase race. The
strategy worked, making for a vastly improved New England product
that became quite marketable during the advent of simulcasting.
Emboldened by a year of moderate success, Sterling Suffolk
Racecourse staged a nine-furlong $100,000 stakes event that looked
suspiciously like the MassCap but was not acknowledged as such in
1993 and 1994, when the main event was sold to a sponsor and christened the "Suffolk Downs Budweiser Breeders' Cup Handicap." It
was not until the following year that the MassCap reemerged as a centerpiece horse race, returning with such a combination of orchestrated and accidental splendor that racing devotees around the country
could not help but take notice of the underdog arrival of Suffolk
Downs as a major player on the increasingly competitive national
stakes landscape.

The modern-day MassCap is the brainchild of Lou Raffetto, the image-savvy Suffolk Downs vice president and general manager. A relentless hustler with high expectations and standards, Raffetto, at age fifty, is that rare breed of industry executive who works hard six days straight at his own racecourse, then can't wait to go off and visit a different track just for pleasure on the seventh. The GM grew up near Monmouth Park, the scenic seaside racecourse on the New Jersey shore, and held just about every conceivable grunt track job as a teenager, from working as mailroom clerk to driving the water truck to replacing divots on the turf course. Raffetto attended Georgetown University and graduated in 1972, but instead of continuing to law school as planned, Lou detoured by claiming a $3,000 horse at a cheap backwater track in West Virginia. The steed won his very first start for his new owner, and "it was like I'd been shot up with adrenaline" as Raffetto later admitted in a *Boston Globe* profile titled "Suffolk's Savior." He worked as a trainer in New Jersey and Pennsylvania for two years before opting for race officiating and management, and by 1974, Raffetto was beginning to parlay minor racing department gigs into increasingly bigger and better positions. After stints heading the racing programs at Laurel Race Course in Maryland and Hialeah Park in Florida, Raffetto returned to his Monmouth roots, accepting the position of assistant general manager. Well known for fresh ideas and bold approaches, Lou was courted heavily in 1991 by incoming chairman Jim Moseley to retool the Suffolk Downs racing program, and it wasn't long before he landed a lucrative deal to pack up and move to Boston just in time to usher in the racetrack's grand reopening as its new GM.

Scheming far in advance, Raffetto prepared a MassCap plan during the winter of 1994–1995 that was systematically designed to lure the best horse in America to Suffolk Downs. A freakishly fast gray named Holy Bull had grabbed racing by the throat with an undefeated record at age two before winning eight of ten stakes and Horse of the Year honors as a three-year-old in 1994. Running roughshod over the classiest competition, Holy Bull was riding a six-race winning streak into his 1995 campaign, and Raffetto wanted badly to pull off a coup that would bring him to Boston to coincide with the highly heralded return of the MassCap. It just so happened that Lou and Holy Bull's trainer, Warren "Jimmy" Croll, were pals from their days together at Monmouth Park, and it didn't take much more than a phone call for Raffetto to find out what the schedule of stakes races was likely to be for Holy Bull that winter and spring. Armed with the information that Croll intended to race Holy Bull in the Gulfstream Park Handicap in Florida before trying the Oaklawn Handicap in Arkansas and the Pimlico Special in Maryland, Raffetto devised a clever incentive plan that attached point values to horses who finished in the money in those very three races. The total purse for the MassCap was to be $250,000, but point-getters in what was unveiled as the Massachusetts Handicap Bonus Series were eligible to race for a much higher winning share. Any horse strong enough to sweep that series of three races and then win the MassCap would receive an astronomical $500,000 *above and beyond* the standard 60 percent winner's share of $150,000, making the enhanced MassCap value the second-richest race on the continent, behind only the $3-million Breeders' Cup Classic.

The concept was novel because it was the first time major stakes events elsewhere had a definite cash connection to a third-party race, and there was really nothing the other tracks could do about it (Suffolk Downs neither sought nor was granted permission to use their races as a bonus tool). The insurance company that underwrote the funding mechanism, which also included lesser awards on a sliding scale, was aware that the likelihood of a sweep was a difficult one even for a powerhouse like Holy Bull, because there was no guarantee the champ would even be entered in those particular three races. But Raffetto, with his inside knowledge of the star steed's schedule, simply sat back, enjoyed the cards he had dealt his own racetrack, and waited for the future to unfold.

Instead of unfolding, the future imploded—violently, immediately, and right in Raffetto's face. The semi-stacked Suffolk Downs deck became an unstable, teetering house of cards before the series even officially started. In what was supposed to be a facile prep race for the first leg of the MassCap Bonus Series, Holy Bull had barely run half a mile in the Donn Handicap at Gulfstream Park when the 3-to-10 favorite took a bad step, bobbled, and was jerked to a halt in distress on the Gulfstream backstretch. Having suffered a severe tendon strain in his left front leg, Holy Bull's career ended on the spot, and apparently so too did Raffetto's chances for bringing a superstar to Suffolk Downs to compete in the MassCap.

A mildly accomplished equine cantered past the stricken champ and into the winner's circle, but no one really paid attention in the aftermath of the tragedy. Raffetto's bonus program looked doomed before it even got off the ground, because now only the second-tier stakes horses would bother to contest the series, and what was the purpose of Suffolk Downs fronting extra purse money to entice entrants who had no marquee value? And with Holy Bull no longer around to scare off the competition, one could be sure that many such second-tier stakes runners would come out of the woodwork to chase the MassCap money. The horse who had just won the Donn would probably now go on to attempt the other MassCap bonus races, and how many people back in Boston cared about him? Still, Raffetto couldn't just abandon his plan now that it was launched. Out of pride for his own idea more than anything else, he felt obligated to track down the connections of the Donn winner and inform them of the incentives available to their otherwise unassuming stakes steed. For the record, that unheralded, largely unwanted horse was named Cigar.

At the time, no one could have guessed that the quiet, ordinary-looking bay with the gentle, white-starred face was on the cusp of being transformed into the greatest racing sensation of the quarter-century, with Suffolk Downs playing a prominent role in his rise and fame. Even in their wildest delusions, neither Raffetto nor the horse's trainer, William Mott, could have been remotely aware of the inherent magnetism of the fragile-kneed underachiever who'd been an early flop. Despite a pedigree that promised grass-course ability, Cigar won only once from eleven tries on the lawn in California before being switched to dirt racing in New York as a last resort.

In October 1994, Mott tried Cigar in an Aqueduct allowance race on the dirt track, and the colt surprised by romping home an easy eight lengths in front. Some steeds simply prefer one type of surface over another—experts say how a horse runs on grass courses or dirt tracks has a lot to do with how its hoof is shaped—but rarely is such a preference so pronounced that it will transform an also-ran into a worldbeater. Yet that's exactly what happened to Cigar. One month later, a seven-length win over Grade I competition in the New York Racing Association Mile solidified his status as a dirt runner, and when Mott shipped south to Florida for the lucrative Gulfstream winter meet, so too did the maturing Cigar. The improving son of Palace Music scored his fourth straight by decimating allowance competition before annexing dirt race number five, a race that in retrospect generates vigorous debate over which star steed would have prevailed had Holy Bull remained healthy in that fateful Donn Handicap in February 1995.

Intrigued by the incentives and flattered by Raffetto's charm, owner Allen Paulson and trainer Bill Mott elected to follow the exact path to Suffolk Downs that the track had laid like an expensive trail of breadcrumbs. As the heavily backed favorite, Cigar dutifully won each of his monthly Grade I stakes assignments at Gulfstream Park, Oaklawn Park, and Pimlico Race Course, sweeping the bonus series. On target for Boston, the five-year-old had now racked up seven straight victories against top competition, and the national racing media had started to take notice with $650,000 on the line. Raffetto now faced an entirely separate problem, though it was one he was glad to have: Cigar had become such a dominant force in such a small window of time that Suffolk Downs was having difficulty rounding up competition to race against him in the MassCap. None of the other five horses who had amassed points in the bonus series—including 1994 Breeders' Cup Classic winner Concern and the highly regarded stakes stalwart Devil His Due—would commit to chasing Cigar, and the first MassCap in six years was shaping up as little more than an exhibition matching the game's new superstar against five hapless long shots. The game's newest superhorse had looked so scary-good during his spring winning streak that none of the sport's top guns wanted to risk humiliation by racing against him.

But the fans didn't seem to care. And neither, quite frankly, did Suffolk Downs. Raffetto switched gears effectively: If the race was going to be little more than a gallop around the track for $650,000, then so be it. It had been decades since the best horse in the land had raced in New England, and the mere fact that Cigar was coming to revitalized Suffolk Downs generated a blitz of Boston publicity that the embattled track could not possibly have concocted otherwise. The entire carnival atmosphere of MassCap Day itself was being structured as a payback to patrons, and bringing the nation's top horse to the festivities was management's way of saying thanks to ardent supporters for enduring tough times through the years. As for the human connections of the steeds entered in the MassCap, Raffetto killed them with kindness, lavishing them with free travel and hotel arrangements, a swank invite-only MassCap dinner cruise, chauffeured cars, prime stabling arrangements, various gifts and trinkets, and just about anything else a MassCap horse owner requested. Obviously, most of these perks were skewed toward Paulson and Mott, but a genuine effort was made to ensure that *everyone* involved with the MassCap felt included, all the way down to the grooms of the no-hopers. Word got around quickly that Suffolk Downs was a track that went out of its way to take care of people who supported its showcase race, and when race day finally arrived and Cigar and top jockey Jerry Bailey effortlessly cruised around the track like the 1-to-5 certainty they were in the wagering, even the grizzled railbirds applauded lustily. The MassCap and Suffolk Downs were back on the map.

The Cigar mystique didn't stop there, and neither did the lovefest associated with Suffolk Downs. The Hollywood Gold Cup in July was Cigar's consecutive win number nine. A trio of important autumn victories followed at Belmont Park in the Woodward Stakes, Jockey Club Gold Cup, and Breeders' Cup Classic. In the aftermath of winning Horse of the Year for his twelve-race winning streak, an obviously touched Bill Mott repeatedly and genuinely credited the Boston track and its fans for playing a major part in propelling Cigar into the stratosphere of the racing world. "Going to Suffolk Downs," he said, "was one of the best things we did. I don't think a day goes by that someone from New England doesn't stop me and say, 'Thanks for bringing your horse to Suffolk Downs.'" While the champ got a three-month break and the media gushed about how the ugly duckling track struck it rich by wooing the sport's most sought-after star, Raffetto was already working ardently behind the scenes to snare Cigar again for the following year's MassCap before anyone could tell the hardscrabble Eastie oval that it couldn't.

The same way he started the previous season, Cigar returned running right off the layoff, capturing the 1996 Donn Handicap in flourishing fashion. Now other tracks were keen to get in on the gravy train, with Sam Houston Race Park in Texas and Arlington Park in Chicago, among others, all willing to put up million-dollar appearance fees just to associate themselves with Cigar. Curiously enough, while others cranked up the dollar offerings in a full-court press, Raffetto had simplified his bonus plan, actually *cutting it* by $150,000, with winner's incentives that maxxed out at $500,000. The reason? Raffetto and Mott were now fast friends, and when it came time to see what it would take to bring Cigar back to Boston, Raffetto very quietly asked the horse's handlers to name the figure they wanted. Allen Paulson, a seventy-four-year-old aerospace pioneer, already had millions of dollars. What he considered more valuable was a sense of trust and an urge to help out the little guy who had first helped him. In March, Raffetto traveled halfway around the globe to the United Arab Emirates to show his interest and support for Cigar by cheering him on in the newly created $4-million Dubai World Cup. And after Cigar won the inaugural running of the world's richest horse race by a dramatic half length, it came as a pleasant but not entirely unexpected surprise when Bill Mott parted company with Lou after the victory party by saying, "See you in Boston, pal."

The rest of the racing world was shocked that the standout steed would be bringing his monumental fourteen-straight victory streak back to Suffolk Downs in what was fast being billed as "The Second Coming of Cigar." In a way, it was like the world's most successful and beautiful movie starlet returning to marry the geeky hometown nerd who had been nice to her in high school. One *Boston Globe* columnist called the return of Cigar "the greatest parlay in recent racing history." In that very same piece, Raffetto readily admitted that "last year, after the MassCap, I remember we all got together and we were saying, 'We're never going to be able to top this.' [Now] I see our ads on TV about Cigar coming and I get chills." The Suffolk Downs publicity department liberally applied the Cigar hype in an attempt to get as much mileage as possible out of the MassCap, but in truth, little hyperbole was needed because Cigar-mania had taken on a life of its own and the craze for the horse was simply snowballing. A lights-and-siren state police detail escorted Cigar's van from the Massachusetts border all the way to the racetrack when he shipped north from New York for the race, with television news helicopters hovering in tow. The city of Boston declared a day during MassCap week in honor of the star steed, and pictures of the champ graced billboards and homemade signs all around the region. The Suffolk Downs media relations department issued a track-record 209 race-day credentials to news organizations from all around the world, and jockey Jerry Bailey, trainer Bill Mott, and owner Allen Paulson were so besieged by autograph seekers and well-wishers that Paulson later said in amazement, "I've never seen anything like that in my life, the way people reacted to this horse. I couldn't take two steps without someone stopping me to thank me for bringing Cigar back a second time."

On the pre-race walk from the stable area to the paddock, the deep crowd lining the grandstand rail gave the 1-to-10 favorite a lengthy standing ovation. As the *Los Angeles Times* put it, "[F]athers hoisted little children on their shoulders. People held their cameras high above their heads and snapped expectantly." The *New York Post* said, "[R]arely has a city embraced an appearance by a horse the way Boston did this week."

Cigar, of course, annihilated the MassCap field in his second coming, winning his fifteenth straight race and edging to within one point of the consecutive-win record set by Triple Crown champ Citation from 1948 to 1950. The attendance of 22,169 was the largest turnout at Suffolk Downs since its 1966 Beatles concert, and the overall betting handle of $3,050,399 established a track record. In its June 2, 1996, edition, even the local *Globe*, with its reputation for going out of its way not to appear overly biased toward home entities, couldn't help but sum the resounding success of the MassCap as such:

> Whatever the final cost of having the immortal Cigar pay us a visit, it was worth every penny for the folks at Suffolk Downs. If people don't come back to this track after their experience yesterday, there is no hope for horse racing in our town.

The track continued to bask in its hard-earned glory through the summer of 1996, but an interesting sidebar about Cigar emerged well after the MassCap. Four days after the race, it was announced that the MassCap king would miss some training because of a stone bruise on his right front foot, an injury so relatively minor that it probably shouldn't even be called an injury. But when you're the horse of the world, no ailment is too small. It was widely reported without question that the tender spot must have emerged during the running of the MassCap. But several months after the incident—Cigar had already gone on to tie Citation's win record at Arlington that July and then lose for the first time in nearly two years at Del Mar in August—Lou Raffetto casually mentioned to me that both he and Bill Mott were aware of the bruise *several hours before* the MassCap, and that for a brief period of time during that anxious afternoon, Cigar's trainer was seriously contemplating withdrawing his horse from the race. In an era where highly valuable horses receive round-the-clock veterinary monitoring and are scratched by hyper-aware trainers if they so much as blink improperly, the importance of this revelation is not that Mott elected to race Cigar to collect some easy cash and glory, but that the conditioner put his career and his $10-million animal's well-being on the line out of respect for Raffetto and in deference to the throng that had turned out to see Cigar. If the can't-lose favorite romped as expected, no one would have to know. And if Cigar had somehow faltered in the MassCap, Mott would have been to blame, big time. For a frenzied eighteen months, the people had supported the champion.

Mott's decision to go ahead and run indicates there are still a few folks at the top echelon of the sporting world who believe that a true champion also has an obligation to support the people.

In the years since, the MassCap has continued its quest for quality. In 1997, the race regained its nationally graded status and Suffolk Downs added a series of extra stakes races to boost the big afternoon's purse total past seven figures, inaugurating New England's Million Dollar Day of Racing. Upon Cigar's retirement, the MassCap torch was passed to Skip Away, champion three-year-old the previous season. He too went on to win the Breeders' Cup Classic and then came back to Boston for a second Suffolk Downs score, setting a track record of 1:47.27 for the MassCap distance while again winning championships at age four and five. When Skip Away moved on to the breeding shed as the sport's leading money winner, a new crop of contenders emerged for 1999, and that year's MassCap featured a fattened $600,000 overall purse and a three-way showdown with international flair: Multiple-graded-stakes winner Behrens outlasted United Kingdom invader Running Stag, with Kentucky Derby winner Real Quiet third.

Now it's the first weekend of February 2000, and once again the Donn Handicap marks the traditional start to the East Coast season. The *Daily Racing Form* headline for today's paper reads, "Spring has arrived," and nearly four months before Boston's big race, Lou Raffetto is once again working his options and angles, having embarked on another world tour to put on another show of shows for the June 3 Massachusetts Handicap. Via cell phone from Gulfstream Park, he calls the Suffolk Downs press box on a dreary Friday afternoon to report an early bit of good news, the stream-of-consciousness sentences flowing excitedly from his mouth like a hyperactive sideshow barker.

"I just spoke to Bond," he says, hurriedly referring to H. James Bond, the trainer of last year's MassCap winner. "Behrens is coming. And the guys in England have been saying all winter long that Running Stag will be back, too. This is it—the matchup of the season:

Behrens and Running Stag, the one-two finishers from last year. Back again. In Boston. MassCap 2000."

The Suffolk Downs racing boss pauses briefly in his rapid-fire delivery and I get a mental picture of Lou standing in the sunny Florida paddock, impeccably dressed in one of his custom suits, framing words with outstretched hands on an invisible marquee, scheming and dreaming for a race that is most definitely his baby, a MassCap that is three months away at a racetrack currently sleeping under the dark chill of winter and a brittle crust of snow.

"Think about it," he continues, slowing down as if considering all the other plausible scenarios before snapping back to the first notion that entered his head. "I mean, why *wouldn't* these guys want to come back to Suffolk Downs?"

ON A BRIGHT MIDWINTER SUNDAY I am cruising through Legends, the stale, dank, paradoxically named sports bar on the second floor of Suffolk Downs. Phlegmy coughs and foul language rule here, and the atmosphere resembles a freaky circus sideshow. Over the past decade, the room has come to attract two distinct types of Boston racetrack personalities: Scary-looking regulars who are, in fact, totally harmless, and another subset of souls who are, without a doubt, truly troubled.

Thanks to the public's demand for increased smoke-free space elsewhere in the track, Legends has become a concentration of carcinogens, one of the few remaining areas where lighting up is not only permitted but enthusiastically encouraged. A thick, blue haze of second-hand tars has tinged the enclosed room's previously white-tiled ceilings a perpetual yellow, its worn industrial carpet is pockmarked with burns, and the large windows that front the clubhouse turn are layered with accumulated cigar and cigarette grime while a liberal spattering of gull droppings ornaments the exterior. When no other passage through the building is convenient, I try to rush through the room as quickly as possible because the stagnant cloud of exhaled tobacco instantaneously permeates one's clothes, hair, and eyes—an unwelcome accompaniment that will linger for the remainder of the day. As if to complement the tainted atmosphere, the Legends food fare tends toward oily and heavy, its waitstaff is notoriously crass, and the security guards are either too indifferent or too damn scared to bother with the intimidating knots of dreadlocked Rastafarians who brazenly commandeer the men's room for reefer-smoking sessions. Passing through during late-night simulcast hours, one is as likely to encounter some skanky couple making out in a lonely, darkened corner of the bar as a paunchy drunk passed out over a table of losing tickets.

The cross-section of today's Legends crowd is typical for an afternoon of live racing: Dispassionate lines of lopsided, shuffling old men call out one-dollar exactas while beefy, insistent Eastie know-it-alls clad in shiny sweatsuits and showy gold-rope chains devour lottery tickets from instant vending machines, scratching away in paranoid desperation. A pair of matronly fixtures—one woman in a bad black wig and another with a beehive hairdo straight out of 1963—take turns screeching at two-inch horses on a bank of small televisions. A mentally retarded gentle giant named Mikey hovers about under constant surveillance because of his penchant for setting wastebasket fires in the stairwells, and once in a while the occasional hard-luck cretin brings in bolt-cutting tools to liberate a mounted television as a consolation prize. To be sure, there are also pleasant-enough oddballs, Legends regulars to whom one says hello for years without really knowing their names: old-timers with emphysema who wheel around oxygen tanks and never bother anybody; night-shift working joes anesthetizing themselves at the bar before punching the clock for evening work; a diminutive widow who likes to hand out candies and mints to friends and acquaintances. But in general, Legends is the gathering place for the most hardcore gamblers at a decidedly rough-edged racetrack, the one room in the joint where the mindset is less about the glories, thrills, and pageantry of the turf and more like "What the hell can I bet on next?"

"Lookit!" shouts one such regular, thrusting a fistful of losing trifecta tickets in my face as I attempt to pass by, simply because I happen to be closest. "I had the 1, 2, 5 with the 2, 3, 6, 7 with the 2, 3, 4, 5, 6, 7! The damn thing came out 2, 5, 6!" The gentleman angrily tosses his tickets on the Legends floor, where they join the litter of countless red-and-white losing slips.

"Those fucking fucks!" an elderly man rages over the outcome of some just-completed simulcast race before advancing to the windows to conquer the next available wagering affair. Along the way, waving his aluminum walking cane in a wide and dangerous arc, he nearly knocks over a tray of drinks carried by a waitress.

At the far edge of the room I notice assistant mutuels manager Tom O'Hearn, whose combat-weary cynicism is a product of having both his father and grandfather precede him in betting-related jobs at Suffolk Downs, all the way back to the track's opening in 1935. Tom is standing off to the side, leaning against a wall with his arms crossed, sternly observing the social spectacle. His gaze is split between the raging octogenarian who has just pushed past me, a squinting old vet in a Korean War ball cap furtively clipping his fingernails while simultaneously eating a cheeseburger, and the small crew of cashiers whom O'Hearn must periodically police to make sure they're attentive to their assigned task of serving the public.

"What's the promotion today?" he asks, eyeing the Legends crowd warily. "Bring a cyclops and get in free?"

Although certain standouts separate the Suffolk Downs clientele from patrons at other racetracks, every pari-mutuel venue harbors a similar sort of caste system, and universally lowest in the pecking order are the so-called stoopers. At once the most interesting and perverse subgroup of customers, these (mostly male) scavengers scour the floors and trash bins for winning betting tickets that have been tossed away in error by unwitting horseplayers. The idea is that since some bettors are unaware of the complex rules regarding disqualifications, dead heats, and "all" payouts (when no single winning ticket has been sold and the next-closest combinations are honored as winners), stoopers can strike it rich based on other people's misunderstandings. At face value there seems to be no harm in letting customers hunt for thrown-away treasure, but things can get out of control when stoopers overturn garbage containers, annoy patrons who have paid a premium to sit in exclusive areas of the track, and sometimes stalk obvious newcomers, scooping up whatever tickets the novices discard on the outdoors apron, banking on the assumed incompetence of rookies. Although entirely legal, it is for these reasons that stooping is considered an unsavory practice, and every track has its own policy on how to deal with it, ranging from immediate banishment by security officers to ignoring it.

At Suffolk Downs, there are two or three regular, everyday stoopers who seriously ply this trade and a handful of part-time wannabes forced to hands and knees out of desperation at the end of a long, losing day. And make no mistake, the amount of money inadvertently thrown away by local bettors is by no means trivial: The annual estimate of outstanding winnings that Suffolk Downs patrons either trash or fail to cash is $500,000. In theory, aside from attempting to file legislation that would have this "outs money" returned to the horsemen's purse account rather than reverting to the general fund of the Commonwealth, it would seem that track management has given up trying to curtail stooping. But in practice, the East Boston oval has stumbled into an accidental policy that effectively contains it.

It works like this: Having come to their own agreement over territorial rights, the two or three "professional" stoopers band together to chase away the part-timers who won't follow the established etiquette. The unspoken protocol calls for not infringing upon the working area of another stooper, making sure no trash is spilled from bins onto the floors while digging through rubbish canisters, and remaining out of the clubhouse box seats and Terrace restaurant until after the final race has gone official. In return, the security force turns a blind eye to the regular stoopers, helps chase away the amateur interlopers, and instructs the cleaning crew not to bag the ticket refuse it continuously sweeps up during the course of an afternoon, instead letting it pile up in secluded corners of the racecourse where stoopers can sift through tickets without falling underfoot of the general public.

Invariably, the largest of these mounds always collects right inside the main entrance to Legends, and the lone stooper who owns that section of the racetrack stands sentinel over his pile like a haggard lord of lost opportunity. But today is about to be that guy's lucky day, and it's almost too much of a coincidence to believe that financial windfall from a heap of broom-piled tickets will be triggered by a horse named—what else?—Sweeping Energy.

A well-bred colt by precocious young sire End Sweep out of a Crusader Sword mare, Sweeping Energy cost $65,000 as a yearling. To date, the four-year-old has earned a total of $14,766 in purses from thirteen lifetime starts, well below the expected return on his initial auction price. Although far from a worldbeater, this afternoon the betting public perceives there are even slower animals entered against Sweeping Energy in the fourth race, and the colt is heavily bet to prevail over a lowly field restricted to horses who have never won two lifetime races. Collectively, his six competitors have amassed 139 luckless attempts among them in their effort to escape this easy non-winners-of-two condition, and Sweeping Energy is pounded to 7 to 5 in the wagering in expectation that he will finally deliver the goods.

Things look promising all the way around the clubhouse turn and down the backstretch for Sweeping Energy, who lays off the pace and looks ready to strike at any moment under Winston Thompson. Overtaking the tiring 7-to-1 High Dollar Count in deep stretch on the outside, Sweeping Energy continues to drift out within the final sixteenth of a mile, unaware that Harry Vega and 7-to-2 shot Time N Half are even wider in the middle of the track and under a furious drive from the back of the pack. Inside the final hundred yards, Sweeping Energy bumps briefly with Time N Half—maybe or maybe not enough to slow his rival's momentum—and the two cross the finish together, inseparable to the naked eye. The photo sign is immediately posted, along with the objection and inquiry lights. On the slomo race replay, no one is sure who won.

After several minutes, the first ruling from the placing judges is that the finish is a dead heat, an exact tie for the win.

But the stewards deliberate further, examining replays of the bumping incident from several different angles while also speaking to both Vega and Thompson via in-house telephone to hear each rider's side of the story.

After nearly ten minutes, the judges eventually decide that Thompson's failure to maintain a straight course in the stretch cost Vega and his mount a clear and unimpeded path to the finish, and the ruling trio decides to disqualify Sweeping Energy from the tie for first and place him second, behind the new official race winner, Time N Half. No one in the press box can ever recall seeing a dead heat and subsequent disqualification in the same race to determine a winner.

High above the finish wire, it takes a good amount of explaining for announcer Larry Collmus to verbally untangle the confusing ruling and what it means in terms of payoffs to various pari-mutuel bets. But many casual customers have already tossed away winning tickets they had assumed were losing ones before the revised order of finish was posted as official, so the explanation falls largely on deaf ears—except for the stoopers, who live for lucrative situations like this.

Downstairs in Legends, capitalizing on the misfortune of novice fans who don't quite understand the rules, the stoopers enjoy an unexpected cash bonanza, taking full advantage of one of the rare racetrack situations when one can literally find thousands of dollars discarded as garbage, randomly strewn and scattered across the chipped concrete floors of Suffolk Downs.

ONE OF MIKE GILL'S most promising prospects is an athletic three-year-old named Lone Storm. He won his first two starts impressively under the care of Osvaldo Rivera, but the trainer made the mistake of letting the colt slip to second place two weeks ago in career try number three. Thus, Lone Storm is one of the first to be yanked from Rivera's shed row and dispatched to new trainer Michael Catalano. Gill tells Catalano that the horse seems fine physically but has acted out of sorts over the past few weeks—shying from training, refusing to eat—without a logical explanation. Upon assessing the new steed,

Catalano asks if Lone Storm's teeth have been checked, but Gill adamantly insists dental problems are not the issue.

Even experienced trainers will overconcentrate on a horse's obvious trouble zones—feet, ankles, knees, hocks, legs—while ignoring an animal's subtle health clues. Bad teeth can be a major source of hidden problems in a racehorse. Poor dental care makes it uncomfortable for a Thoroughbred to chew properly, cutting the athlete's critical food intake. Plus, it is essential to keep a horse's mouth pain-free for control purposes, because that's where a jockey's steering bit attaches to the reins.

Confidently ignoring the assurances of his new boss, Catalano pries open Lone Storm's jaws anyway. He reaches deep inside the Thoroughbred's mouth and almost immediately, a loose tooth comes out in the trainer's hand. By the time Mike finishes probing around, five more follow.

So much for the old adage about not looking a gift horse in the mouth.

AFTER SIX MONTHS of intense rehabilitation, Rudy Baez continues to make substantial progress toward learning a new way of life. Without complaint, the once-dominant rider has applied a forceful, single-minded determination to his rehab regimen, a deep and spiritual dedication that surprises no one who knows Rudy. After spending much of the last half year under the guidance of the world's finest paralysis specialists at the renowned Kessler Institute in New Jersey, Baez is now back home, working his upper body daily at a local gym to compensate for the loss of his legs. Although he still suffers frequent pain and is having difficulty mastering a wheelchair as deftly as he once coaxed Thoroughbreds around a racetrack, Rudy repeatedly tells his wife and three children that he is still the same person on the inside, that he's still their papa, that the only difference is that God has decided he's going to be their papa "sitting down" for the foreseeable future.

During his time at Kessler, Baez lived in room 127, the same quarters once occupied by Christopher Reeve, the actor best known for his role as Superman. The film star was also the victim of a riding accident that paralyzed him in 1995, when a Thoroughbred named Eastern Express balked at the third jump of a cross-country equestrian event, launching the reins-entangled Reeve head-first into the barrier and causing multiple fractures of his first and second cervical vertebrae, rendering him quadriplegic. Reeve used his status as a public figure to crusade for awareness of spinal-cord injuries, and the insuppressible Baez has expressed a desire to become a similar inspiration for others.

After a career that included $30,474,225 in purse earnings and injuries to his shoulder, knee, elbow, both feet, and countless ribs even before his spinal accident, Rudy has made it emphatically clear that he wants to return to the New England circuit in a capacity that includes mentoring young riders. Baez has floated the idea of working as a liaison between New England jockeys and Suffolk Downs management, a position that does not currently exist but would go a long way toward helping each side understand the other during the course of an eight-month season. With no preference for what his title will be or how much he'll get paid, Rudy says he wants to be back on track at all costs, simply because "that's my life."

And today, in a low-key meeting with chief operating officer Bob O'Malley, Rudy Baez is promised any job he'd like at Suffolk Downs, whenever he feels ready to return to work.

In characteristically tactful fashion, O'Malley insists that his arrangement with Rudy Baez be announced with as little fanfare or publicity as possible. But when word begins to spread that Suffolk Downs has also offered to purchase and equip a vehicle with modified hand controls so that Rudy can regain his driver's license and a bit of independence, the story leaks, and Suffolk Downs is in the rare position of having to downplay a good deed in the broader interest of humility.

Rudy's accident didn't even occur at Suffolk Downs, but the story making the rounds is that Rockingham Park has done little to reach out to the Baez family since the tragedy. As one would expect, Rudy remains tight-lipped and refuses to pass judgment, but he has often spoken of the East Boston oval as his home racetrack, and in return, Suffolk Downs through the years has always embraced him as its most favored son in the saddle. Thus, it seems fitting that plans are unfolding behind the scenes for the Massachusetts track to host a day in Rudy's honor in late April—not as a final send-off for a fallen rider, but more of a welcome-back party for a good friend whose presence has been sorely missed.

Tonight is a classically crisp New England winter evening, windless but biting, with a snow ring around the moon that looks like a bright abrasion against the black, perfect sky. After a day at the races, I unwind in the company of horses, tending to barn chores with my girlfriend, Dena, at the suburban stable north of the city where she boards her dressage pony. As a neurology nurse who has seen many cases of hospitalized head trauma and has had a few of her own risky falls from routine horsebacking, Dena is all too aware that the line between everyday, mundane misfortune and absolute calamity that can alter a life forever is a microscopically fine one. She has followed Rudy's story closely since last summer, and as I relate the details about today's news and the encouraging prospect of a new job and new life for Baez, she leads me to a darkened section of shed row separate from the other horses, where a somber chestnut stands calmly under a green-and-orange stall blanket, acclimating himself to new surroundings after recently being purchased as a jumper prospect from an out-of-state owner.

"His nickname is Buck," Dena says as the skittish Thoroughbred retreats from our approach, backing off but maintaining wary eye contact from behind the heavy iron bars that brace his stall door. But, she adds, the horse's registered official name on file with the Jockey Club is Eastern Express.

It takes a moment for the name to sink in. Then the connection dawns on me. Shadows play across Buck's narrow blaze and long, silent face, and I wonder how life would have been different for both horse and rider if Eastern Express had ended up on the track as a racer instead of as a fledgling jumper on some eventing course in Virginia, forever saddled with the burden of being the horse that paralyzed Superman.

Since shipping in several days ago, Dena tells me the steed has been the subject of endless barn gossip and a magnet for morbidly fascinated curiosity seekers from the local equestrian community, parading rubberneckers eager to get a glimpse of a notorious horse. From behind his jail-like enclosure, Buck seems unjustly imprisoned by his past, and he shies from my outstretched palm when I reach to pet him.

"Do you think he knows?" Dena asks me.

Then we turn off the lights and leave the animal alone, immersing ourselves in darkness and the soothing, shifting presence of horses at nightfall.

██

CHAPTER THREE

ANYTHING FOR AN EDGE

Horse racing's an opium dream beyond all dreams
  ever spun,
Where every sad bloke in the mob should have
  won every race that was run.
Did you ever notice, my friend, in the race
  track's grotto of tears,
How many go to the seller's maw—how few to
  the lone cashier?
Did you ever notice, old pal, in the race track's
  dizzy spin
There are ninety ways that a horse can lose—
  with only one way to win?
—GRANTLAND RICE, *Maxims from Methuselah*

O NCE EACH WINTER I escape New England for three or four days in Florida. The trip is relaxing, if something of a working vacation because my father now winters his small string of horses at Tampa Bay Downs from December through April, and on most days I get up before sunrise with my dad and his wife, Joyce, to tend to stable chores and ready the horses for morning training.

I'm not at all the type of guy who enjoys rising early, but I find pre-dawn work with animals satisfyingly therapeutic. After a morning or two on the backstretch, I always end up a bit more appreciative and a touch envious of people who earn a living under a shed row, working hands-on with horses. For some time now, I have been of the strong opinion that the sport would be better off if every industry executive—from midmanagement employees to veteran track officials to corporate bigwigs and anyone else in a coat-and-tie job at the track— had to lace up a pair of work boots and throw on some old clothes to muck stalls, cool out hot horses, fill water buckets, restock hay racks, and clean feed tubs at least one morning a year.

My dad, Paul Thornton, is fifty-nine and has been training Thoroughbreds full-time for three years now, after dabbling with one or two horses off and on for thirty. He won his first race two months after I was born, in 1968 at now-defunct Scarborough Downs, a mosquito-infested oval on the southern Maine seacoast. A long-shot claimer named Midsummer's Eve paid $93.40, winning the final race on the last night of July, and at the time, my father was jubilantly oblivious to the fact that the jockeys had put one over on the betting public. He later found out one of the riders in the race had recently been released from jail, and the tie-up of the nightcap that sweltering summer evening was the jockeys' way of putting together a little welcome-back fund-raiser for their newly freed friend—or so the story goes.

A high school health teacher in a hardscrabble Massachusetts mill town by day and an NCAA basketball referee at night, my old man blew out his knee in the spring of 1997 and decided to take early retirement from both the hoops court and the classroom. Joyce, fifty, had never touched a racehorse in her life, but willfully abandoned her career in retail sales management to help out, and the pair poured their time and energy into building a modest stable that now splits the season between New England and Florida. Last year, they claimed a five-year-old with three sets of screws in his hind ankle (a common but not necessarily desirable medical repair job) for $8,000, and Ben's Quixote went on to become the star of the circuit, winning a pair of $25,000 stakes at Rockingham Park and Suffolk Downs. By the time 1999 came to a close, the determined gelding had scored in ten races overall, a record that had him tied for the honor of most victories in North America. But as racing luck will have it, three weeks ago Ben's Quixote was claimed away by a potent outfit for $40,000 while running third in a Tampa turf try, and there has been a void under the shed row ever since while my dad tries to figure out how to develop one of his remaining five steeds into a top oat-earner.

The early morning temperature is around 50°F, which means everyone down south thinks the next ice age has arrived. But to me, the pre-dawn weather is pleasant as we drive five miles to the racetrack, gliding quietly past endless chain restaurants and strip malls through the dark Florida sprawl, arriving at Barn 6 on the Tampa Bay Downs backstretch by 6:05 AM. I am assigned the task of emptying, scrubbing, and refilling water buckets while my dad and Joyce check in on the charges and ready them for whatever is on the schedule for each horse: a morning workout, a mild gallop, or just a walk around the shed row. In the shadowy mist, forms of horses and shapes of riders pass by en route to the racetrack, clopping over hardened dirt and semi-paved paths while their pilots exchange subdued pleasantries so as not to disturb the impending daybreak. The mixed aromas of sweet feed, fresh hay, raw manure, astringently minty equine liniment, and sulfurous Tampa water carry on the warming air as the sky brightens. Dim images hazily come into focus: An open field beyond the barns, littered with vans, parked fishing boats and unevenly spaced horse trailers, the shroud of fog hiding a far-off herd of deer by the swampy tree line; a gaudy lime-green paint job adorning row upon row of squat, rectangular barns, rooftops alive with small darting birds; glistening horses being hosed down while standing in muddy puddles, exuding steam and snorting playfully; rows of rakes, shovels, muck buckets, sponges, bandages, hay bales, feed tubs, and horse tack. And finally the day brightens enough to reveal a battered fire safety sign at the end of each tired wood and cinder-block shed row that obliquely cautions: Do Not Allow Drunks and Irresponsible Persons in Stable Area.

Stablehands for trainer Javier Contreras, whose horses occupy the remaining nineteen stalls on my dad's side of the structure, are keen to recognize any variation to the routine of the shed row and are quickly aware of a new face hovering by the tack room at the far end of the barn. Although I try to blend into the workplace without committing any obvious blunders that would give me away as a backstretch greenhorn, word spreads fast that I'm "just the trainer's son," in town for a few days and helping out temporarily. Everyone is friendly, but I always feel self-consciously out of place when it comes to working a morning shift on the backside, like the intruding city slicker on a dude ranch who pays for the privilege of cattle-roping, to the disbelief of real cowboys. No matter how well I try to disguise it, it seems that the backstretch lifers always know intrinsically that I'm not really one of them.

The quality of racing at Tampa Bay Downs is roughly comparable to New England, and a number of outfits that spend the summer at Rockingham Park send their stables south to this sleepy Gulf Coast oval as an alternative to the bitter winter uncertainty of Suffolk Downs. The warm weather draws horses from a number of other seasonal northern circuits in Ohio, Michigan, Delaware, Maryland, West Virginia, and Pennsylvania, ensuring a diverse and full barn area for the small Tampa track. The backstretch itself is a kaleidoscope of racetrack ethnicity, with rapid-fire Spanish mixing with broad Bible-belt drawls, transplanted Appalachian patter, and gruff, urban East Coast attitude. Yet despite the melding of various cultures, the overall Tampa Bay Downs atmosphere is also deeply Southern. Distinctly separate knots of blacks and whites sip coffee while watching morning workouts along the backstretch railing, and a disturbingly noticeable number of Confederate flags are proudly displayed atop rifle racks on the many oversized pickup trucks that growl and prowl the track's dusty backstretch pathways.

After the water buckets and stall mucking (as soon as one horse is led out for exercise, the stablehand is supposed to immediately pop in and tidy the enclosure), I am given the task of hand walking Appealing J D, without a doubt the most docile horse in the outfit. Although he is a chronic plodder who has never won beyond the cheap maiden ranks, the five-year-old is lean and in good health, taut and muscular at the end of a worn leather shank. Stall cleaning and hot-walking are the lowest chores on the backstretch totem pole, but these entry-level jobs are also a reliable screening method for a trainer to assess an employee's attitude and desire to advance to more responsible hands-on horse care. The only real instructions for a hot-walker are to keep turning left (to instill familiarity with North American racecourse layouts, whose turns uniformly bank counterclockwise, Thoroughbreds in the United States are approached and handled from the left side, and are always—without exception—walked in a counterclockwise manner under the shed row) and to pay attention to the occasional shouted "Whoa back!" when a horse and walker ahead are stopping or a "Comin' in!" caution when a steed enters the stable from outside. A hot-walker is also taught never to wrap the end of the lead shank around his hand, because if a 1,200-pound animal is startled and decides to bolt, you don't want to learn from personal experience what it's like to be dragged like a rag doll behind a flailing, escaped race-horse.

J D and I walk easily at a brisk, even clip, constantly dodging the curious equine heads that bob, weave, and lunge out at the hot-walk-ers, endlessly curious no matter how many times we circle the shed row, twenty-four stalls up one side and twenty-four down the other. By about the fourth or fifth pass the job grows monotonous no mat-ter how much you love horses, but even the shortest of hot-walking assignments lasts twenty minutes per animal. At the Contreras end of the stable, Appealing J D is reluctant to corner where a high stack of baled hay engages his attention on every turn, and in order to keep the gelding from stealing a bite of alfalfa, I have to nudge him to make the turn each time, coercing his stride firmly but gently by leaning shoul-der to shoulder, bracing my gait against his while breathing in the comforting, dusky smell of J D's clean, copper coat. In the process of passing the same people around the shed row every sixty seconds, you develop odd, disjointed conversations with other stable workers engaged in similarly repetitive stall work. Each time round, I banter back and forth with a ponytailed groom in a faded black Lynyrd Skynyrd T-shirt who absently hoses the legs of a stately gray with bad knees thickly wrapped in muddy, oozing poultice.

"Ain'tcha glad you don't have to do this every day for a living?" the Dixie-accented groom asks with a grin on lap six. Two passes later, he drawls, "I hope you're at least holdin' out for a steak dinner, kid."

At 7:20 AM, just as Appealing J D is tucked safely away in his newly tidied stall, a siren blasts throughout the backstretch, the universal racetrack signal that a horse is loose somewhere on the grounds amid the dangerously heavy traffic of morning training. A frantic page blares over the backstretch loudspeaker—"Horse down! Horse down!"— and a call goes out for the track veterinarian, then *any* available vet, to attend to the five-eighths-pole gap immediately. Although few, if any, workers stop what they're doing, a nervous, furtive glancing silently ensues, with trainers, grooms, and hot-walkers taking mental stock of who's supposed to be where and which, if any, of their own or a neighbor's horses might be involved in the accident.

Within minutes, the news spreads across the backside from barn to barn: A young filly got spooked at the entry gap near the clockers' stand, flipped over backward, and cracked her head on a fence post. The rider fell off unharmed but the horse is out cold, and the track is temporarily closed for training in an attempt to revive the stricken animal. Although a complete shutdown is unusual, it is far from unprecedented, and horse workers, jockeys, and exercise riders dismount from and untack horses who were keen to be led out for a jaunt over the sandy, dewy strip. The situation could be likened to a bad highway accident that has snarled a congested morning commute at its peak, except that no one complains about the subsequent delay the calamity will cause to everyone's routine. Everyone in the Tampa Bay Downs stable area is likely to know the very horse, rider, groom, trainer, and owner involved in the mishap. In Thoroughbred racing, accidents are largely a matter of *when*, not *if*, and life on the backstretch is tempered with a unique kind of empathy, because there are two types of racetrackers: those who have been personally touched by an equine tragedy, and those who haven't *yet*.

By 9:10 AM, the Thornton quintet has been exercised, groomed, bathed, and returned to newly bedded, freshly watered stalls. The final chore before raking the shed row and hosing down the dust is feeding breakfast, which in the Thornton stable consists of a mix of oats, sweet feed, corn, barley, and bran, supplemented with fresh carrots, apples, wheat germ oil, flax seed, salt, and vitamins. The five prepared meal buckets are then brought from the feed-storage shed and emptied into each horse's individual tubs, which clip onto wall mounts alongside the water buckets in each stall.

Horses are intelligent creatures of habit and they most definitely know when it's time to eat. T.G. For Wanda, a moody five-year-old languishing at a low-level claiming plateau, is so excited for breakfast that she kneels down, slides onto her side, then rolls in her bed of wood shavings even while still damp from her bath. The mare is so impatient to eat that she bounces immediately back to her feet, somehow stretches her head three feet outside her stall door, grabs a steel screw-eye that has been bolted to a two-by-four, and rips the entire board from the barn wall with her teeth in an overly enthused demand for service. Appealing J D—who the old man says is one race away from being donated to a good home as a riding pony—has to be allotted his feed in several small rations because he gulps his meals too quickly. He too senses breakfast and reacts by pawing insistently at the rubber mats at his stall entrance, pads that have been strategically placed to prevent him from digging an enormous hole in the dirt each day at feed time. Gold Clearance, a newly acquired gelding who is bred to be fast but has such a small head that my father has difficulty finding a bridle that will fit him, pricks his ears attentively and follows every move of those hovering around him, eyes wide while awaiting the delivery of his meal. One door down, Ladyfolady, a mild-mannered gray who was recently claimed for $10,000 at Calder but was soon discovered to have calcified growths on her ankles that might prevent her from ever racing again, munches contentedly on her hay rack. Oblivious to the excitement that surrounds her, the nonchalant racemare seems to have learned long ago that no matter what, the food will come, because most racehorse trainers would sacrifice a meal themselves rather than have their Thoroughbreds go without a scheduled feeding.

And then, brooding off to the side by himself, is Blackwater.

An impeccably bred and perpetually nasty seven-year-old sprinter, Blackwater seethes patiently in the back of his enclosure waiting for someone, *anyone*, to walk close enough so he can charge the webbing at full force, teeth bared, and jackhammer any moving target within range. When not stalking human prey, the ornery gelding turns his attention to a basketball-sized chew toy suspended outside his stall, intent on assaulting the fake red apple with his angry mouth, viciously slamming the plastic plaything off the dense wooden siding again and again and again. His splenetic rage simmers with self-righteousness. Blackwater *knows* he should be keeping company with world-class racehorses in a faster, stronger pecking order. Deprived of that opportunity, the lean, mean steed has elected to vent his savage wrath on everything in his path, often biting even the very same hands that feed him.

Sure enough, by tracing his race record back far enough, you'll find that Blackwater *did* begin his career against high-class competition in France and probably, in a perfect world, does belong elsewhere. A gifted youngster bred by international powerhouse Juddmonte Farms, his sire, Irish River, was a European champion in 1978 and 1979, and his dam, Frühlingstag, sticks in my mind as oddly familiar, although it vexes me that I cannot pinpoint the relevance of her foreign name. At three, Blackwater won the Prix de Pontarme over the venerable Longchamp course in Paris and earned a berth in the 1996 Prix Jean Prat at Chantilly, where he finished a gallant third against Group 1 (foreign group stakes classifications are similar to American graded stakes rankings, with "1" as the top rank) sophomores. But then the story grows hazy: Somewhere along the line, Blackwater was imported into the United States but failed to attain the same level of success he enjoyed in Europe. A fearsome animal whose nagging physical limitations never allowed him to live up to his true potential, the gelding with the talented pedigree and early precocity devolved into a grizzled warrior of the North American claiming ranks, with the chief culprit being degeneratively sore hock joints. Last autumn he was purchased privately by my father for $16,000 after running against moderate competition in Kentucky. Unraced since then, Blackwater's training so far this season has largely consisted of a strict regimen of rest and relaxation, but the menacing steed has been an unwilling participant in any low-key attempt to rehabilitate his racing prowess.

"Better let me get this guy," my father insists, approaching Blackwater's stall warily with the feed bucket. "He'll take your goddamn head off."

After just one morning underneath the shed row, I know the old man isn't exaggerating. I keep my distance while listening to Blackwater bash his breakfast tub against the side of the stall as he zealously attacks his morning meal.

By 10:15 AM the morning stable work has been completed. It feels satisfying to have finished the bulk of a day's labor by the time I usually stroll into the office back home in Boston. The Gulf of Mexico sun is high, slanting in on the shed row at eye level, and the Florida breeze smells warm and fertile. A radio at the Contreras end of the stable lilts Hispanic songs and the shed-row horses nod their heads to the music. I grab a lawn chair and crack the *Racing Form*, scanning the news items and features before searching for the ever-elusive solution to the daily double.

We head over to the track kitchen for breakfast after a stop at the adjacent Tampa Bay Downs racing office. Nearby is a man-made retaining pond; a pair of baby alligators sun themselves on rocks at the edge of the water. As my dad attends to business inside, Joyce and I gaze at the lazy gators. Rumor is that the filly who reared back and injured herself on the racetrack earlier in the morning is dead. Word has it that the doctors and some bystanders were able to get the dazed animal back on her feet, but the frightened lass thrashed away again and bolted, knocking herself unconscious in an attempt to flee pain and confusion. The severity of the filly's skull injuries left the vets with little choice but to euthanize her.

The cafeteria food—grits and hard toast, biscuits and sausage gravy, chicken-fried steak—is decidedly Southern and the cook is a jolly fat guy who calls everyone "Sir!" and "Ma'am!" while efficiently dishing out orders. Nearly all of the kitchen regulars eating the greasy fare are simultaneously smoking cigarettes. By backstretch standards, 11:00 AM is considered afternoon, and a number of folks are already eating lunch. A growing procession of stablehands line up to buy break-time beers: icy longneck Bud singles and cold, dripping six-packs of Busch. I enjoy a well-cooked western omelet with grits and check out the myriad of winner's circle photos hung on the dining room walls, relics of the days when the little track was known as Sunshine Park and

$5,000 was considered a sizable purse for the meet's top stakes race.

All around the kitchen are large signs asking diners to "Please Pick Up After Yourself," but trays and breakfast residue litter the rapidly emptying room. Food remnants, ashtray remains, newspapers, and yesterday's race entry sheets overflow onto the well-worn floor. The morning rush is over, and a lone worker, a slow-moving older lady wearing a clean white apron and a wearied expression, picks her way through the refuse, methodically clearing tables and straightening chairs. As I rise to bus my breakfast tray into the trash, she meets me at the garbage bin, her leathered face breaking into a wide, beaming smile.

"You, honey," she laughs, gently taking the tray from my hands, "must be new around here, right?"

ON THE AFTERNOON I am scheduled to fly home to New England, my dad is scheduled to race his newest runner, Gold Clearance, a four-year-old who sold at public auction for $92,000 as a weanling but was purchased privately last month from a Gulfstream trainer for a deeply discounted $10,000. The gelded son of Cryptoclearance obviously has (or once had) some sort of problem. He never really lived up to his originally expensive price tag but did pass a conditional vet check as part of the sale agreement and my father is baffled as to what, if anything, is wrong because Gold Clearance has been training up a storm with no obvious physical flaws. Today's $12,500 claiming route at 1-1/16 miles comes up as a tough race on paper, but trainer Thornton feels confident the small, sleek speedster can pull off a minor upset. Since my old man very rarely goes out on a limb and predicts outright victory, I change my flight plans, opting for a later departure so I can stay to see the race and maybe make a small score.

Gold Clearance is not a big Thoroughbred, but what the gelding lacks in size he makes up for in attitude: He prances onto the track for the post parade with his neck arched and chest puffed out, breaking into a strong canter for his warm-up under jockey Jesse Garcia. He opens as the 2-to-1 favorite in the eight-horse field but by post time rises to 5 to 1. Garcia breaks Gold Clearance just off the leaders and tracks the pace into the clubhouse turn. Straightening down the backstretch, they are boxed between rivals, but the veteran rider bides his time. Bending into the final turn at the three-eighths pole, Garcia yells to Juan Umana, the jockey of tiring pace-chaser Colofer, to either go on with his horse or get the hell out of the way. But Umana doesn't budge, leaving Garcia with little choice other than to angle Gold Clearance five wide in search of running room. He engages the leader gamely at the top of the lane, but Core Idea has saved ground the entire race and spurts clear when challenged, leaving my dad's horse 2-1/2 lengths in his wake and a neck ahead of late-charging long shot Novus Scofus. The second-place performance is a decent outing for the new shooter, but as usual, I am left holding nothing but losing tickets.

"Don't go home with a scowl on your face now," my dad says after the race as we drive back to the stable area. He knows I top-loaded Gold Clearance in exotic wagers and didn't cash for a cent even though the horse ran a sharp race. Although any trainer should be happy with a 20 percent piece of the purse and an animal that has returned sound, I can tell he, too, is disappointed but will not show it.

I wait for my dad and Joyce to cool out and bathe Gold Clearance, walking him around and around the shed row to calm him down after the exertion of racing in hot weather, allowing the animal ample drinks from a freshly filled water bucket. Several hundred yards away by the perimeter of the backstretch property, way beyond the brown expanse of burnt-grass meadow, I watch with interest as a group of young men speed recklessly up and down the tree line in a battered golf cart. Every two or three minutes, one of them leaps from the vehicle head first in a flying tackle and wrestles some unseen object to the ground in a cloud of dust while the others in the cart screech to a halt and boisterously cheer the proceedings.

"That's just a bunch of crazy fucking Mexicans," says a cowboy-type trainer who has ambled up beside me, noting my interest while pulling needfully on a glowing Camel. "They're after them armadillos over there by the shade. Sometimes they catch 'em to eat and sometimes it's just for sport. They're out there every fucking afternoon. They're fucking crazy, I tell ya."

I finish shooting the roll of film from my pocket camera by snapping head shots of my dad's horses. While trying to get an angled shot of Ladyfolady, I am sabotaged by Blackwater, who has been lurking in the back of his stall, lying in wait for me to lean close to his webbing.

The gelding nails me good and hard in the left shoulder, not savage enough to draw blood but with enough raw force to leave a deep, purple bruise and a dirty smear of saliva on the clean white shirt I have changed into for the plane ride home. "I told you to look out for him," says my dad as we hustle into the car to make it in time to the airport. "At least you get to leave here with *something.*"

I change planes in Baltimore, and after exiting the aircraft, I realize I can't find the keys for my car back home in the airport parking lot, which is probably buried to its wheel wells in snow. In the middle of the terminal, I rip open my carry-on to search for the keys, flinging clothes, books, and toiletries like a madman before finally uncovering the key ring in one of the zillion or so conveniently hidden side pockets. As I decompress, composing both myself and my luggage while still kneeling on the floor, I hear a familiar Boston accent from behind and above, obviously amused and wanting to know just what the hell I'm doing going berserk in the middle of a crowded airport.

The grinning guy behind the voice is trainer Mike Catalano, who is on the same flight back home to New England after spending a hectic week shipping the first dozen horses to the mid-Atlantic region for new client Michael Gill.

Usually animated and engaging, tonight Catalano is run down and ragged, the victim of a severe head cold brought on by the seemingly endless cycle of arranging for the temporary transfer of horses from Boston to Maryland while simultaneously looking for a place to live and managing from a distance the remainder of his New England division. Bleary, sick, and exhausted, right now Mike just wants to get back to his own bed, but in a few hours, he'll have to wake up and make the forty-five-mile trek in the winter dark from his New Hampshire home to oversee the remaining forty-plus head of horses still stabled at Suffolk Downs.

We sit on the plane together and chat about Gill's ambitious plans for the spring, which tentatively call for Catalano to manage the out-fit at Bowie Training Center in central Maryland while shipping north and west to Pimlico and Laurel before sending the entire stable south to Delaware Park in time for the slot machine–infused spring and sum-mer meet. Catalano is introspective this evening, perhaps even unchar-acteristically tentative about the choices he will be making in the upcoming months. He's getting a chance to manage racehorses for a client whose monthly income is rumored to be measured in millions, but Catalano knows that Gill is very much a loose-cannon owner with a reputation for changing plans abruptly, a man who phones his early rising trainers at all hours of the night with orders and grand plans that can't wait until morning. And in addition to business ramifications, Catalano and his wife, jockey Abigail Fuller, have family plans: The couple is expecting another child in late May, right on the heels of pur-chasing a new house and horse farm, and they just enrolled their other two children in a new school system, thinking that they would not be moving anytime soon. Although the business payoff for partnering with Gill is potentially huge, Catalano admits that some of the lifestyle decisions he faces in the immediate future will not be easy.

"I've been in this game all my life and you know what I just realized in the past three days?" he tells me. "I love working with the horses. I love being with them every morning, taking care of them, planning the strategy, watching them come around, just finding little things to do around the barn. And what I realized, what I just discovered in my mind, is that I enjoy all that stuff even more than the races themselves. The actual races are when I get all worked up. And all the business that goes with it. That's my problem. I'd rather just stay back at the barn with my horses, send the ones that are going to race up to the track with the assistant, and sit back and wait for the results. Then win, lose, or draw, they'd come back to me and I'd just take care of them, fine-tune them with my training. More than the races themselves, it's the horses. That's the part of the game I really love."

The trainer pauses, thinking about what he has just said.

"Does that sound strange?" he asks wearily. "Does that make any sense to you?"

After spending only seventy-two hours immersed in the backstretch, I must admit that what Catalano says makes perfect and absolute sense, and that just wanting to be with horses and filter out the rest does not sound strange at all.

THE ARCHIVED FILES IN the Suffolk Downs press box devoted to the subject "Race Fixing" encompass three well-worn manila folders, each four or five inches thick, overflowing with ragtag bits of newsclip that litter the bottom of an ancient metal filing cabinet. The collection dates from the mid-1960s and includes media coverage of twenty-seven separate New England corruption incidents involving thirty-eight jockeys, twenty-six trainers, and two racing officials, with certain versatile individuals starring in multiple roles. Arranged in haphazard fashion, the files are an intriguing read. But the annals appear to be as sketchy as their subject, with time gaps indicating they are far from comprehensive, and one must also operate under the logical assumption that the best cheating stories remain untold, because the press can only chronicle those miscreants unfortunate, unlucky, or greedy enough to get caught in the first place.

At any racetrack in the nation—perhaps even the world—the first question newcomers always ask is whether the races are fixed. For the most part, the answer is no. An honest analogy is that the sport is like Ivory Soap: It's 99 and 44/100 percent pure. But if you stick around horse racing long enough, the realization eventually settles in that if that 56/100 touch of larceny didn't exist, the game wouldn't be nearly as much fun.

In any sport or business, there's a fine line between getting an edge and outright, blatant criminality. And in a betting-driven pastime like horse racing, deciphering and understanding the advantages that others seek to gain is an advantage in itself, not to mention a highly fascinating and potentially profitable aspect of the game. Still, anywhere the lure of easy money is involved, avarice is certain to follow. It only takes a tiny percentage of offenders to taint the perception of an entire industry, and throughout its checkered history, Thoroughbred racing has never had a shortage of hustlers, hoodlums, thugs, thieves, and con artists who would rather steal 50 cents for the same effort it would take to earn an honest buck.

Although exceptions and offshoots abound, race fixing can be neatly parsed into two categories: drastically improving a single horse's performance by illegal means to bet on that steed, or slowing down one or more heavily favored horses in a race for the purpose of wagering against them. A variation on the latter theme is to mask the talent of a likely winner over a series of races, thus enabling a manipulator to cash a future ticket at inflated odds once the betting public has disregarded the entrant's chances and the animal is finally unleashed at full potential.

Over the years, most of the outlandish behind-the-scenes ploys have gradually been eradicated, thanks to technology. For centuries, entering a "ringer" was a tried-and-true method of fixing a race. But by the 1940s, North American racing had adopted the practice of identifying Thoroughbreds by a unique registration number tattooed on the inside upper lip, virtually ensuring that a superior, similar-looking horse could no longer be substituted for a lowly, slower steed. Equine drugging has long been a problem in racing, ever since nineteenth-century horses were routinely and openly shot up with painkilling and performance-perking concoctions such as heroin. Harsh penalties and increasingly sensitive testing that can detect the presence of banned substances down to the billionth of a gram have effectively deterred widespread use of most notorious narcotics, opiates, and uppers, but new performance-enhancing drugs still rotate into vogue with tidelike regularity. These esoteric and often dangerous elixirs are banned as soon as authorities find a means to detect them, but the cyclical problem is that chemical cheaters are constantly one step ahead of the people who police them.

On the racetrack, the practice of jockeys' blatantly holding back mounts has always been a brazen risk, because putting a stranglehold on a half-ton racehorse is difficult enough without trying to make the hammerlock seem subtle. The most obvious of such skullduggery was quelled by the advent of video patrol cameras in the 1960s. But jockeys who want to ensure that their horse won't win still have a myriad of other options available, such as deliberately disadvantaging an animal's natural running style (taking back on horses who race best with the leaders or gunning a mount from the gate who likes to lope along at the back) or purposely positioning a runner in a pocket or behind a wall of horses, in short, committing "mistakes" that are difficult to distinguish from ordinary bad racing luck or poor judgment.

To shock a Thoroughbred into running faster, some riders will employ a small, handheld electrical device that they press against a horse's neck to produce a fright-induced burst of speed. Although "plugging in" a horse has been universally prohibited for the better part of a century, this practice lives on at lower levels of the sport, with the obvious danger being that even a small jolt of current to a high-strung horse is as likely to send the animal sailing over the inside rail as it is to propel the steed forward in a straight line to the finish. To counter this effect, jockeys will first test-drive a horse with a "battery" during unsupervised workouts. Some reinsmen are so adept at eliciting the desired response that they are able to eliminate the risk of getting caught carrying the device in an actual race by repeatedly conditioning a mount to respond to it in the mornings. By race day, all a jockey has do is grind his bare knuckle into the side of his steed so the horse will think it's about to be jolted, and the animal will take off like a rocket.

Back at the barn, well before the actual race is run, there are numerous immoral ways to hide a horse's true form that are next to impossible to prove, and some of them aren't even explicitly illegal. For example, one New England trainer has long been alleged to "flood" certain horses, meaning that instead of withholding water from a Thoroughbred right before a race (the long-standing and medically sound practice), he'll feed the steed a good, salty breakfast on race day, then let the animal guzzle as much water as it wants right up until it's time to go to the paddock. The result is a bloated, sluggish racehorse that won't run its best but can be bet back next time with confidence, presumably at inflated odds. Another local conditioner is rumored to accomplish similarly poor showings by having an exercise rider vigorously gallop a mount three or four miles the morning of a race, knowing that no one pays attention to that sort of thing with hundreds of horses circling the racetrack during the hectic ritual of morning training. And even veteran bettors might be surprised to learn that it only takes a tiny vial of mercury inconspicuously wrapped under a normal leg bandage to send a 1,200-pound Thoroughbred wobbling like a punch-drunk boxer (the heavy mercury affects the horse's balance), or that a thumbnail-sized piece of synthetic sponge inserted far up into the nasal passage of a racehorse can cut off enough air intake to make the animal stop to a walk in the middle of a race.

It is important to underscore that this sort of backstretch conspiracy is by no means widespread or even typical, and an educated guess ranks Suffolk Downs on par with most other midlevel racetracks when it comes to sporadic incidents of race fixing. Even if the realistic approximation is that a handful of serious incidents *do* sneak under the radar during the course of a calendar year, a 1,500-race season offers a statistical perspective that ranks the likelihood of corruption at far less than 1 percent. The bottom line is that no matter how vigilant the regulation, the clear impracticality of testing or hand searching every horse in every race will always crack the window of opportunity for any nefarious schemer who wants to pull off an inside job right out in the open.

In the 1970s, one Boston-based criminal single-handedly dismantled the nationwide credibility of horse racing, ripping off millions of dollars in the process. Barred from fifty-five racetracks by the time he was twenty-six, the man known up and down the Eastern seaboard as "Fat Tony" operated with reckless, ruthless abandon, openly bragging about his race-fixing prowess with the strong-arm backing of one of the country's most violent organized crime gangs. When this 350-pound felon was finally cornered and caught after a fifteen-year spree,

Anthony P. Ciulla ratted out all his partners, turned over meticulously detailed betting records, and testified before a series of U.S. grand juries about how he earned a fearsome reputation as a self-described "master fixer" who honed his craft, earned his underworld stripes, and stole the betting public blind, right from his boyhood backyard of Suffolk Downs.

Ciulla grew up when Boston racing was in its heyday, the son of a fish merchant who also happened to be an avid horseplayer, and young Tony fell in fast with local hustlers, back when the bookmaking business was all about taking bets on horse races. As an up-and-coming punk in the early 1960s, he shrewdly networked enough inside connections to begin fixing races on the Massachusetts county-fairs circuit, then graduated to bigger and better scams at Suffolk, Rock, Lincoln, and 'Gansett. Ciulla paid his criminal dues with convictions for bribing a racing official in Rhode Island and for drugging a horse at Suffolk Downs, and although he was opportunistic enough to take advantage of any angle he could exploit, he eventually began to specialize in paying off jockeys to hold horses, scripting races while stinging a myriad of New England bookies so that on-track wagers wouldn't depress the odds. By 1973, his business was booming. But that same year the ambitious Ciulla made a crucial betting mistake that could have ended his life. Instead, fortune smiled on Fat Tony, and the wrong move ended up being the most profitable deal of the whiz kid's meteoric race-fixing career.

Ciulla had pulled off a $28,000 betting coup on a Boston bookie who had the backing of the Irish mob. The underworld code is that you don't put one over on powerful criminals without paying for it, and Fat Tony was summoned to a meeting with the merciless mastermind of the brutal Winter Hill Gang. Not only did an angry Howard T. Winter demand that the ill-gotten winnings be returned, but the boss also imposed a $50,000 "fine" on Ciulla to teach him a lesson, and Fat Tony had little choice but to accept the consequences. Then, having settled the matter, the two got to talking about the extent of Ciulla's horse-holding operation. Howie, an opportunist himself, became intrigued enough to strongly suggest that the two merge ventures: Fat Tony would work his race-fixing wizardry, and the Winter Hill Gang would provide muscle, manpower, and money. The two would split the profits while expanding their Boston-based scamming to racetracks up and down the East Coast.

Ciulla's ploy was to pick out races in which four or five trusted jockeys could be bribed to ensure that their horses, usually favorites, did not finish in the top three positions. The going rate in New England was $500 to $2,000 per jockey per race. The key to the scam was to then bet on all the remaining horses who were not being held, and since Fat Tony rigged it so that only long shots would prevail, the payouts were bound to be astronomical. The Winter Hill Gang sent an army of runners to place numerous exacta and trifecta wagers that covered all of the remaining "live" combinations, instructing the runners to discreetly make many small bets at low-denomination windows so as not to arouse suspicion with a single big ticket. At the same time, off-track mob staffers would simultaneously nail rival bookies for win wagers on the horses who were not being held, racking up additional profits. Years later, Ciulla would testify that via this method, the gang fixed hundreds of races, netting several million dollars at thirty-nine tracks over a three-year period in the mid-1970s.

The unscrupulous jockeys who participated in the crooked races, particularly at smaller tracks where money was hard to come by, viewed Fat Tony as a cash cow and did everything they could to adhere to his orders. In some instances, the antics they employed to *not* win reached ridiculous proportions: Riders would leap off horses in the homestretch as if diving into a swimming pool. They'd intentionally steer their steeds to the outer fence, or if unable to hold back a keyed-up horse himself, a jockey would scream for one of his comrades to stop the mount by whipping it in the face. Sometimes, fans reacted angrily when a scripted race didn't play out as smoothly as it was supposed to, or when the tote board flashed an obviously rigged exotic wager payout. In those instances, Ciulla would simply spread some cash behind the scenes to cool everyone out, find a motel room to hide the jockeys taking the heat, then get the hell out of town himself to move on to the next gig.

Very few racetrackers were foolish enough to take Fat Tony's money and not deliver the goods, and those who did were immediately transformed into gory examples of why it was not such a bright idea to cross the mob. Edward Donnally was one jockey who apparently learned the hard way: According to Ciulla's testimony in U.S. district court, Donnally was paid $800 to lose the third race at Suffolk Downs on October 16, 1974. Instead, his horse won, and the rider was ordered to the back room of a local bar to explain his actions. Allegedly, Donnally made the double mistake of mouthing off to the boss, and while an associate repeatedly smashed him in the face with a blackjack, a raging Howie Winter warned the suddenly apologetic jockey that he and his wife could be "put in a [car] trunk and never be missed." Donnally thereafter offered his horse-holding services for free, said Ciulla, who also testified that a Pocono Downs trainer "had his head opened like a cantaloupe" for not staying away from the betting windows as ordered and that a Pennsylvania jockey was beaten unconscious, had his ribs kicked in, and was left for dead in a parking lot when he couldn't keep a mount from finishing second. "These were the kind of people," one state trooper grimly summed in *Turf and Sport Digest,* "that, if you got in the way, would blow your brains out, stuff you in the trash can by the desk in their motel room, and then throw you out the back window when you began to stink."

By 1975, the formidable Winter Hill operation had reached its peak of efficiency, and the gang had infiltrated the highest levels of East Coast racing. According to Ciulla, whose testimony is backed by FBI surveillance records, the Boston mob was known to have contact with some of the biggest names in the New York jockey colony, including Con Errico, Jorge Velasquez, Braulio Baeza, and Jacinto Vasquez. But in a 1978 *Sports Illustrated* cover story titled "Confessions of a Master Fixer," Ciulla recounted that it was superstar Angel Cordero Jr. who was the most skillful of all when it came to holding horses. "He'd have you thinking he was pumping and whipping and hustling more than anybody else in the race," said an admiring Fat Tony. "But Cordero would be almost breaking the horse's jaw with his left hand while only fanning the horse with his whip."

Still, not every jockey could be bought, and in those cases the Winter Hill Gang would not force money on a reluctant reinsman. Instead, the fixers would either pass the race entirely or pay the remaining riders a bit extra to block the jock who hadn't been bribed. Michael Hole is one rider whose name comes up often in law-enforcement documentation about racetrackers who wouldn't accept tainted money. Reportedly, Hole turned down offers of $5,000 and then $10,000 to pull a horse for Ciulla at Saratoga in 1974. But one wonders if the pressure to play dirty or the mob got to Hole first: Eighteen months later, he was found slumped in a car alongside a Jones Beach parkway, dead from an asphyxiation that looked like—but could never be unequivocally proven as—a suicide.

The free ride for the Boston boys came to an abrupt end on Independence Day 1975, when a careless rider at Atlantic City Race Course displayed such ineptitude at holding a horse that the stewards and state police couldn't help but step in and pressure the truth out of him. Although authorities had long suspected that Ciulla was the mastermind behind the endemic rash of race fixing, they didn't get the evidence to convict him until jockey Peter Fantini agreed to wear a wire to record his next meeting with Fat Tony. Locked away on six counts of conspiracy to commit sports bribery, demands mounted on Ciulla to comply with a massive six-state case being built by the FBI in Boston against the Winter Hill Gang. Eager to land his testimony, and well aware that the longer Fat Tony sat in prison, the more likely it was that his co-conspirators would see to it that someone behind bars silenced him for good, the feds offered immunity and entry into a witness protection program if the caged bird sang out against organized crime. "I knew," Ciulla told *Sports Illustrated,* explaining his decision to testify on behalf of the U.S. Department of Justice, "before I got out of jail, I'd [otherwise] be as dead as Man O' War."

Four years later, in 1979, a long and sordid chapter in Boston race-fixing history came to a close when Howie Winter and six others were found guilty in a fifty-one-count federal indictment of racketeering, sports bribery, wire fraud, and interstate travel to commit sports bribery. Seventeen days of excruciatingly detailed testimony from

Ciulla provided the linchpin for conviction, but when compared against the backdrop of hundreds of fraudulent horse races, millions of stolen dollars, and innumerable shattered lives, the punishments seem incongruously weak for the crimes: Winter was sentenced to ten years and a $10,000 fine. But by that time, the leader of the Irish mob was already serving twenty years for extortion and would be out on parole within six years and working as a used-car salesman. The remaining defendants got off with proverbial slaps on the wrist: Jockey Norman Mercier, described by Ciulla as his longtime go-to guy and paymaster to other riders on the New England circuit, was acquitted of all charges after repeatedly asserting under oath that never once in his life did he meet, know, or do business with anyone named Tony Ciulla. Of course, Suffolk Downs itself was never formally charged in the federal proceedings. But to this day, while almost every single one of the characters alleged to have been involved in years of wrongdoing live freely as individuals, the embattled East Boston oval still carries the institutional stigma it earned decades ago of being a safe harbor for scandal— an insiders' joint where corruption and dishonesty are an assumed part of the mix.

Although it is truthful to say that race fixing in New England is a mere fraction of what it used to be when the inmates ran the asylum, the real reason for this turnaround has more to do with raw economics than any honest effort at cleaning up the circuit. Decades of tacit corruption have contributed to the erosion of the betting product, and the dwindling handles on New England races are no longer large enough to support any major criminal plunge into the pools for profit. Repeated burnings by fixers have also made it next to impossible to find an off-track bookie in Boston who will even consider accepting a bet on a horse race, and the few who do usually impose a strict cap on winnings to minimize the risk of getting stung. With the exception of a few wayward horsemen who attempt sporadic larceny or a handful of jockeys who occasionally decide to cut up a race among themselves as a petty form of hazard pay, cheating, it seems, just isn't worth it anymore at Suffolk Downs.

YOU DON'T HAVE TO major in astrophysics and then get an internal medicine degree from Harvard University to become a racehorse trainer. But Patty Meadow did.

And regardless of whether the intelligent, bespectacled doctor is aware or even cares, such lofty scholarly standing combined with a painstakingly reclusive nature is enough to qualify the forty-nine-year-old jockey-turned-trainer as eccentric by default on the East Boston backstretch.

Dr. Patricia Meadow has been a fixture on the New England racing scene for two decades, content to toil in obscurity while pampering a small stable of modestly bred, esoterically named horses that Meadow, for the most part, mates, foals, weans, raises, trains, and races all by herself. In the track program, Patty is listed as the owner, trainer, and breeder of almost every single horse she enters, and because she has experience in the saddle and is one of the few Suffolk Downs conditioners to walk her own animals from the barn area to the saddling paddock for each race, you might as well count her as the exercise rider, groom, and hot-walker, too.

Blending into the workmanlike blur of the backstretch, the demure, deeply shy doctor is distinguished by a constantly furrowed brow and renegade wisps of gray hair that escape the neat bun atop her head as she bustles about her business under the Barn 16A shed row. Her presence as a physician/horse trainer straddles two wildly opposing worlds, but Patty openly resists the label of Suffolk Downs savant. She seems to go to great lengths to keep her Harvard side hidden, does not speak openly about her off-track practice, and no one I know on the racetrack has ever heard the doctor refer to herself by her hard-earned title. Yet the more Patty downplays her education, the larger the myth about her Ivy League intellect grows.

According to press-box veterans, Dr. Meadow long ago asserted her resistance to allowing her unique combination of vocation and avocation to be featured as a media curiosity. The only newspaper clip in her file is a 1980 *Boston Globe* profile of a bashful med-school graduate breaking into the game as an apprentice jockey, a piece that even back then underscored the young doctor's discomfort with publicity. Many years later, in the role of media relations director, my only attempt to talk Patty into a phone interview for a local newspaper went something like this:

ME: Patty? I was wondering if you'd be interested in helping out a reporter who's looking to do a profile on interesting people at Suffolk Downs.

MEADOW: Thank you, but I'd rather not.

ME: Um, all right. Would it be okay if I just asked you a few questions about your background as a doctor and passed the info along to the writer?

MEADOW: I'd prefer to talk about my horses.

ME: Well . . . Okay . . . Could I ask you about some of the offbeat names you've chosen for them?

MEADOW: Which ones do you consider "offbeat"?

ME: Ybbs?

MEADOW: An Austrian river.

ME: Ysaye?

MEADOW: A nineteenth-century Belgian violinist.

ME: Qom?

MEADOW: A holy city in Persia.

ME: Qyrghyz?

MEADOW: A people in Kyrgyzstan. Without the Americanized spelling. Look, I don't like phone interviews, so you really should come down to my barn and talk to me in person if you want to do this.

I stopped by Patty's shed row on several subsequent occasions. But the doctor always seemed to be conveniently out whenever anyone carrying a reporter's notebook or wearing a press badge happened by.

Dr. Meadow races her steeds sparingly and trains them lightly. In all of last year, her entire outfit had only ten total starts, with one win. Although her horsemanship is evident and well-respected—Patty's horses all look nourished, healthily coated, and athletically balanced—

one might argue that her trademark go-slow approach shelters the steeds from the rigors of racing. In the post parade, Meadow's entrants often appear babied and bewildered, as if suffering separation anxiety from a constantly doting caregiver. Once the real running starts, the same trainees are usually content to trail low-level fields at a comfortable canter. Unaccustomed to being banged around in a herd, they routinely lag many lengths behind faster, more aggressively honed foes.

Viewed from afar, the juxtaposition of a Harvard doctor immersed in the rough-and-tumble world of an urban, blue-collar backstretch seems unlikely. But the dynamics of the racetrack have long sustained a stripped-down social atmosphere in which brains and a college degree don't necessarily ensure the same status on the backstretch and in the grandstand as they do in the "real world." Rocket scientists can rub elbows with construction laborers in the Suffolk Downs betting lines, where the only ranking that really matters is who has the bigger bankroll. Similarly, pecking order on the backstretch is garnered according to wins and earnings: At the end of the day at any racetrack, no one asks to see a piece of paper to prove how smart you are, unless that piece of paper happens to be a check for purse winnings.

Meadow grew attached to horses at a young age and only fell deeper in love as the years progressed. Her father, the dean of planning and special programs at Harvard Medical School, gave Patty a docile pony at age six to teach her responsibility. By the time Meadow was fourteen, her parents allowed her to spend three months at a Nebraska horse farm, where the horse-crazed girl gladly handled as many barn chores as she could juggle while honing her rapidly improving riding skills. In exchange for enthusiasm and hard work, Patty had been promised a yearling colt to take home to the family farm in suburban Boston at the end of the summer. But as the hours on the farm morphed into days and then weeks, the excited teen began to increasingly appall her mother and father with talk about staying out of school to continue her hands-on education with horses, maybe even training for the Olympic equestrian team.

It was then that the wise Midwestern rancher gave young Patty a good, long talking-to before sending her back East with her steed. "He sat me down and told me to go to school and finish my education," Meadow reminisced in her 1980 *Globe* interview. "He said I could always go back to horses, but it would be harder to go back to school. Education has always been important in my family, and I knew first things first. But I also knew when I got to a stopping place in my medical career, I wanted to go off and do what I wanted to do—be with horses."

So that's what Patty did. She went to Harvard for four years as an astrophysics major. Upon graduation, she allowed herself a little break, which ended up being two years on a New Mexico ranch. Then she enrolled in med school, landed her second Harvard degree in 1978, and served a rigorous internship at Georgetown Hospital for one more year, certifying her as a doctor. Flush with options, that's when Dr. Meadow decided she wanted to become an apprentice jockey at battle-scarred Sufferin' Downs.

"Neither her mother nor I looks on horses as anything but a large mass of muscle," Dr. Henry C. Meadow explained in the *Globe* piece that profiled his daughter, then twenty-eight, as a fledgling rider coping with her 0-for-42 rookie season. "When she was younger, we thought it would be a good idea for her to have a pony to care for. We didn't know it would develop to this point . . . I'm sure this is an interlude. When people ask me when she's coming back, I say, 'Soon, I hope.' Her mother and I are scared to death she'll hurt herself."

Two decades later, Patty Meadow remains unscathed. But she has yet to outgrow her twenty-year "interlude" at the racetrack.

No longer a jockey but now a trainer, Meadow trudges the length of the Suffolk Downs homestretch long after the winter sun has beaten a hasty retreat behind the grandstand on this Sunday afternoon, coaxing, cajoling, and tugging a worn leather shank attached to a frightened bay maiden named Ypres. The doctor's long-shot first-timer in the last race is the perfect image of equine alarm: Dark eyes wide with terror, ears pinned forward and frenzied, the gelding's gangly legs are splayed every which way but toward the paddock, where the 60-to-1 steed is scheduled to rendezvous with nine other winless rivals, providing entertainment and investment fodder for an edgy betting crowd seeking salvation—or at least a last chance at bailing out even—at the end of the day in the Eastie nightcap.

Ypres—his name is pronounced *Eep*, and it refers to the Belgian battle site where poison gas was first used in World War I—is not at all interested in making the trek from his home stall to the saddling area. And if the resistant gelding's slow series of published workouts are any indication, he will probably be equally unenthused about the prospect of actually having to race against fellow maiden-claiming three-year-olds. Every visual and aural cue on or around the racetrack sends a shock of alarm through Ypres—a darting flock of gulls fighting over a tidbit of trash, a low-flying Lufthansa airliner landing at Logan, the subway train rattling along its tracks more than a quarter-mile away—and Patty Meadow is doing an admirable job just to get her entry into the paddock and over to the identifier in one piece. She holds Ypres patiently and talks to him in a low, soothing voice while the track official deftly flips the animal's top lip to match tattoo numbers with the one listed on his foal certificate, and after having successfully accomplished that task, the gelding is ushered to saddling stall number one. The enclosure is adjacent to the clubhouse outdoor viewing area, but Meadow has little to worry about in terms of a throng of boisterous fans further unraveling the easily spooked maiden: There are exactly three patrons outside on the chilly Suffolk Downs tarmac as the February twilight closes in on darkness, and one of them appears busy way off to the side, muttering to himself while walking around and around in disjointed circles.

Patty seems to be debating a similar roundabout strategy for getting the tack secured on Ypres. Saddling an agitated horse "on the walk" instead of in a semi-enclosed stall is often the best bet for safely accomplishing what can be a difficult task with an uncooperative animal. But before the trainer can decide what to do, her horse abruptly decides for her: Reacting to something that only the young gelding can sense, see, smell, or hear, Ypres rears on his hind legs, then topples past his balance point, crashing backward into the hard-packed mud and stone dust of the walking ring.

Meadow jumps deftly out of the way but quickly darts back to the side of her stricken steed, who has miraculously managed not to land head first. Ypres is given a preliminary examination by the vet stationed in the paddock, and although deemed not seriously injured, the dazed Thoroughbred is logically excused from the finale. The scratch is announced as the remainder of the field straggles out to answer the call to post, and Ypres, now somewhat more sedate, is led back to his barn by his vigilant trainer. Together, the two must now await another day for the reluctant maiden to make his Suffolk Downs debut, while the career of the only doctor-turned-racetracker on the backstretch continues to grind unobtrusively beneath the radar.

WET, SLOPPY RACING CONDITIONS are the order of the afternoon for the Valentine's Day program, and the bogged-down track might bode well for the enigmatic Huckster's Girl, the down-on-her-luck racemare who had to be scratched at the gate last month after flipping in her starting stall. With more than half her $32,393 in lifetime purses earned over "off" surfaces, Huckster's Girl is well known to relish a wet racing strip. After being soundly beaten by a cumulative eighty-five lengths in her last four starts, today the six-year-old will have every opportunity to finally turn things around for herself and struggling owner/trainer Pearl Chain. But the mudlark's perceived chances of success won't have as much to do with the gooey going as they will with an apparent behind-the-scenes battle plan for this afternoon's second race, a $6,250 claiming contest at one mile and seventy yards for older fillies and mares.

Making my rounds through the jockeys' quarters between the early daily double, I stop to chat with Lou Raffetto and several other Suffolk Downs execs who sit at the lunch counter, kibitzing about this and that. After that I nod hello to Norman Mercier, the acquitted former jockey whose lucrative career coincidentally tailed off right after the Winter Hill boys got put behind bars. At sixty-eight, "Stormin' Norman" was rumored to have owned a fairly thick bankroll back in the day; now he must toil as a locker-room valet to make ends meet, polishing boots for rookie riders less than one-third his age. Barely perceptibly, Norman nods back. These days he is a man of few words.

I pass through the swinging door that separates the rec room from the main dressing area, and immediately upon entering the large and busy common room, I encounter Joe Hampshire, whose locker occupies the prime spot adjacent to the less-crowded back wall. But instead of readying for the next race with his valet hovering about him, Hampshire is fully dressed in his riding gear and hunched over the tack table across the aisle from his cubicle. In full view of anyone who walks through the main entrance to the area, Joe has a program open to the second race and is intently pointing out horses and speaking hurriedly to Richard Johnson, a twenty-one-year-old apprentice who just arrived in town this week and has been luckless with five mounts. Johnson listens attentively, nodding his head, absorbing every word. In this race, the rookie has the call on Huckster's Girl.

"Now I'm gonna go to the lead on this horse," says Hampshire, who is riding Fur Will Fly, a consistent veteran racemare with twenty-four lifetime wins and plenty of early speed. She is ranked as the 2-to-1 morning line favorite and is picked on top to win by both handicappers in the track program. "And when we get to the top of the stretch, you . . . "

At this point Hampshire sees me standing in front of him and abruptly stops speaking. But I think I've already heard enough. I continue without a word past the apprentice and the veteran, out into the paddock.

In her most recent start against similar competition, you couldn't find Huckster's Girl with a search warrant. She finished dead last, beaten by 32-3/4 lengths. Three weeks before that, she was scratched after somersaulting backward in the starting gate. Her trainer has not hit the board in four months. Her fledgling jockey has never won a race, anywhere, ever. It has been fourteen races, nearly a full year, since the 4-for-49 racemare last went to post at a mutuel price of less than double-digit odds. In the morning line, Huckster's Girl is 15 to 1, deservedly ranked as the longest shot in the six-horse field.

Climbing the short stairway from the jockeys' room tunnel, I emerge outside to the raw, wet saddling enclosure and immediately cast an eye of suspicion toward the infield tote board.

At eleven minutes to post, the hapless Huckster's Girl is the overwhelming favorite.

Winking next to her number 7 on the tote board, the disturbingly low 8-to-5 price is a beacon of impropriety. Hustling up to the press box, I catch the constantly updated exacta payouts on the various possible win-and-place outcomes on a grandstand television monitor and note another glaring inconsistency: The 7-and-3 exacta combo, with Huckster's Girl atop D.J.'s Gypsy Road, is quoted at $30.00. Using the morning-line odds of the two horses as an estimate, the standard $2.00 exacta payout for a 15-to-1 winner over a 4-to-1 second-place horse should easily be four or five times that amount. In pari-mutuel wagering, the more money bet on a particular combination, the lower the potential payout. A large influx of cash has moved the odds in the win and exacta pools in a very noticeable and conspicuous fashion, and the fact that the bets were made relatively early in the wagering cycle is a red flag that the plays were driven by some sort of inside information rather than by casual horseplayers acting on a hunch.

"They're going to let the new kid win the race," I blurt to the degenerates upon barging into the press office, tossing my program in their general direction for emphasis. I let the guys in on the snippet of conversation I caught, underscoring the oddity of overhearing the leading rider with the mount on a solid morning-line favorite tipping his hand to a rookie rival on the horse who should be the longest shot in the race.

If anyone in the jocks' room knows how well Huckster's Girl moves up in the mud, it's Joe Hampshire, who has won aboard her three times previously, including the mare's most recent victory over a wet surface five starts back. "Check out the flood of action on this horse. I'm guessing Hampshire plans to get the lead but be out of the money. Vega's supposed to be second, I think, with D.J.'s Gypsy Road. Look at the board." The price on Huckster's Girl is rising as more money flows into the pools, but it is still way under par at 3 to 1 as the field steps onto the racetrack for the post parade.

"Are you going to tell the stewards?" announcer Larry Collmus asks, intrigued but not overly incredulous. It would be the right thing to do, I agree, but Collmus knows better than almost anyone else at Suffolk Downs that reporting unusual betting patterns to the judges would likely be an exercise in futility.

A respected veteran race-caller and consummate professional, Collmus is one of the few announcers in the industry who isn't afraid to slip brutally frank criticisms into his race calls or let the judges know what's on his mind when he thinks the game isn't being played by the rules. But an encounter he had with the previous Suffolk Downs Board of Stewards several years ago pretty much sums up the situation: After the announcer had documented complaints about a jockey he witnessed repeatedly holding horses, one gruff, frustrated (and now retired) judge lashed back with a tirade that began "Why are you so bitter? Who'd you bet on?" as if the old-timer could in no way conceive or comprehend Larry's motive for wanting the game to be honest and on the level.

The three stewards at Suffolk Downs, like those at most midsized racing venues, have a difficult job. In addition to overseeing the actual races, they are also responsible for staying on top of a litany of other bureaucratic infractions within the realm of the racetrack, ranging from fining grooms who smoke under the shed row to policing drunk backstretch rowdies to chasing down licensees who fail to fill out proper paperwork. And because judges are often hired from the ranks of retired horsemen (at Suffolk Downs, Association Steward Jim Gigliotti was a local jockey; Commission Steward Bill Keen was a local trainer, and Chief Commission Steward Richard DeStasio was both a New England jockey *and* trainer), enforcement becomes even more problematic when judges have to police longtime friends, acquaintances, and even enemies. Plus, few authority figures like to be informed that they're missing unscrupulous activities right under their own noses, so claims of impropriety are often met with skepticism, indifference, or denial. Even the most vigilant regulators face the paradox of *knowing* when cheating occurs versus *proving* those allegations, so it ends up being far easier to simply quell the whistle-blowers rather than punish the wrongdoers. By default, the industry has historically chosen the path of least resistance when it comes to cleaning up its act, sweeping short-term scandal under the rug at the expense of eroding long-term integrity.

With the clock ticking away to post time, and realizing that anything I could possibly tell the stewards at this point would come down to my word against everyone else's, I decide there's only one course of action available: "We might as well go bet," I say to the guys, dashing for the press box self-service terminal and pulling out my wallet with a minute to post.

The win odds on Huckster's Girl have floated up to a more realistic 10 to 1 as the bulk of outside money merges into the pool. On a slow winter Monday with not many other tracks running in the country, the Suffolk Downs races are being exported to a greater number of simulcast outlets, and the tens of thousands of dollars dumped into the mix by casual players helps to dilute the concentration of early bets on the supposed sure thing, ripening the now-lucrative price on Johnson's mount while the odds come down as expected on Hampshire's favorite. Huckster's Girl settles into the starting gate at a believable 14 to 1, but the 7-and-3 exacta will-pay with Huckster's Girl over D.J.'s Gypsy Road is a still-suspicious $57.00 at the final flash. One of the video directors from the TV control room asks what the big buzz around the press-box betting machine is all about. "Bet the seven," I tell her, hurrying downstairs to watch the race. "I can't tell you why. Just bet."

The field is off and the break is uneventful. Fur Will Fly, at 6 to 5, makes the lead as expected. Once Again Wild, a 6-to-1 steed who didn't beat a horse in her last two tries, engages the favorite from the rail. Lady Schwartzman (4 to 1) and Laurine's Miss (7 to 1) both drop down to the fence and track the dueling duo into the clubhouse turn, while Richard Johnson and Huckster's Girl are allowed to roam unimpeded four wide—without another horse even anywhere close—six lengths off the top with plenty of running room and no mud splashing her in the face. D.J.'s Gypsy Road, a deep closer, is eased back by Harry Vega from post 3, also well away from the spray of slop in the back of the pack.

The pace is moderate, maybe even a touch slow, as the sextet banks into the backstretch. Half a mile from home, the running positions change little except for Huckster's Girl, who has been encouraged to move closer to the top trio while still outside and well away from the others. On the far turn, she overtakes a lackluster Laurine's Miss, while D.J.'s Gypsy Road is also on the move. By the time the field hits the top of the homestretch in a lethargic 1:15-4/5 for six furlongs, Huckster's Girl looks primed to pounce. Galloping easily, the rookie jockey appears on the way to his first career win, and he begins to push just a touch harder on the mud-loving mare, gobbling up ground with every stride, with only two furlongs and three horses between him and the finish wire.

At the quarter pole, Hampshire sneaks a peek behind to see if company is coming, and he catches a glimpse of Huckster's Girl cutting the corner under a full-out drive by apprentice Johnson. But watching through binoculars, I begin to sense that something is not quite right with Huckster's Girl, who in the span of only about a hundred feet coming out of the bend suddenly seems to be laboring, as if she might not be able to continue her bid. Her dark brown legs seem wearied by the weight of four mud-sogged bandages, the mare's head has dropped just a few inches in a tell-tale sign of fatigue, and an alarmed Johnson is now whipping and driving with the gangly, awkward fury of a panicked rookie. Despite a setup that couldn't have been any more ideal, the drained Huckster's Girl just doesn't have any kick left in reserve, that final spurt of speed she needs to surge past the leaders.

Huckster's Girl manages to move into third at the exact same moment that Fur Will Fly—a seasoned mare with no previous history of having trouble on the turns in 117 lifetime starts—all of a sudden and without warning forgets how to turn left at the top of the lane under Hampshire, bolting eight paths from the rail at the three-sixteenths pole, losing precious ground while affording her exhausted competition the generous opportunity to narrow the gap. Johnson, alternating right-hand flails of his stick with an almost pleading, energetic, scrubbing motion, is still five lengths off the top while one furlong from home, not gaining at all despite a commodious and clear path to win. Fur Will Fly's strides also begin to shorten in the 220-yard run to the finish, but Huckster's Girl just isn't making up ground. Almost unnoticed, an onrushing D.J.'s Gypsy Road and Harry Vega come wide and driving, swooping by everyone as if on cue, closing with a flourish in the middle of the track while blowing by the staggering front-runners as if they were waiting for something else to happen. Fur Will Fly lasts for the runner-up spot, but Huckster's Girl is so choppy and tired in the final strides that she even gets passed for third, a sure thing who failed to show up when victory seemed a certainty.

In the winner's circle after the race, the usually animated Vega does not smile when he poses for his picture atop D.J.'s Gypsy Road. Riding back to dismount, Joe Hampshire curses and mutters beneath his breath. Watching from the rail, I am dying to hear his explanation to mercurial horse owner Michael Gill, so I follow Hampshire out of the scale house and over to his scowling boss as the leading rider offers the excuse that Fur Will Fly could have won the race if the mare had not blown the turn. With a shrug, Joe quickly adds that he's not really sure why she did that.

Inside the locker room, the usual post-race chatter is conspicuously absent as the riders remove their mud-soaked silks. Hampshire goes to Vega's locker way over on the other side of the room and huddles with him, speaking briefly before moving on. He puts a hand on apprentice Johnson's shoulder, makes a quick conciliatory comment, then heads to his locker to watch the race replay. He is either too brazen or too careless to notice that I am once again standing behind him while he scrutinizes the television. "I should have gone wider," he muses regretfully, eyeing his turn for home.

At the end of the afternoon, I decide to phone someone higher up the Suffolk Downs totem pole, knowing that I have long since left the proverbial barn door open to report something that I perceived as obvious wrongdoing. Still, I figure it can't hurt. It is a strange coincidence that Suffolk Downs management has just concluded a daylong meeting over safety issues with national and regional representatives of the Jockeys' Guild, who were on hand in the locker room but apparently oblivious to any impropriety that might have occurred. I detail my version of what I saw going on right out in the open, pointing out that even if an overheard sentence or two is circumstantial, the links to inconsistencies in the betting and the bizarre way in which the race itself unfolded certainly seem suspicious when viewed as a whole.

"Well, the outside *was* the best part of the track today," the exec tells me wearily, probably not wanting to deal with this issue at the end of a long day but nonetheless taking the time to watch the race replay while we speak. I also point out how the six jockeys returning to the room after the race were as quiet as pallbearers, and that Harry Vega did not look his customary smiling self in the winner's circle.

"Well, no one was smiling today out there," he counters, loyally defending the very same jockeys track management has been battling all winter. "Would you be smiling if you had to ride under those conditions?"

I decide not to press the issue and instead just drive home in the dark.

Maybe the odd tutorial between Hampshire and Johnson *was* unrelated to what looked like a scripted race, and was instead an altruistic helping hand from a top jockey to a brand-new apprentice.

Maybe it *was* just coincidental that the most hapless horse in the race had a ton of money dumped in on her to win, and that there were remarkable discrepancies in the exacta pools.

Maybe it *was* just a fluke that the favorite inexplicably turned right at the top of the lane instead of heading straight for the winner's circle, where she belonged.

Maybe the quiet tension in the jockeys' room after the race *was* unrelated to a Valentine's Day Massacre that wasn't.

And maybe tomorrow, when the people who toil on the Suffolk Downs backstretch arrive for another freezing morning of winter work in an industry so vitally dependent upon the confidence of bettors who support it, the sun will rise in the West.

At LAUREL PARK, trainer Mike Catalano scores with the first out-of-town starter for his mid-Atlantic invasion, wiring the third race with shipper Boston Pride, an $11.00 winner. One race later, 9-to-1 long shot Premier Imp will come up just a head short of a perfect 2-for-2 start for Team Catalano, earning a photo-finish second.

Mike Catalano stays at Suffolk Downs to watch the Maryland simulcasts, having assigned an assistant to saddle today's out-of-town trainees owned by Michael Gill. But luck is not as good on the home front, where the barn loses with two heavy favorites. Mossad is off the board at 2 to 5 in the third, and Spicy Goto beats but one horse in the nightcap at 9 to 5. Visiting the press box at the end of the day, Mike is nevertheless upbeat despite the split decision.

"I like to drop a horse down to win right off the bat whenever I ship somewhere," Catalano beams, still exhausted but calmly confident at having made the right decision to take his show on the road. "I like to make an impact."

I COME into work to find Bish and one of the press-box interns entranced by the local cable station that televises nonstop reruns of *The Three Stooges* all morning long on Saturdays. I recognize the episode as one of my favorites, the one where Moe, Larry, and Curly get gypped into trading their restaurant for a racehorse who turns out to be a hopeless nag. But the wacky trio soon discovers that Thunderbolt runs like crazy to the nearest source of water when he eats powerful chili peppers, and the boys manage to win a big race by having jockey Larry feed the steed the hot stuff while Moe and Curly circle the track on a motorcycle, coaxing the horse along with a water bucket.

I explain to the intern that during my very first summer working at the track for the *Racing Times*, Bish and I were jammed together in what passed for the press box at Rockingham Park, a claustrophobic 8-by-12-foot cubicle with terminally ill air-conditioning four floors above the finish wire. Every Friday night the track staged racing under the lights, so we'd swat moths the size of softballs, send out for beer and Chinese food, and chase trifectas. Then every Saturday morning we'd arrive bleary-eyed in the smothering New Hampshire humidity, hang cardboard from the press-box windows to block out the painful glare, and return to a semi-human state by decompressing over coffee in front of a never-ending blur of nyuks, knuckleheads, and gratuitous Stooge violence. I tell the college sophomore that at one point, Bish had me convinced that watching *The Three Stooges* was an important Saturday morning tradition for Thoroughbred degenerates in press boxes all across the country. Having never worked at any other track, back then I basically believed everything he told me.

Bish casts us a sidelong glance but does not turn his head away from the black-and-white slapstick blaring from the TV above his desk.

"And you're insinuating to this young man that it isn't?" he asks, mockingly indignant, refocusing his gaze just as Moe delivers an exaggerated blow to Larry's frizzy-haired face with a whipped-cream pie.

A STRONG CROWD is on hand for Presidents Day at Suffolk Downs, and the Monday program features promotional giveaways honoring dead presidents all afternoon in the form of cold, hard cash. But another winter holiday tradition at the Eastie oval—unsafe racing conditions—threatens to submarine the card before the early double is even in the books.

Although the day carries a welcome hint of spring with bright sunshine and 50°F temperatures, the mild climate is also the undoing of a racing surface whose bottom layers have been frozen solid for five weeks. Underneath the deep cushion of sloppy topsoil, the stone-dust base of the track is starting to break apart, leaving uneven footing beneath the mud-smoothed exterior and basketball-sized ice chunks that crack free and float to the surface, bobbing up from the muck where least expected. The second race is delayed for close to half an hour while track superintendent Steve Pini jabbers instructions into a walkie-talkie, ordering his armada of tractors to drag heavy floats across the muddy course to expose the underbelly of the strip to the sun and wind. Calling the winter maintenance shots at Suffolk Downs is a frenetic and inexact science, and Pini's job is a months-long thankless task because everyone—winners and whiners alike—are highly critical of the racetrack's composition.

The jockeys form an odd-looking cluster as they wait for their call to duty, fully equipped, helmeted, and clothed for race-riding; whips in hand, they casually flick at tabletops and chair legs as they lounge and lean by the exit to the paddock, passing time while the heavy equipment slowly circles the oozing, one-mile circumference. Harry Vega slouches in a beat-up, high-backed executive's chair, rolling slowly back and forth on squeaky wheels, mesmerized by the padded stuffing exuding from rips and tears in the tattered blue vinyl. Victor Colon squats on his haunches and grins, Gary Birzer fusses with his threadbare brown and red silks, and Joe Hampshire paces back and forth, just trying to burn nervous energy like the other eight riders. Jose Caraballo chatters nonstop, joking and laughing; the other jockeys are ribbing him because the glib reinsman riled Chief State Steward Dick DeStasio so badly during the mandatory morning films review that the judge completely lost his temper and screamed that Caraballo was an asshole in front of the entire riding colony. Apparently, the outburst came after Jose had the audacity to stand up and ask DeStasio why the stewards have different rules for different jockeys who commit essentially the same riding infractions.

During the hiatus while the maintenance crews finish fine-tuning the quagmire, the jockeys get a surprise locker-room visit from Henry Ma, an affable journeyman who has been out of action since a horrific training accident last July at Rockingham Park. A rider who always struggled to survive near the bottom of the New England pecking order for close to three decades, the forty-seven-year-old Hong Kong native suffered serious neurological damage when a skittish horse he was taking to the track for a morning gallop bucked abruptly, smashing Henry's chin with the jackhammer-like reflex of its rearing head as the animal rose in fright on its hind legs. Unconscious, Ma toppled backward from his saddle and landed headfirst on the racetrack. The spooked horse also lost its balance and crumpled to the ground, landing squarely atop the fallen rider. Henry woke up twelve hours later in the hospital with bleeding in his brain and no recollection of having gone to work that morning.

Ma makes the rounds in the locker room, shaking hands, exchanging greetings with valets and his horsebacking brethren. Henry is an easygoing sort, one of the few riders everyone seems to like. Never one to complain, "The Chinaman" was known on the backstretch as a workmanlike jock who would climb astride anything with four legs and tail to make ends meet. He rarely landed live mounts and only achieved leading-rider status when he ventured to the perilous half-mile Massachusetts county fairs, where the horses are unsound, the turns are tight, and the rewards are monumentally disproportionate to the risks. For several seasons before his accident, times had been tough for Henry: A strip-mall Chinese restaurant in New Hampshire that he owned in partnership with his brother went out of business five years ago, and as recently as 1996, Ma was profiled in a front-page *Boston Globe* sports story that detailed the hardships of a father with a family of four trying to scrape by as a bottom-of-the-barrel jockey. Today, even after a half year of strenuous physical therapy, Ma is still experiencing dizziness and constant, throbbing headaches, and neither he nor his doctors seem to know when—or if—he will ever ride a racehorse again.

"You know when you go out and drink too much and have a hangover? A really bad one?" Henry asks, flashing his trademark toothy grin while leaning his left hand lightly against a table to maintain balance. "That's what it feels like with me. Only every morning it feels like that, and I haven't had a drink in a long time. It just won't go away."

Ma makes amicable small talk, and his comrades seem genuinely glad to see him. But as the jockeys banter back and forth, a barely perceptible twinge of discomfort percolates beneath the surface of sociability: Henry Ma is one of them, but *not* one of them, and the subtlety of the situation is sensed rather than seen. Universally, all riders fear racetrack catastrophe. But even more, they fear talking about it, and jockeys who ride scared don't generally ride for long. Henry Ma standing there in street clothes while everyone else is tacked up and ready to race represents something the reinsmen do not wish to acknowledge: A sudden slip of the saddle, a brief clipping of heels, or just being in the wrong place at the wrong time atop a fully extended racehorse is all it would take for them to be in Henry's shoes. And although it is printed right next to them in big block letters, no one seems to notice that the gang is gathered near a prominently posted sign that the jockeys must pass each time they step out into the paddock:

Under Massachusetts Law, an Equine Professional Is Not Liable for Injury to, or the Death of, a Participant in Equine Activities Resulting from the Inherent Risks of Equine Activities, Pursuant to Section 2d of Chapter 128 of the General Laws.

Or rather, perhaps they all notice. The stuffy winter room is loose with jokes, but the laughter is forced, decidedly different. Outside, the tractors make their final pass, and the riders become even more fidgety for the call to the paddock.

For a number of reasons—his accident occurred during a morning training session and thus away from the eye of the public; the fact that Ma is neither a top jockey nor a household name; general laziness on the part of New England beat writers who don't always report everything they should about the sport—there was never a mention about Henry's debilitating casualty in the Boston dailies or the national racing publications. One day his name just disappeared from the entries, and no one could be bothered to find out why. By contrast, the Rudy Baez catastrophe the very next month at the very same track received substantial national and local attention. And although it may be unfair to compare Henry's neurological difficulties to the paralysis of a fan-favorite leading rider, Ma's career, the use of his limbs, and possibly even his life were just a fraction away from a similar fate, and the real tragedy is that no one took the time to notice.

Despite his physical woes and fiscal hardships, Ma remains upbeat. He jokingly blames himself for today's delay caused by thawing track conditions, claiming that bad luck follows him all around the racetrack. He teases that now he can't go anywhere without his wife by his side, because the doctors say he's not supposed to drive. Finally, the call comes over the locker room loudspeaker for the jockeys to saddle up for the second race. The banter dies down, the big metal door to the paddock clangs shut, and the fallen reinsman is left standing alone.

Henry turns to me and explains in a quiet voice how he is hopeful that he will one day be able to climb astride a Thoroughbred, although the specialists caring for him have bluntly prepared him for the fact that such a day might never come. "Last week they sent me to a psychiatrist," Ma says, shaking his head with distaste, as if his pride had been insulted. "They say I'm depressed. They want to put me on Prozac. I don't want Prozac. I just want to ride."

Henry looks down at the ground and is thoughtful for a moment. When he lifts his head, the characteristic big grin has returned.

"I told them, 'Try not working for seven months. You'd be depressed too.'"

DRIVING INTO WORK on a late February morning, I encounter what old-school New Englanders say is the surest sign of impending spring: the musky smell of skunk in the air. It is usually this time of year that the animals begin to emerge from their dormant winter dens in search of fresh food and mates, and when they come out of hibernation, they're out for good.

Ironically, the skunk smell gets stronger the closer you drive to Boston from the suburbs. These fetid foragers have long since abandoned the woodsy outskirts in favor of the buffet-style dining available in the copious smorgasbord of city dumpsters. Around Suffolk Downs, all the backstretch folk know it's wise not to open a closed trash can or manure bin without first rattling around and making some noise as you approach, because if you give the skunks an opportunity to escape, they will. But corner a skunk in the act of feeding, and you're odds-on to get doused in defense.

One particularly bountiful food bonanza for animals is the Suffolk Downs grain barn on an access road adjacent to the stable area. The large structure is the on-site holding area for New Hampshire–based feed vendor Dodge Grain, and any skunks, mice, squirrels, chipmunks, rabbits, woodchucks, or weasels lucky enough to sniff out the stash must think they've died and gone to animal heaven. In turn, these vermin attract the next logical predators up the food chain, and it is not unusual to see hawks and other birds of prey circling above the vast expanse of racetrack infield waiting for a tasty morsel to make a dash into the open from the shelter of ground cover. At night, I use the access road as a shortcut home to Route 1A, and on my way off the property I usually cruise past the grain shed very slowly, because the raccoons that have staked out territory there are so big and brazen that they won't get out of your way. Some of them are so fat and well-fed that in the dusky glow of distance, they look like medium-sized dogs staring defiantly into a car's high beams.

Tenacity and territorialism also happen to be the subject of today's *Boston Herald* racing column. Joe Hampshire is closing in on career win number 2,000, and after a four-score day on Sunday and another win on Presidents Day, the locker room leader is just thirteen victories away from the milestone mark. Turf scribe Ed Gray speculates that Joe might have already reached that goal "had he not lost his focus last year, slowing his winning considerably." Beset by calamity both on and off the racetrack, Hampshire concurs that the pressure got to him.

"I had tragedies in my life," Joe explains, mentally replaying everything that transpired over the last twelve months. "Between a divorce and my daughter's mother being paralyzed, and the Rudy situation, my mind was in a lot of places other than business." In addition, just before the start of the current season, Hampshire's longtime agent—Max Hall, for decades the best in New England—cashed in his chips and departed in search of a brighter future. "When I came back from Jamaica, I felt refreshed, and Max going to New York rejuvenated me, because it made me work harder. It's making me hustle."

Around the racetrack, one adapts or expires. This universal rule of instinct applies to everyone, from animals who forage at the bottom of the food chain to human characters soaring high and free atop the jockey standings.

THOROUGHBRED RACING'S nationally accepted Scale of Weights has been in the news with increasing frequency. The rigid and archaic system of assigning poundage to jockeys was developed over a century ago, and its stringent guidelines have remained largely unchanged while human athletes have increased markedly in body size. As a result, modern-day riders are forced to resort to a myriad of unhealthy practices to adhere to unrealistic weight requirements. Originally conceived as fair means of equalizing the abilities of equine competitors based on the age of the horse, the month of the year, and the distance of the race, the Scale of Weights in theory mandates assignments as low as ninety-six pounds, with a top weight of 130 pounds. But in practice, most everyday races require a rider to tack no higher than 122 pounds, including silks, underclothes, boots, saddle, irons, and goggles.

Resistance to changing the Scale of Weights is rooted in tradition, with the default industry excuse "Because that's the way it's always been done" most often cited as the reason for keeping things the way they are. Some horsemen claim that allowing jockeys to ride at heavier weights would increase stress and strain on the Thoroughbred, but this rationale lacks merit when one considers that European reinsmen routinely ride at heavier imposts than their American counterparts and that steeplechase jockeys in the United States tack 160 pounds over fence-jumping courses in races run at several miles in length. The only argument that seems to make some sense is the theory that no matter how high the scale—be it 130, 230, or 330 pounds—there will always be jockeys right on the cusp of the guidelines, so that no matter what the breaking point, someone, somewhere will always be trying to reduce frantically to get under the limit.

In Massachusetts, jockeys are allowed to ride at seven pounds above a steed's assigned weight, and any deviation from the published weight in the program must be announced to the public. While a pound or two difference rarely matters to most horsemen (or bettors), few are willing to employ a rider who routinely maxxes out at the top end of allowed overweight. Thus, in order to earn a paycheck, some jockeys are willing to do anything to force their bodies to abide by the unforgiving Scale of Weights, even if it kills them.

For starters, most riders simply eat less, restricting their diets to obscenely low calorie intakes. But even that isn't enough for some jockeys, who will eat only enough to satisfy the feeling of hunger before purging the contents of their stomach by vomiting (in the Suffolk Downs locker room, one bathroom stall is reserved strictly for "flipping"). Saunas capable of reaching 180°F are staples of virtually every jockeys' quarters on the continent, and some riders will take even more extreme measures to sweat off weight by entering these "hot boxes" wearing rubber suits or by lathering up with special creams designed to pull even more water from the body. Drugs—either vile, homemade laxative concoctions of Epsom salts and lemon juice or injectable diuretics like Lasix at doses high enough to be dangerous to horses—are also common, with the belief that flushing the system is the most efficient way to rid the body of liquid weight.

Although effective in the short term, all these methods carry dire consequences. Lifelong patterns of anorexia and bulimia take their toll on the body, resulting in significant health problems. Fatigue from heat-induced reduction and lightheadedness from hunger decrease strength and mental acuity, and stories of exhausted riders slipping unconscious from the saddle are hardly unprecedented (legendary jockey George Woolf, winner of the very first MassCap in 1935, is believed to have died in this manner during the running of a race at Santa Anita eleven years later). Rapid depletion of body fluids causes dangerously low calcium, sodium, potassium, and electrolyte levels, which can cause cardiac seizures and even paralysis. Years of chemical abuse to facilitate weight loss also undermine the human filtration system in cumulative fashion, which means that over time, irreversible liver and kidney damage is a certainty for jockeys who gamble with unprescribed diuretics to fight the natural balance of their own bodies.

When a jockey has reduced to the point that he or she can no longer take any more weight off, then it's time to resort to both legal and illegal methods of shaving poundage from clothing and tack. One common ploy is to weigh out wearing "cheating boots" that have soles sliced so thin as to be utterly useless when standing in the irons, which are then exchanged on the sly for more sturdy footwear before heading out to the paddock. Or, a rider could step on the scale wearing a safety vest with sections of shock-absorbing padding illegally removed before switching to a full-size regulation vest in the bathroom at the last minute. Some Suffolk Downs jockeys—even in the dead of winter—will ride without gloves or socks because every ounce is so precious.

Friendship or outright indifference on the part of racing officials also comes into play when one considers the monotonous process of weighing out and then in again nine times a day, 150 days a year at a track like Suffolk Downs. Scales clerks and their assistants are often retired jockeys themselves, and since few riders naturally make weight without having to reduce in some fashion, these officials can empathize with the dilemma of being a bit over the required weight. Thus, it is natural to assume that, on occasion, officials will look the other way when a jockey is off by a pound or two so an otherwise law-abiding guy can make a paycheck—especially in a profession where it seems preposterous to adhere to the antiquated belief that a few ounces of poundage truly make a difference in a sport where half-ton animals race around a one-mile track.

SUCCESS IS an elusive and odd thing in New England racing. When a horse, jockey, or racing stable reaches the pinnacle of the profession on the local circuit, a move out of town to face bigger and better competition is viewed as breaking out of the minors and into the major leagues. Yet the path to recognition and accomplishment is not always a direct and upward-moving arc, nor is it met with immediate acceptance on the home front. Blame it on envy, jealousy, or old-fashioned, cantankerous Yankee skepticism, but moving up and out of Suffolk Downs is more of a challenge than it seems because a backstretch laden with naysayers always seems to be lying in wait for a prodigal son to return home, tail between legs, so they can collectively chide, "I told you so."

The move to the mid-Atlantic by Michael Gill and Mike Catalano is an obvious case in point. Although it remains to be seen how well they'll fare in Maryland and Delaware, their ambition and aspirations—plus the money and the horseflesh that enables them to attempt the transition—make their breakout attempt a favorably leveraged gamble. Should they manage to strike it rich in the long run, the Gill-Catalano tandem will undoubtedly be embraced by their Boston peers as "local boys who done good." But until they get over that hump, their planned exodus of some sixty horses from an already thin Thoroughbred population can be expected to be met with resistance from the powers behind the scenes.

Director of Racing John Morrissey is the track executive at the helm of the Suffolk Downs backstretch, with implicit power over every single one of the 1,200 horses stabled there. His basic responsibility is the day-to-day scheduling of races, ideally striking a balance between offering an appealing betting product to the public while ensuring that local owners and trainers are content with the varied classifications of races, so that no horse has to wait an unreasonable amount of time between starts. Every two weeks he publishes a "condition book" that outlines which races are eligible to be scheduled on which dates, breaking down each contest by a complex myriad of restrictions according to purse, distance, weight assignments, class, age, and sex. A typical date has between twelve and eighteen separate race offerings. Forty-eight hours before race day, Morrissey's office will take entry applications from horsemen over a period of several hours in the morning, cull the best nine races, assign post positions for each entered horse according to a random draw, then align the races in a specific order on a sheet known as the overnight, which by midafternoon is widely distributed throughout the stable area and grandstand, and to the press. The process is repeated every single day of a 150-date season at Suffolk Downs, and such procedures are mirrored at every single racetrack on the continent, every single day of the year.

But to condense John's job description into one succinct paragraph is a vast oversimplification. For starters, he has to first sell and schmooze the overall Suffolk Downs racing ideology to a wide variety of outfits, pitching his purses to stables that plan far ahead where they're going to be for an entire season, depending on how much money is up for grabs and whether the types of races will match the capabilities of their horses. Once an operation has committed to racing at a given track, a director of racing must then make sure the bigger clients are satisfied with other diverse items such as barn amenities and on-site dormitory accommodations for stable workers. But a typical midlevel track like Suffolk Downs can count on only a handful of large-scale racing stables of forty or more Thoroughbreds to fill its races, so Morrissey must come to terms with hundreds of smaller local outfits, one-horse stables, mom-and-pop Thoroughbred hobbyists, and a litany of assorted fringe players who will supply the horses he needs for his program to grind onward over the course of a season.

Top-quality races with full fields of horses in them are the overall goal of a good racing program, but this equilibrium is difficult to attain. To illustrate, on any given day at Suffolk Downs, Morrissey has no problem filling maiden races at the rock-bottom claiming condition or sprints at the "non-winners of a race in six months" level, because his backstretch is populated with an abundance of owners and trainers whose livelihoods depend on slow steeds running often. Yet John's personal policy is not to card these lower-class events as frequently as he could, because even with full fields of twelve each time around, he knows that inferior claiming races aren't as appealing to bettors, and thus cheapen his overall program while reducing the amount of revenue for the track.

Conversely, the racing office will sometimes have trouble filling richer allowance races—there might not be enough fillies on the grounds who fit an esoteric condition that only comes up every three weeks, or everyone will know that a promising colt from a big outfit is pointing for a certain spot, and none of the rival trainers will want to run against him—but Morrissey will reluctantly allow a six-horse race to "go," even though the starting gate is only half full. His logic is that if too many of the better races in the condition book are scrapped, the bigger stables with talented stock will skip town. Even though the no-frills horsemen always protest loudest when a shortfield allowance knocks a full docket of bargain-basement maidens off the overnight, the unspoken reality is that, quite frankly, these folks can complain all they like, because they're so close to the bottom that they're not going anywhere but out of business anyway.

For the better part of a century, tracks have maintained tight control over the quality and quantity of their horse populations by means of stall allocations. In exchange for committing to a season at a given track, managements extend free stabling to owners and trainers, which is no small cost, considering that current stall-rental rates run anywhere from $100 to $800 per month per horse at public facilities. Although a small percentage of upscale outfits on the national level can afford to train at their own private establishments near major racetracks, getting or not getting stall space can make or break any other racing operation. The nation's exclusive venues—Saratoga, Keeneland, Gulfstream Park—allot stalls only to the most competitive racing stables, and generally their barn areas are completely filled for their short, seasonal meets. But at second-tier tracks, the process is a bit more subjective. Almost any outfit can get stabling at the East Boston oval. But keeping that privilege is another story.

Even when the barn area is announced as "at capacity," there always seem to be empty stalls available throughout the backstretch, matched by down-and-out horsemen whose steeds appear and then disappear virtually unnoticed. In the strange, thorny hierarchy of racetrack politics, a fine line exists between being embraced and being evicted by the people who have power over your stabling: Comments critical of the track or its purse program, failure to enter horses when strongly "recommended" to do so by a racing official, or just rubbing someone in management the wrong way are all perfectly valid reasons for the stall superintendent to come around your shed row one morning to tell you that the director of racing has decided to cut your stabling allotment in half, or wants to move you to a less desirable backstretch location, or worse, that you're out on the street for "not supporting the program."

Attempting to fill five weekly cards against the ominous backdrop of a New England winter is perhaps the most unenviable racing job in the country, and John Morrissey must maintain a hard-line stance when it comes to dealing with a captive cast of participants who race at the mercy of Mother Nature. A blunt perfectionist who can come across as intimidating to people unprepared for his no-nonsense nature, John at times might be guilty of micromanagement but could never be accused of not trying his best to churn out good racing under adverse conditions. Every year the exodus of horses from New England grows—owners and trainers who would rather race in Florida for the winter; smaller outfits that would rather disband because they're no longer turning a profit—and the recent realization that Catalano and Gill will be ripping five dozen horses out of the Boston rotation is hardly welcome news to a man in Morrissey's position. If an average race day at Suffolk Downs features between seventy and ninety entrants, that means nearly a full day's availability of horseflesh will now be running elsewhere.

When the Gill horses were spread among a handful of low-percentage trainers who were essentially puppets for the owner, life was much easier for John Morrissey. Rightly or wrongly, word out of the racing office is that Catalano will have to face the music for aiding and abetting Gill's out-of-town assault. Still viewed as a hothead by some who recall his headstrong, aggressive antics from his younger days, Catalano can expect to be treated as one who has betrayed the system, and at the very least shouldn't anticipate any favors from track management. Unsubstantiated rumors with a vindictive tinge have been percolating on the backstretch about racing officials trying to drive a wedge between Catalano and his remaining New England clients, and how one member of track management with clout on the mid-Atlantic circuit has allegedly attempted to talk Gill into dropping Catalano in exchange for hooking him up with a far more experienced, big-name Maryland trainer. The telltale signs of an old-fashioned racetrack spat are all too evident, but Catalano continues to go about his business, attempting to take the high road by refusing to publicly acknowledge that this Suffolk Downs squeeze is bothersome.

Today Mike is in Maryland saddling Lone Storm—the toothless wonder for whom he has high hopes—to a sixth and last-place finish at Laurel Park. Back in Boston, he has Glockenspiel entered as the 8-to-5 favorite for the Sunday feature, a $13,000 allowance in which the four-year-old towers over a small field of five rivals. But the track surface resembles more of a bog than a racing oval, and despite the shot at an easy purse, Catalano wants to be cautious about the long-term health of a talented horse with a known history of tendon trouble. Glockenspiel is fast but fragile, and Mike wants to take no chances: He tells his Suffolk Downs assistant to call the nagging injury to the attention of the veterinarian who will perform the mandatory pre-race morning checkup, with the request that the animal be allowed to scratch from the race. Such honesty is appreciated by veterinarians, who recognize that sometimes a trainer knows best about beneath-the-surface problems that might otherwise go undetected, and the vet will usually agree to recommend to track officials to have the potentially unsound horse scratched, although the stewards have the final say.

But today—ostensibly because the field for the feature is short to begin with, but in reality, probably because it is Mike Catalano who is involved—there is a problem with this routine formality. By the time the Glockenspiel scratch is requested, track officials protest that they have already allowed Ron Dandy—the leading trainer, known for his willingness to help out the racing office—to scratch C.J. Tejano from the same race for nearly the exact same reason. Scratching a second entrant from the eighth race would mean that the field would be reduced to only four horses, resulting in a loss of revenue for Suffolk Downs because certain bets, such as the trifecta, would not be allowed with so few wagering interests. Despite the pleas from Catalano's assistant that not scratching Glockenspiel could be dangerous to both horse and rider, the stewards refuse to allow him out of the race, insisting that the animal's problematic tendon chance the unsteady footing.

Upon hearing the news via phone in Maryland, the incensed conditioner has three brief emphatic words for his Boston assistant: "Eat the fine."

In other words, Mike Catalano will refuse to remove Glockenspiel from his stall for the race. Instead, he will accept the mandatory fine and hearing before the Suffolk Downs stewards that he knows is now imminent, opting to protect his Thoroughbred rather than risk running—and ruining—the colt over a petty, but growing, grudge match.

My dream is to have enough money so I can retire, not worry and do whatever I want. And then, when I get too old to race—thirty-five or forty—I'll take some business and management courses and go into business. Big business, not any little store, but something big. Maybe the president of my own company. This is just the start of my career. Hopefully I'll be going to New York or California, where the big money is . . . Nobody gives you nothing. You've got to go out and get it.

—HOWARD LANCI, at age twenty,
from a 1979 press profile detailing the young jockey's aspirations
and future plans

I wouldn't wish what I did and experienced on my own worst enemy . . . I'd be up for days at a time. I'd get so paranoid I wouldn't be able to look at a horse, let alone ride one. I'd be scheduled to ride a race, and I'd call the stewards and tell them my car had broke down. They put up with it for awhile. I'm a likable guy, but eventually it caught up with me. I'm not proud of it, but it's part of my life . . . Even though I was a drug addict and a piece of crap in the eyes of a lot of people, I always rode hard. At least I had some standards.

—The same jockey, eighteen years later,
as quoted in a January 18, 1997, *Daily Racing Form* article,
"Lanci Rebounding from Throes of Cocaine"

HOWARD LANCI has been missing in action for the past month. But no one in the jockeys' room seems to have really noticed, because unexplained absences are nothing unusual for the clown prince of New England racing. Throughout a checkered quarter-century career that began when he quit high school in ninth grade, Lanci has been known to be absent from his home state of Massachusetts for months or even years at a time—raising hell at the county fairs; scrambling for mounts in Atlantic City or West Virginia; off on a binge; getting ruled off here and kicked out of there; hustling morning gallops on the mid-Atlantic circuit; and as likely to be dutifully attending Narcotics Anonymous meetings as spiraling out of control on yet another legendary coke bender. Streetwise and cagey, Lanci always finds his way back to Boston—often bruised, usually battered, but never beaten. He simply shows up unannounced and shuffles around the locker room in his familiar frayed bathrobe, acting as if he's never been away, toting nothing more than his weathered riding tack, a handful of racing whips, and an off-color joke or a ribald story straight from the trenches of low-level racing.

When Lanci first burst upon the Suffolk Downs scene, he was supposed to be something special. He grew up in the middle-class suburbs south of Boston in the early 1970s and appears to have fit the bill of class clown right from the outset. In sixth grade, he had a crush on a classmate and followed her home from school. The girl lived on a horse farm, and to gain her favor, young Howard volunteered to help with stable chores. The next thing he knew, he was shoveling horseshit in exchange for being allowed to ride the animals, and eventually he figured out he was more in love with the horses than the girl. In an era where many suburban New England dads got up before dawn to drive their adolescent sons to hockey practice, fifteen-year-old Howie talked his father into toting him back and forth through pre-dawn traffic to Suffolk Downs so he could muck stalls, walk hots, chop ice from frozen water buckets, and eventually, gallop racehorses.

When high school began to interfere with his racetrack education, Lanci decided to drop out. His father—a pool-room operator turned home-improvement contractor who was forever telling people his "heart is at the track"—not only gave his blessing, but arranged for Howard to gain valuable experience in Oklahoma by breaking yearling Thoroughbreds that are just learning to be saddled. At seventeen, when his son returned to Boston to ride his first race at Suffolk Downs, Mr. Lanci hosted a party in the clubhouse. The next day, when Howard hit the winner's circle for the very first time aboard a $20.40 long shot named Bucky Plum, his old man cried.

After one more winter on the farm in Oklahoma (at the time, apprentice jockeys were required to be under contract to a specific trainer, and Howard's boss thought the kid needed further schooling), Lanci hit the road. In 1977, he tried Penn National and Thistledown while still riding greenly. But by 1978, he took leading rookie rider honors at Keystone in Philadelphia. The following year, he edged into second in that track's overall standings, then cracked the tough Atlantic City colony as the meet's fourth-leading jockey. By 1980, Howard was twenty years old, a high school dropout pocketing $2,000 a week in winnings. He was everybody's friend, could really handle a horse, and was riding high.

"Then," Howard recalls, spreading his hands as if to indicate a toppled house of cards, "I came back home to New England. And got into *all* kinds of trouble."

After his apprenticeship expired, partying took precedence over race-riding. For pleasure at first, but later out of sheer necessity, Lanci dove nose-first into cocaine, unaware he was beginning a courtship that would last a lifetime. Blow became Howard's best friend and constant companion, because in addition to providing a powerful high, the drug is favored by jockeys for its role as an infallible appetite suppressant. His still-growing body was filling out, and after four years in the saddle Howie was no longer the 104-pound wisp of a rookie he was the first time around Suffolk Downs. After all, he reasoned, if he couldn't make the weight, he couldn't ride.

But the diet-by-narcotics regimen was destined not to work for long. Up all night, Lanci began to miss morning workout assignments, which led to missed mounts in the afternoons when trainers became annoyed with his unreliability. His wins became fewer and farther between, and weeklong suspensions for routine riding infractions were little more than an excuse to stay home and do even more drugs. Soon the benders spiraled to the point where Lanci stopped coming around the track in the afternoons as well, and the backstretch was rife with rumor, a whirlwind of wild talk involving booze, girls, guns, and drugs.

According to the Association of Racing Commissioners

International, the ruling body that compiles licensing statistics for the Thoroughbred industry, Howard Lanci has been cited for a litany of racetrack offenses in five states since 1976, ranging from careless riding (twenty-one times); repeated failure to honor riding engagements (nineteen); interference to another horse (fourteen); assorted violations regarding disrespectful, vulgar, obscene, or threatening language toward a racing official (six); various counts of causing an altercation, striking another jockey, or "riding to retaliate" (six); and a handful of misuse-of-whip infractions (five). Lanci's rap sheet further notes he courted trouble by being arrested in Massachusetts for possession of a controlled substance in March 1981, possessing marijuana in the Suffolk Downs jockeys' room nine months later, and being arrested again in 1984 for Class B and D narcotics while also carrying an unlawful firearm. In 1991, Lanci failed an agreed-upon test for cocaine that was a condition for retaining his riding license, and two years after that he violated a similar agreement by refusing to submit to another mandatory narcotics screening. In 1985, 1989, and half of 1991, Howard's conduct was judged to be so egregious that he was barred from licensure altogether, and since all North American racing jurisdictions abide by reciprocity rules, he couldn't set foot on a Thoroughbred backstretch anywhere on the continent for nearly three full seasons.

Yet at the same time Lanci was systematically dismantling his life through the 1980s, some sort of charmed aura always seemed to accompany him in that he could never kill off his career—or himself—completely. Raised to be courteous, tell the truth, and accept responsibility for his actions, Howie usually did just that when faced with a disciplinary hearing, so it was difficult for the sport's administrators to rule him off entirely when Howard appeared genuinely eager to reverse his wrongs. And Lanci's numerous second chances were by no means limited to the regulatory system. His press box file of clips culled from yellowed snippets of newspaper reveal him to be an alley cat who's been allowed way more than his allotment of nine lives: There's a 1981 photo of Howie falling off a horse right at the Suffolk Downs finish wire, miraculously suspended in midair with only his left arm wrapped around the animal's neck. A separate clip carries the headline "Lucky to Be Alive" and tells of a filly who died of an apparent heart attack on the far turn, collapsed to the ground, then rolled right over Lanci, who walked away unhurt. Another tells about a newly installed flexible racetrack safety rail, designed to cushion the blow of any jockey unlucky enough to fall on top of it; Howard, of course, ended up being the first to try it out. Best of all is Lanci's very first *Daily Racing Form* interview. He was an apprentice in Pennsylvania and had just left the track after morning training when the Keystone beat writer stopped by the backstretch looking for him. Sensing an opportunity for good publicity, his agent called the young rider at home and told him to rush right back. An exuberant Howard obliged, but in his zeal to be interviewed, he totaled his car pulling out of his apartment complex. The veteran reporter appeared more stunned than the rookie jockey when he wrote, "Undaunted and uninjured, Lanci climbed from his wrecked car, walked to the nearest pay phone, called the track and was interviewed as if nothing had happened."

Half a lifetime later, Lanci had worn out his welcome in New England. By age thirty-four, the western Massachusetts county fairs were the only tracks where he could land live mounts, and the remaining eleven months of the year were basically maintenance so he could thrive on the half-mile bullrings of the leaky-roof circuit. In 1993, he never made it that far into the season. In late July, Lanci got into a beef with the Rockingham clerk of scales. Unaware that the official had picked up the in-house phone to alert the stewards that their favorite habitual offender was once again out of control, Howard threatened bodily harm to the clerk, and his profane utterances were broadcast via speakerphone directly to the judges. He was lucky to get off with only a $250 fine. But one week later, Lanci again flew into a rage at the Rock, directing his anger toward the part-time laborer who washes and sets out the jockeys' silks. This time, the stewards ordered Lanci to submit to an immediate narcotics screening. Instead of taking the test, The Howitzer took off.

Sitting out yet another long suspension, Howard didn't resurface on a regular basis until mid-1995 at Charles Town, a track that at that time was considered one of the cheapest on the eastern seaboard, a dumping ground for talentless Thoroughbreds. At six furlongs in circumference, its narrow oval is a quarter mile longer than a county-fair bullring, and the West Virginia track ran under the lights and trotted out the same tired horses every single week of the year. The riders and backstretch lifers were largely an insulated colony of good ol' boys scraping along as best they could, and newcomers looking to horn in on the small stream of revenue were hardly welcomed with open arms. If such a newcomer also happened to be an abrasively vocal Yank with a rough riding style, forget it.

Lanci won few friends in the Charles Town jockeys' room while managing four suspensions in his first four weeks. Off and on, Howard persevered for a season or two, and the unofficial word that filtered back to New England was that the West Virginia jockeys were trying to band together to refuse to ride against Lanci because of his reckless on-track antics. But the story behind the story was that his peers couldn't stand Howard because he wouldn't conspire with them to tie up races.

Such integrity just might be the hidden link in the Howard Lanci story, the one overriding reason that the racing gods have allowed him to survive for so long in a sport that is ruthlessly efficient at culling and casting off the weak, the sick, and the greedy. You can flip through all 100 rulings in Lanci's ARCI infraction file and not unearth one penalty that pertains to race fixing or cheating. And Howard knows it, too. In spite of his many other flaws, Lanci wears his honesty like a badge, a piece of equipment as essential to his vocation as a saddle, whip, or riding boots.

"That's the only thing that kept me from getting blackballed," Lanci admitted in a 1997 *Racing Form* interview that comes across as both candid and practical, considering his widespread reputation as a narcotics abuser. "There's jockeys out there who can't buy a mount because they did drugs and held horses back, and the trainers know it. But even if I took the money—and $500 is a lot of money to a drug addict—I wouldn't have held a horse back. And what would've happened then? That's all I needed was to go to the track and have nine guys want to break my legs."

This morning, Howard Lanci waltzes into the Suffolk Downs locker room after his latest unexpected absence like he hasn't been away at all. Claiming sobriety for nearly seven years now, The Howitzer's infamous rants have mellowed with age, even taking on a self-mocking tilt at times. But his slapstick antics still convey something true, a surreal subtext of deckful-of-jokers racetrack wisdom. In short, people tend to like Howard not because he's unafraid to jeer at the emperor for wearing no clothes, but because he'll think nothing of stripping down to nakedness himself so the poor guy won't have to be laughed at all alone.

Howard grins when I stop to say hello to him. With a wild shock of sleep-matted hair, a mouth that has kissed the racetrack at thirty-five mph more times than the journeyman jock can or wants to recall, and wide, darting eyes magnified by a powerful pair of prescription glasses, Lanci sits in the jockeys' room beneath a black-velvet painting of a group of dogs playing poker, and he is literally hungry to ride. I ask where he's been and what he's been up to, and The Howitzer tells me that instead of being involved with "big business" or "big money" like he long ago predicted he'd be doing, he's been spending time in the "big house." After his twenty-fourth arrest or criminal citation—his ninth for driving with a suspended or revoked license—Lanci has returned to work to hustle mounts.

On this particular Wednesday, Lanci has been named to ride only one horse, Standard Raise, a steed known to be habitually lame who was ordered scratched by the stewards on the advice of the track veterinarian two weeks ago. But lady luck smiles on Lanci, as she often seems to do: Fellow jockey Tammi Piermarini is out sick with the flu, and the three mounts she has vacated are eagerly snatched up by Howard. Win, lose, or draw, each ride is worth $35 just for stepping out onto the racetrack, plus a piece of the purse if any of the runners manage fifth or better. But—as also always seems to be the case with The Howitzer—there is one minor problem.

Lanci appears overweight by at least seven, maybe eight, pounds.

He is called to report to an assistant clerk of scales, and the two commiserate in guarded voices. Lanci and the assistant know each other well from their years together on the county-fairs circuit, and today the fill-in official happens to be in charge of the weighing in and out of riders in the absence of the head clerk. Although not privy to their discussion, from afar I can see Howard nodding his head in grave fashion. After this brief exchange, Lanci scurries off to his corner of the locker room, where he readies for the first race. Suddenly subdued, he tries to remain inconspicuous and waits until the final possible moment to check in for the official weigh-out. He steps on and off the scale quickly, before the digital numbers have a chance to truly register, and it is further in his favor that the state police trooper assigned to monitor the jockeys is either indifferent or unaware about this process. The Howitzer hustles out to the paddock, perhaps or perhaps not tipping the scale at the required 122 pounds assigned to his 0-for-11 maiden mount in the opener.

If the assistant clerk is indeed going to cut Lanci a break in this fashion, he is hardly going to let Howie get away with blatantly jeopardizing either of their positions. The substitute official is overheard telling Lanci not to eat anything the entire day, fearing that his weight will balloon yet another pound or two during the course of the afternoon. Once Lanci checks out for the first race, the assistant clerk gives orders to the locker-room snack bar manager not to let Howard start a meals tab. With forty confined athletes all watching their weight, the lunch fare in the Suffolk Downs jockeys' room is astonishingly replete with poor nutritional choices: While many jockeys manage to quell hunger by chewing ice cubes or chugging Gatorade all afternoon, it must be tempting to see rows of snack cakes, pastry, muffins, dessert specials, ice cream treats, and racks of potato chips surrounding a french-fry cooker and sandwich grill. There is no yogurt on the menu, and fresh fruit is only occasionally available. With ventilation not at its best in this basement eatery, the aroma of deep-fried onion rings and sizzling bacon permeates the premises, hardly the ideal fragrance if you're forcing yourself not to consume calories while waiting all afternoon to ride some hapless long shot. It's probably even tougher if, like

Howard Lanci, you've just gotten out of jail and have only $3 in your pocket.

Decades ago, when he was a rookie, the fledgling rider acquired the rhyming nickname "Fancy" Howard Lanci. But one look at the journeyman's anxious, animated horsebacking style is all you need to see to believe that his other moniker—The Howitzer—is far more appropriate. Although Howard lands few live mounts, he makes the best of whatever he's offered, and if nothing else, he's known for getting even the most sluggish of Thoroughbreds out of the starting stalls with alacrity. Howie's aggressive, hell-bent, gate-busting technique has made him a blue-collar fan favorite, and his perilous feet-on-the-dashboard riding style makes him easily recognizable from half a mile away. Like wildly flapping flags that trail his every movement, Lanci's silks almost always come untucked from his riding breeches, and when he pulls a horse up while galloping out after a race, he leans far back in his stirrups, like a schoolboy scolded too many times not to tip backward in his chair.

In the opener, the horse he picks up from Piermarini is a 21-to-1 maiden invader from Charles Town. Howard guns Painted Colors to an impossible lead, threatening to upset the field at a breakneck pace. Turning for home, he maintains a two-length advantage while caught five wide, but the weary front-runner has nothing left for the straightaway and is passed by four horses in the stretch. Still, Lanci rides his mount hard to the wire and is beaten only a quarter-length for third by a 99-to-1 shot. Painted Colors manages to finish ahead of four other runners—three of them are either pulled up or eased before the finish—earning The Howitzer $48 (his percentage of the fifth-place purse plus the mandatory $35 mount fee) for his effort.

In the second race, Lanci again outbreaks the entire eleven-horse field aboard Standard Raise, but the sore old gelding stops to a walk and fails to beat a single horse, while Richard Johnson—the young apprentice who failed to win aboard sure-thing Huckster's Girl nine days ago—finally obtains his long-awaited first career victory. The twenty-one-year-old goes wire to wire atop Hoop Coyote Hoop, who, despite being winless in four years and being ridden by a jockey who had never won himself, goes off at even money in a talentless $4,000 bottom-level claiming contest. After the race, Johnson gets a congratulatory announcement over the public address system, and a small group of fans ring the winner's circle to applaud the rookie rider. On the rite-of-passage walk back through the paddock to the locker room after his first lifetime win, Johnson is greeted by his fellow riders with the traditional racetrack dousing of water, eggs, shaving cream, boot polish, snow, mud, and whatever else the jockeys have handy to pelt him with in a long-standing ritual of congratulation.

Howard Lanci takes advantage of the celebratory tumult by sneaking back into the locker room ahead of everyone else, evading the preoccupied eye of the assistant scales clerk. He furtively bribes the fry cook into handing over a couple of candy bars, then scurries off in the direction of the unoccupied sauna. Never one to let opportunity slide by, The Howitzer is back on track at Suffolk Downs and finally able to enjoy a meal in peace.

VETERAN HORSES are in the spotlight on the final Saturday of February, and the feature is a good one. A field of six faces the starter for the Waquoit Stakes, a $25,000 event named in honor of the 1987 MassCap upsetter. The three heavy hitters in the 1-1/16 mile race are King Roller, a fast sprinter with three wins and four seconds from his last seven starts; Galloping Gael, the Mike Catalano trainee who ran in last year's MassCap; and old warhorse Prolanzier, who seeks lifetime win number twenty-nine.

The affair is a tactical chess match right from the start. The jockeys know that if reputable sprinter King Roller gets the lead by himself, he's as good as gone. They also know that if Prolanzier and King Roller slug it out in a speed duel for the first six furlongs, the race plays right into the hands of Galloping Gael, the big closer. Winston Thompson elects to send the 2-to-1 Prolanzier for the lead as soon as the gates open, but not at a fast clip, putting to the test the old racetrack adage that pace—or lack of it—makes the race.

Thompson milks the early action into the first turn and deftly guides

Prolanzier to the rail ahead of even-money favorite Galloping Gael and 31-to-1 fence-sitter Lion Prince. King Roller, at 5 to 2, is forced to chase the leader while losing ground on the outside. Bending into the backstretch, Thompson still has Prolanzier under confident restraint, practically standing up in the irons to throttle back the speed of his steed. The first fraction is :25-4/5, a ridiculously slow opening quarter mile for any caliber of horse at Suffolk Downs, let alone the circuit's top Thoroughbreds. Whenever Jose Delgado edges King Roller closer, Thompson lets out another notch on Prolanzier, but only as much as he has to in order to maintain the lead.

The pace is still a dawdling :50-3/5 for the half mile, with Galloping Gael trapped behind 14-to-1 Personal Moon and eager to run. But Harry Vega is cautious about gunning too soon with his one-run horse. Prolanzier's lead is still a measured half-length on the far turn, yet no one has made a serious move. The entire field is grouped under collective restraint as in a long-distance European race, where the horses merely canter for miles before launching into an all-out frenzy nearing the finish.

And that's just how the race unfolds at the top of the stretch: Prolanzier kicks on for home after a six-furlong fraction of 1:15, which plays distinctly to his advantage. He didn't have to run hard to make the lead and keep it, and now the only question is whether he will have enough gas left in the tank to finish. A furlong from the wire, Galloping Gael is set down into an all-out drive but appears to have too much ground to make up and not enough time to do it. Vega tries to muscle him forward, but bumps with Personal Moon in deep stretch. When challenged, Prolanzier kicks in again, opening up by three-quarters of a length. Thompson pumps his fist like he has just won the Kentucky Derby, stopping the timer in an excruciatingly slow 1:47-2/5. But when the track cuts Prolanzier's winning purse check or engraves the official stakes trophy, the final time won't matter one bit.

The winner's circle ceremony is a jubilant affair, and a small crowd gathers on the grandstand apron, with even the most wizened diehards coming out of the woodwork to pay respect to a resilient racehorse. Jockey Thompson hugs Prolanzier, and in turn, assistant trainer John Assimakopoulous hugs Thompson. In the press box, several degenerates will use the word "masterful" to describe Winston's winning ride, and even the Equibase statistician, a veteran notoriously stingy with praise, will insert a *clever rating* comment in the official past performance chart of the race.

In the jocks' room before the nightcap, I follow the noise and find Thompson in front of his locker, receiving congratulations from fellow riders. The Suffolk Downs jockey colony is competitive but close-knit, and when one of their own accomplishes a feat worth accolades, praise flows.

"He's never gone 1:15 in his life," an exuberant Thompson is saying about the lethargic pace he was surprisingly allowed to set. "I knew there was no speed in the race and I knew they wouldn't catch me with an easy lead. You don't give a horse—especially Prolanzier—that kind of pace and expect to beat him."

Jose Caraballo offers a more humorous explanation of Thompson's winning tactics. "You should have heard him out there. It was like he was singing a lullaby. He had all the other riders hypnotized. We just went to sleep." Caraballo elaborates, crouching into a riding position and singing off-key, mimicking Thompson: "Rock-a-bye baby, on the treetop; when I turn this motherfucker loose, he ain't never gonna stop . . . "

SARATOGA RIDGE, the venerable roan recently claimed by Mike Catalano, is taking a step up in class to the $12,500 claiming level for his new connections. The gelding who loves to finish second is installed as the 5-to-2 second choice in the betting.

Chasing the leader, the Ridge stalks in second for a half mile of the six-furlong race. But the eleven-year-old appears to be toying with pacemaker Outen Delight as the two splash down the backstretch and through the far turn.

Inside the final furlong, Saratoga Ridge looms boldly to get on even terms with his front-running rival, then hesitates ever so slightly. Just as it looks as if the old warrior will play the runner-up role to perfection for the thirty-fifth time in his career, the game claimer decides he wants to dive for the lead inside the sixteenth pole. His see-sawing gray head makes the top, hangs back yet again to wait for someone to catch up, then when the speedster packs it in and the onrushing closer comes too late, the Ridge ends up nodding home on top in a dicey three-way photo.

In the winner's circle, the victorious gray exudes a confident air of indifference, casting a cagey eye in the direction of his competitors, who trudge back slathered with the slick sheen of brown spray he has kicked back into their faces. Barely winded, Saratoga Ridge looks as if he could go around the track again with nary a change to the outcome of the race.

THIS AFTERNOON marks the second attempt at a first career start for Ypres, the high-strung maiden from the stable of Dr. Patty Meadow who flipped out in the paddock two weeks ago.

This time the wild-eyed Ypres doesn't even make it anywhere close to the saddling area, which is bad for the horse but probably a benefit to the general safety of everyone in the paddock. On the walk up the homestretch from the stables, the three-year-old fights free from his owner/breeder/trainer and bolts back to the barn, careening through the maze of shed rows at full throttle with a leather shank dangling dangerously between his spinning front legs.

At least it looks as if the gelding knows how to run. Now all he has to do is make it to the starting gate.

CHAPTER FOUR

MUD SEASON

*Politics isn't imposed upon racing from time to time; it's in the
weave. It's in the statutory straightjacket; it's in the geogra-
phy, history, and calendar of New England racing.*
—BILL VEECK, *Thirty Tons a Day*

THE SUFFOLK DOWNS admissions director is having difficulty
with his front-gate clerks. He has to constantly hound them to stay
at their positions manning the main entrance, but once the boss walks
away, the employees wander off for a cup of coffee, a cigarette, or a
chat with their co-workers, leaving the turnstiles wide open for fans to
stroll in as they please without paying. Because the Suffolk Downs
staffers are union workers, all the director can really do is write them
up, transfer them to a less desirable location, and hope that they either
quit or learn their lesson. Neither usually happens.

"You move a guy to a different spot," he laments at the staff meeting that kicks off the month of March, "and every politician in Revere
and East Boston starts calling Mr. O'Malley to complain that Suffolk
Downs is picking on their people. You can't win."

Political patronage is big business at Suffolk Downs, although the
track is hardly the unloading zone for the well connected that it used
to be in its glory days. Elected officials never seem to have a shortage
of people they need to reward for contributing to campaigns, and for
decades, ever since the state's four pari-mutuel facilities began offering
the only legal gambling in Massachusetts, all a politician had to do was
pick up the phone and "suggest" that a friend or relative be "taken

care of," and a track official would willingly oblige. If no such cozy place on the payroll existed, one would be created on the spot, lest the racetrack risk offending the same public servant whose payback on pari-mutuel matters might someday—and in Massachusetts, there always *will* be a someday—end up detrimental to the well-being of the establishment's betting business.

Innovative baseball executive Bill Veeck briefly ran Suffolk Downs thirty years ago, and when the smoke settled after his tumultuous two-year trial by fire, the patriarch of sports promotion minced few words in his memoir when chronicling his distaste for the Commonwealth's exasperating practice of ironclad cronyism. Although Veeck refused to play by the insiders' rules, at least he had a clear understanding of the way the process was supposed to work, as explained in his memoir, *Thirty Tons a Day:*

> The pols believe that horse racing was created by a bountiful heaven as their own private grazing grounds. And not without reason. The control of racing is in the hands of the state legislature. Your license to operate comes from the Racing Commission, which is the creature of the legislature. Your racing dates, which are what you live by, also come from the Racing Commission. The commissioners are appointed by the Governor. Their legal adviser, whenever a problem arises, is the Attorney General. (pp. 78–79)

Veeck escaped town (or was run out of it, depending on whom you believe) in 1971. Later that year, the Bay State inaugurated a 50-cent weekly sweepstakes. In the twenty-nine years since, state-run gambling has swollen to a $4-billion sacred cow that directly employs 400 workers. With combined revenue at Suffolk Downs, the greyhound tracks at Wonderland and Raynham-Taunton, and the harness track in Plainridge now accounting for a mere 15 percent of what the Commonwealth rakes in with scratch tickets, daily numbers games, weekly mega-prize pools and every-five-minutes Keno drawings, it is no surprise that top insider jobs now cluster in the Massachusetts State

Lottery. Presumably, just like when the racetracks were in their heyday, many staffers land there simply because they know somebody capable of pulling the right strings to clear the way for a cushy career change.

At today's staff meeting, the longtime program sales manager chimes in with firsthand knowledge about the legendary clout of ground-level Suffolk Downs employees and the drastic measures they'll take to protect their jobs.

"Twenty-seven years ago I started working here when I got out of the service," the Eastie native recalls, grinning at the memory. "The very first week, we go on strike. I'm new. I like my job. And I don't have anything against the track. But the guy who got me the job says to get my ass out there on the picket line with everybody else. So of course, out I go."

"We're picketing out on the street, over by Beachmont, when a truck pulls up and about eight guys get out. I'm told they're our guys. But they don't work with us. I've never seen 'em. They've been sent to strike with us, to support us. And as they're getting out of the truck, two guns fall to the ground."

"'Jeez,' I said. 'This is gonna be a fun job.'"

"'You got that right, kid,' an old-timer says, calmly pointing to the loaded weapons as if the guns were ordinary workplace tools. 'Around the racetrack, whenever the unions are concerned, you can bet it'll be a bang.'"

THERE WAS a fistfight on the backstretch this morning. A horse trainer with a grudge allegedly assaulted a newspaper reporter, right by the rail at the top of the homestretch. I must be careful to refer to the attack as "alleged," because, despite the presence of scores of Suffolk Downs onlookers watching hundreds of Thoroughbreds being jock-eyed around the track during training gallops, not a single witness could or would step forward to detail what they saw to security officials.

In fact, the only person not afflicted by a sudden onset of amnesia is Steve Myrick, the writer who says he was blindsided by Bobby

Raymond, the racehorse conditioner with a checkered past. In addition to being amnesia-free, it seems that Myrick is also immune to that pervasive and long-standing racetrack malady known as the backstretch code of silence, which, without a doubt, directly contributed to today's confrontation.

"I was standing at the gap watching workouts, and all of a sudden I saw Bobby standing next to me," Myrick explains to me in the press box, fully aware that a *Lawrence Eagle-Tribune* piece he recently wrote about Raymond had made the trainer—the same gentleman whose hermaphrodite horse was the talk of the backstretch several months ago—livid with anger.

"I nodded hello even though I know I'm not his favorite person. He kind of did a double take, started in on me verbally once he recognized me, then came after me. We danced around a bit, then Mario [DeStefano, the president of the local horsemen's union] came out of nowhere and stepped between us. It was over really before it even started."

Raymond and Myrick are both big, husky guys, and neither Raymond's hostile behavior nor Myrick's unruffled "I kind of expected this" attitude surprise me. Although Steve is not a turf writer who is at the track every day (his full-time job is in news production for a Boston TV station), the observant and even-keeled freelancer is in many ways the best informed and most journalistically balanced racing reporter in New England.

The dispute stems from a feature-length story Myrick wrote in December about the demise of OK By Me, a once-fast horse whose career plummeted from top-notch graded stakes to bottom $4,000 claiming competition before suffering a fatal injury shortly after coming under Raymond's care. The circumstances of the incident were both grotesque and highly visible: The horse was euthanized after rupturing a tendon directly in front of the Suffolk Downs grandstand on a packed Saturday afternoon, and customers complained to the media relations office for weeks afterward about Raymond spewing profanity at fans who booed him for risking a once-valuable steed in a lowly claiming race. Yet while no other writer on the Boston racing beat even mentioned a word of this controversy in print, Myrick had the courage to seek out answers to tough questions about the life and death of a prominent Thoroughbred and a trainer who has had more than a few scrapes with the law.

In a well-researched investigative piece, Myrick detailed Raymond's litany of racetrack-related suspensions, which range from a 1981 felony guilty plea in connection with an armed tractor-trailer hijacking to a seventeen-month drug suspension by the Massachusetts State Racing Commission in 1994 after a cache of injectable equine medications, syringes, and needles was found in his barn. Despite being stonewalled by the Suffolk Downs stewards and having the trainer himself point-blank refuse two offers to explain his side of the story, Myrick penned a thorough piece that questioned whether someone with a felonious past should be allowed to hold a license in an industry whose business model depends on integrity. The article was fair in its summation that even though ethics and common sense might have dictated otherwise, no actual rules or laws had been broken by allowing a once-proud horse to sink to such a sad level. With an objective eye and a balanced tone, Myrick's investigation managed to tactfully raise awareness about criminal behavior and animal welfare, two uncomfortable subjects that few in the game are willing to admit is of concern, let alone write about in detail.

As expected, the story struck a raw nerve with many in the back-stretch community simply because it violated the cardinal racetrack rule of keeping the truth out of the public spotlight "for the good of the game." In short, the collective mindset around Suffolk Downs— both on the backside and in the front offices—is that the sport should cover up controversy and protect insiders at all costs, based on the strangely insular logic that outsiders can never truly understand what really goes on behind the scenes in day-to-day backstretch life. Yet the reverse argument can easily be made that insiders *themselves* are the ones who have a skewed viewpoint of racetrack reality: Like a blink-ered racehorse, they are too embedded in their own world to glimpse it clearly, and it is in this vein that racing has always preferred to stomp the messenger rather than expose and eradicate the root causes of its problems.

For years, the racetrack mantra has been to keep horse racing's secrets within the "family" and to not air any dirty laundry where outsiders can see and smell it. Instead of adopting a proactive stance—making an explicit example of how the game will not tolerate violators; pointing out how a system of checks and balances ensures that lawbreakers are punished—administrators instead revert to the ostrich mentality whenever trouble arises, thereby becoming implicit partners with the very same problems that harm the industry. And in the process of opting for loyalty over truth, they sell themselves, their customers, and the game short.

The reasons that this outdated mentality persists are as varied and fragmented as the industry itself. First, understand that Thoroughbred racing remains largely rooted in the past. Tradition is a definite part of the allure and enjoyment of the sport, but in terms of day-to-day attitude, many tracks still put forth a public facade that seems better suited to the halcyon days of the game when everyone was fat and happy. For decades, Thoroughbred racing operated in a PR vacuum where there was little criticism or objective comment on the part of the press. The industry bible, *Daily Racing Form*, refused to print critical commentary until the 1990s, and old-school newspapermen were simply paid off to write rosy features about how great everything was. For certain, these practices existed in other sports—Major League Baseball teams kept writers on the payroll well into the 1960s—but in racing, the custom continued for years thereafter. As a result, the industry evolved into a thin-skinned beast unaccustomed to the discomfort of probing questions.

Upon being promoted to media relations director, I was reminded by longtime Suffolk Downs boss Bob O'Malley that the job used to consist of little more than ghostwriting columns for lazy reporters in the mornings and "making sure there was enough ice and tonic for the gin" to keep media members pleasantly buzzed throughout the afternoons. Now, the vocation of racetrack media relations work has shifted from being a publicist to being more of an apologist for the sport, and over the past several years I have harbored a quiet discomfort with that notion. I keep waiting for the industry to step up and share some of this uneasiness, but that's a long-shot proposition in a game where old habits die hard and change is glacially slow.

"I get the feeling Bobby could have broken free and gotten to me if he had really wanted to," Myrick admits with a shrug, chuckling at the memory of his adversary holding himself back while not really being restrained by the union president who stepped between them. "But I know that's the way he operates. Basically, he's a bully."

BACK IN TAMPA, Blackwater, the sprinter with the jackhammer head and mean-spirited temperament, is entered at the $5,000 claiming level in a restricted race for horses who have not won three races in half a year. The drop in class is sizable, about half his usual claiming price. Mulling his options, my old man figures the horse has been a bit ouchy in recent training and hasn't produced a winning paycheck all meet. The gelding hasn't earned his oats, and every day that the excitable and aggressive animal lives under the Thornton Racing Stable shed row, the odds tilt in favor of equine mayhem.

The class-plunging Blackwater is pegged to 19-to-10 odds by the Tampa bettors, bearing the burden of favoritism squarely on his broad, dark bay shoulders. He lays second and tracks the pace intently for a half mile, launches a bold bid on the turn, engages the leader at the top of the lane, and wins under a confident drive by an open four lengths.

Not surprisingly, the gelding is claimed by a new outfit, and after cooling out and providing the mandatory post-race urine sample at the backstretch test barn, Blackwater is handed over to the groom representing his new trainer. The partnership that owned Blackwater for four months will just about break even on its initial $16,000 investment, considering training costs, vet bills, and a smattering of purse money the gelding earned from four races.

The loss of stock is not professionally a problem for my father, and one would think that he and Joyce would even be somewhat relieved to have the most disorderly and dangerous horse removed from the shed row. But every time he loses a horse, whether the animal is a winner or a plodder, my dad seems sad to see an animal go. Like good coaches in other sports, effective racehorse trainers condition themselves not to become emotionally attached to the equine athletes they train. Still, it can be difficult to care for an animal every single day, for months or even years at a time, without feeling some small bit of personal sentiment when faced with a suddenly empty stall.

And in the case of the explosively ornery Blackwater, Paul Thornton also has legitimate concerns that this volatile Thoroughbred will accidentally—or intentionally—hurt a new handler unfamiliar with the animal's ferocious personality.

THE ENIGMATIC MAIDEN Ypres is in the first race on the first Monday in March, and the gelding manages to arrive in the paddock with relatively little disruption, just some minor bucking and kicking when he makes his way in front of the imposing concrete-and-steel grandstand. Well proportioned but rough around the edges, the three-year-old sports a distinctive white blotch of hair on his bay forehead and an unruly black mane that cannot be tamed. His eyes are wild and ears active as he is being saddled by breeder/owner/trainer/groom (and doctor) Patty Meadow, almost as if he is planning another escape from the confines of the walking ring.

For safety reasons, everyone in the paddock is acutely aware of the horse's presence. But young Dyn Panell mounts without incident and leads the field onto the track as the prerecorded bugle blares the field to post.

As soon as Ypres hits the dirt surface of the main track, he locks his knees and freezes in place, refusing to move. Then he props backward on his hind legs in a spooked attempt to dislodge his rider. Meadow, who has accompanied the gelding all the way from the quarter-mile walk from the stable area to the paddock and has led him onto the track, feels that the whip that the jockey is holding is somehow upsetting the skittish animal, even though Ypres can't see it. So Panell is instructed to drop his stick, which is then retrieved and handed to one of the out-riders (officials on horseback who escort the horses and keep order in the post parade), who will return it to the jockey once the field nears the starting gate. Surprisingly, this tactic does manage to soothe Ypres, who immediately breaks off into a gangly trot and heads for the back-stretch.

"He's scared of the whip, that's all," Patty says in a quiet, nervous voice. She paces back and forth in the paddock; wanting to watch, yet not wanting to watch, as her maiden warms up into a light jog.

"Scared of life is more like it," mutters a rival groom in passing.

"I hope those guys working the gate all got their insurance paid up," retorts another.

By random assignment, Ypres has drawn post position number 1. Traditionally, the innermost starting stall is considered a plus, because the paths closest to the rail represent the shortest way around the race-track. But post 1 can be a disadvantage for young horses, especially first-timers unfamiliar with the ritual of the gate. The horse who loads first has to wait for the rest of the field to step into line, and confine-ment inside a stall can be claustrophobic. Another drawback to the rail is that Thoroughbreds who hesitate slightly at the break tend to get shuffled to the back of the pack, because those who make it out of the gate alertly are gunning all out to secure a position close to the fence. Generally, these obstacles can be overcome with experience in after-noon races and repetitive schooling during morning training, but even some veteran steeds never get over the phobia of breaking from the inside. Despite being forewarned that the troubled maiden has already had to be scratched twice within the past month, the public supports Ypres to a respectable 13 to 1 in the betting. In the track program, analyst Jim Bishop has bluntly summed up the unlikely colt's chances as such: "His worktab is nothing to get excited about, and it will prove a moral victory if he can just get this one under his belt."

As it turns out, the starting gate does not appear to be the fearsome enemy of Ypres this afternoon. He loads first, with Panell calm aboard his back and an assistant starter right there in the stall with him, petting the gelding the entire time. The outside maidens are the ones who are disruptive, and the field proves to be a chore to load, most notably Gumpas Pond, who escapes from his handlers and jogs around to the front of the starting gate before being restrained and reloaded. It takes just shy of four full minutes—a ridiculously long time for seven horses—to have the first race field properly settled for a start.

To his credit, Ypres is the best behaved of the bunch. But in horse racing, good manners are no replacement for raw speed: When the gate springs open, Ypres staggers out dead last, totally mistiming the start.

Panell doesn't panic, but deftly rushes the gelding close to the early action, seizing an opening at the inside, immediately darting past four horses. Ypres tracks a moderate pace and lays close enough to be third, six lengths off a dueling duo, as the maidens bend from the backstretch straightaway into the far turn. Saving ground on the rail, he lopes into second when Irishing, one of the pacesetters, calls it quits at the top of the stretch, then swerves into the lead when the other one, Pebble Jet, throws in the towel. Gumpas Pond makes a half-hearted effort to get to the new leader inside the final sixteenth of a mile, but Ypres scoots home untouched in a very slow 1:18 for six furlongs, undefeated in his first official start despite requiring three tries to finally make it to the races.

In the winner's circle, Patty Meadow looks more surprised than anyone. The good doctor manages an edgy smile as her pensive eyes quickly scan her winded homebred horse for possible damage.

"Twenty-nine seconds it took them to make it down the homestretch," Bish says in the press box, unimpressed with the lethargic final quarter-mile yet giving credit where it is due. "But he ain't bad looking, you know? If he can ever figure out the game, he looks good."

Larry Collmus comes down from the announcer's stand and offers a similarly complimentary comparison.

"He almost looks like a real horse."

AN ELDERLY WOMAN calls the press box today to ask a myriad of questions pertaining to her upcoming, first-ever visit to a racetrack.

"Is it *nice*?" she wants to know, right off the bat.

That's a tough one to answer. It depends upon your perspective, but I don't tell her that.

Public relations at Suffolk Downs has become a dual paradox over the course of the last several seasons. The logical outward appearance of the task includes efforts to promote the track as a viable and respectable entertainment option, as a safe and historic sporting establishment where you can bring the kids, eat a nice meal, see the pomp and pageantry of Thoroughbred racing, and maybe make a buck or two while doing something different for a casual afternoon. But those external efforts are internally paralleled by an equally intense push to get the word out to Massachusetts politicians that Suffolk Downs is a foundering battleship of a business in dire need of legislative attention, the cornerstone of a $622-million statewide pari-mutuel industry whose dicey existence touches some 6,000 constituents. These two conflicting strategies appear to be at cross-purposes, but the reality is that Suffolk Downs is compelled to present a dual-headed image because its two primary audiences are grounded in opposingly divergent beliefs: Potential customers largely seem to accept that horse racing represents a dying game languishing past its prime, while the political machinery hums along under the smug assurance that state racetracks are fat, money-churning mills of greed always on the hunt for more. Neither assumption is correct, but elements of each argument are distilled together somewhere in the very hazy middle of the overall picture.

Three weeks from today, the much-anticipated "blue-ribbon committee" will hold hearings at the State House, and the thirteen-member panel appointed by the Senate, House, and Governor Paul Cellucci has been assigned the task of gathering input that will purportedly lead to a sweeping overhaul of the Massachusetts racing industry. In preparation, the media relations department at Suffolk Downs has focused on gathering an array of information to support management's main public thrust of preserving jobs and increasing revenue for the Commonwealth by bolstering purses for live racing. Like an onion, one must first peel away a few layers before coming to the crux of the proposal, which is that the mechanism for funding those purses should be increased gambling, either by the legalization of casino-style betting on track property or via new laws permitting off-track, phone, and Internet pari-mutuel wagering.

Politics and Massachusetts racing have always danced a curious, sidestepping tango of reluctant coexistence, and within the puritanical halls of Beacon Hill it is considered a breach of political etiquette to actually come right out and *ask* for liberalized gambling, lest legislators be reminded that betting is a sinful endeavor only tolerated because it provides a sizable chunk of change to the state's coffers. Like the elephant in the living room that party guests politely refuse to acknowledge, wagering can be a dirty word in certain Boston power circles, and my superiors at Suffolk Downs have gone so far as to instruct me to omit the words "gambling" and "betting" from the track's legislative literature, replacing those terms with the slightly more sanitized "gaming" when such a reference is absolutely necessary. So instead of mentioning Thoroughbred racing's principal means of generating revenue, the spotlight will turn to the plight of the people who depend financially upon the sport to earn a living, tangibles that politicians and the press can more easily grasp.

Humanizing the impact of horse racing in Massachusetts goes deeper than accounting for the 400 employees who draw a paycheck directly from Suffolk Downs and the estimated 1,600 horse owners, trainers, jockeys, exercise riders, stable employees, veterinarians, farriers, and vendors who do business on the backstretch. The economic ripple effect of the racing industry also includes neighborhood businesses, restaurants, services, and stores that surround the track, plus the local real estate markets that provide housing. Some sixty Thoroughbred horse farms operate within the Bay State, and in addition to providing jobs, these breeding and boarding operations ensure the existence of open space and environmental greenery that might otherwise be subject to development. Demand for hay and grain is high when racing thrives, creating additional business opportunities for Massachusetts farmers and jobs for the folks who process and deliver those goods. Since reopening in 1992, Suffolk Downs has paid out $89 million in purses to its horsemen, and it is rational to suppose that, in addition to the $13 million that the track has shelled out for capital improvements during the past decade, much of that money gets cycled back into local and state economies. The number most often bandied about when assessing the annual gross domestic impact of Suffolk Downs on the Commonwealth of Massachusetts is $241 million. But when welfare, unemployment benefits, and lost revenues from taxation are factored into the equation assuming closure of the track, that figure rises to $255 million.

In 1989, before then-struggling Suffolk Downs closed, the average daily purse distribution (the cumulative amount the track paid out to horse owners each afternoon) was $40,000. Now in 2000, that figure has more than doubled to $84,000. But such respectable advance pales in comparison to the slot-infused competition at other East Coast tracks: Once-moribund Delaware Park—with 2,000 video slot machines mandated by state law to return 10 percent of net revenues to horse racing—can offer the clout of $250,000 in average daily purses. A decade ago, it used to be that New England horses who had reached the end of the line would be banished to West Virginia, where they would dominate the sorry locals in a downward move akin to falling off the face of the Thoroughbred planet. By the start of the twenty-first century, thanks to similar legislation, both once-dingy Charles Town ($115,000) and rural Mountaineer Park ($125,000) now far outpace the money offered to Boston horsemen. The tide has turned, with steeds who can no longer earn their keep in Appalachia routinely showing up to throttle their equine peers at Suffolk Downs.

But even though purses have improved at tracks with slot machines, few in the racing industry mention how this arrangement sort of resembles a deal with the devil: The old-timey aesthetics are gone from these racetracks-turned-casinos that are now referred to as "racinos," and nearly every one resembles a tacky, Vegas-themed warehouse full of one-armed bandits in which customers are forced to walk through a maze of chirping, clanging slot machines before they can see a living, breathing Thoroughbred outdoors on the racetrack. As obscene amounts of gaming dollars roll in and the horse-racing aspect of the operation continues to be marginalized, the eventual danger is that regulators in gaming-friendly states will begin to start questioning why a slice of the profits is even earmarked to subsidize the antiquated pastime of horses running around in circles. The very gaming mechanism that was enacted to save the sport just might erode it away over the long haul.

Part of the package that will be presented to local legislators includes profiles of owners and trainers who have departed Suffolk Downs to race in other states. The task of compiling the biographies and phoning the horsemen for quotes is at once depressing and enlightening—depressing because the list is so long, enlightening because those interviewed are emphatic about returning to their home state if Massachusetts will just enact laws to aid the industry. Despite New England's relatively high cost of living, its notorious winter weather, and the long-term deterioration of regional racing, home is still home to most folks, and the consensus seems to be that it wouldn't take much to lure Bostonians back to work and live where they grew up and learned the game.

"I sure would like to race at Suffolk Downs again on a regular basis," says Bill Perry, a former four-time leading Suffolk Downs trainer who uprooted his family from Revere in 1995 in search of a more realistic return on his equine investment. Speaking from his Gulfstream Park stable, Perry readily agrees to be quoted on behalf of the legislative effort. "We miss the area. But to give you an example, I claimed a filly in Florida last winter . . . If I sent her to Suffolk, the purse for that allowance race is $12,000. I sent her to the same race in Delaware and the purse was $24,000. Financially, how can I tell the owner I want to race that filly in Boston?"

Joe Vaccaro, a longtime horse owner who relocated his operation to Florida and Delaware in 1994, echoes Perry. "This is forced on us. No one left Suffolk Downs because they didn't want to be here. They left because it was economically impossible to stay. Our position is that we are prepared to come back to Boston once the purse structure is there. If slot machines are what it takes to make this happen, to get the purses competitive enough, we'd be back at Suffolk Downs tomorrow."

Ned Allard, who won three Suffolk Downs training titles before jumping ship in 1992, agrees. "These are New England people who love to see their horses run in New England. What happened at Delaware was amazing. Slots picked it up and put it on the map. Positively, I'd come back."

I am mentally shuffling through these disheartening financial statistics while trying to sound upbeat and positive to the woman on the phone, cajoling her into believing that the "Day at the Races" promotional giveaway to which she has been invited is not some scam and is, in fact, a legitimate marketing attempt on behalf of Suffolk Downs to encourage and introduce new patrons to the sport. After a while, the skeptical old lady is enthused to learn that the freebie includes a complimentary buffet, admission, and programs. She is also pleased to hear that the track has a shuttle service that runs the quarter-mile distance between the subway stop and the front entrance, although she is mildly perturbed that Suffolk Downs won't detour its bus fifteen miles to her home in Wellesley to pick her up at her own front door. If she bet enough, I jest with her, we probably would.

"Do you *bet* there?" she sputters, suddenly alarmed.

"Do I bet?" is my reply, not fully understanding the question.

"No, people in general. People actually *bet* on horse races?"

"Well, we hope they do."

"But do you *have* to bet?" she persists.

"No, you don't have to," I explain. "You can just watch the races if you prefer. It's a fun afternoon either way."

There is a long silence, and I'm not sure if the woman is still on the other end of the line or if the scandalous news about racetrack wagering has shocked away another potential Suffolk Downs customer.

———

"DID I TELL YOU we lost Blackwater?" my dad says on the phone from Tampa, his voice terse and edgy even a few days after the claim. I figure he must be going senile because we already had this exact same conversation the other night.

"No, you don't understand," my father continues, irritably. "The horse is *lost*. Gone. No one can find him."

Now I really start to think something is wrong with the old man. And I still don't know what's going on.

"They took Blackwater back from the spit box [the post-race drug testing area] and put him away in his new barn. The guy must have been drunk or wasn't paying attention. My guess is he didn't latch up the stall guard correctly and Blackwater rushed the webbing like he always does. He broke through, ran around loose all night and escaped. No one on the backstretch has seen him and no one knows where he is."

The Tampa Bay Downs stable area is bordered by dense scrub and swamplands. It is no secret that alligators are abundant in the area, and my first thought is also the worst: that Blackwater ran headlong into the wetlands, got stuck, and is thrashing and struggling chest-deep in some bog, captive prey to carnivorous reptiles.

"I'm not too happy about it," my father says, sharing the same unspoken fear. "And if this horse doesn't turn up safe sometime soon, I'm going to make sure people hear about it."

As THE FIELD barrels down the homestretch in the opener, a star-tled cat darts directly across the track at the eighth pole, scampering madly from the infield to the outer rail, narrowly avoiding being tram-pled by the onrushing six-horse pack.

Mercifully, it is not black.

Larry Collmus catches the frenzied feline out of the corner of his eye. Missing only an imperceptible beat, the announcer regains com-posure to matter-of-factly mention the bizarre happenstance in his call. The horses take little notice of the panicked barn cat, and loose-on-the-lead favorite Lake Jacqueline sails home by six lengths under Ramiro Herrera, who manages to celebrate his thirtieth birthday with a rare trip to the winner's circle.

In the fifth event, Herrera is the 3-to-1 second choice astride Lucky Dad, who owns an anemic 1-for-24 lifetime record and knees that glisten with medicated salve. No cat runs across the track this time, but the magic continues for the birthday boy, who ambushes the field by an easy 5-1/2 lengths.

The pair of victories doubles Ramiro's seasonal win total, from two to four.

With his purse winnings just now breaking the $20,000 mark for the meet, a rough estimation of Herrera's take-home pay this winter averages out to $200 per week, before taxes.

It's no wonder that just last week, the journeyman jock was seen after the races mingling with the territorial grandstand stoopers, scouring the Suffolk Downs floor in search of mistakenly discarded pari-mutuel treasure.

THE VERBAL SPARRING in the jockeys' room has simmered down in recent weeks, but the have-nots are still feeling a bit bitter toward the haves, resenting the seemingly unequal clout the top riders have over their struggling brethren when it comes to dealing with track management and canceling races. There is talk that several jockeys—Harry Vega and Jose Caraballo, second and fourth in the standings, respectively—are ready to jump ship when Delaware Park opens in early April, and the fear is that their impending departures will cause them to act indifferently about group decisions. One week ago, leading reinsman Joe Hampshire attained the milestone mark of 2,000 lifetime wins, and the absence of a number of fellow riders from the traditional post-race congratulatory ceremony only accentuated the division between the jockeys who call the shots and those forced to follow.

Howard Lanci—now eligible to eat at the locker-room snack bar but still having difficulty maintaining both his riding weight and a reliable stream of clients—is sitting on a stool at the lunch counter, deeply involved in one of his maniacal rants about the injustice of racetrack politics. Grinding along with only two wins from forty-seven tries so far this season, The Howitzer has scavenged only one mount this afternoon, aboard an eight-year-old mare with a 1-for-56 lifetime record, a 30-to-1 no-hoper on the morning line.

"I know where all the bodies are buried around here!" he bellows at the top of his lungs, apparently to no one in particular. "I'm coming clean! I'm gonna bring this place *down!*"

Then he turns to one of the startled interns sent to fetch the press-box lunch order and continues methodically in a softer tone, as if imparting some important hidden knowledge.

"And you know what, kid? The strange thing is, I'm not even fucked up right now."

ONCE EACH DAY I unburden myself from business in the press box and take a stroll through the grandstand, way down to the barren section of the aging concrete plant amid the sectional rows of steel pipe and vacant orange seats that are sparsely populated by a sprinkling of diehard fans. Some of these regulars have been sitting in the same spots for decades, day after day, race after race. For the most part loners and outsiders, some of them are very sharp handicappers with their own intricate systems, a knowledgeable knot of curmudgeonly retirees who keep to themselves and take a glimmer of pleasure in their own collective cantankerousness.

An informal, likable lot, these old-timers know each other more by habit and congenial exchange than by actual name, and they seem content not to bother with unnecessary details of each other's lives outside the communal custom of the racetrack. When one of them doesn't show up for a few afternoons in a row, the remaining grandstand denizens accept it as racetrack fate that the guy must be either hospitalized or has galloped off to the great big winner's circle in the sky, because for these folks, serious illness and death are the only fathomable excuses for deviating from the ritual of racetrack routine.

"Yep, old Cadillac Louie got the pneumonia," one of them says to me today, "and then the pneumonia got *him*."

This spurs a racetrack debate among the orange-seaters about the prospect of afterlife, with one pari-mutuel veteran lodging his request to have his cremated ashes scattered across the Suffolk Downs finish line.

"Aw hell, you can just sprinkle mine at the eighth pole," one cigar-chomping crank cracks in response. "I've died there enough times already."

A VALET—which only in the convoluted world of the racetrack rhymes with *mallet*—performs one of those thankless behind-the-scenes jobs that no one pays attention to until something goes dreadfully wrong.

Aside from laying out the equipment for three or four jockeys— boots, riding pants, safety vest, helmet, goggles, whips, gloves, and undergarments—a valet is also expected to have a correctly weighted saddle and a fresh set of silks ready for each mount his riders have on the program. In addition, the valets share rotations for the saddling and unsaddling of horses before and after each race, and they must also accompany their assigned jockeys to the scales for the official weighing out and weighing in for each contest. Between races, valets basically act as personal servants, providing fresh towels, shower shoes, soap, deodorant, and an assortment of other basic necessities at the request of their riders. Valets must also be adept at basic repair such as mending, tailoring, waterproofing, and boot shining. In the heyday of the sport, a good valet would also be responsible for ironing a jockey's suit, shirt, and trousers so he looked sharp at the end of the afternoon, but now the only time a Suffolk Downs rider shows up in the locker room wearing a coat and tie is with great reluctance, and probably for a funeral.

Perhaps the truest indication of the anonymous role of a valet occurs when his jockey wins a race and it's time for the winner's circle photograph: Racetrack tradition dictates that the valet must stand *behind* the flank of the winning horse so that he does not show in the picture, a throwback to the gentrified days of the sport when the blue bloods would be horrified by the uninvited presence of hired help in their carefully framed portraits of victory. The basic day rate for a Suffolk Downs valet is $45, supplemented by tips and a standard 10 percent cut of purse winnings from each of his riders (and that's 10 percent from the *jockey's* own 10 percent share, not the overall purse).

The job of racetrack valet usually defaults to former jockeys, creating an odd circle of closure to the profession of riding Thoroughbreds. Almost every jockey breaks in doing racetrack dirty work—mucking stalls, washing feed tubs, walking hots—and a significant number of riders end their autumn years in similar fashion, scrubbing mud, polishing boots, and performing personal chores for a younger generation of reinsmen. One of the game's most poignant examples of locker-room camaraderie is the willing immediacy of valets to take up a collection for an injured rider or a fellow valet who has taken ill, and when the jar gets passed in any jockeys' room in the country, it's a safe bet that those who have the least are the ones who give the most.

Sal DiMeo is a sixty-six-year-old valet who has worked the locker rooms in New England for decades. Sal is strictly old school. He broke into the game half a century ago, and he walks the walk and talks the talk of a sharp-tongued, silver-haired character straight out of a Damon Runyon story. DiMeo is quick with a wisecrack, yet politely calls everyone "sir," even the rookies who were born long after Sal retired as a rider himself. He struts about his business with a peppy gait, often whistling some long-forgotten tune while expending a terrific amount of elbow grease and energy. Sal takes meticulous pride in his work, and on the few occasions I've used the Suffolk Downs locker room to shower, DiMeo has always insisted on caring for my clothes and providing toiletries. At first it seemed as if he was going overboard in fishing for a tip, but Sal has repeatedly refused whenever I've tried to slip him a few bucks. Instead, he and the other valets prefer to be compensated in the form of coveted clubhouse passes, which are a prestigious kind of underground racetrack currency that dates back to the glory days of patronage at the East Boston oval.

Once, one of the other valets asked me to do him the favor of looking up Sal's riding record from his days on the old Rhode Island circuit. I knew that decades ago DiMeo was a blue-collar jockey but had
never heard him speak of specific mounts or big races that he won.
Searching through the dusty chart archives, I soon learned that the
reason Sal never crowed about past accomplishments the way other ex-
reinsmen did was because there didn't seem to be very many, or at
least none that I could unearth in the leather-bound annals buried in
the back of the press box. The numbers were so disheartening that I
stopped checking and made up some story about the chart books
being missing when the guy reminded me about the request. Yet no
matter how you quantify it, Sal still shows up at work every morning
with a smile, a good story, and unbridled enthusiasm, admirable qual-
ities that can never be codified in terms of racetrack statistics.

The complete record of a horse named Jeremy Hill is far easier to
pinpoint: He's a three-year-old Thoroughbred who has never finished
a race, having been eased or pulled up in his only three career
attempts. Today, Sal DiMeo and Jeremy Hill will cross paths in the
Suffolk Downs paddock before the first race, and the intersection will
not be pretty.

The opener is a cheap maiden sprint, and despite the horse's laugh-
ably bad past performances, Joe Hampshire has accepted the mount
aboard Jeremy Hill, who is returning to the races off a six-month
absence. Reacting with irrational exuberance, the betting public is
backing this sorry steed to 10 to 1 in a classic lesser-of-evils race that
someone has to win, collectively assuming that if the leading rider is
taking the call, the maiden must be ripe for a turnaround.

Sal DiMeo isn't too concerned with the odds on Jeremy Hill when
he ascends the tunnel stairs from the locker room to the paddock on
this early spring afternoon. Hampshire is not in Sal's "corner" (in
another inexplicable example of racetrack slang, riders assigned to a
particular valet are considered to be in that valet's "corner" even if all
their lockers are lined up in a straight row), but DiMeo has drawn the
random duty of helping the trainer and the jockey tack up the num-

ber 3 horse in the opener. If Sal hasn't already looked at the maiden's especially poor form and made the logical guess that Jeremy Hill might be an unruly sort who just doesn't agree with or enjoy the concept of racing, the valet finds out as soon as he enters the walking ring with Hampshire's tack, where the unschooled animal is frantically bucking and rearing, ears pricked straight up in a signal of fright, eyes wide and searching for an escape. To start the racing day, it will be the diminutive valet's job to secure and strap the racing saddle and its accompanying girth, chamois, cushion pad, number cloth, and irons underneath and around the back of the obstreperous Jeremy Hill, who in full view of everyone in the paddock is the living embodiment of the natural Thoroughbred instinct of fight or flight.

Even past the age of retirement, DiMeo is more agile than his compact stature might suggest, and he nimbly dances and sidesteps around the paddock along with Jeremy Hill's groom and trainer as they attempt to settle the nervous horse into a position where they can quickly get the girth around him and securely cinch the saddle. The accepted racetrack practice for tacking up a difficult horse is to saddle the animal while he's moving, with the belief that removing him from the small saddling stall will both calm the steed and minimize the risk for injury. Jeremy Hill isn't buying this theory however, and he makes several antsy turns around the walking ring, wheeling and dragging his frustrated human counterparts in tow before ending up right back where he started, squarely in front of stall number 3 with ten minutes to post and the remaining six maidens in the race all saddled up and ready to hit the track.

Thoroughbred handlers are taught that when dealing with an anxious Thoroughbred, it is wise to stick close to the animal, even though this tactic might seem counterintuitive. The closer you stand to a horse, the less chance he has to really wind up and nail you with his head or hooves, and the close contact also serves as a subtle alert system when a steed can't see what's going on behind him or at his sides. By moving cautiously around the hind end of a horse and always touching him on the rump to let him know you're there, it decreases the chance that the animal will lash out in defensive reflex. DiMeo is well aware of these rules of equine engagement, and with five decades of experience, he is certainly not afraid—cautious at times, but definitely not scared—of a racehorse. Sal knows that even the best horse handlers take their lumps on occasion, even when they're doing everything exactly right and by the book. And by the book is how DiMeo is playing it when he sidles up alongside Jeremy Hill, speaks soothingly to the wild-eyed colt, and deftly starts to slip the girth around the chestnut four-year-old's midsection.

With a muscular explosion of his hind quarters, Jeremy Hill violently launches Sal DiMeo headfirst and backward with a sudden and volatile thrust of his hips, propelling the helpless valet a good dozen feet through the air before he lands squarely on his back on the hard-packed walking ring. Sal's skull ricochets off a cement border designed to safeguard the fragile paddock grass but not to cushion the impact of an unprotected human head. Half in a puddle, with Joe Hampshire's saddle and riding tack scattered about haphazardly, DiMeo is out cold, limbs so spread-eagled that he looks like a vaudeville actor doing an overly exaggerated job of pretending he's just been shot. The scary part is, everyone knows the valet isn't faking.

The track ambulance is on the scene within two minutes. By then, DiMeo has regained consciousness and can move all his limbs and digits, although he is woozy and disoriented. A group of onlookers form a loose circle around the stunned valet—racing officials, security guards, veterinarians, outriders—but everyone does a good job of respecting the medical technicians' request to back off and not crowd the scene. Former jockey Abby Fuller, who is seven months pregnant and in the walking ring working as the track's between-race TV handicapper, kneels beside DiMeo in the mud and holds his hand the entire time. Howard Lanci, already tacked up and awaiting a rare chance to ride the 9-to-5 favorite in the same race, also crouches nearby, a scowl of quiet concern clouding his usually animated face. One of the paramedics is asking Sal if he can recall what happened, and if his vision faded to black when he hit the ground. The other is fitting DiMeo for a protective neck brace. In the midst of this ruckus, Jeremy Hill has somehow managed to be successfully saddled by his caretakers. The groom keeps him away from all the other horses in the paddock, and the colt paces a nervous circle on his short shank.

"Don't put that thing on me!" DiMeo pleads with the EMT as the rigid stabilizing collar is placed around his head. "Please! I'm claustrophobic!" he explains. Despite dizziness and an open laceration on the back of his scalp, DiMeo does not want to go to the hospital. In fact, he insists, he'd rather just sit with an ice pack for a bit before heading straight back to work.

Reluctantly, the paramedics relent on the neck brace, but they are adamant about taking the valet to the emergency room so a doctor can examine his injury. "Anything to do with your head, Mr. DiMeo, it's really better to have it checked out sooner rather than later," the EMT implores, and a few of the onlookers chime in with similar encouragement. Still, the more persistently they argue the case for medical attention, the more stubbornly Sal digs in his heels and says he wants to stay.

"Sal, you better go," pipes up Lanci, ever the realist, attempting to be helpful. "A guy like me gets whacked in the head, it ain't gonna matter much. But you—a man of your age—you really should go."

DiMeo finally agrees to go. After a delay of seventeen minutes waiting for a backup ambulance, the field goes to post for the first race.

Jeremy Hill chases the pace, comes up empty when asked for his run, and ends up passing three horses, including one who fails to finish the race. The fourth-place try is the best ever in his brief career, thirteen lengths behind the winner. Not great, but it could have been worse. The same holds true for Sal DiMeo, who, several hours later, returns to the track immediately upon his release from the hospital. Wearing a bloodied bandage under his off-kilter Suffolk Downs baseball cap, the valet is back in action in time for the ninth race.

"Christ, I can't be taking days off," Sal says, searching for something to do, pretending to be annoyed that his fellow valets have covered his share of locker-room duties. "I mean, this is a racetrack. This is my job. I'm here to work."

BOSTON IS HIT with a late-season squall on St. Patrick's Day. Although the amount of snowfall is not much by New England standards, every year when a storm rolls in after a few nice weeks of spring, people forget what winter is all about and everything gets gridlocked again. Yesterday it was 70°F and weather records were shattered all across the region. Today, on a Friday with no live racing scheduled, it's an absolute whiteout.

Track superintendent Steve Pini, easily the most second-guessed Suffolk Downs employee on the payroll, makes the call by midafternoon to allow the snow to be harrowed into the track instead of letting it accumulate and get plowed off. Based on several decades of experience, Pini knows whichever decision he makes is bound to annoy or irritate someone: If the storm becomes more severe than expected and he has chosen to rake the snowfall into the dirt surface, he has made a grave error that will result in too much frozen precipitation being mixed into the top cushion of the track. With cold nights and warm days, the track will drain and thaw unevenly, making for an unsafe surface that can take weeks to rectify. If the reverse happens—Pini seals the track tight with rollers, lets the snow build up overnight and plows it all away the next day—that means an automatic cancellation of morning training for the grading machinery to do its work. So if it doesn't snow enough, Steve then looks foolish because he has cost the horsemen a precious morning of workouts, gallops, and gate schooling just so the plows can remove a surface dusting of snow.

With the Atlantic Ocean and its constantly shifting winds less than a mile away, handicapping Mother Nature can be a more daunting risk than picking the ponies at Suffolk Downs.

RIGHT DECISION, wrong outcome.

Morning training was cut short today because of the three inches of snow that were plowed into the racetrack. That small an amount is not a problem under normal circumstances, but with plenty of late-winter sunshine and temperatures above the freezing mark, the racing strip becomes a quagmire, muddy and thawed on the surface but still frozen and chunky down below in uneven, rutted sections.

Steve Pini can't win. But at least he goes down swinging.

Operating on little sleep, Pini directs his battalion of harrows and floats around the racetrack in frenzied fashion—or at least as frenzied as a team of ultraheavy equipment can get while topping out at seven or eight miles per hour. The John Deere tractors claw at the muddy surface, ripping it open to expose pools and pockets of moisture. Then the massive rollers float away the water, and even out what's left. To be effective, this process has to be repeated again and again. Watching from the press box, there seems to be no pattern, no method to the repetitive madness. But by noon Steve has worked earthen wizardry, miraculously transforming the track into a freshly groomed corduroy dirt surface.

It appears as if the show will go on after all, and announcer Larry Collmus is given the go-ahead to play the National Anthem recording and read the race-day changes. The fans file through the turnstiles, some of them spilling out onto the concrete apron to enjoy the wildly fluctuating weather, which has once again shifted suddenly warmer. The horses make the walk from the backstretch barn area to the paddock for the first race. The jockeys make their pre-race preparations. A maintenance worker trudges out to the infield tote board and hangs the sign that denotes the official track condition: Fast.

But in the half hour prior to first post at 12:45 PM, with the sun at its zenith, the track starts to unravel. Or rather, it melts. With the sun beating down strongly, temperatures shoot upward, approaching 50°F. All over the strip, subsurface pools of mud bubble up from beneath, oozing to the top like crude oil. The view of the track from several stories above is like watching a thick, brown lake come alive. There is also another problem: Just as the horses are about to leave the paddock for the opener, it is discovered that the hired ambulance is not on the grounds. Apparently, the company with whom Suffolk Downs contracts for emergency service misunderstood the earlier decision to cancel morning training. Thinking that the afternoon races were also called off, the paramedics went home and neglected to inform track officials they weren't coming back.

A frantic call goes out to the ambulance contractor and replacement paramedics are dispatched. The horses circle, plodding counterclockwise in the soupy walking ring. The jockeys sit and wait. Casual fans have no idea what's going on, while cynical sharpies, based on past precedence, think that management is deliberately stalling to try to fix the racetrack. The thaw continues at a record pace. On the infield tote board, the Fast sign is replaced with Good and then Muddy.

"By the time the ambulance makes it," says a discouraged Lou Raffetto, one eye on his watch and another on his liquefying racetrack, "It might be a moot point anyway."

Raffetto seems resigned on the issue of cancellation today. Probably reasoning that this will be the last time this season he'll have to deal with winter weather, he is understandably weary of bickering with the jockeys over whether it's safe to race. And although it's easy to make the call when your neck isn't on the line, there seems to be general consensus among management, the local horsemen, and even some veteran riders that the standard for what's hazardous and what isn't has been gradually lowered over the past several years. The joke in the press box is that it's a good thing the jockeys' locker room is in the basement level without any windows, because the riders would pull the plug every time a black cloud loomed threateningly on the horizon.

Twenty minutes late, the field hits the sloppy surface for the first race, shadowed by the ambulance. In the locker room, the jockeys who are not riding are already packing up for the day, changing back into street clothes or heading off for a hot shower, laughing and joking as if the cancellation of the remainder of the card is a foregone conclusion. On the track, once the gates open, the riders who do have a mount appear to be going through the motions. As a group, they ride cautiously and without any real effort, strung out and spread far apart. The goal seems to be to just make it around so no one gets hurt, or even too dirty. For the record, Wilfredo Lozano Jr. loops the field on the turn and wins going away on Song of Night at 7 to 1. Joe

Hampshire sits tight aboard odds-on favorite Countach and finishes up the track, far behind the top finishers.

Spring is in the air, it's a beautiful sunny Saturday, and the program is canceled for the seventh time this season at Suffolk Downs. After months of relentless battering by harsh winter elements, the problem this afternoon is that the weather, believe it or not, is far too pleasant to race.

MY DAD is on the phone telling me about the horse he claimed to fill the vacancy in his shed row, a hard-hitting six-year-old racemare he thought was a bargain pickup for $12,500. One of the leading stables at Tampa Bay Downs is disbanding, offering sharply discounted horse-flesh because its principal owner is about to be indicted on charges of embezzling $5 million from a Massachusetts vocational school where he served as longtime treasurer.

"That's not why I called," I tell him. "Whatever happened to Blackwater? Did they find him?"

"Oh yeah," my father answers. "I forgot to tell you. They found him in an unused stall, way back in an empty barn on the far side of the property. A little hungry and thirsty maybe, but otherwise okay."

In fact, Blackwater had hidden himself in the very same stable from which the accused embezzler from Massachusetts had just pulled out. My old man tells me it's eerie in that section of the Tampa backstretch: One week it's a vibrant, working Thoroughbred shed row, the very next an equine ghost town.

"That horse might be mean," my old man muses, as if reminiscing about a lost equine love, "but, man, can he take that aggression and channel it into running straight out of his skin."

NEW ENGLAND has always carved out a niche as a fertile region for producing horses and humans who go on to bigger and better things. Chalk it up to the ferocity of the competition or a backbreaking

Yankee work ethic, but no matter how you account for it, racetrackers from the Northeast always seem to emerge as a shrewd, hard-boiled lot, and the locals who do manage to rise above the repetitive toil usually count on wits, guts, and persistence rather than finesse, flourish, or flash to deliver the goods.

The mighty Seabiscuit has been popularized as the rags-to-riches epitome of an underdog Bostonian who struck it big. Knock-kneed and homely, fate rescued this unwanted steed from Suffolk Downs obscurity in 1936, and "The People's Horse" ended up captivating the nation for years to come. Although hardly as prolific, equally appreciated homegrown talents include Timely Writer (scored in the Hopeful, Champagne, and Flamingo Stakes before winning the 1982 Florida Derby), Mom's Command (swept the 1985 Filly Triple Crown), and Waquoit (a late-1980s graded-stakes gray named after a Cape Cod beach). As for jockeys, local boy Tony DeSpirito rose from Massachusetts poverty to national prominence, establishing a then-record 390 wins as a sixteen-year-old apprentice in 1952. All-time earnings leader Pat Day rode briefly in New England as a 1970s rookie, and Boston-born hall-of-famer Chris McCarron is widely accepted as one of the city's most favored sporting sons. When one adds to the list scores of capable trainers, numerous successful stable owners, several noted racing journalists, and a handful of key industry executives, the roster of graduates who cut their teeth in the trenches of New England becomes impressive quite quickly.

Good people always go on to bigger and better things, but the recent exodus from New England racing is difficult to put into perspective compared to the glory days. Then, only the crème de la crème left for bigger and better opportunities after outgrowing regional competition. Now, in 2000, roughly the top one-third of racing outfits have either left the circuit or are contemplating doing so because they can't break even in the current Thoroughbred economy. The choice comes down to either leaving home or leaving the industry, and writer Steve Myrick articulates the situation poignantly in the March 19, 2000, *Lawrence Eagle-Tribune*:

Find me a trainer on any Thoroughbred race track in North America who does not gripe about purses, and I will show you a trainer who has not looked at his books lately.

Grumbling comes naturally to trainers, and owners, too. It is a predictable consequence of a system where the people who invest the money and do the work have little control over what they get paid. But this spring the grumbling seems to be a little bit louder, and there are some concrete signs that dissatisfaction with the prize money offered here in New England is causing the top trainers and jockeys to seek fortunes elsewhere . . .

The migration to more lucrative venues, along with the usual strain of a long winter, is already evident. Suffolk is currently carding four programs per week, with only nine races per day. That means only 36 chances per week for all the trainers, owners, and jockeys to earn a paycheck . . .

The history of wrangling over racing regulations on Beacon Hill offers little cause for enthusiasm. Attempts to bring off-track betting (OTB), phone account wagering, or video slot machines at the track have fallen victim to widely differing interests among horse tracks, dog tracks, and anti-gambling legislators . . .

"It's a crucial, critical time," said [Lou] Raffetto. "I don't have an answer. We are trying to run a first-class business that means something to Massachusetts. There's really not a whole lot anyone can do, short of legislation to help the racetracks."

The ironic thing is, according to the spreadsheets that land on my desk every week, total betting volume is actually *up* 4 percent for 2000, compared to the previous year. But this short-term blip on the radar screen does not reflect the overall, decade-long downward trend for the live product, because the vast majority of wagering Suffolk Downs now handles is on out-of-state simulcast races, from which the track gains a smaller cut. Nor does this slight increase tell the true story about how betting money trickles down to horse owners in the form of purses, and how the East Boston oval can no longer keep pace with gaming-bolstered entities that offer much fatter rewards for essentially the same risks and expenses.

"I haven't gone up on my day rate [the fee charged to horse owners] in ten years," says third-generation trainer Aimee Hall, who discloses in the same *Tribune* story that she and husband Jose Caraballo, the third-leading local jockey, will be packing up their family, racing stable, and breeding farm to make the move to lucrative Delaware Park. "How can you go up on your day rate? It's not fair to the owners. The price of grain, bedding, everything else goes up."

Ron Dandy, the leading Suffolk Downs conditioner for five out of the last six race meets, concurs: "How long can you keep your owners here?" he says, offering the anonymous example of a top, longtime client. "He's staying here because he wants to see his horses run. It's getting to a point, he doesn't even want to do that."

These are not empty threats from frustrated New Englanders grinding away at the game in an eroding little corner of an otherwise flourishing industry. The daily departure of huge, lumbering horse vans from the Suffolk Downs stable area can attest to that. Usually, this is the time of the season when outfits traditionally begin returning to the region. This year, the flow has been reversed, to the point where one might more accurately call it a flood. But perhaps even more disturbing is the seldom-discussed Plan B for the wealthy partnership members who own Suffolk Downs: If Massachusetts does not enact favorable legislation to aid the industry, they will simply sell the most lucrative 190 acres of development property in Greater Boston and walk away from the racing business with a huge windfall. Everyone else at the ground level of the game just, well, walks away.

"It gets your attention," says Lou Raffetto, whose grim racetrack now has little choice but to face reality head-on. "We're always concerned, because you wonder, will they come back?"

AFTER MAKING an impact by winning with his first starter in Maryland, recently relocated trainer Mike Catalano has been mired in a 1-for-20 slump. The weather is warming, his horses are cooling, and the pressure to perform is being ratcheted up by impatient power client Michael Gill, an owner who demands immediate return on his equine investments.

Even the sharpest racing stables hit the skids every so often, and the timing of such droughts is wildly unpredictable. A month into its mid-Atlantic invasion, Team Catalano has been stymied by tough luck, poor rides, bad post positions, nagging illness, and minor injury. Faster rivals and clever competition have also played a role in keeping the Boston boys out of the winner's circle, but by and large, Mike must examine his shed row from the inside out to get back into the groove.

Once-promising stakes candidate Lone Storm has done nothing but spin his wheels in two starts. Crossano is getting a reputation as a hanger—a horse who looms boldly but can't finish the job—after consecutive runner-up efforts. The usually reliable Hanover Street has been slow from the gate. The other day, Glockenspiel got hung out to dry from post 11, and Cut The Cards looked like a certain winner, leading every step of the way before faltering in the final few strides. Flying Max was recently up the track as the longest shot on the board, Premier Imp got claimed just when he was sitting on a big effort, and Saratoga Ridge, that venerable gray blur of reliability, has yet to be seen in the Maryland entries since his win at Suffolk Downs last month. Countless other steeds have raced or trained so lethargically that Catalano himself is a bit off kilter, scrambling in an unfamiliar environment, and the results-driven Gill doesn't give a hoot how these problems are addressed. All the boss wants—expects, really—are wins.

Barely six weeks into his new job, Mike Catalano is learning the hard way that being second-guessed can be a whole hell of a lot worse than being in second place.

ON THE WEST COAST of Florida, Blackwater continues to terrorize Tampa Bay Downs.

Over the course of the last nineteen days, the sleek black epitome of equine rage has unleashed his pent-up fury upon racetrack foes with the same reckless abandon he usually reserves for human handlers. After his easy $5,000 win on March 2—the afternoon he was claimed away from my father and went AWOL in the stable area—the frenzied gelding roared back nine days later with another decisive score, despite stepping up one level in class. Today, Blackwater's current connections have elected to run their streaky steed right back again for that very same $6,250 claiming tag, engaging in that time-honored hit-and-run backstretch bluff known among claiming trainers everywhere as "ramming one down their throats."

From a handicapping perspective, what's a bettor to do when assessing a horse like Blackwater, who has hit upon a sudden reversal of fortune in such a small window of time? If you assume that the animal has truly turned the corner to bigger and better things, you must also then logically question why his owner and trainer are risking losing such a productive steed who has proven ability at this $6,250 level. Or putting it another way, if the horse wins so easily at his current plateau, then why aren't his connections gunning for fatter purse money at a higher claiming bracket? Could the horse be damaged goods and they're *hoping* someone claims him? Or, could it be that the horse is sound enough to win *today* but those closest to him know that a nagging injury or infirmity will make itself evident a few weeks down the road? Most racing stables like to strike while the iron is hot, pouncing on a streaky Thoroughbred the way a day trader capitalizes on short-term movement of stocks. But some outfits use reverse psychology, dropping a horse in class so precipitously as to arouse suspicion when nothing is even remotely wrong with the animal.

It's a game within a game, and sometimes horseplayers who peer at *Racing Form*s far too long assign logic that just isn't there to begin with: Maybe alimony payments have to be made. Or an owner needs to kick-start his cash flow to make the mortgage. Or a racing outfit is going out of business or moving to a different circuit and it wants to cut the size of its stable. Extremely likely, but rarely considered, is that a trainer could simply be making a stupid mistake. All of these factors could be true, or none of them could be true. At the racetrack, whether the gamble occurs at the betting windows or behind the scenes at the claiming box, bold moves never guarantee delivery of certain reward. The only absolute in the equation is risk.

Either way, Blackwater is heavily favored, at 4 to 5, to win today's sixth at Tampa. He settles into last place early, picks off horses willingly on the turn, and canters past his overmatched rivals one by one. Not once does Blackwater feel the sting of his jockey's stick; at no point in the race does victory seem in doubt. He wins handily, by 4-1/4 lengths, and the son of a European champion prances into the tiny winner's circle in condescending fashion. Although the seven-year-old hardly looks winded, a practiced eye can detect a barely perceptible imbalance in his rear legs, a slight asymmetry that signals he is favoring one, or perhaps both, hock joints. Several trainers have dropped slips into the claim box, and one of them will be chosen by a roll of the dice as the new owner of a fast horse compromised by his own conformation.

"Imagine if he was totally sound how good he'd be?" my father wonders, brushing aside any regrets he might still secretly harbor about letting Blackwater go for five grand. "Christ, with that pedigree and attitude, a horse like this could win the MassCap."

WITH SIX DAYS to go before the highly anticipated blue-ribbon racing hearings on Beacon Hill, today I meet with Larry Overlan, an economist who has been hired by the track to compile a detailed public policy report that Suffolk Downs will be able to use as ammunition in its legislative push.

Dressed in drab tones of gray and sporting an unanimated demeanor, the guy certainly looks the stereotypical part of a no-nonsense number cruncher. Bluntly, Overlan tells me that one of the key points on which the Massachusetts racing industry has been misfiring for the past decade is its collective plea for bailouts and subsidies. Too much emphasis, he says, has been placed on the "We're a good bunch of guys in an industry that a lot of people depend on, so you have to help us out" mindset.

Instead, the economist believes our strategy should focus on how the state has created an unfair marketplace in which Suffolk Downs would otherwise be successful if it didn't have to fight the monolithic Massachusetts Lottery or operate under legislative constraints that prevent the track from competing against rival gaming operations in nearby states.

"Because let's face it," Overlan shrugs. "In terms of employment and revenue to the state, someone could just as easily write a similar study that says a shopping mall on this piece of property could equally or better serve the needs of the community."

BEHIND THE CLOSED DOORS of the Suffolk Downs locker room, one of the veteran riders has been bragging that he's been dating a dancer from The Golden Banana, the seedy strip club up on Route 1. Of course, no one in the jocks' room believes him. Until today, that is, when the proud reinsman invites his lady friend to the track for her first-ever visit to the races. Jaws collectively drop in the paddock when a big-haired blonde with a petite body conspicuously snakes her way through the overwhelmingly male crowd to join her beau in the winner's circle after his big score in the Saturday stakes feature.

Strutting confidently in a black leather jacket, skin-tight jeans, and high-heeled motorcycle boots, the lithe young lady certainly looks the part of someone who is used to turning heads. As her boyfriend accepts the trophy and shakes hands with the winning owners, his babe appears quite comfortable posing for photographers and the in-house TV cameraman as they focus on her instead of the ceremonial post-race presentation.

Although it is against the rules for unlicensed guests to be allowed in the jockeys' room during the racing day, the jockey escorts his girlfriend back to the locker area to meet and greet his buddies. A group of valets and male jockeys form a small crush of humanity around the perky visitor, all eager to exchange pleasantries and get an up-close look at the sweetheart, who doesn't seem to mind being the center of attention. The clerk of scales is not at all amused with the uninvited distraction. He has difficulty gathering the troops for the weigh-out for the final race, but the Suffolk Downs official is clearly outflanked and outnumbered.

"Hey, you're pretty light!" remarks one of the jockeys in the crowd, making conversation.

"You should step on the scale!" says another.

"Go ahead! You're probably light enough to ride!" chimes in a third, adding a dig about the tough time her boyfriend has recently had making riding weight.

"Actually," the vivacious cutie says with a coy smile. "I weigh less than *he* does. One hundred ten pounds. I rub his face in it all the time."

A brief, awkward pause ensues. One of the valets, off by himself in a corner readying tack, mutters a comment that comes out louder than intended, breaking the silence.

"Oh, I bet you do, honey. I bet you do."

THE DAY is bright and breezy, with a hint of early season sweetness in the air. Surprisingly, the usually combative commute into East Boston is free from hassle and aggression. My morning coffee is strong and fresh, the car windows are fully open, the radio is belting out some funky jazz from a local college station, and I'm musing over several promising MassCap candidates as if the big race was right around the corner instead of ten weeks away. Having completed the advance work for tomorrow's much-anticipated State House hearings, there are no ominous projects looming over the media relations department today, and it is one of those rare occasions when my biggest challenge of the afternoon will be trying to unlock the mystery of the daily double. It's such a pleasantly perfect day and the vibe is so good, that by the time I hit Revere Beach Parkway for the turn into Suffolk Downs, I don't want the ride to end because I figure life can't get any better than this.

But it does.

My favorite end-of-the-row parking spot is available, and I snag it.

Then, as soon as I step out of the car, I'm blinded by the shimmer of morning sun glinting off a shiny new penny, the angular bearded face of Abe Lincoln pointing straight up for enhanced kismet.

I pocket the 1-cent piece and walk toward a stooped old man who sets up shop near the press entrance to indulge his passion for feeding shore birds. His name is Francis—just like the patron saint of animals—and even though this gentleman lives out of a rusty station wagon and looks as if he barely has means to secure food for himself, he takes time almost every single day to toss bread scraps to gulls and pigeons who converge upon him in a shrieking cyclone. Many of these birds are stained an unsightly, tarry black from caustic oil residue off the nearby tankers, and the feet of larger gulls who hang out at the airport are tinged a queasy, fluorescent green from runway de-icing toxins. Yet to gentle Francis, who rarely speaks to people, this indistinct flock of mutants contains uniquely individual friends who lend pleasure to his daily ritual. I don't even mind knowing that by the end of the day, his benevolence will cause my car to be covered in waste droppings, because according to old racetrack superstition, being shit upon by birds is a sure sign of good luck. With twenty-four hours to go before the legislative hoopla commences, I figure Suffolk Downs needs all the help it can get.

The good omens continue when I enter the building. A scruffy Jamaican who calls himself "Bunny" usually camps outside the jockeys' room entrance, where he accosts incoming riders for betting tips and hounds track employees for free programs. But today Bunny is in a jovial mood, and instead of scowling, he opens the door for me with an exaggerated, overly formal flourish. "All the best to you today, sir!" he utters in grandiose fashion.

On the way up to the press box, I share an elevator ride with Track Superintendent Steve Pini, who informs me that his crew "nitrogen bombed" the dormant turf course with fertilizer over the past forty-eight hours and that the chlorophyllic reaction has been both intense and immediate. The winter blanket of snow is long gone, and when viewed from atop the grandstand, the suddenly verdant expanse has turned overnight into what has to be the lushest spring lawn in all of

Boston. For a change—and for the first time in a long while—it appears as if the grass is greener on the Suffolk Downs side of the fence. Tomorrow we'll find out if this positive perspective holds true from the imposing vantage point of Beacon Hill.

THE MASSACHUSETTS STATE HOUSE is seven miles away, but worlds removed from Suffolk Downs.

The building itself is architecturally imposing—magnificent red bricks, immaculate Corinthian columns, steep granite steps, and a shimmering golden dome topping the southern crest of storied Beacon Hill. Covering two entire city blocks, the "new" State House was built in 1798 and stands as the oldest building in the oldest, most gentrified neighborhood of the nation's oldest metropolis. A palpable sense of history dominates the grounds: Statues of prominent pilgrims and patriots adorn the wide front lawn; somber portraits of colonial leaders and religious martyrs are affixed high above the gleaming marble corridors; freedom-fighting murals echo centuries of heritage and evoke generations of influence with iconic Boston names like Adams, Hancock, Revere, Webster, and Winthrop. Fusing past with present are the modern-day political contemporaries who populate these hallowed halls, imparting a heightened sense of purpose and urgency to the business of the Commonwealth: Well-dressed aides and eager young staffers scurry to and fro; small knots of elected officials engage in impromptu, low-toned debate; and the silent, watchful gaze of state police troopers uniformed in full formal dress lend an impression of order, security, and stability. The Massachusetts State House feels, to a visitor, like something right out of a civics textbook, a rich blend of tradition and social progress locked in seamless function for the sole betterment of citizenry.

This illusion is shattered, however, as soon as I inquire at the information kiosk for the location of the special pari-mutuel committee hearings. I figure that since the blue-ribbon racing panel is such a high-profile affair—the agenda shows the entire day booked solid in fifteen-minute blocks, with overflow time allotted in anticipation of the proceedings running past 6:00 PM—that the testimony will almost certainly be heard in the main chamber. But the large central assembly hall is vacant, save for a handful of tourists and schoolchildren snapping photos and gaping at the infamous Sacred Cod, the cheerless, oblong wooden carving that looms large over the legislative entryway.

"You're looking for *what?*" exclaims the baffled attendant behind the info desk, caught off guard by a constituent requesting directions to an actual hearing. "Is there a horse-racing thing here today?" he asks a co-worker, irritably flipping through a clipboard of schedules. "Oh, here it is: 'Special Commission on Horse and Dog Racing Industry in the Commonwealth.'" The gentleman's intonation is condescending, implying that I should have inquired by using the full and proper name of the committee. "That's over in B2—down in the annex."

Down in the absolute bowels of the State House is more like it, and apparently next to the boiler room, judging by the suffocating heat.

It's fifteen minutes before the scheduled 9:45 AM start for the hearing, and the place is already jammed with anybody and everybody having to do with pari-mutuel racing in Massachusetts, as well as a supporting cast of blue-collar characters awaiting a legislative decision on their future. The warm spring morning had begun with unexpected rain showers, and the combination of damp weather, a standing-room crowd in heavy winter coats, and a full-blast heater that no one seems to know how to shut off has conspired to make everyone uncomfortable and edgy. Packed, cramped and hot, room B2 reeks of wet, humid wool, bringing to mind the old cliché about lambs lined up for slaughter—and this is *before* any testimony on the state of the sport even begins.

Disturbingly, the only empty seats are in the front of the room, at the tables reserved for the thirteen blue-ribbon panelists. Several of the committee members are not present, and a few other regulators and legislators rotate in and out of the proceedings without a word, presumably to attend to important business elsewhere. The early speakers on the agenda are oddly matched and disjointed: A representative from defunct Great Barrington Fair—the Berkshires bullring that hasn't hosted a horse race since closing amid allegations of scandal and insolvency—practically *demands* that the committee consider his racetrack for any perks that might be granted to other licensees, until a panelist reminds him that his venue has not held a valid racing license for nearly three years. An animal-rights group called Grey2K testifies in favor of abolishing dog racing at Wonderland and Raynham-Taunton. But a committee member familiar with the organization's shock tactics gets the spokeswoman to admit that her graphic photograph of an abused greyhound was *not* taken at one of the state's two dog tracks as implied, but in actuality is an oft-used file photo that originates from Spain. By the time the head of the Massachusetts harness horsemen's union delivers a rambling, unfocused plea on behalf of his embattled brethren at Plainridge Race Course—the testimony is so vague and ill-defined that a reporter standing next to me quietly inquires if I think the man is drunk—the first four hours of the blue-ribbon hearings have already unfolded as an excruciating blur of petty griping without an obvious game plan. And although Suffolk Downs has yet to have its say, I can't help but get the sick, sinking feeling that if you are a panelist on this commission and don't know one party from another, the disjointed clashing of individual entities only serves to degrade the entire industry as a whole.

The lone common thread in most of the presentations is that Massachusetts racing is a runaway train going nowhere fast, and that the state had better step in and apply the brakes before the industry self-destructs. For years, this has been the catch-22 that has enabled the clannish Massachusetts legislature to sidestep the issue of true pari-mutuel reform: Regulators constantly point out that fragmentation among the state's forever-squabbling racetracks is what prevents them from passing meaningful laws that would revamp the industry. Wonderland Park (the Sarkises) and Raynham-Taunton (the Carneys) have been family owned and operated for decades; both dog tracks are well-connected politically. Suffolk Downs is by far the largest provider of racing industry jobs and revenue, but as a cumbersome limited liability company, it negotiates change with the alacrity of an ice floe.

Plainridge and the whole Standardbred set are fringe players, just pesky enough to get in the way. Although everyone seems to agree that changes to the current structure are needed, infighting over details and minor percentages always ends up forcing a stalemate that sinks legislative action. Yet on the few occasions when the four Massachusetts tracks *do* manage to present a unified front, Beacon Hill turns instantly suspicious and hesitant, as if the very nature of group agreement must mean that the racetracks are conspiring to hatch a plan of unprecedented greed and avarice. As a result, nothing gets accomplished under those defensive circumstances, either, and the Bay State racing industry goes back to finger-pointing and internal arguing, with nothing to show for its trouble.

During the hearings, the feedback from panelists on the blue-ribbon committee is emphatic and single-minded: *Slot machines are not a realistic issue; don't even ask for them. Of course, we'll have to toss you a bone because otherwise the Commonwealth will have all of these unskilled, unemployable people on welfare, but it will not be nearly as big a bone as you hope, want, or need.* It is both insulting and disheartening to hear people who know very little about the inner workings of the sport operating with such a reactionary, robotic mindset. Perhaps I shouldn't have been naive enough to expect it, but there is no talk of proactive overhaul, no mention of Massachusetts aspiring to become a leader in the pari-mutuel industry, no overall goal of the state setting an example rather than following the herd. It is alarmingly evident that this specially appointed body has no progressive tools up its sleeve that it will recommend to the legislature, nothing to raise the profile of the game and revenues for the state, nothing other than a fresh Band-Aid and a pat on the back.

Leaning against the back wall of this blazingly hot basement, I know it is only a matter of time before one of the committee members puts in his two cents' worth about how the racetracks better get their collective act together *before* petitioning this busy group of lawmakers, and it is Senator Michael Morrissey who is first to chide the pari-mutuel participants with this familiar, well-worn Beacon Hill scolding. "I would urge the tracks to work out a solution," he brays, pausing at the podium for dramatic emphasis to allow the news cameras to click and flash. "Because you may not like the solution we come up with."

Still, the hearings provide a few bright spots. Jim Greene, an active proponent of education, health assistance, and substance-abuse treatment for Suffolk Downs backstretch workers, offers poignant remarks about people who toil below poverty levels to support higher-ups in the food chain. Aimee Hall, whose Massachusetts family has been involved in Thoroughbred breeding and racing for three generations, gives emotional testimony about how she and her husband, jockey Jose Caraballo, have to pack up and move their family out of state to earn a modest living, following a too-long list of friends and acquaintances who have been forced to do the same. In a way, it's like hearing people give a eulogy at their own funerals.

Suffolk Downs is poised to give a polished presentation, but by the time our 1:35 PM time slot arrives on the agenda, nineteen other groups have already had their turn at the microphone. For months, Bob O'Malley has strategized how he will use the track's allotted fifteen minutes to convince legislators and regulators to help, but like anything else, timing and placement are everything. With the scheduled lunch break still an hour away, the blue-ribbon panelists entrusted with the improvement of our industry could not possibly look any more pained, bored, or annoyed with the repetitive proceedings and stifling surroundings. Sterling Suffolk Racecourse needs to impress upon these political powers that Thoroughbred racing is important, that the shackles of the state must be loosened for it to flourish, and that *purses, purses, purses* are the linchpin in the whole $622-million betting equation that churns an additional $255 million in economic impact. If the Commonwealth of Massachusetts will clearly define which competitive tools it will make available to racetracks, the industry can most definitely survive, and possibly even thrive.

Armed with potent fiscal information, the articulate O'Malley is flanked by a pair of highly qualified experts retained by Suffolk Downs to drive home these emphatic points. He first introduces Michael Shagan, the renowned New York attorney credited with inventing the legal framework for the nation's largest OTB system and for crafting the federal legislation that became the landmark Interstate Horse Racing Act of 1978. Then Bob presents Reverend Richard McGowan, S.J., a leading gambling researcher and well-respected professor of economics at Boston College. The presence of a Jesuit priest mixed up in the business of betting raises more than a few eyebrows in the muggy hearing room, and the panel moderator cannot resist slipping in a rhetorical quip that unwittingly serves as bleak summation of the insiders' overall tone toward pari-mutuel racing.

"I can only assume," the moderator says with a smirk, nodding in the general direction of Father McGowan, "that Suffolk Downs is hoping for some sort of divine intervention?"

CHAPTER FIVE

SPRINGING ETERNAL

That which does not kill us makes us stronger.
—FRIEDRICH NIETZSCHE,
Twilight of the Idols

AN ANONYMOUS CUSTOMER leaves this sarcastic request in the grandstand suggestion box today: "Sirs—You need more obscene yelling. It makes it more enjoyable here."

At least I think the writer means it to be sarcastic.

To say Suffolk Downs is rife with colorful characters would be the understatement of the century. Sometimes, when immersed in the day-to-day atmosphere of a large, urban betting factory, it is easy for the distinction between acceptable racetrack behavior and what passes for "normalcy" in other environments to become blurred, if not outright obliterated. To outsiders, the racetrack can be an intimidating, mystifying place with odd people performing unusual rituals. But diehard racetrackers view the ways and social structure of our own insular, timeless enclave as a welcome sanctuary from the maddening sameness of the so-called real world. One jaded press-box regular, a retired Boston narcotics detective who's seen his share of strange folk, recently put it like this: "In society, there's no such thing as dysfunction anymore. In fact, to be *functional* is now a dysfunction. At least at the racetrack, you can safely operate under the assumption that everyone here is off-kilter, because for the most part, our weirdos are all relatively harmless underneath."

That analysis helps explain someone like The Pimp, a customer we in the press box have studied both up close and from afar over the years. No one seems to know The Pimp's real name, but guessing by his appearance and demeanor, it is very likely that this gentleman would approve of the nickname bestowed upon him by the PR staff. An imposingly large older black man, The Pimp struts about the grandstand in a vintage 1970s suit, sporting enormously wide lapels, a feather-and-fur fedora above his gleaming, gold-toothed smile, and a ram's head cane that he waves recklessly in alternating fits of euphoria and rage. The Pimp follows the races only sporadically, but his real talent is handicapping fellow members of the betting public, attempting to charm them into parting with a couple of bucks for a wager to tide him over until he strikes it rich, or if he's lucky, money for a bet *and* a little something from the bar.

Once, while riding the Green Line downtown on a day off, I caught sight of The Pimp at the other end of a crowded subway car, unintentionally terrifying a group of college girls with his charismatic shtick. To defuse the situation, I walked over and started talking horses. The Pimp forgot all about the sorority sisters and started sizing me up, trying to figure out how I knew he liked the races and probably also attempting to calculate how much of a mark I might be. "*Everyone* at Suffolk Downs knows you, my man," I told him. "You hold court in the grandstand every single day." By the end of the train ride, The Pimp had invited me home for dinner to meet his wife. "My bitch makes the best damn pork roast in all of Boston," he bragged, playing up his old-school gangsta demeanor, hoping to pique my interest. I declined, but pitched in five bucks for a bottle of wine so he wouldn't have to go home to his old lady empty-handed.

There are other endearingly eclectic racetrackers who float in and out of the Suffolk Downs periphery. You see them every day for months, then they're gone. But as soon as something clicks in your brain and you start wondering *Whatever happened to* . . . the character in question shows up as if he or she had had never been away, right back in the same place with the same routine and mannerisms as when you'd last seen that person many moons before.

Any hardscrabble inner-city racetrack counts among its core customers various loners, lost souls, laborers, tipsters, street toughs, cops, and criminals, all grinding and gambling in collective desperation, all in search of an edge against the fascinating vagaries of logic, luck, and life. These characters are not just the cogs of a small, struggling track like Sufferin' Downs but are the unacknowledged supporting cast for an entire industry. They don't get counted in marketing surveys, and their voices aren't represented in roundtable discussions or symposium panels. But they certainly do have opinions, although largely they remain content to restrict their prejudices to the maddeningly fascinating game of moving money through mutuel windows. At so many levels, horse racing is an every-man-for-himself endeavor. As one of the few betting games in which players must outfox each other rather than leverage cleverly against the house, it doesn't take long to figure out that the truly successful bettors are the ones who keep quiet about it. Egos abound at the track, but it's a pretty safe bet that the anonymous handicapper on the roof taking wind measurements or the poker-faced gent in the last row of the grandstand with his multicolored felt pens is a more formidable foe than the loudmouth in the Turf Club who crows about being comped for valet parking, brags about how much he bets, demands free meals, and pompously overstates his winnings.

One thing that always surprises outsiders is the almost total lack of violence among racetrack patrons. In fact, I can't recall ever seeing a single instance of physical aggression in the Suffolk Downs grandstand. I've heard local railbirds spew vitriol-laced tirades. I've seen brawls on the backstretch, short-fused jockeys taking a pop at one another in the locker room, and even tipsy track executives battling at holiday parties. Yet despite all my time at the East Boston oval, I have never once seen a horseplayer throw a punch at a fellow racing fan in anger.

Sit in the boozy bleachers on a summer evening at Fenway Park or wade through the rowdy tailgaters in the aftermath of a New England Patriots football game, and I guarantee you'll see fists flying sooner rather than later. But fighting among patrons at the racetrack, that alleged incubator of all degeneracy? Never at Suffolk Downs, as far back as I can recall. Even the track's infamous mobster shootout in

1982 comes with a humorous sidebar that illustrates the reflexive priorities of horseplayers in the face of mortal danger: Caught in the crossfire, legend has it that clubhouse fans scrambled madly for cover—but only after first making sure they had snatched their *Racing Forms* and track programs from the tables so they wouldn't be inconvenienced when the gunshots ceased. Or like the other day, when the fire alarm screamed to life while I was walking through the mezzanine before the sixth race: Not a single soul got up to leave, nor did anyone seem even remotely concerned that a ferocious blaze might be ripping through the grandstand. The calm was surreal while the piercing (luckily false) alarm blared, and the collective attitude seemed to be "Who the hell can worry about being trapped in a burning building when post time for the next race is just two minutes away?"

On July 4, 1966, thanks to a colossal coincidence of impulse and fate, the most bizarre incident in the history of Suffolk Downs was also captured on film as one of the most vivid strange-but-true images in horse-racing photography. As a field of talented two-year-olds soared through the homestretch to decide the Closing Day feature, Happy Voter and Taunton emerged to lead the Mayflower Stakes pack inside the final furlong. At the same time, a fan later described in press reports as having "emotional problems" vaulted both the chain-link grandstand fence and the outer rail of the racetrack, sprinting straight into the path of the onrushing Thoroughbreds.

Dressed in a dapper suit and tie—underscoring the nostalgic tidbit that *everyone* used to get dressed up for the races, even those contemplating suicidal acts—the flailing gentleman arrived at the finish wire at the same time as Happy Voter and startled jockey Frank Ianelli, who swerved his horse just enough to spin the waving, screaming fan directly into the path of favored Taunton and Joe Spinale before scampering free to win the race. Although knocked off stride, the man on the track never fell, only grazing Taunton before miraculously avoiding certain trampling by the trailing horses. Track photographer Henry Carfagna instinctively activated a backup camera affixed to the inner rail, and by the luck of the shutter, when he developed his film, a perfectly framed close-up of the ordeal appeared on print. The infamous photo was picked up by wire services, shown in next-day newspapers as far away as Europe, and shortly thereafter featured in a full-page spread by *Life* magazine.

Yet the zany story doesn't end there: Allegedly, when the now-defunct *Boston Record-American* ran the shot, a copy editor tagged the picture with a headline that highlighted the "deranged fan" who caused the chaos. According to press-box lore, the man in the photograph—after being released from police custody and, presumably, psychiatric evaluation—took offense at the editor's choice of terminology and sued the *Record-American* for libel. Since the newspaper could not substantiate its claim that the gentleman's highly atypical behavior was enough to legally brand him as "deranged," the fan is said to have scored a sizable judgment for defamation of character.

So what's the moral of the story?

You can label Suffolk Downs fans anything you like. Truly, they are a fervently diverse and unusual breed.

Just don't call them crazy.

AFTER THE STATE HOUSE HEARINGS, I hit the road over the first weekend in April for my last chance at consecutive days off until the season ends after the MassCap, taking the train to New York City for a visit with a college frat brother who has recently passed the bar exam. It is strange to sleep in late and to experience what people actually *do* on a Saturday other than go to the racetrack. It is pleasant to have the afternoon off, but still, I have this uneasy feeling that I am missing something, that I should be somewhere else.

On several occasions over the weekend, I am asked what I do for a living. If the small sample of responses are any indication of how the general public perceives the Thoroughbred industry, the game just might be in need of an image upgrade.

At my buddy's law office, a seventy-year-old attorney tells me he hasn't been to the races in a few years, since a retirement party for his pal "Cappy," the longtime announcer at Belmont Park. After informing me that the game just ain't the same as back in the good old days, he then asks if jockey Con Errico—"a smart, smart Italian kid"—still rides on a regular basis.

My guess is that it's been more than "a few years" since this gentleman visited a racetrack. The announcer to whom he refers is Fred Caposella, who retired around the time I was born, nearly three decades ago. I explain that it's been quite a while since Con Errico was in the saddle, although I elect not to mention that the reason is because Con lived up to his name by earning a ten-year federal prison sentence for race fixing back in the 1970s.

The next evening in a Brooklyn bar, a foreign-affairs graduate student tells me that she knows nothing about horse racing other than that her friend's uncle was a harness driver who got mauled in a vicious accident at Monticello Raceway. But, she adds, that's not what truly bothers her about the sport.

"It's that *environment*," she exclaims with apparent shock and a touch of sympathy, unable to comprehend that I actually enjoy the racetrack. "How do you *deal* with those *people* on a daily basis?" Keep in mind that this graphic perspective of horror comes from a young lady who, several minutes earlier, told me that she recently completed a ten-week project interviewing prison-camp survivors in war-ravaged Azerbaijan.

Either things aren't as bad as I thought in Eastern Europe, or they're worse than I ever imagined at Suffolk Downs.

THE FIRST NEWS that greets me when I return to work after my April Fool's excursion is that Roger Goyer, a fifty-seven-year-old trainer from Montreal with a scrape-along reputation and a two-horse stable that hasn't won a race all year, was arrested by Revere police over the weekend on charges of selling crack cocaine through a hole in the Suffolk Downs stable fencing. Allegedly, the cops had been lured to his setup by following the increased traffic of prostitutes who had begun to flock to the area in broad daylight, lining up to score a narcotics fix like people ordering coffee at the Dunkin' Donuts drive-through across the street.

"Welcome back," says Bish.

But today I have little time for quelling public-perception fires. This afternoon I am subbing in the announcer's booth for Larry Collmus, who has flown out of town to interview for a race-calling position at a prestigious top-tier track. Although no one at Suffolk Downs wants to see Larry leave, no one can blame him for scouting around for greener pastures, considering the uncertainty surrounding racing's future in East Boston.

Collmus schooled me to be his backup at Suffolk Downs in the winter of 1992, my first full season in the Boston press box. In a vacant room adjacent to the announcer's booth, I would call practice races into a tape recorder, then after each contest was made official, Larry and I would huddle in his office with the sound turned down on the TV replay while he critiqued my style and cajoled me to improve. Race-calling basics are easy to articulate—be informative rather than entertaining, rely on the jockeys' silks rather than saddle-towel numbers, and when you get in a jam, regroup at the top of the pack—but putting those skills into practice is another ball game entirely. The first time I went live on the mike can be likened to the first time I had sex: I was too nervous to know what was really going on, it was over quicker than I thought it would be, and all I *really* knew for sure was that I liked it and wanted to do it again.

To this day, I can recall both the winner of the first race I ever announced (a speedy young filly named Please Answer) and, shortly thereafter, the name of the first horse I mistakenly called a winner (Faces Up, a thirteen-year-old gelding whose muddy silks, saddle towel, and markings were indistinguishable to my untrained eye during a rainstorm). Art form or not, I quickly learned that the key to competently calling races is to recognize that the fear of making an ass out of yourself can be an outstanding motivator. The argument could easily be made that calling a live horse race is the most difficult job in all of sports announcing, and a detailed job description might look something like this:

You must correctly and quickly identify up to a dozen unpredictable animals charging in a pack at thirty-five miles an hour in tight formation in variable weather conditions and under limited visibility from upward of a half-mile away through a set of binoculars. The names, numbers, and multicolored silks will change for every one of the nine (or more) races per day, although the one visual certainty will be that the fast-moving group of horses will almost always be the same color (brown) against a noncontrasting (also brown) dirt background. Once you have identified each horse, you must verbally call out each running position and offer an instantaneous but brief bit of commentary for each runner as it occurs without the benefit of hindsight, replay, or close-up angle, and you must furthermore call out this information in an accurate, concise, and intelligible manner over an open microphone before thousands of live viewers and tens of thousands of others watching via satellite. Performing these tasks correctly will guarantee you nothing, but one simple screwup gives paying customers license to excoriate your very soul and cast aspersions in your general direction, often invoking or implying the character of your mother or other loved ones.

It's also worth mentioning that the pay isn't great at first, you work every weekend and holiday, and that no matter how good you are, there will always be people who just plain don't like your style or much prefer the guy who was there before you. In addition, there will always be rank amateurs certain of the fact that they can perform this thankless task much better than you ever could, and if you *do* ever consider stepping away from such a coveted position, there will be no shortage of professional and wanna-be word-slinging horse hollerers ready and willing to take your place.

But the flip side is obvious: You get paid to call horse races for a living. How can you beat that? Working as a racetrack announcer is a definite rush. And any race-caller who denies this delirious, ego-boosting aspect of the job is most certainly lying.

I haven't announced a race since Closing Day at Suffolk Downs the previous summer, and admittedly, I am not exactly feeling my best for today's program, probably because my throbbing body feels as if it needs a vacation as the result of overzealous vacationing with an old drinking buddy over the course of the previous three days. Right off the bat, the rust on my race-calling skills is evident—I stumble over the wording of the first two finishers in the opener, then blow the photo call for the show position in the fourth race, inverting Plucky Lady and Buckaroo's Lady at the wire. But as the day goes on, I get into a groove, calling several tight finishes (correctly this time). As the afternoon comes to an end, I feel as if I'm hitting my best stride. Any gambler in the grandstand knows this feeling: As soon as the final horses of the day cross the finish wire, that's when you finally feel like you've got it all figured out.

"Just like falling off a bike, right?" says Bish when I return to the press box after the ninth race, binoculars in tow.

"It's the one time I'm glad we're in the midst of a horse shortage," I reply, battle scarred but not beaten, ready to medicate myself with a good, strong cocktail. "Thank God I only had to call six or seven in each race."

VETERAN CONDITIONER Al Borosh, who holds the Suffolk Downs record for most training titles with nine and is currently second in the seasonal standings, becomes the latest local to join the exodus south to Delaware Park, which opens on Saturday for its eight-month embarrassment of riches disguised as a race meet. He is quoted by Ed Gray in the April 4, 2000, *Boston Herald* as being reluctant to leave, but like fellow trainers Mike Catalano and Aimee Hall, the decision for Borosh is one of economics over emotions.

When you want to continue to run a first-class operation, it's just not very profitable right now to race at Suffolk Downs at this time. I've been here since 1973. I consider this my home, even though I'm originally from Philadelphia. I've dedicated so many years to the business in this area. It's been good to me and I like everybody here. Unless the state is to get something going for the horsemen, the Massachusetts breeders' program and the owners, the future is bleak here. I don't want to have to make the move permanent, but it might have to come to that.

In the grandstand this afternoon, a gentleman I do not recognize flags me down amid the sparse Tuesday simulcast crowd and asks when I'm leaving. I figure he must have me confused with somebody else.

"Where am I supposed to be going?" I ask him.

"Oh, I don't know," he replies. "I just figured sooner or later, you'd be jumping ship like everybody else."

JOE HAMPSHIRE gets another win on this early April afternoon, expanding his runaway lead in the local riding standings to seventy-three tallies. Since Jose Caraballo and Harry Vega, tied for second at fifty-one wins each, have both bolted Boston for Delaware Park, Hampshire's next-closest competitor is intense rookie Dyn Panell, who has forty-two wins while riding forty-four fewer races than the leading veteran. Hampshire's sole score doesn't come easily though, as the victory aboard Buddy's Georgy in the second race comes sandwiched between twin spills from the starting gate in races 1 and 4.

In the opener, Hampshire has the reluctant call aboard dangerous maiden Jeremy Hill, the horse who roughed up valet Sal DiMeo last month. Joe almost manages to get his fractious steed settled during the post parade and pre-race warm-ups, but the four-year-old viciously assaults the starting gate in the short time between being loaded and waiting for the latch to spring. Firmly planting his forward feet as a brace, the rangy, awkward colt torques his hind end against the rear of the padded steel enclosure. Then, without warning, he shifts gears and launches himself forward, bashing his neck and shoulders against the front of the barrier. Hampshire, jostled and off balance but still in the irons, elects to bail out the back of the stall but does so just as Jeremy Hill springs back into reverse. The jockey lands awkwardly in the deep dirt behind the starting gate, dusts himself off, shakes his head, and remounts.

As they leave the six-furlong chute, Hampshire breaks Jeremy Hill to the back of the pack and keeps him outside and away from potential trouble all the way down the backstretch. He manages a halfhearted turn of foot around the bend, but at the top of the lane it is clear that Hampshire does not have the horse to finish anywhere even close in this lowly $5,000 maiden claimer. Give Em Your Best, in career start number twenty, finally hits the winner's circle, wiring the field by 3-1/2 lengths. Through binoculars, I watch a good three-way photo-finish battle for last place between Jeremy Hill and double-digit long shots Fames Case and Cryogenic. Joe wins this race-within-a-race by a nose over the two longest shots on the board.

"Yeah, there's something wrong with that horse," Hampshire grumbles while eyeing the replay above his locker and changing for the second event. "I don't know if I want to deal with him any more."

Prior to the fourth, Hampshire is rocketed out of the back of the starting gate, this time right in front of the stands while attempting to calm another rowdy mount, 17-to-1 long shot Who Is Absent. With a strenuous flick of her flank, the angry filly bucks the 116-pound jockey high off her back. Hampshire lands hard and limps around for a half minute before ambling back up the back of the starting gate and climbing aboard for a forgettable sixth-place finish.

"Another day at the office," he says after the race, stripping down and suiting up for the next contest.

EVERY DAY for six weeks I have been checking vigilantly for the name Saratoga Ridge to appear in the entries. When the eleven-year-old last won for Mike Catalano on February 27, I had hoped he would remain in Boston with the trainer's Suffolk Downs division. But the Ridge finally resurfaced on the Delaware Park workout listings last week, so I knew his next start would be on the mid-Atlantic circuit.

This afternoon the roan gelding is entered at Pimlico Race Course in Baltimore, his first start outside New England in nearly five years. Although I would rather see my favorite gray competing locally for purely sentimental reasons, I figure Saratoga Ridge has as good a shot as any steed to turn things around for the struggling Team Catalano. Mike's horses in Maryland have only won once in the past three weeks, continuing an uncharacteristic cold streak, and rumors are rampant that Michael Gill, his wheeling-and-dealing boss, is ready to pull the plug on their rapidly souring business relationship.

The more I learn about this intensely driven mortgage tycoon turned horse trader, the less I like Michael Gill. By all appearances, Thoroughbred racehorses are little more than commodities in his profit equation, disposable entities that must either win or get written off. Rocky relationships with the trainers Gill employs—six have been hired, fired, or are somewhere in the middle so far this season—indicate a similar impatience with people who provide the hands-on care for his equine investments. Although Gill justifies his impulsive decisions by making it emphatically clear he is a businessman first and not a horse hobbyist who intends to waste money, the methods behind his madness look far better on paper than they do in real life.

Recently, an incident that underscores Gill's mercurial personality occurred on the Suffolk Downs backstretch. The Media Relations Department had received an e-mail from a horse worker in South Carolina who was trying to track down a Thoroughbred she once helped raise as a yearling. The woman had learned that the horse was plodding along in Boston for a $4,000 claiming tag, and she wanted its present owner to know that if and when the gelding was ready to retire, she would like a shot at purchasing him to ensure the animal had a safe home after his racing days were over.

I dispatched one of the press-box interns to the barn area to track down Gill, who had recently claimed the horse in question. I figured that at the very least, as the racetrack's leading owner, he would like the opportunity to acknowledge the woman's kind offer. The student volunteer found Michael beneath one of his shed rows, vociferously chewing out one of his rotating racehorse conditioners, and the benign act of delivering a copy of the e-mail soon escalated into a skirmish reminiscent of trying to serve someone a subpoena. Unleashing a tirade of profanity, the high-profile horse owner allegedly told the quaking intern that he wanted nothing to do with any sort of horse offer from a stranger, didn't want to discuss or even read the e-mail, and furthermore, demanded to know what the hell some unknown youngster was doing snooping around his racing stable. Then Gill unceremoniously ordered the kid to leave.

"Maybe he was having a bad day," I explained to the shaken intern, regretting that I had sent him. But then, I thought back on everything I knew about Michael Gill—a history of equine drug violations, lengthy suspensions, aggressive claiming tactics, conspiracy theories, and abrasive personnel firings fueled by a ruthless, win-at-all-costs attitude—and I didn't really believe the apologetic pretext spilling out of my mouth in the man's defense. I got the feeling the intern didn't buy my lame, half-hearted explanation either.

Looking at the Pimlico program, I am surprised to see that Catalano has elected to start the Ridge in blinkers today, a piece of equipment that the ancient gelding hasn't worn in seven seasons. The sudden switch strikes me as odd because the addition of a restrictive eye covering is something a trainer is likely to try with a young horse who has trouble focusing attention, not a seasoned eleven-year-old with 124 lifetime starts under his girth. Then another subtle change in the simulcast program catches my eye: Since his last start at Suffolk Downs, the ownership of Saratoga Ridge has also changed. Previously, the steed had raced under the listing "Cat II Stable," the name used by Mike Catalano for his personal Thoroughbred interests. Now the ownership line reads "Michael Gill," and I cringe to make the connection between the abrupt transfer of the horse, the inexplicably rash alteration of his equipment, and what it all means in the long run for a hard-trying horse in the declining years of a highly competitive, entertaining, and productive career.

The race itself is an afterthought, a mere prelude to my concerns over what will happen next to Saratoga Ridge. The old gray tries in vain to chase the pace, never really sinks his teeth into the steering bit, never truly digs in, and backpedals to fifth, beating only one horse in a six-horse field.

A DRY, hot wind is gusting from off the mainland, way hotter than usual for early April. At first the warm air feels welcome, but slowly, instinctively, I pick up the ominous vibe that something is amiss with the elements. Wind pummels the glass-and-concrete grandstand in surges, opposite from the way the breeze usually blows in off the sea. The infield flags are straight out horizontal, and small but powerful cyclones of losing tickets, newspapers, dirt, leaves, and concessions debris whiplash endlessly in tight circles on the concrete grandstand apron.

About the time the seventh race goes off, something is obviously burning either nearby or in the ductwork that feeds the press box. I jump up onto my desk to sniff the air vents for signs of trouble but can't quite pinpoint the source.

"I think it's out there," says Bish, pointing in the general direction of the racetrack.

I glance outside and catch a glimpse of the bright and breezy home-stretch suddenly obscured and overshadowed by a large cloud that abruptly blocks the soft April sunlight. Moving to the windows and craning my neck higher, I look up to see that the shadow is not caused by a cloud at all, but by an enormous and persistent belch of dark, foul smoke wafting over the entire racetrack from something ablaze upwind in the waterfront area of East Boston.

"Smells like an insurance claim to me," says Bish, dropping a maudlin hint about the region's notorious arson-for-profit reputation while closing our windows to avoid the heavy, cloying fumes.

Taking the back stairway to the roof, I see that something big— *really* big—is burning just south of Suffolk Downs over by the airport. Although I can't tell exactly where, a dense, noxious column is rising rapidly about a half mile away, framed by the Boston skyline in the background and the thirty-five-foot-tall Virgin Mary shrine on the adjacent hill to the fore.

Downstairs in the press box, we see on TV that several local news channels already have helicopters at the scene and have interrupted programming for a breaking-news alert. A nine-alarm blaze engulfs the century-old Orient Heights Yacht Club, and the fire has already ravaged a half dozen boats and destroyed two homes in the tightly built neighborhood. Over 200 firefighters have been called in for containment purposes because the blasting wind is shooting the flames sideways, spreading glowing embers all around the area.

At one point, it becomes difficult to even see the horses on the track. Fans vacate the open outdoor grandstand concourse on an otherwise fine spring day, but the industrial smell of charred soot penetrates the building and follows them inside. Still, without interruption, the show goes on.

The afternoon elapses, live racing comes to a close, and down the street, the fire is brought under control. The racetrack property is spared from damage, but the acrid, caustic taste of devastation lingers all night, waiting for the winds of change to clear the air at Suffolk Downs.

THE PUNISHING GUSTS continue, but racing does not after only four events on the Sunday program.

Being located adjacent to the Atlantic Ocean does not exactly help, but the severe Boston breezes do not limit their damage to Suffolk Downs. Downtown at Fenway Park, maintenance work for tomorrow's Red Sox season opener has to be halted when part of the left field screen atop the thirty-seven-foot-high Green Monster is ripped from its moorings by a 50 mph blast. At several other racetracks as far west as Ontario and as far south as Pennsylvania, the blustery conditions cancel racing completely.

"When the horses are blowing around, you can't be righteous with the public," jockey Joe Hampshire says to one of the interns sent to

NOT BY A LONG SHOT

gather locker-room quotes. Several press-box degenerates chuckle at the jockey's sudden concern for the fans, noting that none of Hampshire remaining mounts looked "live" enough to win anyway.

"I don't really have a problem with this," says a weary Bob O'Malley, explaining management's position to media members. "They are 100-pound people trying to steer 1,000-pound horses."

It is the eighth overall cancellation at Suffolk Downs so far this season. The track has now lost either a full or partial racing card because of cold temperatures, snowfall, a frozen surface, a thawing surface, human error, and on at least one arguable occasion, apathy. An overabundance of hot air can now be added to that unique list.

IN THE EIGHTH RACE, Bish gives out improbable bomb Wanton Discovery in his program handicapping selections. At 51 to 1, the colt rallies smartly to nail third. He pays $17.60 to show and keys a juicy $1,359.20 trifecta. Both prices are huge, considering the favorite won the race.

There are horseplayers in the Suffolk Downs grandstand who swear by Jim Bishop's race analysis, many of whom blindly bet the horses he ranks 1, 2, 3 for each race. Considering that the unlikely long shot had been soundly beaten in each of his last four starts, I am perplexed by the method behind Jim's madness and ask him to explain the logic behind his selection of Wanton Discovery.

"Well, we ordered out for Chinese food the other night when I was making program picks," Bish retorts, dismissing my mistaken credit for handicapping genius. "It was right in front of me on the menu. Who could resist such an obvious hunch play?"

THE NEW ENGLAND TURF WRITERS ASSOCIATION meets tonight for its semiannual dinner meeting. Although once a robust and active sporting club, the organization has evolved into an anachronistic formality over the decades, now more of a social and charitable entity whose main purpose is to drum up publicity for the sport. Formed in 1943 by an avid gang of racing scribes, the NETWA has its roots in the heyday of horse racing, an era when the Thoroughbred beat was a coveted newspaper position and numerous Boston dailies competed for a racing-hungry readership by jamming the Suffolk Downs press box with as many as three or four staffers per publication. Over time, as interest in major league team sports skyrocketed and pari-mutuel racing slipped into the monotony of a year-round grind, New England tracks went from a position of power to having to resort to begging for ordinary ink and headlines. Now, every few months or so, another local paper decides its sports pages can do without the old-fashioned agate typeface of horse entries and race results.

One by one, as the region's racing journalists die off, they are rarely replaced, and the few who do remain on the beat don't seem to enjoy the ribald camaraderie the old-timers always talk about. After a day at the races, press-box cronies no longer while away the evening over cocktails and companionship, nor do they go out to ball games together or take in a greyhound program under the lights at Wonderland. Once the last race is posted official, the few degenerates who still do show up just go their separate ways and seem glad to be able to do so. Quite frankly, you could roll a bowling ball through the Suffolk Downs press box on any given afternoon with little fear that the sphere would strike a single member of the fourth estate.

Still, at this evening's meeting, there is plenty of business on the turf writers' agenda. Several new members are up for induction, candidates for the annual scholarship awards are discussed, and Larry Collmus is unanimously elected to a third consecutive term as the organization's president. Yet even though the current Suffolk Downs announcer wields the gavel and presides over the proceedings, it is a former Boston race-calling legend who steals the show.

Jim Hannon, or "Big Jim" as he prefers to be called, was the long-time voice of New England racing, with announcing stints at every track in the region at one time or another from 1953 through 1994. Considered one of the most personable horse hollerers of his era, Big Jim also manned the mike at Delaware, Charles Town, Beulah Park in

Ohio, and old Timonium in Maryland, and he is said to have once turned down the prestigious gig of calling the Kentucky Derby at Churchill Downs because he didn't want to uproot his family from Boston to Louisville. A gregarious showman in the old-school sense, Hannon was a natural fit for variety skits and vaudeville acts in his spare time, and for many who tuned in daily for his animated live radio broadcasts, Big Jim *was* New England racing. After twenty-one straight seasons on the job at Suffolk Downs, his trademark booming bass voice went down with the ship when the track closed in 1989, but Hannon resurfaced for a final race-calling fling two years later when Rockingham Park's eccentric announcer was busted for growing marijuana in a secret greenhouse inside his home.

Welcomed back warmly by fans, Big Jim presumably could have called horse races at the New Hampshire track for as long as he wanted. But a single fateful slip of the tongue was his swan song: One afternoon in 1994, after an abysmally slow and particularly forgettable cheap claiming race, Hannon wryly commented to a friend in the announcer's booth about the sorry quality of racing at the Rock. The innocent witticism would have gone unnoticed had Big Jim not forgotten to first turn off his microphone before uttering, "They're all rats. How can anybody even bet on these things?" The gaffe was piped loud and clear to thousands of on-track patrons and co-workers, and was also broadcast to innumerable far-flung simulcast customers, many of whom might have shared the same opinion. But Rockingham management heard the wisecrack, too, and didn't take the remark lightly. Regardless of the truth in his statement, Jim Hannon was ignobly asked not to return after the end of the racing season, and he finally hung up his binoculars for good.

Now, at age seventy-three, Big Jim toils as a mutuel clerk in the Suffolk Downs grandstand, five stories and many memories removed from the prestigious position he once occupied. It is disheartening to have to see a gentleman in his autumn years forced to revisit the sport, hat in hand, accepting practically any job offered just to make ends meet, yet Hannon can always be counted on to be at his good-natured, jolly best at these turf writers' reunions. Immersed among old friends and spouting a never-ending geyser of wistful humor about the glory days, Big Jim reverts to what I imagine he was like at the prime of his personality: mixing, mingling, and swapping fables, jokes, and rumors with his long-retired press-box buddies.

The laughter and the liquor flow, and certain stories always resurface whenever wizened Boston turf writers gather: tales about Big Jim napping between races, waking midrace to call a finish as if nothing had happened. The story about one turf writer who used to bring his dog to the races, until one fateful day the pet pooch became overly excited by seagulls outside the press-box window and fell a hundred feet to his demise. The legend about Hannon's predecessor, ol' Babe Rubenstein, who got blown from his rooftop perch while braving the elements at Rock during the hurricane of 1938. Babe loved to bet, and this yarn is *always* spun whenever Big Jim gets on a roll: One afternoon, Rubenstein suffered a heart attack before the races. As he was being wheeled out of Suffolk Downs on a stretcher, Babe became distraught, insisting that the medics first call his press-box buddy before taking him away in the ambulance. Rubenstein made such a fuss that they waited until Eli Chiat, the longtime *Racing Form* chart-caller, rushed down as instructed. Eli took Babe's outstretched hand and leaned down close, expecting to hear his friend's last gasp. Instead, the announcer slipped his pal a folded sawbuck. "Here's ten bucks," wheezed the Babe. "Make sure you bet the two-two double for me."

Perhaps it's merely the glow of nostalgia that imparts life to these legends, but hearing about an era when racing had true seasons and when going to the races was an actual social *event* makes it seem as if everyone associated with the greatest show on turf back then was a minor celebrity, bit players in a perfectly scripted play that no one ever wanted to end. The racetrack was a microcosm for the lifestyle of postwar America in the mid-twentieth century, a gritty yet grand place where you could dream, scheme, and socialize; win and cry; lose and laugh; or just roll with the punches, knowing that everything would be all right by post time tomorrow. It should come as no surprise that the sport's tragic flaw is the same volatile combination that did in the societal concept of "Americana" itself: Innocence, coupled with an unwillingness to change, eventually reveals itself in the long run as a sucker's bet.

That's not to say that there aren't plenty of young guns willing to embrace an old game under new terms. This evening a new member, a Suffolk Downs press intern, is up for nomination into the NETWA. The impending vote is about to be unanimous so we can move on to other important business—namely dinner—until Big Jim holds up the proceedings by chiming in to voice his opinion.

"What I want to know," Hannon roars—Big Jim doesn't hear so well these days, and his resonant diction raises a few decibels higher every time I hear him— "is does this gentleman meet the *official* criteria for membership?"

The intern looks lost, maybe even a bit worried, because we've already assured him the vote is a mere formality. But every one of the two dozen NETWA members in attendance knows what's coming next: Hannon's rhetorical punch line to an annual fraternal prank.

"I mean does he like to *drink* and *gamble* just like the rest of us? Ah, Ha, Ha, Ha, Ha, Ha, Ha, Ha!" Big Jim's belly laughter sounds like a motorboat roaring to life.

The intern passes both prerequisites with flying colors, then it's on to the eats. But the comedy routine doesn't stop there. Big Jim frequently likes to say he's never met a meal he didn't like. Upon dinner being served, he stands up and cautions everyone with another classic Hannon quip.

"Dig in, boys. But remember: The white part's the plate. Ah, Ha, Ha, Ha, Ha, Ha, Ha!"

Later, when the meeting winds down, the old-timers file out to the parking lot while some of the younger guys, mostly the Suffolk Downs press-box clan, line the bar for a nightcap. Before heading out himself, Jim Hannon makes it a point to stop and congratulate the new intern. Alone by the door, shrugging on his coat, the voice of New England racing pauses, then quietly offers a few words of sage advice to no one in particular.

"One thing to never forget," Big Jim reflects, lowering his tone to its most somber pitch of the evening. "Is that in this game, you always meet the same people on your way back down the ladder of success who you once passed on the way up."

LAST WEEK, nearly eight months to the day since the accident that changed his life forever, paralyzed jockey Rudy Baez obtained his license to operate a motor vehicle using hand controls. Relentless in his physical therapy, the fifty-year-old dean of New England riding is intent on getting back to the track and is eager to accept the open invitation to work for Suffolk Downs in a yet-to-be-determined ambassador-mentor position.

Behind the scenes, management is busily preparing for Rudy Baez Day three Saturdays from now. The homecoming gala will include a meet-and-greet session with fans in the grandstand, special presentations to the fourteen-time leading Suffolk Downs rider and his family, and a rededication in Rudy's name of the $25,000 Faneuil Hall Stakes, a half-century fixture at Suffolk Downs that Baez had won in each of the previous two seasons. Also on that afternoon, Rudy has expressed a desire to be able to drive away from the winner's circle festivities in his specially equipped vehicle, a new car that has been purchased by Suffolk Downs as a discreet gift.

From the first days after his tragedy, almost as soon as Baez regained enough coherence to realize that he could not walk, the deeply religious reinsman made it known that it would be important for him to act as an inspiration to others and to show people that determination, perseverance, and faith can overcome any obstacle, even the loss of legs. Rudy has always been stubborn. He disputes the belief of his doctors that he will never walk again, and many months ago, while enduring the grueling regimen of rehab, he got the idea into his head that he wanted to be able to get into his car under his own power, start it up, and drive out of the winner's circle and up the length of the Suffolk Downs homestretch in front of his fans. He is not at all comfortable with the notion that the last time the New England racing community saw him leave the racetrack, he was a cripple being carried away on a stretcher.

"Everything is going along nicely," Rudy is quoted in today's (April 9) *Boston Globe*. "I'm working hard at my therapy, and I'm getting better. I'm getting there. I feel good. It's time for me to come and see my friends at Suffolk Downs."

Bob O'Malley and Lou Raffetto are just as eager to have Rudy on board, although one thing the Suffolk Downs bosses are adamant about is downplaying the racetrack's role in assisting Baez. Both executives have underscored their desire for the East Boston oval to capitalize as little as possible on the publicity of Rudy Baez Day. Although news about the creation of a special job for Baez and the secret that Suffolk Downs purchased Rudy's hand-controlled Toyota Avalon have already leaked, other sizable expenses—such as the installation of a wheelchair lift to allow Rudy to get from the paddock to the jockeys' room—have remained under the radar of the press and most folks on the backstretch. For an embattled racetrack that has become notoriously frugal, the powers that be are sparing no expense in doing the right thing.

"They have been real humble about that," said a touched Judy Baez in the same *Globe* article about her husband's progress. "We're going to display the car on Rudy's day, to show everybody how he gets around. They don't know it yet, but I am going to put a sign on it that says it was donated by Suffolk."

IN FLORIDA, my dad is in the process of finalizing preparations for shipping his stable north to New England. For the past several weeks, he has been vacillating over whether to take a stab at reclaiming Blackwater, the tenacious sprinter with bad wheels and an even worse temper. He theorizes that the deeper, sandier Suffolk Downs racing strip could help the gelding's notoriously ouchy hocks and that the cooler weather just might be the key to taking the edge off the seven-year-old's malicious attitude.

But it looks as if Paul Thornton has missed his opportunity. Blackwater is entered this afternoon at Tampa Bay Downs, but not for a claiming tag. Riding a three-race winning streak, the gelding's new connections have selected an allowance race for the high-strung steed, and it figures to be a logical spot. Sent off as the 8-to-5 favorite, Blackwater chases a quick pace and is well positioned to pounce. The only trouble is that those fast fractions are set by Irish Bacon, another horse in sharp current form, and his blazing early lead proves insurmountable. Irish Bacon wins by an open ten lengths, and Blackwater is clearly second, 3-1/4 lengths ahead of everyone else in the ten-horse race.

"I'm leaving town in three days, and I guess we won't be seeing this horse in Boston," my father muses. "Still, I've always wondered what the *real* story was with Blackwater, why he didn't pan out in Europe, and how he ended up over here. Now, I guess we'll never know."

The peculiar thing is, as my dad and I chat on the phone trying to fill in the blanks, the key to this mystery is sitting right on my Suffolk Downs desk, buried amid an ever-growing stack of paperwork. Although less than a foot away and staring me straight in the face, the pedigree printouts for the sixty-first Massachusetts Handicap are the last place I would ever look to connect Blackwater's past with his present, because the chasm between world-class graded-stakes racing and lower-level claiming contests is just too huge a gap to be a factor in this particular equine equation.

Or is it?

At the racetrack, part of the allure is that one never knows.

HOWARD LANCI is sporting a new T-shirt today that says "Shut Up and Ride" in big block lettering. In the finale, he does just that.

Crouched atop a 6-to-1 maiden filly named Vitrify, Lanci stalks Joe Hampshire and favored pacemaker Fast Storm all the way around the track before collaring the leading rider and his 8-to-5 shot inside the eighth pole. Lanci and Hampshire hook up in an all-out duel headlong through the final furlong, bobbing back and forth, brushing, thrusting, and banging off each other until the last jump, when Vitrify nails Fast Storm by a nostril at the wire.

The Howitzer, as usual, is ecstatic upon hitting the winner's circle.

He pumps his right fist high. He soars his whip high into the air for his valet to catch. He jauntily removes his helmet for the ceremonial victory photograph, grinning like he's just won the MassCap. Few fans adorn the outdoor apron after the last race on a Saturday, but the handful of remaining customers are treated to an entertaining show even if they didn't bank on hard-luck Howie. Lanci hits the ground running from a leaping dismount, but instead of heading in the direction of the scale for his official weigh-in, Howard abruptly detours the opposite way to take care of another matter first.

For most of the day, a young girl, maybe five years old, has been eagerly watching the colorful spectacle of horses and jockeys with her mom from just behind the winner's-circle fence. Mother and daughter haven't strayed too far from the paddock the entire afternoon, gleefully taking everything in. Yet for the most part, their presence has gone unnoticed or ignored by the boisterous winners who have crowded in and out of the victory enclosure to have their pictures snapped after each race.

Howard Lanci, however, has seen them watching and waiting while dismounting from his own long-shot losers throughout the day, and on a whim he spontaneously decides to give the little girl a thrill on what is very likely her first visit to a racetrack. Looking like a gawky, clumsy kid himself, Howie hops through the tiered flower boxes and shrubbery that line the fence between the public and the paddock, reaches over the railing, and gives his racing goggles to the young fan, fitting them atop the girl's head and grinning proudly when she beams back at him.

Half undressed, flak jacket hanging loosely from his ribcage, Lanci banters and chatters happily with the remaining riders in the locker room as the valets break out the traditional end-of-day cooler of Budweiser. Together, the group watches the full race replay, with Howie narrating his strategy while the others needle Hampshire about how The Howitzer rode the pants off the top jock. I approach Howard in the corner to congratulate him for his well-timed, workmanlike effort, but more importantly to thank him for going out of his way to make an afternoon at the races special for at least one future fan.

"You know, I wish I was a leading rider," Lanci tells me, gazing away for a long, pensive moment before locking his eyes with mine. "I'd give away all my whips, all my saddles, everything. When I won, I'd just give it all away if I could."

AS SUFFOLK DOWNS nears the six-week mark to the region's richest and most historic horse race, to be held on June 3, the behind-the-scenes prep work for the sixty-first MassCap is kicking into high gear. Already, the press office is fielding credential requests for New England's Million Dollar Day of Racing, and recruitment wizard Lou Raffetto now phones or stops by several times daily with updates and additions for the showcase race at the Eastie oval.

Although MassCap Day will draw the biggest crowd of the season with the largest on-track betting handle, it is imperative to point out that the concept of the race as an *event* is much more important to the track in the long run than any short-term profits derived from that single afternoon of racing. The Massachusetts Handicap is the calling card for Suffolk Downs, the one ace in the hole that makes it possible for the gritty urban racetrack to get noticed by key industry players on a national level and by potential customers and skeptical politicians on a local scale. At the sport's major venues, six- and seven-figure graded stakes that draw the sport's top human and equine stars are a ho-hum given. But at a worn-out joint like Sufferin' Downs, where respect never comes easily, a big race is a once-a-year occurrence whose value doesn't go unappreciated.

Lou has just returned from California in an attempt to lure top West Coast horses to Boston for his Grade II baby. If the constant wining, dining, and schmoozing is an effort or a strain for Raffetto, he hides it well. Two years ago I accompanied Lou on one of his infamous recruitment trips, to the Preakness Stakes in Baltimore, and watching him line up horses for the MassCap and its undercard was like observing an indefatigable field marshal aligning troops for battle, all the while relishing the process as much as his end product. Raffetto can simultaneously work a cell phone, entertain guests at his clubhouse table, dart off to the jockeys' room, run into half a dozen old friends and acquaintances on the way back, and still manage to check in with the home front in Boston to see how business is doing, maintaining a witty sense of humor all along the way. On the road, Lou is the first one up in the morning and the last left standing at the end of an evening, and he won't dream of letting anyone else pick up a tab in between. When Raffetto makes a promise, he not only remembers, but delivers, and if one of the consequences of all this self-strategizing and one-man wheeling and dealing is that Lou sometimes holds his MassCap reins a bit too tightly, he has certainly earned that right by investing his emotions and staking his reputation on the outcome.

In the press box, we have mounted a large whiteboard on the back wall of the office to keep track of leading MassCap contenders and their likely status for the race. Lou loves to come up and tinker with the rankings, and this afternoon between races I find him standing behind my desk, arms crossed, staring transfixed at the magic-markered horse names as if willing them to leap off the wall and into his paddock five stories below. As is usually the case whenever the racing boss makes his rounds in the press box, a small entourage of reporters, media staffers, and racing officials soon gathers, and it is not long before Lou begins rattling off probabilities and possibilities for the main event.

At the top of the chart are Behrens and Running Stag, the one-two finishers from last season's MassCap. Next on Raffetto's wish list are Lemon Drop Kid, winner of the Belmont and Travers Stakes, and Vision and Verse, the horse who ran behind him in both races and who also happens to be trained by Bill Mott, Raffetto's old pal from the Cigar days. An up-and-coming Brazilian horse, Out Of Mind, is also supposed to be the real deal, and lesser-known but talented horses like The Groom Is Red and David are also on the bubble. "If it all falls right," Lou says, "this could be our most competitive MassCap."

But "if" is a huge word in horse racing, and Raffetto knows it. He discusses some of the difficulties he anticipates in lining up a stellar MassCap field, not the least of which is the timing of the June 3 race. The handicap division for horses three years old and up is glutted with top money races in late spring, with the Pimlico Special in Maryland scheduled three weeks ahead of Boston's big race and the Stephen Foster Handicap in Kentucky two weeks after it. Both competing stakes boast $750,000 purses, or $150,000 higher than the MassCap. Further complicating matters is the fact that the Foster Handicap will be run over the same track as this year's Breeders' Cup Classic, and smart conditioners will want their horses to have an insurance race over the quirky Churchill Downs strip in case they end up gunning for the $4-million season-ending jackpot. Travel logistics are another issue, as Suffolk Downs must arrange and pay for equine air transport from California and Kentucky if it expects to attract horses stabled in those parts of the country.

"If we have a rematch between Behrens and Running Stag, we'd have a story with some steam," Raffetto explains. "One of the things we're up against is that trainers are going to be looking for a race over the track in the Foster. But still, our race has become an important one on the handicap calendar. Gone are the days when I had to tell Bill Mott where Suffolk was. Cigar and Skip Away both won here, then went on to win the Hollywood Gold Cup. That's a selling point for us.

"There's a possibility, if everything comes together, that we'll have seven or eight top quality horses in the MassCap," Lou continues, thinking realistically yet waxing optimistic. "You know, despite all the competition, we could end up with the best race we've ever had."

AFTER A 1,200-MILE DRIVE from Tampa Bay Downs, my dad arrives home in New England. His first stop—like any road-weary horse trainer—is not the welcome comfort of his own house, but rather the backstretch shed row where his horses will be stabled until the close of the Suffolk Downs season in a little more than a month and a half.

My father has timed the trip to arrive with his carload of tack and training gear one day before the steeds are scheduled to van into Boston via commercial equine carrier. Shipping an entire racing operation, even a modest-sized stable, can be a grueling endeavor. Joyce, his wife and ace assistant, stayed behind to oversee the departure of the outfit and will fly back to Boston tomorrow; this is the way they usually have to work it so that one or the other is always there to personally onload and offload the horses. Thornton Racing Stable now numbers eight Thoroughbreds, with only one—Gold Clearance—remaining from when I visited Florida in February. The old man says he is happy with the turnover of stock but is dead tired from his solo car trip. I volunteer to throw on some old work clothes and leave the press box before the late double to help him unload equipment, set up stalls, and prepare the next morning's breakfast mash so the horses will have a hot meal waiting upon arrival.

A light spring rain is falling but the chilly backstretch air carries the unmistakably pleasant smell of horses, wet straw, fertile mud, and new grass. Although only a quarter mile away from the bustling grandstand and just a tall fence removed from gritty urbanity, today the Suffolk Downs stable area is as close as it ever comes to being tranquil during daylight hours. Most trainers and stablehands have fed their horses early this afternoon, and the few remaining stragglers after 4:00 PM are those who either just had a runner in or have one entered for the nightcap. My line of sight into the far turn is blocked by a wall of shrubbery, but I first hear, then feel, the distant rumbling and muted pounding of Thoroughbreds as they cut the corner for the featured eighth race. From the backstretch point of view, the races are always different: Seen from a gap in the bushes at the three-eighths pole, the thundering field is an indistinct, amorphous blur coming straight at you. There is no cheering, no audible race call, and only a brief flash of color and clarity as the herd splashes into and out of the turn at fifty feet per second. You hear adrenaline-fueled chatter as the jockeys rocket by in tight formation, sharp cracks of leather into horseflesh from reinsmen who sense they have enough underneath them to make a winning move, and the instinctive "Lemme out!" shouts from rivals who know their steeds are spent and have no business being pinned down on the inside rail. After the rhythmic, concussive splashing of the trailing hooves becomes muted by the mud, there is a slight pause before an ambulance and then the track veterinarian's jeep roar by, realistic reminders of the sport's palpable peril. Then it's just wind, rain, and the haunting screech of far-off seagulls, the after-echo of horse racing as it exists in a perfect vacuum without winners, losers, or even an identifiable outcome.

The backstretch PA system blares and breaks the spell, but only momentarily. "Bring 'em on up for the ninth race! Bring ya hosses up for the ninth race, puh-*leeze*!" A young groom wearing head-to-toe rain gear leads a blanketed, bay maiden along the puddled earth-and-asphalt walkway. I wish the smiling girl good luck and we exchange pleasantries. The next Secretariat could be hiding under that dripping nylon sheet at the other end of her shank, but I neither inquire nor care to know the identity of the low-slung horse with curious, attentive ears. Sometimes it's best to step back and take in the anonymous equine atmosphere without clouding one's mind with the myriad of names, statistics, and information that are so integral yet so overwhelming to the basic enjoyment of the game. Purses, betting handles, breeding fees, simulcast surcharges, and profit-loss ledgers drive the frontline economics of pari-mutuel racing. But the promise of possibility exists on every racetrack backstretch, and if you can spot that elusive quality in the eye of a run-of-the-mill racehorse trudging through the mud, you'll blindly invest your entire soul in this sport, no matter the cost.

Back under the cover of Barn 22, I hoist bale after bale of pre-packaged wood shavings—"3.4 Cubic Feet Per Parcel," each one says in big block lettering—into freshly raked stalls as the spring drizzle patters on the rooftop and blows sideways into the plastic-covered stable windows. The shed row is well insulated from the outside world, and the only sound is a repetitive and satisfyingly hollow *whunk* as my work boot splits the center of each brown-papered package, spilling fragrant pine wafers into neat mounds on the damp clay floor. At the entrance to each stall, my dad vertically chalks the nickname of each horse in anticipation of tomorrow's arrival, carefully plotting who he wants stabled next to whom, based on various equine quirks and personality traits. Close scrutiny of the wooden slat walls inside any backstretch barn will reveal layers of the past, season after season of similar hiero-glyphics: faded names, training abbreviations, feeding instructions, and lip tattoo numbers, all once part of some previous tenant's master plan, eventually and inevitably eroding into a jumble of inscrutable Thoroughbred graffiti. Horses and trainers come and go, new plans and aspirations are hatched, and the cycle repeats itself anew.

IN AN ERA of multi-million-dollar races, purse earnings are what sep-arates Thoroughbred racing's glitterati from your average run-of-the-mill racehorse. Without a doubt, big money drives the economics of the industry.

But the overlooked truth is that without the supporting structure of day-to-day low-level claiming contests at small and midsized racing venues nationwide, the upper crust of the profession would cease to exist. Not every Thoroughbred can be a championship-caliber race-horse, and there wouldn't be year-round racing without the meat-and-potatoes steeds who provide the day-in, day-out betting product. For every elite equine superstar who commands a six-figure breeding fee, there are thousands of others who fit the "non-winners of a race in six months" $4,000-level claiming condition at Suffolk Downs, the low-est category there is. For every precious, valuable pearl, someone has to swallow the rest of the oysters.

When it comes time to dole out the Eclipse Awards for the sport's annual championships, the term "winningest horse" is almost exclu-sively understood to mean the horse whose bankroll is the biggest at the end of the season. A top-flight Thoroughbred who wins a handful of high-profile races can immediately vault to championship status based on purse earnings alone. But a steed who cranks out the most actual trips to the winner's circle is highly unlikely to attain front-page status in the *Racing Form*. Arguments abound over which of these two tasks is tougher, but the logic is simple enough: Million-dollar horses shoot for national stakes and have their campaigns carefully mapped out months, if not the entire year, in advance. Conversely, to win a lot of races, you have to enter a lot of races, and that takes its toll on even the most robust runners. Long-range planning on the part of a hard-knocking claimer usually goes as far as the current condition book, or about three weeks.

Although it's only mid-April, a Suffolk Downs horse is tied for second on the national win list. Yashima has quietly gone about business the hard way, favored in nine straight races while overachieving in unlikely situations. She has bounced around in four different barns already this season (Michael Gill has claimed her three times in five months), and with a 5-for-8 record this year, it is no surprise she's popular at the claim box.

It's also no secret that the modestly bred chestnut is not the most physically gifted of horses. One tip-off that a Thoroughbred might be damaged goods comes when new connections drop an acquisition by a level or two right after they've claimed the horse, signaling that the animal might not be worth what they just paid for it. Earlier in the meet, I bet against Yashima for several races in a row simply because she looked so ouchy during pre-race warm-ups. Another time I overheard a couple of jockeys at the lunch counter saying that Yashima was so crippled that she would fall down if she ever raced in the mud. Of course, all this occurred during the fragile-footed mare's three-race win tear in March, and I have since given up trying to beat her. It's bad racetrack karma to root against a horse whose desire vastly exceeds ability.

Today, gunning for the national win lead, Yashima will try $8,000 claiming company, and Jose Delgado has the call because top jock Joe Hampshire has elected to ride Headin Home instead. Stepping into the starting gate, Yashima is 9 to 2 in the betting, her highest odds in more than half a year. She breaks alertly, engages the leaders between fillies at the front of the pack, but then starts to fall back steadily on the turn. Just when it looks like the six-year-old is ready to pack it in, Delgado swings her outside, steering clear of the mud being pelted back by the tiring pacemakers. Yashima pricks her ears and skims swiftly over the oozing surface, gliding atop the slop without difficulty.

When Yashima hits the winner's circle, she is winded and somewhat cranky, not wanting her handlers to touch her or remove the sludge-plastered tack that covers her slick, filthy underbody. The mare doesn't seem to care much for people. Then again, most people don't seem to care that the winningest Thoroughbred in the country rasps out a pay-check-to-paycheck life on the hardscrabble East Boston backstretch.

"She's not the soundest of horses," says Abby Fuller in the press box once the race goes official. Even while several months pregnant, Fuller galloped the delicate mare in the mornings last autumn during the brief time that Yashima resided in her husband's stable. "But she's got it right here," Abby says, lightly tapping her own heart with an index finger, "and you can't teach that."

LONICUT, an undistinguished ten-year-old with a 1-for-34 career record, has gone down in defeat by double-digit losing margins in each of his last five outings at Suffolk Downs. But on this rainy Wednesday, the 4-to-1 old-timer is victorious in the opener, a $5,000 claiming route race restricted to horses who have never won twice.

It is a racing rarity that a Thoroughbred so old is still eligible to compete at a preliminary level populated by young horses who have just broken their maidens, and our computerized database in the press box doesn't go back far enough to ascertain the date of Lonicut's only other career score. Curiosity compels me to the paddock to check out the official Jockey Club foal papers on file with the track identifier, where I learn that the gelding's only other lifetime win came seven years ago, in an $18,000 maiden-claiming sprint at Calder. Glancing at the track program, I notice that none of the five steeds Lonicut beat for lifetime tally number two today were even born the day he broke his maiden back in 1993.

"Some horses," the identifier tells me, tongue firmly planted in cheek, "just take a while to round into their best form."

———

THE FRONT-PAGE HEADLINE atop the April 20 *Boston Herald* bellows, "Pols Boozed, Slept Through Budget Spending Spree," in huge, oversized type and even greater tabloid hype.

The article goes on to explain how during a controversial all-night legislative session last week, "House lawmakers partied, drank and slept their way through an unprecedented spending spree, quaffing beer and wine and napping for long stretches between amendments that added nearly $200 million to the state budget." As the day unfolds, subsequent follow-ups by local media outlets add embarrassing detail to the gluttonous sideshow, with claims that some politicians openly cast ballots for members who were not there and how at one point an inebriated gang of lawmakers shouted a speaker from the floor with chants of "To-ga! To-ga!" in a surreal scene reminiscent of the zany party movie *Animal House.*

Juvenile antics aside, not a single piece of legislation dealing with the survival of the Massachusetts racing industry was voted upon during the bloated budget passage, even though the staggering fiscal extravaganza amounted to nearly twenty times more than Suffolk Downs annually pays in purses to keep its horsemen afloat.

I speak to a beleaguered Bob O'Malley to get his view on this disheartening piece of news. He says our lobbyists think the racing industry is still on deck—yet admits that no one seems to know if the lack of an invite to the raucous Beacon Hill bash is a good or a bad omen for things to come.

But considering that the House has already met thirty-eight times this year, that the legislative session is set to expire at the end of July, and that the special blue-ribbon racing committee has yet to issue a single statement or finding on the subject after more than four months on the job, the odds that pari-mutuel reform will be a priority for Massachusetts politicians are getting longer and longer with each passing hour.

UNDER ORDERS from Michael Gill, trainer Mike Catalano has entered Saratoga Ridge, that stalwart, stubborn gray, for a $7,500 tag at Delaware Park today, the lowest, cheapest level of claiming competition the overachieving gelding has ever faced in 125 lifetime starts.

Catalano continues to sputter on the mid-Atlantic circuit. The horses he has saddled are a collective 4 for 55 since leaving Boston, and the starters at Delaware—the track with astronomical purses that was supposed to be the focal point of the Gill-Catalano invasion—are slogging along at a luckless 1-for-26 pace. Statistics do, on occasion, lie, and to his credit, the usually steady Catalano is starting to see a small turnaround in productivity. Of those twenty-six Delaware steeds, five have run second, with three others finishing third, for a respectable 35 percent in-the-money ratio. But, as Mike is reminded on a daily basis, his boss didn't pump hundreds of thousands of dollars into new horseflesh just so he could say, "Nice try, we'll get 'em next time!"

With his once-cocky boxer's ego giving way to doleful, and at times lonely, introspection, the humbled trainer suffers the consequences of self-doubt as best he can. With both business and reputation at risk, and a wife due to give birth in less than a month, Mike Catalano is spinning his wheels, 350 miles from home and running out of time on his leveraged gamble of striking it rich on the road.

At age eleven, Saratoga Ridge is more than twice as old as any of the five horses entered against him in today's eighth event, and only a few years younger than his teenage apprentice jockey, Abel Castellano Jr. The gray takes in his new surroundings stoically, nodding with indifference as if the quiet, tree-lined Delaware Park paddock is nothing special to him, as if the hustle and bustle of the gritty Boston backstretch, with its low-buzzing jumbo jets and constant clatter of the subway, is more his style. Eyes narrowed and white, wizened head free to gaze all around (Mike Gill's experiment with blinkers lasted exactly one race) the roan gelding with the renegade cowlick sizes up the competition, determining by instinct where he belongs in the pecking order. Adopting a defiant, on-toes stance, the Ridge struts out onto the muddy racecourse, blissfully unaware that a win this afternoon will launch him over and above the $300,000 lifetime-earnings mark, a figure unequaled by his five equine rivals even with every single cent of their career purse totals combined.

The betting public is also sizing up the situation, and when Saratoga

Ridge settles into post position number 4, he is the clear choice to win the race at 13-to-10 favoritism. The wet racetrack should be no problem for the ancient gray, considering he has performed consistently multiple times in the mud. But that's assuming that even though he appears today in front leg-wraps (a bandaged horse is akin to a slightly sore human athlete who tapes his ankles for support), he's still sound, and an honest measure of his true value might be tipped off by the absence of claiming interest in the eleven-year-old. No rival trainer has anted up the seemingly bargain price of $7,500 to purchase Saratoga Ridge, and it is most likely the suspicious nature of his recent races that has scared away any suitors. Claiming a racehorse for relatively short money is like evaluating a used car: Even though there is no obvious body damage, there are lots of miles on the odometer, and it's anyone's guess whether the current owner is bluffing or just wants to unload his property to churn a profit.

When the field bursts from the gate, Saratoga Ridge breaks with the pack, but his young apprentice rider is indecisive. The horse to his immediate left rockets to the lead from post 3, while the gelding to his right stutter-steps from stall 5 and comes out last. Backseated in the saddle, the kid in the middle appears momentarily panicked, and the Ridge gets shuffled back to fifth, an unenviable position from which he must chase a freewheeling pacemaker who has opened a ten-length advantage on the gray in the first sixteenth of a mile in a six-furlong race.

Saratoga Ridge knows what he's supposed to do, even if his fledgling jockey doesn't. With a burst of annoyance, he takes off without being roused, darting to the outside upon sensing the loosening of the reins by his apprentice passenger. This is what's known as "giving a horse his head," and if a jockey allows an uncontrollable speed demon to dash off at an intemperate pace, the horse will burn himself out without saving any energy in reserve.

The Ridge has gunned down far faster horses than this group, and he is on the hunt into the far turn, widest of all and picking off challengers one by one. At the top of the homestretch, only front-running Klondike Gold stands between the classy warrior and the winner's circle. Heads apart, they match strides until the eighth pole, when reality finally kicks in: Saratoga Ridge had to work way too hard to reach his contending position—tardy at the start, widest on the turn, pelted by mud every step of the way—and he is homing in on the thirty-fifth second-place finish of his life, thanks only to the gloriously complex combination of muscle memory, stamina, and raw equine desire.

IT'S FOUR DAYS and counting to Rudy Baez Day on April 29, and the press office is fielding a flurry of interview requests from media outlets that want to feature the fallen jockey as an example of determination and courage. During the course of the afternoon, I phone the Baez residence to verify a few last-minute logistical details and to check in with our man of honor, pretty much like I've been doing every few days over the past several weeks. Today I'm told by one of his children that Rudy can't come to the phone, so I figure he's gone to the gym for a workout and leave a message.

It is not until several hours later that I learn from Rudy's agent, Mike Szpuk, that the reason Baez couldn't come to the phone was not exactly because he had stepped out of the house for a little bit. In actuality, the paraplegic jockey has abruptly left the country, and no one is sure when he'll be coming back.

Szpuk tells me Rudy received urgent word over Easter weekend that his elderly mother was fading fast in the Dominican Republic. Complications from multiple heart attacks and hip replacement surgery have been further compounded by a recent stroke, and relatives informed Baez that if he wanted to see his mom one more time before she was called to heaven, he had best book himself on the very next flight back home.

The bond between mother and son is exceptionally close in the Baez family. Even before his tragic accident, Rudy often credited this amazing lady with instilling in him the drive and ambition to succeed not only as an athlete, but as a caring, compassionate human being. Baez has not seen his mother in over two years, and although the seventy-three-year-old woman knows her boy was hurt in a very serious racing crash, Rudy has opted not to tell her that he has lost the use of his legs and must now use a wheelchair to get around.

The sudden trip will be an arduous and challenging one for the former jockey, who tires easily and still struggles in silence with life's most basic tasks. It is also unclear whether Mrs. Baez will be conscious or coherent enough to acknowledge her son's presence. But even though Rudy lacks the mobility that most able-bodied folks take for granted, he was long ago hardwired with intense determination and incredible strength of spirit. And now is the time for him to pay respect to the person who gave him not only life, but the special will and faith to live it fully.

At precisely high noon, one of the TV control room staffers comes into the press office to advise me of something that might interfere with the finish-line camera shot on this unseasonably raw, snow-spitting Wednesday in the last week of April.

"I don't know if you want to call someone or do something about this," she says, choosing her words carefully. "But there's a dead *something* on the track under the rail right at the wire. I don't know what it is, but if you look under the fence, you can see the crows are pecking at it pretty good."

In a mad scurry as fast and as calamitous as the start of a twenty-horse field in the Kentucky Derby, every degenerate within earshot lunges for binoculars and rushes to the press-box windows, eager to see the morbid freak show. The carnage is assuredly the remnants of some small animal—something grayish-brown that until very recently had four legs and a tail—limp in a drainage puddle exactly 2-1/2 lengths out from the finish wire.

"What the hell is it?" asks one of the interns, peering through the sleet.

"Yep, that's definitely a critter," asserts a press-box veteran, surveying the scene through high-powered field glasses. "Or a varmint."

"Okay," says another wiseguy, shifting fluidly into bookmaking mode. "I'm giving 6 to 5 that it's a rat. It's 5 to 1 to be a barn cat.

And just for fun, 30 to 1 on a small otter because we're so close to the ocean."

"That's one big fucking rat," says the intern, grimacing. "*If* it's a rat."

A third onlooker calls the play-by-play of the crows goring the carcass. But the guy can't tell if the circle of red around the animal's neck is blood or a cat collar. "I hope it's not that cat who ran across the track during a race last month," he says.

"I'm offering 100 to 1 on it being a mink," the bookie chimes in. "You also get to keep the pelt if it is."

After ten minutes of bloodthirsty entertainment without definitive classification, I phone the building operations manager and ask him if he can have one of his workers shovel away the remains.

"Is that where that muskrat ended up?" he asks, instantly knowing the identity of the animal without being asked. "Nikki got one again yesterday."

Nikki is the pet retriever who lives on the premises with the head groundskeeper and whose ultimate joy and goal in life is to chase Canada geese off the Suffolk Downs turf course, romping around in a never-ending effort to keep the pesky birds from destroying the racetrack lawn with their ravenous grazing and copious discharge of greasy droppings. "One bite to the eye and then she lost interest in it," he tells me, unfazed. "I'd say that's about the twelfth or thirteenth one this season."

A laborer trudges through the ninety-foot span of homestretch quagmire, chases off the crows, and disposes of the carcass. Upstairs, no money changes hands because not a single handicapper wagered on muskrat, which was generously offered at 10 to 1.

FROM A SOCIOLOGICAL STANDPOINT, the racetrack is a closed community where the collective mindset fluctuates wildly between long-entrenched, never-questioned beliefs and haywire short-term memory. The result is a bizarre clash of universal half-truths whose central ideas are firmly rooted in legitimate precedent but remain untempered and unchanged by the insistent prodding of recent events.

For example: Tomorrow, Suffolk Downs management has scheduled a companywide meeting three hours before first post on Rudy Baez Day. At the behest of Bob O'Malley, the marketing director attached an official memo to everyone's paycheck the last two weeks to make sure word got out.

Any employee who has worked at the East Boston oval for any part of the last decade should recognize this notification for exactly what it is. Every spring, right before the final push leading up to MassCap Day, track management schedules some sort of pep rally—a company picnic, a suggestion contest, box lunches in a tent on the grandstand apron—to let the workers know their efforts are appreciated, and to ask everyone to put their best foot forward during a time of year when we have our best chance to attract new customers. The employees all get hats, or a tote bag, or some other token item that is scheduled to be given away in a promotion sometime soon, and the operating officials take turns infusing the troops with a sense of pride for the racing product.

But this is Suffolk Downs, currently a cauldron of skepticism and panic, where the sky always seems to be falling awfully damn fast. So rather than thinking back exactly twelve months to the last time such a pep rally was held, the masses instead flash back a dozen years, rewinding to the troubled 1980s, when the thought of an embattled Bob O'Malley addressing the worried multitudes was a surefire preamble to imminent shutdown. For the past fourteen days, racetrack gossip has been rampant that the track is bankrupt and can't pay its massive mortgage; that the plant is going out of business and won't even make it until the MassCap; that everyone will be out of work before June and a Wal-Mart or Home Depot will be up on the site by next Christmas. A swift-moving alternate version of this tale of woe is that Mr. O'Malley is about to ask everyone to take a 10 percent pay cut in order to help keep the track afloat, and this latest innuendo has union officials rankled about unfair labor practices and lawsuits.

"Good," says the staffer who authored the memo. He is mildly amused that his innocent missive has caused such a furor. "Maybe I should start writing more memos."

Shortly thereafter, I run into an elected official for the mutuel clerks union who is strutting about the grandstand in a huff, spreading the latest outlandish rumors among the workforce. When he tries to pry me for information that doesn't exist about tomorrow's big "announcement," I can't resist the opportunity to toy with his political pomposity. "Sorry," I tell him, trying my best to appear evasive. "I know, but I'm not allowed to say."

"Boy, will everyone be surprised when they get baseball caps instead of a pink slip tomorrow," the marketing director quips.

Then he imparts to me the best news I have heard all week: Rudy Baez has returned home safely from the Dominican Republic. His mom is still alive, and he will be back on track in time for tomorrow's meet-and-greet ceremony.

The favorite son of Suffolk Downs will be tired and maybe not quite feeling his best after a week of hectic travel, but he's assured track officials that he will show up. Baez is a man of his word, yet it is fair to assume promises to other people are eclipsed by a separate, silent vow Rudy made to himself eight months ago, flat on his back in a hospital bed, alone with his thoughts: One day, whatever it took, no matter how long it took, he *would* grace the winner's circle yet again. The return visit would be by his own power, and—Lord willing—on the jockey's own terms.

THE LATE APRIL SKY is cloudless and bright blue for the first time in ten days. As I gaze down from the grandstand rooftop, the racetrack is alive with morning training activity. Purposefully crouched men and women perch atop tightly coiled Thoroughbred beauty, coaxing order from instinct, sequence from chaos.

None of us mention it, but we in the Suffolk Downs press box share the shameful guilt of having taken part in some off-the-cuff racetrack sarcasm gone bad. Our stupid inside joke started sometime during the decade of the 1990s, when year in and year out, Rudy Baez single-handedly dominated the local stakes schedule. He would win the feature race of the week almost every Saturday, and as part of the duties of the media relations office, one of us would be assigned to gather post-race quotes for reporters on deadline.

Invariably, having to interview Baez as the winning stakes jockey was a near-verbatim repeat of his previous performance. No matter which horse he rode and no matter how impressive or unique the margin of victory, Rudy's take on the race was always the same unchanging mantra—"I just want to thank God for letting me ride this horse; I want to thank God for giving us all the opportunity to make it around the track safely; I want to thank God for blessing me with the talent to be a jockey"—and so on and so forth without any real insight or comment on the race itself. Certainly, there is no doubt that the humble jockey was genuine in his religious sentiments. It's just that his heartfelt quotes didn't make for very good copy.

As Rudy's numerous stakes victories all morphed into one, so too did the press-box wisecracks: "Don't bother to send the intern for quotes, we can just recycle last week's release. Hey, if God was in on Rudy's sure thing, how come the horse went off at 12 to 1?"

Win, lose, or draw, no one was planning to interview or quote the perennial king of the local riding colony when he guided Gator Bait into the Rockingham Park starting gate for that otherwise unremarkable $5,000 claiming sprint on August 4, 1999. And to be sure, since that date, no one in a New England press box has ever again spoken in jest about anyone else's religious inclinations. Although we never intended to be hurtful, we learned the hard way that our snide remarks were hollow and callous, even if Rudy never heard them. Proper apologies aside, the only reason I recount the incident here is to underscore how many of us take for granted the simple gifts that life has bestowed upon us.

Baez rode in 28,609 horse races, and every single time I saw him step out into the paddock, he made the sign of the cross before saddling up. Afterward, whether the ride resulted in one of his 4,875 lifetime wins or an up-the-track finish, he blessed himself again. If, after the race, the occasion warranted someone approaching with a notebook or tape recorder, Rudy would set them straight about how truly thankful he was that his creator allowed him to race horses for a living. Baez didn't care if he had said the same exact thing only a week before or if the person jotting down his feelings understood or connected with them, because those words came from Rudy's heart. Time after time, on so many Saturdays, I witnessed the jockey with the lilting Spanish accent and direct, intense eyes standing before his racetrack locker, thanking God.

And today, alone on the rooftop watching workouts, I find myself praying for those roles to be reversed for just a single afternoon; for God, in some small way, to thank Rudy Baez for all the lives he has touched at Suffolk Downs.

WHEN A PERSON becomes paralyzed, it takes nearly two full years after the onset of trauma for the body to adjust to a loss of functionality. Even then, to a great degree, it never does, and the mind must find ways to compensate for and overcome a myriad of nagging difficulties.

At first, Rudy's immune system fought itself, and the high risk of infection to his kidneys and bladder necessitated the ingestion of "about a hundred pills a day" just to maintain a steady state. Being robbed of mobility is an obvious problem for a paraplegic, but few folks realize that the loss of musculature from the chest down also means a person with a spinal cord injury cannot cough to expel mucous from the lungs, nor can bodily wastes be removed without the aid of a urinary catheter or daily disimpaction of the bowels by hand.

Although the support group he attends has helped Baez cope with the frustrations of being unable to perform a whole slew of "normal" everyday activities—just opening and closing a sliding door to get out onto his deck on a sunny day is a major undertaking—Rudy has learned the hard way that his body can give him trouble even when he isn't trying to do *anything*, because his old racing injuries, such as a previously broken neck, stiffen when he is still for too long. The former jockey was never one to sit around anyway, which is good because

Rudy calls himself "dangerous" with time on his hands to allow depressing thoughts to eat away at his spirit. So for mental distraction as much as physical therapy, Baez attacks his upper torso weight-lifting regimen with zeal, and he says his entire body really feels good when he lowers it into the warm water of an indoor swimming pool to pull lap after lap with strong, thick shoulders until blissful exhaustion sets in. But just getting to the gym one mile from his house can be a challenge: Rudy has already fallen a few times trying to get his wheelchair into the car, and he is stubborn enough to accept help only when he absolutely needs it.

Rudy Baez Day festivities are scheduled to commence at noon, with a meet-and-greet session in the grandstand followed by a feature-race presentation in the paddock and a round of media interviews in the winner's circle. Although the event has been months in the making—and even considering that extra staffing was built into the plan to handle an overflow crowd—I can sense as soon as the admission gates open that Suffolk Downs has vastly underestimated the outpouring of support that Rudy's homecoming will generate. By 11:30 AM, half an hour before the man of honor is scheduled to make his appearance, the line of well-wishers is already extended out the grandstand door, and the usually irascible Eastie throng is surprisingly patient, enthusiastic, and upbeat about the chance to shake hands with their horse-backing hero. Being wrong at the racetrack rarely fills a degenerate horseplayer with pleasure. But we weren't even *close* on the count of how many people would turn out to share their sentiments, and as the ever-swelling crowd continues to queue, I feel fortunate to have contributed to making this particular incorrect assumption.

Rudy is dressed smartly in a tan sport coat and patterned tie over a crisp white dress shirt. If he is weary from the trip back and forth to Santo Domingo, his game face hides it well. Baez nods briskly as we discuss the timetable for the afternoon, and his intense but polite demeanor reminds me of how he used to look when receiving riding instructions from a trainer before a big race. When it comes time for him to move, Rudy does not like his wheelchair to be pushed; he has opted for a lightweight non-motorized model and propels himself wherever possible, even around tricky angles, wearing a determined look and fingerless gloves with extra leather padding in the palm.

As he makes his way through the grandstand, the parting crowd applauds boisterously. Positioning himself at the head of a long table near the paddock windows and arming himself with a Sharpie autograph pen, Baez then begins to receive the long, snaking line of racetrackers. "These," he says to a television camera that has leaned in close to capture his first fan interaction, "are my people."

THE LINE of humanity files past Rudy for three straight hours. The crowd never lets up, and neither does the jockey with the iron grip and gentle voice. It is an inspiring experience just to stand off to the side and watch as Baez chats with admirers, some of whom are crying or are shaken up to say how much they've missed him. In cool and collected fashion, the man in the wheelchair bolsters the spirits of the very fans who have turned out to encourage *him*, declining to take a rest break or even a single sip of water the entire time. People bring gifts, religious icons, framed photos, and tokens of remembrance, and the appreciative public is uncannily diverse: One guy holds up a handmade sign that says "Rudy for President," and soon enough, the slogan is all around the grandstand. An average joe decked out in a Red Sox cap, Bruins jersey, and Celtics sweatpants is overheard telling his two sons in matching Little League uniforms how jockeys, pound-for-pound, are the planet's strongest athletes, and that even though they have never heard of Rudy Baez, he thinks it is "important for them to meet the man." The largely Hispanic contingent of cleaning-crew laborers who toil for minimum wage doing the Suffolk Downs dirty work have been excused from the afternoon shift to pay their respects, and one has a tattered Rockingham simulcast program he picked up off the floor the day Rudy went down. The janitor and the jockey had struck up a friendship years ago, and the worker says that one day when he was down on his luck, Baez let him in on a long shot he knew would run well. To this day the laborer remembers the winning tip, because the money allowed his family to avoid deportation back to abject poverty in El Salvador.

More than a few of Rudy's visitors are in wheelchairs themselves. One man in particular, a thirty-four-year-old quadriplegic, hands Baez a letter to read later. Four years ago, Wayne Ross was attempting to set a Guinness world record by bicycling the world's longest contiguous land mass, some 16,000 miles from Alaska to the tip of South America. Halfway through, he crashed into a bus in Guatemala and broke his neck. "I feel like I share something with Rudy," the air force veteran says. "Biking was my life and I broke my neck on a bike. Horses were his life and he broke his neck riding a horse." He invites the jockey to call him—but not to talk about hardships they have in common. Rather, Ross says, "to talk about his new life."

The meet-and-greet session extends beyond its scheduled three hours, and we have to hustle Rudy out of the grandstand for the homecoming presentation, promising the remaining fans in line that Baez will be available afterward in the paddock to socialize with anybody who got shut out. Four Boston television stations, including the local Hispanic news channel, plus several radio stations and a full press box of print reporters, are on hand to cover the event. The media office has issued its largest number of credentials in a single day since last year's MassCap.

Surrounded by his wife, three children, the entire New England jockey colony, and all the locker-room valets, the ceremony begins with a video montage of Rudy's career highlights interspersed with pre-taped tributes from a dozen national riders, including Chris McCarron, Pat Day, and Julie Krone. Red Sox superstar pitcher Pedro Martinez, a fellow Dominican who helped raise $62,000 for the Rudy Baez Assistance Fund, also sends along his best wishes and some souvenir baseballs. Trainer Charlie Assimakopoulos awards the jockey a commemorative photograph on behalf of all of the horsemen, then announces that the first-born foal from his prized mare Speedland will be named in homage to Rudy, because Baez rode her to so many local stakes victories. Through it all, Baez is somber and stoic. The only sign of sentiment comes when the most personal gift of all is unveiled: Over the course of the spring, Suffolk Downs has collected signatures and notes of encouragement from over 500 racing fans on huge wall-size sheets of art stock. These words surround a color action shot of Rudy bearing down on horseback, and the entire package has been custom framed alongside a befitting quote from Andrew Jackson—"One man with courage makes a majority."

Before making the trophy presentation to the winning jockey of the $25,000 feature race that has been newly renamed in his honor, Baez pauses to compose himself, then takes the microphone to offer several difficult but concise sentences of appreciation, the emotion in his deliberate speech echoing and reverberating against a backdrop of respectful silence:

> I'm very happy I'm here with everybody—with all the ponies and my family.
>
> I want to thank God you guys all meant this for me: Suffolk Downs management, Lou Raffetto, and everybody else; the jockeys, and all the people here behind me. The people that make the races, the people in the gate—everyone here, God bless you all. You people are all so nice. God bless you all.
>
> I hope that people don't [stop coming] here just because I'm not here anymore. All the jockeys here, they're probably better than me.
>
> Coming here, you can be sure that things are going to go on like I was here. I'm not here, but my heart is here.
>
> I thank you all. I thank my wife Judy—she's the best—and everybody else.

Lost in the shuffle is the new Toyota Avalon, which true to her word, Judy Baez has parked adjacent to the paddock with a large sign thanking Suffolk Downs for its donation of the custom vehicle.

As we make our way to the winner's circle fence so Rudy can shake even more hands and sign another round of autographs, Baez and I banter about plans for the future, and he seems relieved that the hoopla of the afternoon is behind him. Rudy tells me that he's looking forward to driving the car to the racetrack for work next season, and how in the meantime, he'll just enjoy taking it easy, chauffeuring his kids back and forth to various activities. This summer, his eleven-year-old son will start Pop Warner football practice. With a grin, Baez adds that his thirteen-year-old daughter will need a lift to a local riding stable—the little girl, he says, wants to take horseback-riding lessons.

HOURS LATER, long after the racetrack has gone dark, I get a call informing me that Rudy's mother passed away late Saturday afternoon.

Upon returning home to Wakefield to host a small after-races party among family and friends, the paralyzed jockey received word from the Dominican Republic that his mom had too much to overcome in the aftermath of her stroke, and was mercifully called to peace.

The timing of Mrs. Baez's death coincided almost exactly with Rudy's return to the Suffolk Downs winner's circle.

One would like to think that some higher power arranged it that way, so a mother could look down upon her son's greatest accomplishment and beam with pride.

■■

CHAPTER SIX

KING OF SPORTS

Far back, far back in our dark soul the horse prances.
—D. H. LAWRENCE, *Apocalypse*

I N A STATISTICALLY TYPICAL breeding season—1997, for example—35,139 registered Thoroughbreds will be foaled in North America.

Of that number, only 23,014 will make it to the races. Thirty-five percent will never see the inside of a starting gate.

Of those who do start, 15,886 will eventually graduate to the winner's circle. That means roughly three out of every five members of the foal crop will never finish in front of a pack of peers in an actual race.

Culling the herd further, barely 3 percent of the total class of 1997 (1,140 horses) will lay claim to victory in some sort of stakes race. Of the entire crop, only a select six-tenths of 1 percent (223) will manage to win a graded race, the highest classification of competition.

In an industry where even the very best owners, trainers, and jockeys know they're going to lose at a 75 percent clip, dreams, aspirations, and compulsive desires persist in clashing against blunt reality.

If you foaled a Thoroughbred in 1997, today—the first Saturday in May 2000—is the day you had circled on the calendar from the moment that baby horse's legs hit the ground. Realistic or not, nearly everyone in the business hopes to someday start a promising three-year-old in the world's most famous horse race, the Kentucky Derby.

This afternoon, nineteen survivors from that original 1997 crop of 35,139 will line up for the 126th Derby at Churchill Downs. Just making it to the race is an honorable accomplishment. But only one horse will win it. Defying the odds, that victor will be Fusaichi Pegasus.

In many ways, a glorious future was foretold from birth for this highly hyped colt. Purchased for $4 million as a yearling, Fusaichi Pegasus was earmarked as an exceptionally talented runner even before he ever stepped onto a racetrack. He was impeccably trained through a carefully mapped set of prep races, winging along undefeated in his first five starts this year en route to becoming the first betting favorite to win the Run for the Roses in twenty-one years. But let's get ahead of ourselves and indulge in a bit of literary fast-forwarding, a luxury that is never available in the here-and-now world of the racetrack.

Two weeks from today, in his quest for the elusive Triple Crown, Fusaichi Pegasus will be soundly beaten in the Preakness Stakes, inexplicably listless as the 3-to-10 favorite. The colt will then injure himself in his stall prior to the Belmont Stakes, necessitating a scratch, followed by several months on the sidelines. Fusaichi Pegasus will return to score in one more late-season stakes, an easy tune-up for the Breeders' Cup Classic. But in the continent's richest race, he will finish sixth as the 6-to-5 favorite, seemingly without excuse.

Not allowing an underachieving race record to deflate an exceedingly lofty reputation, the colt's handlers will promptly syndicate this star steed for a record valuation before whisking the Derby winner off to a Kentucky breeding shed, where well-connected bloodlines enthusiasts will shell out $135,000 a pop to have their mares serviced by the world's only $60-million stud. One need not blur the historical boundaries to note that the staggering market value of this single stallion is exactly one and a half times the 1997 purchase price for all of Suffolk Downs, which changed hands for $40 million the same season Fusaichi Pegasus was foaled.

History, as the saying goes, gets written by the winners. But losers have the best, most intriguingly honest, tales to tell.

This afternoon, few folks will witness Patty Meadow, who bypassed a Harvard career in medicine to chase an equine dream, sending out *her* three-year-old homebred this first Saturday in May, at Suffolk Downs instead of Churchill Downs. Ypres is 20 to 1 in the morning line to win an entry-level allowance race scheduled half an hour after the Kentucky Derby simulcast crowd has vacated the East Boston grandstand in droves, and Dyn Panell scrubs briskly at the gelding's neck as the gangly Thoroughbred lopes around the far turn in dusky twilight, ears cocked, seemingly enjoying his surroundings far off the front-runners. But cutting the corner for home, a good ten lengths behind the freewheeling favorite, Ypres suddenly *gets* it, extending and striding out fully when hooked by 26-to-1 Timely Whirl while far behind the leaders. Even though they are not close to winning, the two long shots duel in their own private midpack match race for the final eighth of a mile, alternating furious head bobs to the wire. The raw intensity of these two modestly bred three-year-olds slugging it out is lost on practically everyone busy focusing on the front-runners, but their battle culminates in an unnoticed yet tight photo-finish for fifth, with Ypres on the losing end at the last lunge. Horse and rider return in a canter after galloping out around the clubhouse turn, and both Panell's squinting face and Ypres's broad chest are peppered with moist, sandy loam.

Another noteworthy horse whose story will never be featured alongside the likes of a Derby winner is Blackwater, the ferocious gelding from Florida. While a younger generation of fashionably bred horses is running for roses, this claiming warrior appears to have slid slowly off the grid. Today is closing day at Tampa Bay Downs, and Blackwater's name has not appeared in the entries or workouts for nearly a month. Efforts to locate the regally bred runner have devolved into reliance on backstretch rumor: A friend of a friend heard that the talented but troubled son of Irish River recently resurfaced at Philadelphia Park. A stablehand who made the trek north to New England said he thought the ornery sprinter was sent to a farm somewhere outside Ocala, Florida. My old man speculates that those degenerative hock joints finally caught up with the grizzled veteran, and that Blackwater, for better or worse, is gone for good.

Then there is the saga of Saratoga Ridge, who also gets a start on Derby Day. Having outraced—not to mention outlived—an enormous percentage of his 1989 foal crop, the resolute roan goes this afternoon for another $7,500 claiming tag at Delaware Park. The recent downward career curve of the eleven-year-old mirrors the perplexing path of his hard-trying trainer: After a sharp start back in February, the unshakable Maryland slump has shadowed the stable to Delaware, where Team Catalano has crashed and burned to a 1-for-42 record.

Much like Saratoga Ridge, this season Mike Catalano has often shown up second (eight placings) or third (seven). But impatient owner Michael Gill has made it resoundingly clear that he did not invest in a major Thoroughbred outfit to churn out a 36 percent in-the-money mark if his horses aren't winning, and it is an open secret that Catalano's job is in jeopardy, with short-term statistical aberration severing what was anticipated to be a long-term business deal.

The hard-trying gray does not run poorly. Then again, Saratoga Ridge does not win, either. Breaking from the extreme outside, the gelding forces the early pace, gets to within a neck of the leader at the quarter pole, then backpedals to fifth, beaten three lengths at the wire. If he follows his previous pattern of stable management, owner Gill is going to insist that Catalano find softer competition for Saratoga Ridge, which might mean returning the horse to the Suffolk Downs rotation. And if word comes down from the boss that second-stringers will be banished to Boston, the trainer could very well find himself back on the same van north with his horses.

Oblivious to the irony, the Delaware Park chart-caller could just as well be writing about hard-trying Mike Catalano's ill-fated foray to the mid-Atlantic when he pens this afternoon's performance comment for Saratoga Ridge in the game old gelding's 127th lifetime start: *Broke alertly to prompt the pace, faded in deep stretch.*

THE DAY AFTER the Kentucky Derby, the *Boston Sunday Globe* runs a two-page photojournalism spread about street nurses who work for low pay in high-risk areas of the city giving care to the homeless. Some of the pictures show elderly people and war veterans who must resort to sleeping under bridges, dead-broke shelter folk rummaging through trash dumpsters for meals.

One stark, black-and-white photograph prominently depicts a down-on-his-luck Suffolk Downs backstretch worker being examined by a visiting caregiver who has long attended to human residents of the East Boston barn area. The sparse text accompanying the photograph quotes the nurse as such:

At Suffolk Downs, who gets better treatment, the horses or the people?

The horses. Definitely, without any question. The horses are an investment. Here somebody could get hurt and walk away and there's somebody else to do the work. They are cheap labor and the horses are the moneymakers. They [the horses] are well fed and taken care of.

LOU RAFFETTO is in full-blown MassCap mode, and his enthusiasm is effusive and contagious. The next whistle stop on his whirlwind recruitment tour is this weekend's Pimlico Special, followed by a return visit to Baltimore the following Saturday for the Preakness, where he will unleash a final blitz of lobbying aimed at the connections of the nation's top horses. New England's Million Dollar Day of Racing is now just twenty-five days away, and amid a season of uncertainty, the Suffolk Downs general manager is acutely aware that a successful showcase race featuring marquee horses and top-name jockeys will go a long way toward determining whether his track sinks, swims, or even treads enough water to stay afloat until the next race meet.

Still topping the MassCap wish list is last year's defending champ, Behrens. Trained by a down-to-earth Saratoga horseman who goes by the dashing, spylike name of H. James Bond, the nation's top older handicap horse most recently ran second in the world's richest race, the $6-million Dubai World Cup, and the brawny bay six-year-old has a full slate of options for his next stakes start. But Raffetto and Bond are on excellent terms, and Lou has already extracted a promise from the conditioner that a return trip to New England is in the cards for Behrens. In fact, the two are so tight that Bond quietly tipped his hand to the GM weeks ago about coming back to the MassCap, enabling Raffetto to do some advance planning of his own: Based on this behind-the-scenes agreement, Suffolk Downs ordered several hundred snazzy MassCap promotional banners emblazoned with Behrens's likeness, which will be hung from street lamps all around downtown Boston to herald the coming of the region's most historic horse race.

Last season, a British invader named Running Stag nearly stole the MassCap show, and he too has been committed to this year's race in an effort to even the score with arch-rival Behrens. Dismissed at odds of 8 to 1 in a field that featured Kentucky Derby winner Real Quiet, trainer Philip Mitchell came close to orchestrating one of the greatest MassCap coups of all time: Because his horse had primarily raced in England, France, and Germany, Running Stag was perceived to be a typical one-paced European plodder unaccustomed to—and thus disadvantaged by—the relatively quicker North American style of gunning hard from start to finish. All week long in advance of the big race, the main topic in the press was how fast and grueling the early MassCap fractions would be, and all week long the highly personable Mitchell—a five-time amateur jockey champion in his native United Kingdom—gladly and glibly encouraged this reasoning, providing ample entertainment to backstretch reporters while bemoaning the obstacles his horse would have to overcome.

Yet when the starter sprung the latch for the 1999 MassCap, it was Running Stag who rocketed right to the lead, with jockey Shane Sellers zipping along at a brisk clip as per his trainer's explicit instructions. The surprise strategy succeeded in dueling 4-to-5 favorite Real Quiet into defeat, but Behrens didn't buy it. He and Jorge Chavez sat off the pace and pounced, nailing Running Stag in the shadow of the wire after the two hooked up in a furious stretch fight. Mitchell lost the war, but he won all the important battles in between, including the toughest sell of all: The diehard Suffolk Downs railbirds gave the second-place Brits a more rousing ovation than the winner when the horses galloped back after the race, and Mitchell himself was hailed by the turf writers as a colorful, quotable mad genius who immediately vowed to return for another, full-blown "Stag party" in MassCap 2000.

Against the odds, and with very little fanfare, Lou Raffetto's MassCap story line has held together quite well since February. Behrens crushed the Gulfstream Park Handicap field as the 3-to-10 favorite before chasing Europe's best horse, Dubai Millennium, in the World Cup. Bond has rested his star steed since that late March foray to the Middle East, and only two weeks ago resumed serious training with Behrens. Running Stag spent his winter racking up frequent-flier miles, finishing second in the Hong Kong Cup before checking in seventh in the World Cup behind Behrens. Opting to forgo a strenuous set of public workouts, Mitchell will fly his horse into the United States from England next week to sneak his globe-trotting traveler into a New York allowance on May 24, a race that will serve as Running Stag's final screw-tightener before taking aim at the MassCap.

Raffetto is wise enough to know that a big race lineup is never a certainty until the horses reach the starting gate. So while actively wooing Bond and Mitchell, he is simultaneously laying the groundwork for an alternate cast of characters who will either strengthen the field or be thrust into a leading role should one of the top two stars withdraw at the last minute. Few trainers are as prepared as Jim Bond, though. While Raffetto is out hustling "insurance" horses, the calculating conditioner has his own understudy waiting in the wings: By anteing up an additional nomination fee, Behrens's second-string stablemate Pleasant Breeze has also been nominated to the MassCap—the equine equivalent of having a frankfurter on hand in case the filet mignon falls into the fire. Bond, if nothing else, is a thorough horseman who keeps all his options open.

A COLD RAIN pelts the Massachusetts shoreline, and by midafternoon, a relentless thunderstorm rips through the region. Two miles down the road at Logan International Airport, flights are delayed and air traffic is grounded because of the dangerous conditions. Yet at Suffolk Downs, where the faint smell of scorched ozone lingers in the chilly air, the game goes on as scheduled.

About the only thing colder than the unseasonably raw 46°F mid-May weather is jockey Howard Lanci, who is mired in the depths of his 0-for-26 losing streak. But in the fifth race, with too-close-for-comfort electrical bursts darting all around, Lanci gets loose on the lead with Runaway Cargo, the longest shot in a seven-horse claiming sprint. Amid sheets of rain, bright white flashes of lightning, and the concussive reverberations of enormous thunderclaps, the 12-to-1 gelding sloshes home by three lengths. The Howitzer guides his steed straight to the winner's circle, where like a crazed horseback warrior, he hoists his riding helmet high, points his upturned, grinning face to the slate-colored sky, and beams a defiant victory salute to the elements. While Howie cackles and basks theatrically in a rare bit of glory, the others in the winner's circle—groom, valet, photographer, clerk of scales, and security guard—stomp and mutter impatiently, wishing that the maniac reinsman would move the hell along so they could all dart inside to shelter.

The entryway to the locker room is jammed and chaotic. Jockeys crowd the clothes hamper in the narrow hallway, complaining and hollering, cursing the conditions. They shake themselves like drenched dogs while stripping off layers of racing silks, safety vests, helmets, Saran-Wrapped goggles, boots, breeches, and wet cotton underclothing. The official weigh-in is futile, because each rider has picked up pounds of water and mud while trolling the Suffolk Downs bog. Tammi Piermarini has a bloody lip; she doesn't even know until someone tells her, and has no recollection of being hit. She says her main concern was just keeping her head down and getting her horse around the track safely in one of the worst downpours she's ever experienced. Several riders echo Tammi's sentiments about the pelting rain, but those who have a call in Race 6 suit up and head out, bracing for the next encounter with the elements.

Amid the raucous din, almost everyone manages to take a moment to come over and congratulate Howard Lanci. He's the court jester, the one who keeps the comrades loose, and his underrated role is embraced by an unspoken code of racetrack karma: It doesn't take much to make Howie happy. The other jockeys know this, and perhaps also perceive that when his sprits are high, Lanci's effusive devil-may-care energy rubs off on everyone else. Members of this unique clan spend a good chunk of their lives locked together in a small room beneath the Suffolk Downs grandstand, and it's almost as if in order for the group to collectively remain on an even keel, the wackiest guy of the bunch has to be all wound up in full-blown, grab-life-by-the-balls performance mode to serve as welcome distraction from reality. Without The Howitzer's mortal diversion, the tragic flaw of riding racehorses for a living might inadvertently become exposed, and the entire group would have to confront the can't-last-forever predicament of their profession.

Still breathing hard, Howie plants himself in front of the largest television set in the jocks' room and savors his victory. Untamed hair fractious and wild, a drenched towel draped around his skinny shoulders, Lanci is absorbed in his winning ride, ghosting along in tandem with his own lanky image on the TV screen: throwing crosses, slashing his steed's flank right, left, and then right again before wrapping up the reins and driving home first under the finish wire.

After watching his pantomime, one of the valets jokingly asks Lanci if the zaps of lightning and the massive thunder booming down from above were the *real* keys to startling Runaway Cargo—who hadn't won a race in five months—into the winner's circle. "Yeah," Howie replies with a sly, knowing grin. "He must be a *machine horse!*" Lanci's comment provokes a round of snide laughter, because every single soul in the locker room recognizes the term as racetrack slang for a Thoroughbred whose performance can be illegally enhanced by a jolt from a concealed electrical device.

"Except today," the clown prince of the jockey colony cautions, adopting a mock-serious tone and cocking a finger to the heavens. "That sonofabitch thought he was gonna get plugged in by *God.*"

SUBSTANTIATING MY FEAR that the local future of Thoroughbred racing is being pulverized to bits by the grinding, ravenous gears of the Massachusetts political machine, both the *Herald* and the *Globe* today run wildly disparate updates about the state of the sport and how it's being legislated (or not) on Beacon Hill. Below are the headlines and lead paragraphs of two separate stories covering essentially the same issue on May 11,2000:

Boston Herald: **Simulcast Expansion Talks Still at Impasse**
Bay State racetrack owners, their industry already under attack from out-of-state gambling competitors, may now face the potentially devastating loss of televised betting.

Boston Globe: **Simulcast Betting Optimism Expressed**
A key member of a special legislative panel reviewing the state's parimutuel industry said yesterday that he will recommend an expansion of simulcast betting at the state's two horse tracks and two dog tracks.

The *Herald* story quotes an unnamed legislator as saying there is "no guarantee" that any compromise will be reached on the political impasse before the end of the legislative session in July. Yet the *Globe* cites State Racing Commissioner Robert M. Hutchinson Jr. as on the record that the legislature "wants to do something that moves toward solving the problem." Although their conflicting remarks seem to indicate otherwise, both sources have been working together on the same blue-ribbon committee for close to half a year now. Confused, I ask Bob O'Malley which of the two stories is the real deal. His answer is even more enigmatic.

"It's all a big poker game," the track's Beacon Hill point man comments dryly. "Sometimes you just have to bluff if you want to stay in the game."

THERE IS no political mudslinging today, but this afternoon someone finally unearths the true dirt at Suffolk Downs.

We've had some offbeat requests for racetrack memorabilia over the years. Old programs, saddle towels, and horseshoes usually top the list. Even mundane Suffolk Downs promotional items such as umbrellas, key chains, and baseball caps routinely get posted for sale on the Internet at jacked-up prices only hours after being given away at the turnstiles for the price of admission. Nowadays most so-called collectors are nothing more than opportunity sharks looking to churn a buck on other people's sentiments.

But today Bish doesn't even bat an eye when a fan all the way from California finds his way up to the press box to request permission to step out onto the Eastie oval to obtain a sample for his collection of—get this—racetrack dirt.

The fan, a horse owner and self-described student of Thoroughbred breeding, enthusiastically explains to us how he began accumulating racetrack loam while on a tour of Kentucky horse country several years back. He asked the guide if he could obtain small specimens of the Keeneland and Churchill Downs racetracks, and although his query was met with a quizzical look, he was allowed to take home a soil sample. He keeps his ever-growing collection in labeled display jars and is genuinely surprised that no one else seems to have thought of the idea of souvenir soil.

Then again, the fan reasons before going down to collect his dirt, "I guess if everyone requested dirt, there wouldn't be much left for the horses to run on."

LOU RAFFETTO is between recruitment trips, and this morning I sit in his top-floor office absorbing a MassCap debriefing in the aftermath of last weekend's major stakes events. On the East Coast, six potential Suffolk Downs starters slugged it out in the $750,000 Pimlico Special. They swept the first six positions in the eight-horse field, yet the only horse to emerge from the Pimlico Special raring to race right away is the Jim Bond–trained Pleasant Breeze, the second-stringer who up until now has been known only as Behrens's understudy. At 35 to 1, he ran the race of his life despite getting caught flat-footed at the break, checking back sharply the entire run through the clubhouse turn, and steadying again at the top of stretch before closing willingly for second. He was the only horse truly gaining on the race winner, and Bond later confided to Raffetto that Pleasant Breeze managed such a stellar effort even though his left hind leg was badly bloodied by continuous crowding on the turns. Luckily, the cuts turned out to be superficial, and now Bond has the enviable dilemma of having two sharp horses at the top of the older male handicap division.

While Lou was wining and dining potential clients in Maryland, another trainer friend of his had a good news–bad news type of day 2,500 miles west at Hollywood Park. Richard Mandella, a conditioner known for repeated success with importing overlooked Thoroughbreds from South America and transforming them into U.S. stakes winners, saddled both Chilean stalwart Puerto Madero (second in the 1998 MassCap) and newcomer Out Of Mind (a Group 2 winner in Brazil) in the Mervyn LeRoy Handicap. The race was supposed to be a cakewalk for the former, and more of a "Let's see what we've got here" try for the latter. Yet it was heavily favored Puerto Madero who spit the bit after seizing the early lead, while unheralded stablemate Out Of Mind blitzed from the back of the pack to soar home first in shockingly easy fashion.

What all this means for the June 3 MassCap is anyone's guess, but Lou is clearly a man on a mission when it comes to orchestrating his Million Dollar Day of Racing. He sets the scene in rapid fashion, rattling off the names of prominent owners, trainers, jockeys, and agents, putting ideas into words as soon as they form in his head but clearly in the know about which horsemen are bullshitting him, which are not, and which ones *think* they are but really don't have a clue. I scribble notes about each potential MassCap starter, jotting down story lines and impressions about horses and humans who would make good copy in advance of the race, while Raffetto articulates a volley of Thoroughbred knowledge about the sport's handicap division. All the while, Lou simultaneously attends to the everyday business of running a racetrack—signing checks, approving requests, authorizing work orders, and assigning special projects for the fast-approaching MassCap. Although his constantly ringing phone is politely screened by a well-informed assistant, Lou still must pause to seamlessly field about a dozen calls in a twenty-minute span. Many of the people on the other end of the line are the very owners and trainers we were just discussing, and whether he is in the mood to engage in amicable discourse with them or not, Raffetto greets each one with the same gregarious charm and rakish wit of a modern-day horse hustler trying to get what he pays for if he's hosting a seven-figure racing extravaganza.

AESTHETICALLY, Suffolk Downs in springtime is a far cry from the beleaguered bleakness of the winter months. Mother Nature plays an obvious role in awakening the bountiful infield flora, but the exterior landscaping gets a big boost from track management, which budgets heavily for cosmetic improvements in the weeks preceding the MassCap. Almost overnight, the grounds get a meticulous manicure, the paddock is vividly abloom in flowers, shrubbery, and fresh paint, and even the gigantic glass wall of windows that fronts the grandstand is given its annual power scrubbing, a top-to-bottom, three-day affair that requires an industrial cleaning company working from an elevated bucket truck. Eight years ago, the old-style clubhouse entrance was restored to its original 1935 facade, and this area too gets a detailed makeover, so that the ornately styled brickwork and proud, stone-carved equine statues can greet racegoers in much the same fashion as they did during the halcyon era of the sport when the track carded only sixty programs all year and *every* day of the meet was a major event.

This year, Suffolk Downs has budgeted $20,000 for landscaping to beautify the property for New England's Million Dollar Day of Racing. Although that figure might seem superfluous, much of the cost goes to cover extensive replanting of the same greenery over and over again because of a strangely local malady unique to those who gamble and garden in East Boston: Each spring, the grounds crew scrupulously sows lavish rows of flowering trees and plants alongside the concourse leading up to the track's main entrance. And like clockwork, each spring, green-thumbed thieves with a penchant for ripping off other people's petunias back up their cars, dig up a bush or a row of flowers, and liberate the plants as racetrack freebies, leaving little more than a hole and some leftover dirt in about the same span of time that it takes a Thoroughbred to gallop six furlongs.

In the front courtyard, adjacent to the long walkway that leads to the main entrance, a grizzled Suffolk Downs maintenance supervisor is in the process of assigning a work crew to plant a bed of annuals. Over the track's in-house two-way radio, I can hear him haggling with the security shift boss over why he needs a guard to stand watch over flats of pansies until his laborers return from lunch.

"Because in five minutes, somebody will steal all our fucking flowers, that's why!" screams the exasperated landscaper.

If we could only train the locals to help themselves to the snow and ice that blankets the joint in January, then the entire ordeal of seasonal racing at Suffolk Downs would go off without a hitch.

THE MASSCAP is a dozen days away, and the pretenders are beginning to be culled from the contenders. Having spent the better part of the spring pitching New England's Million Dollar Day of Racing, Lou Raffetto must now put on his racing secretary hat and attend to the delicate business of assigning weights for his $600,000 handicap. Although initially invented as a theoretical means of equalizing the chances of all entrants in an important stakes race, the practice of adding and subtracting poundage has largely gone the way of the horse and buggy in this modern era of Thoroughbred racing, and the tedious task of ranking steeds by handicaps has devolved into a watered-down anachronism now more likely to offend than entice the connections of top horses.

In the first half of the twentieth century, being top-weighted in a handicap race was an unavoidable badge of honor for the sport's star horses. Seabiscuit (in 1937) and Whirlaway (1942) were both asked to tote 130 pounds en route to their respective MassCap victories, conceding as much as thirty pounds to lesser foes. In those days, a sizable spread in the rankings was not uncommon. Big-money races were few and far between, and trainers had to accept the challenge of racing as a formidable highweight because the only other option was to keep a fast Thoroughbred in the barn until the next major stakes rolled around—and that race might be clear across the country, where the horse would likely *again* be heftily weighted. Over time, though, the advent of year-round racing led to the demise of handicap racing: By the 1990s, six-figure races existed almost every single weekend on the national calendar, and this new explosion of options shifted power from race organizers to horsemen. Now, trainers openly take advantage of the glut of graded stakes by playing one track's weight rankings against another's, and in a business where leverage never comes easily, no one can blame them. If a conditioner feels his horse is unfairly burdened by Suffolk Downs when the weights are announced this Saturday, skipping the MassCap is no big deal, because similar graded races with different handicaps are right around the corner at Churchill Downs, Belmont, and Hollywood Park.

Lou—and everyone else involved with the race—knows he has to make Behrens the top-weighted horse, but the thorny part of the equation is by how much. The defending MassCap champ owns $4,259,000 in lifetime purse earnings and top billing on the influential National Thoroughbred Racing Association poll, so even the most diehard skeptic would have difficulty arguing that Behrens should be dethroned from the top slot in any track's handicap rankings. Even trainer Jim Bond would candidly concede that his horse is the one to beat, so Raffetto will use 121 pounds as his high-end benchmark— exactly one pound more than Behrens carried in his most recent victory—and work down from there to achieve the assignments for the other twenty-two MassCap nominees.

Racehorse trainers aren't so much concerned about the actual weight an entrant must carry as they are with the spread of poundage between their horse and other rivals. Run-of-the-mill $4,000 claimers successfully lug 122 pounds every single day at Suffolk Downs, but in general, few of them ever carry a load more than six pounds higher than the lightest competitor in the race. In the MassCap, the distribution of ability ranges from the nation's top horse to a handful of local long shots whose connections hope to pick up a $20,000 fifth-place piece of the purse, so Raffetto must broaden the gap between Behrens (121) and an ambitious Boston allowance lightweight like Makeyourselfathome (107). Although the distinction in ability and achievement between those two animals is obvious, wedged in between are numerous seasoned Thoroughbreds with hard-earned stakes credentials, and that is where Lou will have difficulty smoothing out the details. In fact, considering that Behrens's return to Boston has been an open secret among Suffolk Downs management for the better part of a month now, I am somewhat surprised and more than a little unnerved to read in *Daily Racing Form* that Jim Bond is emphatic about not allowing a lightly weighted rival to turn the tables on Behrens. "I am not going to let a horse at 110 [pounds] beat this horse," the trainer said, alluding to the fact that he could always send his top gun to Kentucky for the Stephen Foster Handicap if he doesn't like the weights for the MassCap.

Lou stops short of acknowledging that his friend might be trying to exert a little bit of last-minute strategic influence via the press, and he brushes off Bond's implicit threat that Behrens won't show up at Suffolk Downs. Instead, Raffetto reassures me by pointing out a few tricks he has up his own sleeve that will balance out the handicap process, lessons that Lou learned the hard way during twenty-five years as a racing official known for making big races come together.

For example, Raffetto will probably weight Lemon Drop Kid at 119 for the MassCap, which is only two pounds behind Behrens. This makes it appear as if Suffolk Downs has ranked a competitor hot on the heels of the highweight, but of course, Lou may elect not to divulge to Bond—or anyone else—that he found out definitively five days ago that Lemon Drop Kid won't be entering the race. Similarly, Golden Missile is the up-and-coming new challenger in the older horse division off his win in the Pimlico Special. But with trainer Joe Orseno leaning toward other options, his horse can safely be installed at 117 without insulting anyone. Running Stag is logically next at 116, and although this is three pounds more than the British invader was asked to shoulder in last year's slugfest, such a weight assignment cleverly preserves the five-pound cushion that Stag enjoyed last season when Behrens was 118 for the MassCap.

Out Of Mind (114) is likely to be Boston-bound, but Raffetto realizes that he is gambling with too high a weight assignment for an on-the-bubble horse who has to ship cross-country from California. But his ace in the hole is that he knows Out Of Mind's regular rider, Eddie Delahoussaye, has trouble tacking any lighter a weight assignment. Essentially, Lou is banking on trainer Richard Mandella not protesting for a lower handicap because his jockey would have to report overweight anyway. Pleasant Breeze—although beaten only two lengths by Golden Missile—gets a feather-light ranking of 111. This sizable ten-pound concession is another carefully crafted nonissue: Pleasant Breeze won't even have to step outside his Saratoga stall, because stablemate Behrens is the one who'll be trekking four hours east as the favored MassCap highweight.

After ten minutes sizing up such weighty issues, I am left with the dual feeling of how outmoded and petty the whole handicap system is, while at the same time yearning for the bygone days of the game when true champions of the sport packed on the pounds, and anyone bold enough to try and run 'em down in a race like the MassCap simply saddled up and took aim.

"It's all politics," Lou agrees, unfazed. "A mind game."

EVERY DAY of the season, horse vans lumber into and out of East Boston, delivering and deleting an ever-shifting rotation of Thoroughbreds for new beginnings, second chances, and last resorts. The armada of equine carriers ranges from small mom-and-pop hitch trailers to long, padded commercial rigs booked to capacity after stops at tracks up and down the Eastern seaboard. Racing's trickle-down economics ensure that cheaper horses from pricier tracks eventually find their way to a midlevel haunt like Suffolk Downs, either in passing or in permanence. Next week, that role will be reversed when the glitterati of the game arrive in style for New England's Million Dollar Day of Racing, and press photographers, TV crews, and a curious throng of locals line up to greet the pampered pros. But the backstretch gawkers will have missed an equally remarkable import who slipped past the stable gate days earlier for an unnoticed homecoming: Overlooked in the MassCap hustle and bustle, Saratoga Ridge, the ancient gray claimer admired for his tenacity and determination, has returned to the grounds after a three-month exile to the mid-Atlantic.

So, too, has Mike Catalano, who at once seems unburdened yet mildly dispirited to be back where it all began—again. Assuredly, the trainer had aspired to return to Suffolk Downs under different circumstances, perhaps with a MassCap horse of his own this spring. Instead, the ex-boxer is back in Boston looking to regroup in the wake of a nightmarish 1-for-50 losing skid, and over the past week the notation "Previously trained by Catalano, Michael L., Jr." has appeared in the Delaware program alongside each and every Michael Gill entrant. As a consolation prize, Mike has been given the option to return north with the stable's second-stringers, barely three months after he agreed to uproot his family and business by committing to the travel-dominated demands of his boss. Catalano will now oversee only the New England division, and although his pride has taken a hit, Mike will first call a shot of his own before agreeing to these new terms. For the remainder of the race meet, he will step aside and designate an assistant to tend to Gill's horses, because Team Catalano has a more important arrival on the home front: Weighing in at eight pounds, eight ounces, Mike's wife, Abby, just gave birth to a healthy, angelic baby girl the couple have christened Micayla.

At the racetrack, life goes on, impervious to the outside world. This afternoon, Saratoga Ridge gallops postward solidly backed at 9 to 5 in the fourth event, and I wonder if even a single soul in the grandstand is concerned about where he's been and what's happened to his trainer since the two were last seen in the Suffolk Downs winner's circle on a raw, sleety Sunday in February. Cantering to the starting gate for the 128th time—today with top jock Joe Hampshire in the irons—the

Ridge appears poised to pounce in an $8,000 claimer, a five-furlong sprint switched off the grass course when drenching rains rendered the turf unusable. A number of older, ouchy steeds have been scratched by their trainers today because the main track resembles a mud bog, but the eleven-year-old still manages to excel over gooey going, having earned five of his nineteen wins and $73,900 in purses in the mud. It is dangerous and often wrong to attribute human emotions to animals, but peering at Saratoga Ridge in the pre-race warm-ups, he clearly looks like he's relishing the rich, brown soup as if glad to be back in Boston, eager to outrun the nine equine peers who have dared line up against the salty veteran on his own home court.

But whether Saratoga Ridge—or even the bettors—realize it, the old roan *has* lost something off his fastball. He rears in his stall just as starter Tom Schwigen springs the latch, causing him to break awkwardly in the air for the first time in his life. A five-furlong, one-minute race at Suffolk Downs is no place to try to launch a long bid from far off the tailgate, so Hampshire immediately pumps furiously at the gelding's neck while the pair are pelted by mud in tenth and last place.

The Ridge is one of those game, seasoned warriors, who, as they admiringly say on the backstretch, "will run over broken glass to get there first." So when he senses his jockey's urgency, he cranks his hindquarters into overdrive and fires past half the field with a wide, quarter-mile drive around the turn. With a bold bid, he gains on the leaders at every call, launching into third place by the final furlong. Then, just when it appears as if Saratoga Ridge is about to power past, he pauses—for a brief but perceptible beat.

Throughout his career, the cagey gray has earned a reputation as a runner who "waits" on other Thoroughbreds, allowing beaten competition to rejoin the chase before surging past late in a race. Popular consensus is that some horses behave in this manner simply to enjoy the raw, animalistic pleasure of asserting equine dominance over inferior rivals, and today's slight hesitation seems not to deviate from the eleven-year-old's usual catch-me-if-you-can tactics. But what *is* out of the ordinary is that his final closing kick never comes. Saratoga Ridge digs in and doesn't give up, yet no explosion accompanies his frenzied sense of purpose. Crossing the finish wire 1-1/4 lengths behind a pair of unimposing claimers, the Ridge gallops out in a four-legged funk, an erstwhile magician suddenly stunned to realize he no longer possesses enough power to summon the rabbit from his hat.

After the race, plodding back to be unsaddled in front of the grandstand, Saratoga Ridge is blowing hard. His whitish-gray coat is smeared filthy brown, and as the only horse in the race who didn't wear blinkers, his dark eyes are crusted shut with racetrack sludge. The gelding shakes his head from side to side in an effort to clear his vision and never sees a racing commission employee affix the small numbered tag to his bridle that indicates he has been claimed away from owner Michael Gill and trainer Michael Catalano. Unaware of the circumstances, the Ridge turns and trudges the opposite way up the homestretch, a proud workhorse in decline led down a well-worn and familiar path.

RUNNING STAG cleared quarantine in time to beat the daylights out of a damn good allowance field in New York yesterday, cementing his status as the main danger to Behrens in next Saturday's MassCap. The race included five horses who had either won or placed in graded stakes, but jockey Shane Sellers made it look as if the 8-to-5 favorite was simply out for a stroll around the sweeping Belmont Park oval, scoring by an unpressured length and a half after loping past the leaders on the turn. Stag galloped out strongly past the finish wire, stubbornly tugging on the steering bit in an insistent manner that served notice to his passenger that the bay Brit wanted—and was capable of—more strenuous work.

"Shane never really had to ask much of him," trainer Phil Mitchell tells me from his home on the historic grounds of Epsom Downs in southeast England, where he stayed up late into the evening to catch the satellite broadcast of Stag's stateside win. "He just lengthened his stride and took off. He ran on his own power. Once he hit the front, he was where he wanted to be."

Although Running Stag's monster effort was the talk of the track, it is Behrens who continues to command the lion's share of ink in the morning's headlines. Zipping over the Saratoga training course, the nation's top-ranked racehorse breezed an energetic five furlongs in the mud the other day, and the move was impressive enough for conditioner Jim Bond to commit for the first time in print that the six-year-old would return to Suffolk Downs to defend his MassCap title, while stablemate Pleasant Breeze would trek to Kentucky for the Stephen Foster. "Behrens has traveled enough," Bond says in the May 25 *Daily Racing Form*, alluding to the hectic schedule that whipsawed his star steed from Florida to Dubai to upstate New York through the first six months of the season. "Boston is only four hours from Saratoga. I think it's the smart thing to do."

THE GREAT MYTH of horse racing is that the game is the regal and royal Sport of Kings.

Those who rake in the lion's share of racing's profits and the people who market the industry would prefer if folks stuck to the storybook pomp-and-pageantry notion of the sport as it has existed for ages: a blanket of roses in the winner's circle. The dreamy image of a racemare nuzzling her newborn foal in the misty bluegrass. Seven-figure championship classics. Fancy hats, big cigars, and mint juleps. But like many so-called certainties of the turf, these images don't represent the reality of the racetrack.

Not by a long shot.

At one level, there is nothing wrong with ascribing such lavishly elaborate imagery to the sport. Yet from a separate perspective, racetrackers are only fooling themselves if they seriously buy into the fanciful, contrived notion that in horse racing, beauty must always equate to "pretty." To paraphrase a famous Massachusetts statesman, the enemy of truth is not the deliberate lie, but the persistent, persuasive, and unrealistic myth.

Every spring in East Boston, when the $600,000 Massachusetts Handicap looms as a viable and desirable target for the fastest horses in the land, two divergent worlds pass briefly through each other's elliptical orbit. And when the rough-around-the-edges people and ponies of New England collide with the high-profile jet-setters of the game, the result is fascinating ascertainment that Thoroughbred racing—while far from the Sport of Kings—is, without a doubt, the king of sports.

The stable area at Suffolk Downs is both physically and sociologically separated from the outside world: a dirt-and-asphalt enclave of barns, dormitories, tack rooms, and storage sheds fenced off and heavily guarded from the surrounding sprawl of urbanity. On the backstretch, time defers to the resolute routine of the racehorse, whether on a daily clock dictated by the unwavering regimen of training-feeding-racing-feeding-rest or the broader calendar that measures seasons in terms of track openings and closings. Many of the grooms, hotwalkers, and fringe players who work the New England circuit live on site in subsidized housing and rarely get a chance to venture beyond the confines of the property, except to dart across Revere Beach Parkway to the mega-supermarket or out the back gate for a pre-dawn cup of Dunkin' Donuts coffee. Since most of these laborers lack access to an automobile, the farthest they will venture all year is a thirty-five-mile van ride up the highway with their horses when racing switches to Rockingham. If one compounds the captive monotony of the local Thoroughbred culture over the blur of many racing seasons, it is no surprise to learn that a significant chunk of the Suffolk Downs working population might toil for years in this secluded equine commune without ever once crossing the Mystic River into downtown Boston— a journey of barely three miles, but so far removed from the perspective of a backstretch lifer that the notion of a big city across the bridge might just as well be another out-of-reach racetrack rumor.

Backstretch folk fully ingrained in the game tend to be an even-keeled bunch—not overly excited when things are going great, never too low when the breaks are bad. At Suffolk Downs, the fast-approaching MassCap is no exception, yet the impending main event evokes a contrast in attitudes when New England's Million Dollar Day of Racing is considered from the viewpoint of a laborer who barely clears $200 a week. Whereas media relations employees and fans in the grandstand are immersed in anticipation, the hired help shoveling shit out by the salt marsh are only grudgingly aware of the main event. If anything, the prevailing attitude is one of fascination tinged with resentment.

"Lookit this," says a groom to two cronies in the backstretch kitchen over breakfast, stabbing at a sprawled-out *Racing Form*. I sit one table away, attacking scrambled eggs while glancing through the same edition of the paper. "A million bucks in purses. Some horse will ship in from New York or California to take the money and run, and we won't see a fucking penny of it—as usual."

The guy does have a point. The last time a local won the MassCap was in 1987, when Waquoit narrowly defeated national powerhouse Broad Brush. Now, the cash up for grabs on New England's Million Dollar Day of Racing equals roughly 10 percent of purses for Suffolk Downs' *entire* six-month race meet. As far as most of the backstretch is concerned, the $600,000 MassCap itself could be better divided to fund 150 separate races for the hard-knocking bottom claimers who run at the track's minimum claiming level for barely $4,000 a pop.

And it's not just a money issue: After trudging through a long winter under working conditions devoid of many basic amenities, it can be a slap in the face for a stablehand to suddenly see a single barn—the one that will house the high-profile stakes shippers for just a few days—newly whitewashed with gleaming paint and freshly clayed floorings, the bedding of each stall cushioned thigh-high with enough straw and shavings to last half a month for the average Suffolk Downs steed. A large sign will be erected at the stable gate to welcome out-of-town guests, and complimentary round-the-clock security will be provided for their visiting horses. In addition, the MassCap owners, trainers, and even their *grooms* will be offered gratuitous hotel rooms, rental cars, perhaps with chauffeured drivers to take them to and from some of the swankiest restaurants and nightspots in the city, and an entire week of parties and festivities will be capped off by a lavish Boston Harbor party cruise on a private yacht the night before the big race. Considering the circumstances, it is easy to see why those who do the Suffolk Downs dirty work might feel slighted, sort of like the girlfriend deemed fine for a roll in the hay 364 days out of the year, but out of luck when it comes time to be shown off on the arm of track management come prom night.

Still, however collectively snubbed the backstretch lifers might get over the annual outlay of generosity, the bitterness is almost always fleeting. Once the horses and the TV cameras start arriving for the MassCap, the atmosphere of the entire stable area shifts perceptibly, taking on an air of importance, as if the presence of sleek, strong equine athletes weighing in for a truly big prize fight has rekindled some long-dormant spirit for the sport, that alluring feeling of boundless possibility that initially attracts most racetrack lifers but later gets bludgeoned to bits by the monotonous grind of the game. This newfound feeling spreads rapidly by simple, social association, and diehard racetrackers begin to feel good just by being connected in some small way with the big event: They'll offer to let shippers borrow some inevitably forgotten piece of equipment, show the grooms where to get ice for their buckets, or pitch in just by offering a friendly face or a pleasant bit of conversation. And in turn, whether they know it or not, the visiting horsemen reciprocate by showing the locals that they actually have quite a bit in common with the Eastie backstretch clan, that the only real difference between one hardworking horseman and another is the presence or absence of a really fast Thoroughbred under the shed row.

When high profile trainer Bob Baffert came to town with Derby winner Real Quiet last season, the most enjoyable aspects of MassCap week were the impromptu chat sessions that sprang up outside his stakes barn after the silver-haired horseman had dutifully answered every question from the swarming media. It was only after the last of the reporters drifted away that the affable Baffert plunked himself down in a folding chair and rattled off his *best* off-the-record stories about pain-in-the-ass owners, cantankerous racehorses, and low-level racing hijinks from days gone by in the bush leagues. His backstretch audience consisted almost entirely of Suffolk Downs grooms, security guards, and one-pony tricksters who could laugh both *at* and *with* the big-time trainer, and Baffert himself seemed most at ease when doing nothing more than shooting bull on the backstretch. It was a similar atmosphere when Sonny Hine saddled champion Skip Away to back-to-back MassCap wins in 1997 and 1998, as scores of old-timers came out of the woodwork to reminisce with the veteran conditioner about blasts from the past on the old New England circuit. Even amid all the hoopla surrounding the second coming of Cigar in 1996, stoic trainer Bill Mott managed to endear himself to grizzled locals by quietly slipping some anonymous groom a hundred-dollar bill to comb through Cigar's deep straw bedding on hands and knees just to make sure the star steed wouldn't step on some unseen sharp object. Word of this generous act spread rapidly throughout the barn area, but the aura of awe had less to do with Mott forking over a hundred bucks than the gracious impression it made upon the Eastie horse workers who thought, "Damn, this guy really must care about his horses."

I continue to eavesdrop on the brutally frank MassCap criticism flying back and forth between the stable workers at the next table, and as they grow increasingly irate at management's decision to budget $600,000 for a single race, I want to turn around and explain to these guys that their thinking is all skewed, that you have to think of all that cash as marketing money, and not as purloined purses. I want them to see the big picture, to know that in the long run, the exposure of New England's Million Dollar Day of Racing will benefit *everyone* on the circuit, and that no matter how good a job these grooms do with their $4,000 claimers, we sometimes have to pay a premium for big stars to show up so the local industry can reap some badly needed media exposure. It's important to get the word out that the sport still exists and can even thrive under the right circumstances, and it's also critical for everyone who earns a living at Suffolk Downs—from executive board members to backstretch lifers—to know that grand expenditures earmarked for a single Saturday in June buy the track more than enough credibility to last an entire year of racing.

But instead, I keep my mouth shut and say none of this to the grooms. I am the interloper out here on their turf, just another suit from the front office venturing into the stables full of theory and talk. Marketing buzzwords and long-range mumbo jumbo don't get you very far on the East Boston backstretch, where winning a single six-figure horse race is nice, but plainly subordinate to the much more arduous accomplishment of simply surviving, season after season.

THE WEIGHT ASSIGNMENTS for the sixty-first Massachusetts Handicap have been released, and to the shock of no one, Behrens has been pegged as the 121-pound highweight. Not counting the horses that we already know aren't coming, his next closest competitors for the $600,000 showdown include Running Stag (116), Out Of Mind (114), Vision and Verse (113), David (113), Gander (110), and The Groom Is Red (109).

"I think that the weight assignments are pretty fair," trainer Jim Bond tells me when I call him for his media quote on the MassCap weights. "When you are a multiple Grade I winner, you should have to carry the highweight."

Bond's casual acceptance of the poundage allows Suffolk Downs to exhale a silent sigh of relief. No one wants to upset the trainer of the top racehorse in the nation at this stage of the game, and Lou Raffetto was right on the money about the process of handicap weighting being little more than a tedious exercise in racetrack diplomacy. Bond's verbal stamp of approval means that Behrens is as good as in the entry box for the MassCap, because after proclaiming the weights as fair, a conditioner of his repute would never intentionally pull a fast one at the last minute by substituting a lightweight like Pleasant Breeze (111 pounds) in lieu of the stable's star.

"We're excited to bring him back to Boston," Bond continues. "He'll be formidable, tough to beat. Anyone who thinks Behrens will be a bit rusty the first time back can put up their money and try to beat him on MassCap Day."

I REACH trainer Philip Mitchell via telephone from across the pond, and the Brit jauntily fields questions about Running Stag and his rematch with arch-rival Behrens. Just this morning, Mitchell was forced to part ways with Shane Sellers, his anticipated U.S. jockey, after an accidental double-booking of mounts led to a riding conflict in a Kentucky stakes race the same afternoon as the MassCap. Sellers was torn between riding two fast stakes horses in two different parts of the country on the same day, but Mitchell made Shane's choice easy by dispensing with the bullshit and instead awarding the mount on Stag to up-and-coming John R. Velazquez. Ever the diplomat, Phil explains to me that as long as his horse is in fine form, it really doesn't matter which of the nation's top riders climbs aboard Running Stag's broad bay back for the MassCap.

"It's not a problem," Mitchell explains. "John was supposed to ride Running Stag in the MassCap last year, but then *he* had another commitment. Shane picked up the mount and he caught on with us for the rest of the year. Running Stag? He's wintered really well. After some time off, he came back looking absolutely like a million dollars. He's completely physically changed; I'd say he's 30 percent better than last year. This is something we always knew he'd do, or rather always knew he *could* do, from age five to age six. He's in great shape. Running Stag is better than ever. We're ready."

Mitchell outlines travel plans for what he's glibly billing as his "Boston Stag Party." In three days, the horse will van five hours north from New York with two assistants from his temporary barn at Belmont, arriving on the East Boston backstretch late Tuesday morning. The trainer himself will fly in from England two days later, "just in time for the Red Sox game." While most horsemen are all business in the days leading up to a major stakes event, Phil is the antithesis of tension. Although he does not come right out and say so, it is easy to get the feeling that Mitchell treats his transatlantic endeavors as a gift bestowed upon him by the racing gods, an opportunity to explore the world thanks to a truly talented racehorse. Although years of difficult work are evident in Phil's impeccable standing within the international racing community, he is hardly one of those people who needs to be told to take time to stop and smell the roses. To him, Thoroughbred racing is a one vast garden of strange and stimulating flora, and the privilege of being allowed to cultivate one of its blooming specimens is as much of an enjoyable journey as a final destination.

WITH THE ARRIVAL of MassCap week, the press box at Suffolk Downs—like any track hosting a major event—becomes a blur of activity. My chief duty as media relations director now becomes maintaining daily contact with the trainers of top contenders, because the working press will be expecting notes and quotes to help round out their stories as the region's richest horse race approaches.

In this role, it is imperative to respect a fine line between a horseman's privacy while obtaining enough information to help the media assemble credible coverage. Some old-school trainers prefer not to be bothered at all with what they consider to be mindless pre-race meddling by the media, and they neither desire nor recognize the need to publicize the sport that provides them a livelihood. Others don't mind speaking on the record about their racehorses, but are simply too shy, awkward, or unaccustomed to the spotlight to grant smooth interviews. A handful are natural talkers who know exactly what to say, when to say it, and to whom, but such racetrackers—a publicist's dream—are few and far between. So what I try to do as the media relations guy is strike a balance right off the bat: I phone the major MassCap players about a week in advance and ask to prearrange a certain time that works best for *them* so I can check in for daily updates on their starters. As incentive to cooperate, I point out that if they block off five or ten minutes each morning for me, it will preempt a horde of individual reporters with essentially the same questions from hounding them the rest of the day. Even the most crabby conditioners usually see the logic of this arrangement, and the end result is that Boston beat writers get to fill their notebooks with ample quotes while trainers enjoy peace of mind without the phone ringing all afternoon long.

Jim Bond is one of the better horsemen to deal with. After speaking with him regularly during his two previous forays to the MassCap, I can attest to the trainer's punctuality, reliability, and frankness. A forty-two-year-old straight shooter from western New York, Bond began helping his father with show horses at age six. The stable eventually morphed into a racing outfit based at Finger Lakes, where on his sixteenth birthday, the elder Bond gave his son a choice between training his very own $1,500 claiming filly or the gift of a new car. "I won a couple of races with her," Bond admitted years later in a press profile, "but let's just say I probably should have taken the car."

On his own ever since, Bond improved in leaps and bounds on the upstate circuit, yet it wasn't until the late 1980s that his career hit a major upswing, when he was first asked to train a stable of horses for Virginia Kraft Payson, a high-profile horse breeder with deep pockets. Soon enough, Jim found himself with a barnful of real runners and success began to blossom, which then enabled him to attract other major clients. Within a decade, the plainspoken guy from the backwater track in central New York was wintering down south in Florida, winning prestigious Grade I stakes such as the Travers at Saratoga, and jetting to—and placing in—far-flung international racing events like the $6-million Dubai World Cup.

Several years ago, on the advice of an aunt, the modest trainer decided to play up the famous moniker he shares with the fictional spymaster from the movies. Now, H. James Bond sends all his horses to the training track wearing saddle towels bearing the "007" secret agent logo, and when I phone his racing stable for an update this morning, an assistant informs me that's exactly where Mr. Bond is at the moment, preoccupied with observing a key workout for one of his stakes horses. The way the young lady relays this information to me, at a terse but courteous clip, even makes the whole thing sound like some sort of covert espionage maneuver. But I figure Jim must be busy with Behrens, so I leave word that I will try him later that morning. Even though I can't obtain quotes from the trainer just yet, at least I know what my lead item for the press notes will be. I decide to sit back and wait for the official workout times to be published before getting back to Bond to flesh out the details concerning the MassCap champ's final tune-up before Saturday's big rematch.

The Saratoga workouts pop up onto my computer screen just a bit before noon. Only trouble is, the name Behrens is nowhere to be found on the list.

Exasperated that the clockers were so incompetent as to miss the morning training move of the top horse in the nation, I phone Bond immediately, knowing that the trainer is sharp enough to hand-time all his own horses anyway. Waiting for Jim to answer, I scan further down the list to see that Pleasant Breeze worked six furlongs in preparation for next month's Stephen Foster, but that doesn't help me with Behrens. By the time someone at the stable finally tracks down the boss, I can sense that Jim is in no mood for idle chat. It's obviously been a busy morning, but Bond is one conditioner who never ducks the media. Like a fastball straight down the plate, Jim can be brusque and businesslike when he has to. But at least the guy keeps his word and allocates time for daily interviews with the host track that is putting up the $600,000 his top steed will try to earn in a little under two minutes come Saturday.

The timing snafu has nothing to do with lazy clockers. Behrens, it turns out, simply didn't train.

"No, everything's good," Bond tells me, and I take his word for it because I can't detect any sort of wavering or stress in his tone. "As we get closer to the race, Behrens is doing fine. We didn't work him today. Maybe Tuesday. Maybe Wednesday. I'm not sure yet. He'll probably go a half mile." Racehorses are disciples of custom, and so are their conditioners. Yet Thoroughbreds routinely reveal themselves to be highly adaptable animals, so who's to second-guess a world-class trainer just because he puts on his game face and tweaks his training regimen a little bit? There's no rule on the books that says Jim Bond has to tip his hand five days before a big race.

But there's also no law against wondering if the absence of power-house Behrens from the Saratoga worktab was an orchestration of accident or design.

IT'S EARLY for a press-box degenerate like me, but nearly a full day's work is already in the books by backstretch standards when I speak to

Jim Bond a bit after 8:00 AM on Tuesday. He is standing by the rail at the training track across the street from historic Saratoga Race Course in upstate New York, speaking calmly into a cell phone, patiently explaining to me that it is no big deal that he has once again decided to postpone the final pre-race blowout for his defending MassCap champ.

"Behrens just galloped two miles today," Bond tells me matter-of-factly. "We're going to send him out three-eighths—maybe a half mile—tomorrow morning."

Jim downplays the sudden switch in pre-race strategy for Behrens, who hasn't raced in sixty-five days and has now skipped public workouts in each of the last seven, after a pattern of regularly spaced training runs dating back to April 25. But Bond is noticeably tight-lipped. He curtly declines to elaborate further on the issue of workout recency, and instead asks if he can help me out with any other questions before he has to get back to work.

I ask the first thing off the top of my head, just to be able to provide more copy for the press notes. But Jim is equally ambiguous when I query about how he envisions Saturday's race will unfold, especially considering that Running Stag nearly caught the MassCap field napping by seizing the lead last year. Will Bond's star be positioned closer to the early action this time around? Does he fear a "race-within-a-race" setup that might force a headstrong Behrens to choose between winning the internal pace battle at the expense of losing the overall war?

"I really can't tell you that," Jim counters, adding that he defers all the actual race-riding to first-call jockey Jorge Chavez, a capable veteran. Although I find it difficult to believe that Bond, a master tactician, won't have a strong say in how he expects the MassCap to play out, I understand his desire not to have his game plan divulged in print. By way of explanation, he instead brings up the recent Pimlico Special—in which Pleasant Breeze stunned the field for second at 35 to 1—as a good example of what happens when pre-race pace plans go right out the window. The race just totally "fell apart," he says, when several key speed horses ran into trouble shortly after the start.

"So," H. James Bond adds cryptically, sounding more and more like his secret agent namesake as MassCap Day approaches, "you never really know what's going to happen in this game."

DESPITE WHAT BOND SAYS, one thing I *do* know for certain is not going to happen—now that I'm spending every morning of MassCap week in close proximity to tightly wound Thoroughbreds—is that I am *not* going to put myself in a position to get jackhammered by a racehorse again, the way the feisty Blackwater tagged me with his teeth back in February. A purple souvenir of soreness lingers on my shoulder as evidence of that savage encounter, so it is with a wary eye that I note the nearest route of escape when Running Stag emerges from his souped-up horse van inside the main Suffolk Downs stable gate. His level, intelligent head is cocked in defiant curiosity, and he struts down the loading ramp with an air of aloof superiority that suggests the confident challenger is haughtily unaware that he finished second here last year in the MassCap, not first.

A well-proportioned athlete with a radiant bronze coat that tapers to black at his thick shoulders, muscular hindquarters, and dappled, tucked-up belly, Stag practically drags assistant Roger Teal over to a patch of backstretch grass and begins methodically sampling the Suffolk Downs foliage, tearing into the choicest tidbits of turf. The van ride from Belmont Park was uneventful, says Teal, an affable, likable Brit who has circled the planet as Running Stag's constant traveling companion. Roger also doubles as the six-year-old's regular exercise rider, and the two have shipped as a team to Hong Kong, the Middle East, and all over Europe and the United States so many times during the last several seasons that, as Teal puts it, a five-hour van trip from Long Island to Boston is just "another walk in the park" for a seasoned, globe-trotting bloke like Stag.

One glance at Running Stag's past performances—thirty-six starts with nineteen in-the-money finishes at twenty separate racecourses in six different countries—and it is clear that this runner is not fazed in the least about having his passport stamped. If such a thing as "travel tolerance" can be bred into a racehorse, Stag's diverse pedigree would also indicate an innate ability to bed down in a different stall every few weeks without any adverse effects on performance. Bred by global powerhouse Juddmonte Farms, Running Stag's sire, Cozzene, is an American-born champion miler whose own father, Caro, was an Irish-bred champion in France. Running Stag's dam, Frühlingstag, is a French-bred mare whose lineage reads like a *Who's Who* of German breeding influences. Yet Running Stag's hectic touring schedule is only partly dictated by the whims of his human connections: Earlier in the week, trainer Phil Mitchell floored me by explaining the litany of agricultural restrictions imposed upon livestock shipments in and out of Europe. Basically, a racehorse can leave the continent for up to thirty days without triggering an additional thirty days of quarantine upon reentering Great Britain. So if Stag flies to New York for a May 24 allowance race followed by the June 3 MassCap and maybe the June 11 Brooklyn Handicap back at Belmont, he must then go all the way back to England to prepare for his late-summer assault on Saratoga. Otherwise, he's over the thirty-day limit, stuck somewhere in a European quarantine barn, and Mitchell would rather risk an expensive air-freight bill than deal with the consequences of an entire month of missed training.

It would seem that the far more reasonable solution would be to simply leave Running Stag in the United States all the way through to the autumn Breeders' Cup Championships. But Mitchell dismissed that idea outright as soon as I suggested it. His reason? "Purely because," he intoned playfully, as if trying to explain something that everyone involved with Stag already knows to be a universal truth, "this horse *does* get bored."

Barn 6 on the Suffolk Downs backstretch used to house the horses of trainer Al Borosh, but the longtime New Englander uprooted his operation and rumbled out of town last month, vacating the premises. The structure has been newly minted as the stakes stable, and the pristinely prepared stalls on the eastern side of the shed row have all been left intentionally open so that the two British trainees (Mitchell has also sent a sprinter named Mister Tricky for the $250,000 Moseley

Handicap) can enjoy some privacy during their short stay as guests during MassCap week at Suffolk Downs.

Mister Tricky, a five-year-old chestnut, has one of those white blazes that runs diagonally down the length of his nose before curling under his lip, and the gelding steps into his stall obediently, twitching his ears and sniffing at everything new—the salt breeze off the Atlantic, a bulldozer going by, the Hispanic chatter of hot-walkers riding by on bicycles. Running Stag, however, has neither time nor interest in local sights and sounds. The decidedly more dominant of the duo is all business, lashing out at a row of empty water buckets groom Tony Bishop has lined up at the perimeter of the shed row to fill with bottled water. Satisfied at having sent the heavy plastic containers scattering, Stag allows himself to be wrestled by Teal into stall 17 ("he *has* to have the corner stall; he always wants to be where the action is"), where the horse commences to torpedo his head into his knee-deep cushion of wood shavings, coming up for air with an intimidating snort that sprays fragrant, wafer-thin chips of bedding in all directions.

Stag then bares his teeth in a wide-mouthed leer probably intended to be menacing, which isn't when you stop to think how cartoonish the posturing, wild-eyed beast looks in the throes of his attention-getting antics: bulging eyes glowering from beneath an unruly mop haircut reminiscent of Moe from *The Three Stooges*, his jet-black mane peppered with wood shavings.

"Careful now, he'll go after you if you let him," Teal warns me, smirking as I flinch instinctively from what I'm quickly learning is an all-too-familiar Running Stag rampage. "He's a bit of a character, you know?"

THE EQUINE HOOF is a marvel of durability. The horse is a single-toed animal, bearing two-thirds of its weight on two front legs, with the final bone of each hoof (the "toe") encased in tough layers of protein fed by a microscopic complex of blood vessels. The feet of a healthy racehorse can absorb an incredible amount of shock. But a pinprick of impact in the wrong place at the wrong time can cause stress to even the most resilient of soles, resulting in an almost undetectable hematoma on the underside of the hoof. Some intuitive trainers and farriers are better than others at diagnosing such "stone bruises," which are at once one of the most common yet widely misunderstood equine injuries.

When a stone bruise is fresh, it is likely to cause mild lameness. The tenderness usually dissipates within a few days, or can otherwise be corrected with temporary padding or a change in shoeing. Many horsemen (and horses) simply choose to ignore them, and it is a back-stretch certainty that a handful of Thoroughbreds on any given day at any given racetrack will compete with varying degrees of stone bruises, running right through the mild pain. A stone bruise is hardly a life-threatening ailment—the human equivalent would be stepping on a pointy rock at the seashore with bare feet—and most steeds tolerate them from time to time with barely an impact on their everyday schedules.

The exception, of course, is when a stone bruise occurs to the top-ranked racehorse in the nation. Then the Thoroughbred world veers madly off its axis, tilting off course for a rotation or two before the gravity of the game gently tugs the sport back into rhythmic syncopation. In other words, shit happens.

I know something is up when I can't get the usually dependable Bond to return my Wednesday morning phone calls. A slew of beat reporters has crowded into the Suffolk Downs press box in anticipation of today's MassCap press conference. Half an hour before the post-position draw, with the trainer of the heavy favorite missing in action, I hustle over to Lou Raffetto's office to see if the GM can yank a string or two to ensure that Behrens's connections will be available to field questions from the assembled media.

But Lou is busy. In fact, he's on the phone with Bond himself, who is explaining why it is highly unlikely that he will be able to honor his commitment to run the defending champ in the sixty-first Massachusetts Handicap. The track executive and the trainer exchange veterinary lingo in rapid-fire succession, but the bottom line on Behrens can be best summed by an old racetrack cliché: No hoof, no horse.

At dawn this morning, Jim Bond once again canceled the scheduled workout for the MassCap favorite after detecting a minor injury his instincts sensed had been simmering since last weekend. Behrens had begun favoring his left front leg, and although the hitch in his step was oh so imperceptible, it did not escape the watchful eye of his conditioner, who had been hoping against hope that the ailment would pass. Jim himself admits that Behrens's mild soreness could still wear off by the end of this afternoon, but even if his injured millionaire makes an immediate recovery from his stone bruise, it still means Bond won't be able to hone his top gun to the peak of fitness with only seventy-two hours before the big race.

What Jim is willing to do, he tells Raffetto, is wait and see how Behrens acts tomorrow morning, and then maybe take a last-chance test drive around the Saratoga training track to find out if his horse is fit enough to race. But, the conditioner cautions, the more likely scenario come Saturday will be that understudy Pleasant Breeze will make the four-hour van ride east to Suffolk Downs as a last-minute substitution for the most recognizable name in the game. Lou Raffetto's MassCap, the pet project he's been nursing for nearly twelve months now, has just fallen completely apart. To his credit, the man barely blinks.

Raffetto, after all, is a horseman himself. He understands the randomness of freak injuries, and the merciless measure by which they are doled out by the racing gods. Maybe—and Lou is a superstitious person—Suffolk Downs already got its big break in the stone-bruise department when Cigar was sent to the MassCap starting gate despite one on his right front hoof in 1996. But on that afternoon Cigar was the 1-to-10 favorite in what amounted to little more than an exhibition match, and he could have run around the track backward under Jerry Bailey and still finished first. Raffetto requires no apology from Bond for wanting to withdraw Behrens at the last minute, because Lou understands there's nothing you can do when a horse steps the wrong way and wrenches his foot. The media, on the other hand, will be hounding both Bond and Raffetto for explanations, and with the conference set to start in less than fifteen minutes, I am told to just get the press lined up in the banquet room, start serving the buffet, and keep quiet about the Behrens defection until after the post-position draw.

But the reporters pick up on the vibe in the press box, and the degenerates begin to question the interns when they catch them frantically running off copies of Pleasant Breeze statistics for the media kit, literally at the last minute. In addition, several scribes have already queried why there are no official press notes about this morning's Behrens workout, and the air is rife with rumor. Since I'm not a very good liar, I simply tell any writer who asks me directly that yes, Behrens is injured, and that no, I'm just as in the dark as they are. We'll know more, I assure them, when Jim Bond gives us the official blow-by-blow rundown, which I figure will occur shortly after the post draw but just before the last of the media members avail themselves of a second helping of chicken Kiev at the press luncheon.

At the media conference, the sixty-first edition of New England's richest and most historic horse race officially draws a field of nine, lined up as follows:

Grade II Massachusetts Handicap, 61ˢᵗ Running			
$600,000 Purse (winner's share $400,000), 1 1/8 Miles			
No. Horse	Jockey	Trainer	Morning Line
1 Behrens	Chavez, J.	Bond, H. J.	8–5
1A Pleasant Breeze	Chavez, J.	Bond, H. J.	8–5
2 Gander	Bridgmohan, S.	Assimakopoulos, C.	15–1
3 Vision and Verse	Bailey, J.	Mott, W.	6–1
4 The Groom Is Red	St. Julien, M.	Zito, N.	15–1
5 Makeyourselfathome	Open Mount	Bazeos, P.	30–1
6 Out Of Mind	Delahoussaye, E.	Mandella, R.	9–2
7 David	Gryder, A.	Hushion, M.	5–1
8 Running Stag	Velazquez, J.	Mitchell, P.	5–2

It is a Suffolk Downs tradition to have one totally unexpected, out-of-left-field long shot enter the MassCap at the last minute without being on the radar screen of racing officials, and in this year's edition, it is local lightweight Makeyourselfathome—the horse with the unwieldy name and starry-eyed connections willing to risk $2,000 for the privilege of entering and then another $4,000 to start in a $600,000 stakes. The gelding recently won an allowance race at the Eastie oval by 12-1/4 lengths, but his 107-pound handicap is so light that trainer Peter Bazeos can't even name a jockey at the time of entry because no local rider is capable of tacking so low an impost.

On the other end of the scale, Behrens gets in at 121 pounds, favored as part of a two-horse entry, but it is announced to the media that the defending MassCap champ is a very unlikely starter and that stablemate Pleasant Breeze, entered as his backup, is the more probable of the two. Then trainer H. James Bond does what too few people in the game—horsemen and industry executives alike—are able or willing to do: He steps up to the microphone, via speakerphone from his Saratoga stable, and faces the music.

"Behrens carried just a little bit of heat in his left front foot this morning," Bond begins, speaking slowly, not stopping until each and every media question is answered, even the glaringly redundant ones. "It was ever so slight. Behrens is far too valuable to me and his owners to do anything borderline. You don't work horses unless they're 110 percent. At six o'clock this morning, he was in an ice tub. I did X-rays on both feet, just for my confidence. We've got a little bit of softness on the inside of the left heel on the left side. We've got a few remedies, and hopefully the good Lord will help us get him ready."

"I was originally going to work him three-eighths of a mile this morning. I had to cancel that this morning. The bottom line is I'm just going to wait and see with Behrens and see if I can get a work into him tomorrow or not. In my heart, I cannot take this horse over and work him unless he's 100 percent. He's been too good to me and it's just too long a year. This was supposed to be this horse's coming-out party, and I want to show the rest of the world what a great horse I get to train."

"We've had a lot of rain, about eight days of solid rain. I usually don't have any horses with foot problems, and now I have two horses with stone bruises. It's just a situation that he stepped on something. Unfortunately, when it rains, the stones arise. Nobody will ever know what it was or what it is. It's like people: Some people just wake up in the morning and have a sore leg and they come out of it in 24 hours or less. Everyone's an individual."

It is almost as an afterthought that a reporter finally asks Bond about Pleasant Breeze.

"He's training incredible," Bond replies, seemingly relieved that he can finally put a positive spin on the situation. He adds that regardless of which stablemate starts, the lone certainty is that his longtime go-to guy, Jorge Chavez, will be in the saddle in Boston.

"If you didn't have Behrens in the barn, you wouldn't feel bad bringing Pleasant Breeze anywhere in the country. He's my pinch-hitter right now, and I'll see if I need him for the big race."

THURSDAY DAWNS hot and hazy, and the first day of June offers a sultry hint that the long, humid New England summer is settling in to stay. Two miles south of the track, I'm wincing into the morning glare of the heat-blasted tarmac of Logan Airport, peering eastward in the direction of a screaming jet engine, waiting for a specially booked horse charter from Louisville to roll into view on the cargo runway. Inside the huge, unmarked Boeing 727 is MassCap entrant Out Of Mind, who has flown from Los Angeles after a brief stopover in Kentucky, where he was joined by Run Johnny, the favorite for Saturday's quarter-million dollar Moseley sprint.

Suffolk Downs has picked up the $2,500-per-horse tab for these two highly pampered first-class passengers, an expense that is both a courtesy to their respective connections and a leveraged gamble for the media relations department to try to parlay a bit of last-minute publicity for New England's Million Dollar Day of Racing. When the mighty Cigar shipped into town for his highly hyped second coming in 1996, the East Boston oval went all out to ensure that the media event blossomed into a full-blown promotional circus. The track hired state police details to escort the New York van from the state line all the way to the stable gate, instructing troopers to blast their sirens and flash their blues the entire journey east on the Massachusetts Turnpike. Press-box interns called in "urgent traffic alert" memos to all the local television stations, ensuring that every news helicopter in the region would be hovering above the equine spectacle by the time the entourage snaked its way into the city. With a legendary winning streak on the line, the MassCap was an easy sell that season. But this year's effort falls short of drawing even a fraction of the same media attention, because—let's face it—the airport arrival of a Brazilian steed whose only claim to fame is a long-shot West Coast stakes victory is hardly as compelling as the grand appearance of the number-one horse in the universe.

But still, since track management must make these flight arrangements anyway, and because it's not every day that a Thoroughbred flies into Boston for a big race, it is worth a shot to try to round up a few reporters and camera crews to record the arrival of the MassCap Day contenders. Often, the success of such a media pitch relies more on what is *not* happening elsewhere, and unfortunately for Suffolk Downs, this morning does not appear to be a slow day for breaking, graphic news: A local youth baseball coach has been arrested on child-molestation charges, violent racist threats scrawled on a bathroom wall have closed a suburban high school, and city planners and the Boston Red Sox have scheduled a joint press conference to unveil a new ballpark blueprint that could call for the demolition of venerable Fenway Park. Only one media member—a beleaguered Associated Press photographer who keeps checking her watch—even bothers to show up for our so-called event, and I fear we are in danger of losing her in the next few minutes because the airport press official who is supposed to grant us access into the heavily secured off-loading area has yet to show up to act as our escort.

As chance would have it, the Logan staffer not only zooms up in an air-conditioned shuttle bus just as the AP photographer is about to bail, but he has also managed to round up a trio of TV camera crews and several floating newspaper reporters willing to cover the MassCap deplaning. "Sorry I'm late," the harried airport PR guy says by way of greeting, explaining that the assembled media had swarmed his office twenty minutes ago in search of sound bites to accompany a 500-pound marijuana bust at a separate terminal. "Lucky for you," the publicist quips, snickering at the misfortune of the drug smugglers that led to the unexpected herd of news media for the Suffolk Downs photo-op.

Run Johnny, a compact gray, is led down the high, heavily padded arrival ramp first, followed by Out Of Mind, who clops down the incline at a leisurely, relaxed clip. As the old saying goes, horse racing ain't a beauty contest, but if it was, track officials might as well hand over the MassCap trophy and winner's share of the $600,000 purse check here and now to save this striking steed a trip around the track. A large, well-proportioned, dark brown animal with an almost metallic sheen to his coat, the five-year-old Brazilian could be mistaken for nothing other than a fast, finely honed racehorse. With a square, muscular rear end, Out Of Mind's hindquarters stand a good several inches above my eye level, and the sleek, calm Thoroughbred is the epitome of understated power: muscle on muscle, glistening skin shrink-wrapped around taut sinew.

"Wow, is that the winner of the race?" one of the reporters asks me, totally unaware that the MassCap has yet to be run, a general-assignment scribe sticking around only because his editor told him to.

"You know, he just might be," I reply, similarly mesmerized by Out Of Mind's poised, handsome head, symmetrical, prancing gait, and carefully coiled equine intensity. "Come Saturday, he just might be."

THE ANTICLIMAX everyone has been expecting comes in the form of a midmorning phone call from Jim Bond, who confirms two days before the race that Behrens will indeed not be traveling to Boston for the Massachusetts Handicap. The slightly injured favorite—two months of meticulous preparation derailed by a single step on an unseen stone—has definitively been withdrawn from the $600,000 stakes, although it is very likely that the robust racehorse has no idea he is hurt. Behrens enjoyed a light jog around the Saratoga training track shortly after daybreak, but his trainer's keen eye discerned that the warm-up was not sharp enough for the fragile champion to attempt a more strenuous workout, thereby eliminating the nation's top horse from the MassCap mix.

"He's been in my barn for four years. I know Behrens like the back of my hand. Unfortunately, I probably know him better than my children, and there was just too much tenderness there to send him out for his workout. I don't want to do any damage to him. He's just too good, too classy, to take a chance. I've probably taken more ulcer medicine in the past 24 hours than anyone in the country, but I know in my heart that I'm doing the right thing for Behrens."

And understudy Pleasant Breeze?

"He galloped a mile and a half, very workmanlike. Now we're just sharpening him to get ready to go into the ring on Saturday."

ALTHOUGH THE DEFECTION of the defending champ would be an entirely valid reason for the MassCap pre-race hype to abate and deflate, media interest actually intensifies after the scratch of Behrens, or at least becomes more crystallized as the lead story line switches to the charismatic, globe-trotting British challenger and his affable cast of quotable blokes. Running Stag will almost certainly inherit favoritism in the betting for the $600,000 showdown, and with trainer Philip Mitchell expected to jet into Boston by 3:30 PM Thursday, local turf writers are eager to interview the witty conditioner in the stakes stable as he arrives to inspect his star steed.

In fact, more media will request credentials to visit the Suffolk Downs backstretch this afternoon than during the previous five months of the season combined. As a loose cluster of print reporters, press-box staffers, backstretch workers, and TV cameramen gathers in the sunshine outside Barn 6, even the most critical members of the fourth estate are genuinely impressed with the paint job and general cleanup of the stabling accommodations. The degenerates banter back and forth about the quality of the MassCap and its undercard, and everyone seems to have a competitive opinion about who will win on

Saturday. It's a calm, restful day in the barn area with no live racing scheduled, but it's also one of those rare times that the East Boston oval is infused with anticipation, when everything about the racetrack and its highly charged behind-the-scenes atmosphere seems aligned—even destined—to unfold in fortuitous fashion, delivering a rare slice of the dream that makes the daily grind of the rest of the season bearable.

Then—just as I'm standing there soaking up the aesthetics—a fist-sized brown rat darts out of the cover of the nearby marsh grass and scampers in a panic among our loosely clustered group.

The frightened rodent scuttles in a frenzy in search of the closest escape, which he hastily decides will be up and over the feet of one of the interns and under the cover of the shed row near Running Stag's corner stall. The rat zips frantically into a narrow hole between two bottom barn planks, his thin, twitching tail snaking behind him as he angles downward for the cool, damp safety of clay beneath the stakes stable. The flustered reporters compose themselves by falling back on that old racetrack standby, black humor, threatening to forgo their features on the MassCap in favor of a more sensationalistic exposé about backstretch rodents in East Boston.

"Just make sure you call it a vole, not a rat," cracks one media staffer, ever vigilant about the racetrack's reputation yet unable to resist tacking on a jibe. "You know, the friendly MassCap vole. He could be our mascot. That sure sounds a hell of a lot better than the MassCap rat."

Trainer Mitchell arrives on the scene shortly thereafter, as punctual as a man can get despite Boston's excruciating afternoon traffic. Warm greetings are exchanged all around—Phil is the type of guy who can make even a complete stranger feel like a long-lost friend—and the British conditioner immediately checks in on his charge in stall 17, where Running Stag has suddenly begun thrashing his head up and down as if energetically nodding *Yes!* After a few brief words with his assistants and a look at sprinter Mister Tricky, Mitchell then commences holding court, first answering questions from the group before offering himself up for on-one-one interviews.

A glib, succinct horseman who has benefited from additional experience as a popular television pundit for a U.K. racing channel, Phil perfectly fits the role of gregarious, articulate Englishman. A likable chap who always seems nattily attired in a sweater-vest regardless of the weather, Mitchell comes across as candid and intriguing while managing to remain tactful at all times. He fields the usual assortment of pre-race prattle—why he chose to return to the MassCap, how he regards his horse's chances, which other entrants loom as the main dangers—before several reporters start to dig a bit deeper, curious about how Phil came to acquire the feisty $1.1 million oat-earner in the first place.

Oddly enough, Running Stag was not the initial object of Phil Mitchell's desire. At first, the veteran trainer explains, he was much more intrigued by the raw potential displayed by Stag's older brother, a horse also bred by international bloodstock powerhouse Juddmonte Farms. In France in 1996, Mitchell had watched that particular three-year-old score with style in a difficult stakes at Longchamp before finishing a gutsy third against Group 1 competition at Chantilly. But by the time Phil got around to making a serious offer on the talented son of Irish River, the steed's stock had risen and he was no longer for sale.

Unsure exactly what happened to the horse who initially caught his eye—he believes the animal ended up being shipped to Southern California—Mitchell instead set his sights on acquiring the very next foal that had been produced by the same Juddmonte dam Frühlingstag, a two-year-old colt who had just finished dead last, eleventh, then second in his first three races in France. Based on bloodlines alone, Phil went out on a limb and made a speculative "mid five-figure" purchase on behalf of client Richard Cohen. He allowed the baby colt to mature for four months, and over the winter, the headstrong son of Cozzene easily trounced every other youngster in the Mitchell training yard, including horses who had already broken their maidens. In his first start at age three, Running Stag scored by seven lengths, and the dominant bay has done nothing but win major stakes events all around the planet ever since.

Captivated by the tale, one writer asks Philip if he can recall the name of Running Stag's unlucky older brother, the horse presumably doomed to obscurity.

"Of course," the detail-oriented Brit fires back instantly, without so much as a pause for breath. "I remember him well. The name of that horse was Blackwater."

I nearly choke when I hear those three syllables.

Blackwater? The very same ill-tempered sprinter trained by my old man in Tampa? The ouchy, grouchy gelding with bad hocks but a furious, admirable win-at-all-costs disposition? The same ornery steed who took a slice out of my shoulder? Although the reporters gathered around the stakes stable dutifully scribble Mitchell's comments about the lost equine brother of the leading MassCap contender, the absurd irony of the revelation is meaningless to everyone but me.

"That horse could run," Mitchell says wistfully. "I still wonder whatever became of him."

THE MORNING before the MassCap, the *Boston Globe* leads its sports section with an extensive feature on Jorge Chavez, the first-call rider for H. James Bond. Although the jockey and trainer must now revert to Plan B with Pleasant Breeze, the huge color picture that accompanies the piece—a shot of the thirty-eight-year-old champion astride the muscular Behrens in last year's Suffolk Downs winner's circle—serves as a final photographic reminder of the untimely scratch.

Jorge, the article goes on to reveal, is not too proud a man to openly admit he has a lot to be thankful for. Fearlessly aggressive on the track but generous and soft-spoken away from it, the talented Peruvian overcame an unbelievable combination of abject poverty, lack of formal education, and preposterous odds to rise through the ranks and achieve his dream of riding racehorses.

"Always when I ride, I remember how it was," Jorge reflects in a quiet tone. "Where I came from, I will never forget that. That will always be a part of me. Something I will never forget."

Tomorrow the aggressive Peruvian will partner with the backup horse from the Behrens barn, but the buzz around the press box is that the jockey's keen talent and winning touch just might enable Pleasant Breeze to spring a mild upset. And considering what's gone wrong for Jim Bond so far this week, his choice of rider for the sixty-first MassCap might be the trainer's best—and final—advantage.

BY 7:30 AM FRIDAY, Running Stag has been out for a light trot over the Suffolk Downs surface, dragging traveling companion and exercise rider Roger Teal along for the ride. As has been his custom, Teal allows the curious bay to stop along the outside fence near the six-furlong chute to take in the action on the track and adjacent subway rail, which captivates the attention of the new favorite for the MassCap on this warm, late-spring morning.

"He only literally jogged around there," says Philip Mitchell, entertaining guests, onlookers, and a handful of media members outside Barn 6. Off to the side, Running Stag enjoys a bath and mugs for photographers in a manner that suggests the horse knows he's the center of attention. "He just went for a circuit to stretch his legs. He only ran ten days ago, so we really don't want to do much serious with him."

If Mitchell is relieved that Stag's arch-rival Behrens will be passing on the MassCap, he does not say so. If anything, one gets the sporting sense that Mitchell had been relishing the rematch as an opportunity to turn the tables.

"I think it would have been a very neat race," Mitchell muses, speculating on how the MassCap might have shaped up. "I know my guy is better than last year, and we still would have made a few alterations. But Behrens is the top handicap horse in America and still would have been very tough to beat. I'm not saying his absence will make it any easier. A $600,000 race is not going to be a pushover for anybody. It's going to be a very competitive race. It's always tough for $600,000. But if Stag is fortunate enough to get a win on Saturday, I would put him second-best to Behrens in America."

One of the more refreshing aspects of the Running Stag road show is the open and friendly atmosphere around the Brits' section of the stakes stable, which at many racetracks is a restricted, off-limits, heavily guarded area. Even though management has assigned round-the-clock security to monitor the entire barn, Mitchell and his staff encourage and seem to enjoy being the focal point of the backstretch community. Grizzled, veteran stablehands who never get to lay their eyes—let alone hands—on a championship horse are welcomed under the shed row to pose for pictures and pet Running Stag. Mitchell, Teal, and assistant Tony Bishop answer any and all inquiries, and in return always have a few polite queries of their own about the peculiarities of American racing and training. One visitor who stops by to greet Mitchell is Paul Thornton. After hearing the news that he once trained the older brother of the MassCap favorite without realizing it, my dad has brought the winner's-circle photograph from the day Blackwater pulled his infamous disappearing act on the Tampa Bay Downs backstretch.

"Yes, I *can* see a bit of Stag in him!" Mitchell exclaims, scrutinizing the photograph of the horse he initially coveted but missed out on training. "I remember he was Group 1 placed in France—ten furlongs. Had a real smart closing kick." Led back to his stall after his bath, Running Stag shoots an icy glare in Mitchell's direction upon the mere mention of his name.

My father fills in some of the blanks for Mitchell, picking up Blackwater's tale pretty much from where Phil left off yesterday with the group of reporters: After landing stateside in California, Blackwater struggled at the allowance ranks on the grass before being transferred to Kentucky, where he similarly spun his wheels at Churchill Downs and Keeneland. Soundness and ability deteriorating in slow, inevitable tandem, the horse—eventually gelded somewhere along the way—dropped into claiming company in Ohio, where he finally won sprinting on the dirt at River Downs. Shortening up in distance and adapting his tactics to a more front-running fashion, Blackwater kicked around the Midwest at the low allowance and midrange claiming levels for several seasons at Ellis Park and Kentucky Downs. After finishing up the track at 20 to 1 when entered way over his head at Keeneland, my father was offered the once-regal runner through a sales agent in November for $16,000. Aware that the gelding had hock problems, Thornton then shipped Blackwater to a Florida farm for six weeks of rest before gradually gearing the animal back into action at Tampa Bay Downs.

Mitchell is curious to know if Blackwater, at seven, owned the same fractious, stubborn, headstrong attitude as Running Stag at age six. In lieu of answering, my old man rolls up his sleeve to reveal a months-old war wound courtesy of the older sibling. "Ah yes," Mitchell acknowledges in agreement, sneaking a look over his shoulder at his own malicious steed. "The hot temperament runs in the blood."

But it's what Mitchell *doesn't* say that makes for the true difference between the equine brothers. While the two horses might be genetically similar, their separate environments, flukes of fate, and rigors of racing have conspired to sculpt entirely different physical packages. The legs are the be-all and end-all for any racehorse, and even a casual comparison of the two brings to immediate light the chasm between their abilities: Running Stag's legs are supple, well-proportioned, and thick with sinew. Even standing still in his stall, his limbs resemble pliant saplings. The legs on Blackwater are angular, bony, and slightly crooked, and even in a photograph taken moments after victory, the gelding appears uncomfortable bearing weight on his hind feet, shifting in restless agitation. Fire-breathing attitude, heart, and inbred passion simply aren't enough in this sport, where the wheels are definitely the distinction between horses who travel the world and those who strain to survive for a nickel claiming tag, the distinction between being favored for a $600,000 stakes race and getting lost in a swamp at Tampa Bay Downs.

As the two trainers part, Running Stag lingers, coiled in the back of his stall, ready to strike. The embodiment of pent-up energy, it is impossible to discern what he is sensing—other horses, people, competition, an air of expectancy. The moody dark bay lies keenly in wait for whatever is coming next around the corner, ready and willing to lash out and attack.

———

ON THE OPPOSITE SIDE of the stakes stable, Out Of Mind is led counterclockwise around the shed row by groom Ruben Mercado while trainer Richard Mandella looks on. The Brazilian horse has been given a rest from on-track training after his transcontinental journey, but once morning workouts have officially ended, the meticulous Mandella plans to supervise a schooling session in the paddock, hand-walking his horse the length of the empty homestretch to the saddling enclosure so Out Of Mind can familiarize himself with the surroundings.

"Look at him," says a pleased Mandella, alternating quiet commentary with fluent, firm Spanish instructions to his groom. The forty-nine-year-old conditioner is a man of few words, but it is obvious that he holds this steed in high stead, almost as if Richard harbors an unspoken, scary suspicion that Out Of Mind may be improving faster than he, or anyone else, realizes. "He looks fabulous. He looks like he never left home."

A winner of numerous high-profile stakes races, the West Coast trainer's hallmark is his patient handling of older male horses, many of whom, like Out Of Mind, are South American imports still racing soundly at age six or seven. Although he is a multiple winner of Breeders' Cup races, Mandella is perhaps best known for saddling long shot Dare and Go in the epic upset that snapped superhorse Cigar's sixteen-race winning streak in 1996. Mandella knows a good horse when he sees one, and he demonstrates an uncanny ability to do exactly what needs to be done to bring out the best in each animal that comes under his care.

"Since we switched him to the dirt, which is what he prefers, he's been a pretty good horse." Mandella explains, understating the obvious. "We just let him fall back and he had a pretty devastating run at the end. So we did the same thing in the LeRoy Handicap, and it worked well. We're certainly not going to change it now."

Under the observant eye of his trainer, the burly Brazilian goes about his business in focused fashion, bobbing his massive head while walking at a measured, even pace. Mandella, too, abstractly nods his head in time as Out Of Mind passes by.

"He's real strongly made," the trainer sums. "He's muscular. And he's in the prime of his life."

IT IS NOW twenty-four hours before all the out-of-town MassCap horses must be officially signed into the Suffolk Downs stable area, and the remainder of the stakes shed row is quiet. The New York–based runners—The Groom Is Red, Vision and Verse, David, and Pleasant Breeze—will arrive later today or tomorrow morning. Although some horsemen are big believers in the idea of advance preparation and early shipping (like Philip Mitchell and Richard Mandella), it is worth noting that a number of others (such as H. James Bond and Bill Mott) manage to win a fair share of major stakes by vanning horses to tracks on race day whenever feasible, enabling them to strike quickly, take the money, and run.

Gander and Makeyourselfathome, the two local long shots, don't have much of a choice about MassCap accommodations. Both have been stabled at Suffolk Downs for the duration of the season, and it's a pretty safe bet that neither would be shipping elsewhere to face top-quality stakes horses in a $600,000 graded event. But the allure of big bucks in their own backyard makes it worth a shot for their respective owners to put up the $6,000 starting fee to contest the MassCap, and in the days leading up to the main event, trainers Charlie Assimakopoulos and Peter Bazeos have both been touting the familiarity angle as a factor if the local hopefuls are to upset the richest race of the Suffolk Downs season.

The final publicity prep work before race day is wrapped up by 3:00 PM. With nothing left to do but wait, the attention among media relations staffers now focuses on decompressing over cocktails aboard the MassCap Eve dinner cruise, a gala affair aboard the *Odyssey*, a posh luxury yacht rented by the racetrack for a sumptuous sunset tour of Boston Harbor. With no live racing scheduled on Fridays, the Suffolk Downs crew whiles away the afternoon by betting on assorted simulcasts and kibitzing with local racing writers, and there is no shortage of opinion on tomorrow's outstanding fourteen-race betting card.

Overall, the press box mood is jovial, but the tone of the day—and by extension the entire MassCap—instantly turns somber with the running of the second race from Belmont Park.

The New York race is a maiden event at a mile on the grass. Jockey Jorge Chavez—as usual—is riding first call for trainer Jim Bond aboard a first-time starter named St. Forlene, and the sleek bay appears ready to make a winning move at the top of the stretch. Surrounded by the pack and advancing gamely, head-and-head with the leader, the 9-to-1 shot is poised to kick clear at the quarter pole when Chavez nudges her for acceleration. Like a smart filly, St. Forlene quickens and responds on cue. Horse and rider move in tandem coming off the turn, seemingly set to shoot the gap and stride clear to victory. Then the graceful fluidity, raw power, and vivid elegance of the scene is shattered, disintegrating to confusion and chaos.

Even after repeated viewings of the head-on replays, it is difficult to discern exactly what starts the horrific, chain-reaction accident. Horses scatter, spill, and veer wildly in all directions to avoid a sudden entanglement of limbs, reins, and a downed rider thrown hard to the ground. Jockeys bolt upright in the irons and attempt to jump, swerve, or otherwise avoid high-speed carnage, controlling their mounts by sheer instinct and adrenaline. Seven runners in all are involved in the accident, and three fillies do not even finish the race. One of them, apparently the main cause of the calamity by virtue of a bad step, is the Bond-trained and Chavez-ridden St. Forlene.

Emergency crews arrive on the scene, and only two things are clear in the immediate aftermath: St. Forlene, who rose to try and scamper away with loose, riderless reins flapping behind her, has suffered a compound fracture of her right front medial bone. While Bond's filly is being euthanized via barbiturate injection, a dazed Jorge Chavez lies near her, crumpled and unresponsive on the racecourse. "That's the worst possible place for a spill to happen," says a subdued Larry Collmus, watching in silence along with an equally gloomy cast of press-box degenerates. "A grass race, coming off the turn, sitting second at the quarter pole in the middle of the pack—you've simply got no shot for the other guys to get out of your way."

After several stony moments of silence and a companion shot of the blank Belmont Park tote board, New York race-caller Tom Durkin haltingly informs patrons that Chavez is still prone on the ground and being attended to by the ambulance workers. A few more interminable minutes pass. Everyone in the Suffolk Downs press box is glued to the television monitor. Flailing for a glimmer of good news, a tentative Durkin finally tells the crowd that the champion race-rider does, at the very least, appear to have movement of his limbs. Delicately, the jockey is placed on a backboard and loaded into the waiting ambulance. The issue of whether the cover boy from today's *Boston Globe* will be able to ride Pleasant Breeze in the MassCap very suddenly and scarily becomes secondary to whether the guy will ever be able to walk again.

Then the authoritative, unflinching "Official" sign goes up, horse racing's hollow cue to look away, turn the page, and segue straight into the next scheduled event.

CHAPTER SEVEN

SHOWTIME

A horse gallops with his lungs, perseveres with his heart, and wins with his character.
—FEDERICO TESIO, *Thoroughbred breeding theorist*

VIOLENT THUNDERSTORMS rip the Atlantic seaboard all through the night. Shortly after dawn, I surface from sleep with the sensation of being reeled upward through deep water in super-slow motion, emerging from a racetrack dream in shapeless, vague stages. First I hear the sound of chirping birds and bickering gulls. Then, from below, syncopated horse hooves clopping and splashing through mud, followed by chatter, laughter, and backstretch camaraderie. I discern the warmth of early morning sunlight, the smell of freshly mown grass, and can practically taste the salty-sweet breeze off the ocean. In my half-slumber state, I marvel at how the feeling is so realistic and pleasant, a glorious hallucination of what it would be like to awaken to a perfect day at the track, a day so full of promise that you know— absolutely *know*—that it's never going to end.

Then I hear the shrill voice of an outrider cussing out an insolent exercise jockey whose reckless horsebacking practically forced some poor pony girl over the inner rail, and it is only then I realize that I *am* waking up at the track, groggily regaining possession of my faculties on a beat-up futon mattress on the floor of the Suffolk Downs announcer's booth.

Ever year I harbor harrowing anxiety about oversleeping on the morning of the MassCap and can never get a good night's rest. I hazily recall that this season, I wanted to avoid that by bringing my sleeping bag, shaving kit, and new suit of clothes to the track one day in advance. After the booze cruise last night, I opted to crash in the press box rather than risk the thirty-mile drive home, so now here I am, five stories above the finish wire at 6:30 AM on the morning of New England's Million Dollar Day of Racing.

I hit the backstretch by 7:15 AM to find Phil Mitchell holding court outside Barn 6, chatting easily with a group of locals. On the opposite side of the stable, Richard Mandella has sent Out Of Mind to the track under his exercise rider for an easy jaunt. The horse van from Belmont Park has arrived, and The Groom Is Red—owned by Boston Celtics basketball coach Rick Pitino—is being walked counterclockwise around the shed row while MassCap veteran Bill Mott tends to Vision and Verse and three other favorites for the undercard stakes. Pleasant Breeze is also on the grounds, but when Jim Bond ships in from Saratoga, he prefers to stay away from the hoopla. He and trainer Bobby Raymond are close pals from back in the days at Finger Lakes, and although the internationally known stakes conditioner and the surly trainer of a hermaphrodite horse seem an unlikely pair, Bond knows that the Raymond stable is a nice, quiet spot where reporters or curious onlookers are unlikely to venture.

I get a cup of coffee in the jockeys' room and see that the *Boston Herald* has given the MassCap double coverage on both its front and back pages. Page one of the morning tabloid features a big color portrait of roguish Running Stag nibbling on a gushing water hose, and the back depicts local hopeful Makeyourselfathome preparing for an unlikely upset. The *Boston Globe* also prominently trumpets the big day of horse racing on the outer cover of its sports section, where Michael Madden waxes poetic about the MassCap in a column titled "Suffolk Center of Thoroughbred Universe Today:"

. . . Suffolk Downs once again will do very well. It will be the centerpiece of all Thoroughbred racing in America today.

It has been this way for six years, and even in retrospect, the accomplishment is amazing. Lotteries, casinos, scratch tickets, untold gambling opportunities and the shortsightedness of horse racing itself—for decades racing feared television, thus losing generations of new fans—have reduced horse racing's interest level to that of . . . well, soccer.

Major league sports cities usually have very minor league tracks. Philadelphia, San Francisco, Seattle, Detroit, Cleveland, Chicago, Washington-Baltimore, St. Louis, Houston, Phoenix and on and on have races at the level of Triple A baseball all the way down to Single A. And yes, Boston, too, is in that mix. Only New York, Los Angeles, Miami (in the winter), and Kentucky truly have major league racing.

But for one day of the year Suffolk Downs is most unlike all those other middling tracks. It is the place where all horse racing eyes are on the Massachusetts Handicap run in East Boston.

Today is that day.

After reading the race-day coverage, I put down the newspapers and get the real news of the day from the Suffolk Downs clerk of scales: Jorge Chavez managed to escape serious injury after yesterday's grisly spill in New York. Although his X-rays are negative, the Eclipse Award–winning jockey is too sore to ride this afternoon and will have to give up his MassCap mount. Caught in a pinch, with nationally ranked riders already booked to Saturday commitments all across the country, trainer Jim Bond has awarded the last-minute ride aboard Pleasant Breeze to Boston's top jock. This afternoon, Josiah Hampshire Jr. will have his shot against the big boys, and dame fortune has arranged it so the leading local rider will be able to show the racing world what he can do on his home court.

IN THE OPENER, a fleet local filly named Ms. Sadira wires the field at 3 to 1 under a confident Joe Hampshire, and the screaming grandstand erupts in a crescendo of cheers.

On the occasion of the region's only major horse race, the Suffolk Downs throng always arrives ready and willing to get pumped up for

Thoroughbred revelry. Nooks and crannies of the cavernous concrete facility that go unused 364 days out of the year come alive on MassCap Day, and one doesn't have to walk too far into the plant—past roving entertainers, Dixieland quartets, clowns, and organ-grinding monkeys—to realize that this is a major urban sporting event with a spirited atmosphere. By noon, the outdoor beer garden is wall-to-wall with college students. Big cigars, binocular cases, and thick wads of cash overflow the clubhouse box seats, and sporty gentlemen in seersucker suits accompanied by fashionable ladies in classy hats occupy every available table in the open-air Terrace Dining Room. All the grandstand apron benches are taken, and beyond that, a crush of lawn chairs lines the asphalt beach all the way to the eighth pole, where fans slather on sunscreen and soak up the vibe being pumped out by a local reggae band. Gleeful children queue up for free pony rides, balloons, and face painting, and kids of all ages try their hand at interactive horse-racing games sponsored by the National Thoroughbred Racing Association's Racing Experience "fan van." The flavor of the afternoon is refreshingly festive, and even though the gravity of a $600,000 horse race lends an expectant air and feeling of importance to the proceedings, in short, this is the one day of the season that the embattled East Boston oval truly *rocks*.

Carousing aside, New England's Million Dollar Day of Racing has come up as a gem of a betting affair. In addition to the MassCap, the fourteen-race program contains the $250,000 Moseley Breeders' Cup Handicap, a $50,000 grass stakes, and a trio of $25,000 supporting stakes. Eight solid allowance races with mostly full fields round out the wagering mix, with nary a single maiden or claiming contest on the card. Making the pre-race walk past the crowd from the stables, the horses look healthy, athletic, and on the muscle, and it is obvious that somewhere behind the scenes on the backstretch, Suffolk Downs grooms and caretakers have painstakingly taken the time to braid manes and clip their steeds so their animals make a sharp appearance in the paddock before the biggest crowd of the year. Even the hard-luck horsemen who usually show up in the saddling ring looking like they've just rolled out of bed have put on a sport coat or tie for

MassCap Day, and the quality of racing is at once complex and high-ly competitive.

In the second race, hard-trying long shot Starship Ensign gets loose on the lead and escapes to the tune of $55.40. The advantage swings back to favorite players in the third, when intense rookie Dyn Panell aggressively hustles home Valid Miss Chain at 2 to 1, driving to the wire under a relentless, heady hand ride without using the whip. From the roof of the grandstand, I can see cars are backed up all the way past the grain barn on the access road, almost out to Route 1A, a good six furlongs from the track's main parking lot. Reporters arriving late tell me that the highway from downtown Boston is backed up for three miles all the way to the airport tunnels, and even the most senior degenerates cannot recall the last time they missed the daily double because of racetrack traffic. Downstairs among the masses, business is brisk, and the only major complaint is that there aren't enough mutuel tellers to handle the onslaught of new fans who've suddenly caught a highly contagious case of betting fever.

Lou Raffetto, as usual, is adeptly juggling about seven MassCap tasks at once. He has briefly commandeered my desk and phone line in the press office to crunch the early returns with the mutuels man-ager, projecting a blistering betting pace based on the day's first few races. So far, everything has gone according to plan, including the one key item that is out of anyone's control—the serenely sunny weather.

"So did you somehow manage to arrange for a nice day, too?" I kid Raffetto, who only a few hours before daybreak was facing the prospect of nasty thunderstorms that threatened to waterlog his rac-ing surface, turf course, betting card, and season-high crowd of cus-tomers.

"Actually, no," Lou responds, serious but smiling. "You know who always takes care of that." It takes me a moment to figure out what Raffetto is talking about, but then the memory comes back as clearly as the bright, breezy sky outside.

In 1995, when management was readying for its revival of the MassCap after a six-year absence, Jim Moseley, the man responsible for the return of racing to Suffolk Downs, was badly sick with lymphoma.

Despite toughing out a slew of caustic cancer treatments, Mr. Moseley still wanted to do whatever he could to pitch in and make the MassCap a success. Aware that the well-respected chairman of the board would sacrifice his own health at the expense of a horse race if allowed to overwork himself, Raffetto half-jokingly entrusted Jimmy with but one tough task—delivering sunny weather for the risky venture.

The impossible assignment became a running gag between the two track execs, a lighthearted way to relieve the pressure of a serious illness while allowing the benevolent boss to remain involved. That year, MassCap Day dawned cloudy and stayed overcast until the main event. But when the horses came out in the post parade for the big race, radiant, luminous sunshine streamed down upon the track.

Mr. Moseley presented the winning trophy to the connections of Cigar that afternoon, and would only live to see two more editions of the showcase race he loved so proudly. But Jimmy must still be exerting his influence in some fashion, because every single year since his passing, the weather has been bright and brilliant for the Massachusetts Handicap at Suffolk Downs.

VETERAN WARHORSE PROLANZIER—the ten-year-old who gashed his leg open en route to a gritty winter victory back in January and once ran third behind Cigar in the MassCap—steals the show in Race 5, scoring lifetime win number thirty, leading at every call. Again, the rider is Joe Hampshire.

The top Boston jock is riding "in the zone" this afternoon, achieving that Zen-like state of horsebacking in which every instinctive move is a winning one. With two tallies and a pair of seconds from the first five races, Hampshire's luck continues into the seventh, even though he is forced to check back sharply on High Above when making what appears to be a winning move. But soon after the horses cross the wire, the stewards launch an inquiry into the stretch drive, and after reviewing the replays from several different angles, they determine that the infraction by the leader was enough to keep Hampshire's mount from scoring, so they elevate High Above from second to first. Oddly enough, this particular race is named in honor of the winning trainers of the last five MassCaps, so in the ceremony after the disqualification, Hampshire gets to pose for a picture in the winner's circle with H. James Bond, exactly three hours before the visiting conditioner will give the leading rider a leg up aboard Pleasant Breeze.

"That's the beautiful thing about horse racing and being a jockey," Hampshire tells me in the jockeys' room after stopping to sign autographs for a crush of kids lining the paddock fence. "You've got to be in the right place at the right time.

"Now," he adds, referring to his MassCap mount, "I've got to make it count."

On the other side of the Suffolk Downs locker room, Jerry Bailey sits by himself, engrossed in a *Racing Form*. Alone, aloof, wearing shades indoors and conversing with almost no one unless he has to, the nation's winningest rider (top money earner four of the last five years, with $180 million in lifetime purses) is a case study in making it count when the stakes are high. A poised, polished master of finesse who also happens to know how to articulate slick sound bites, the forty-two-year-old superstar's standoffish nature does not exactly endear him to his race-riding contemporaries, or so it seems. Then again, that attitude seems justifiably reciprocal, because being number one in any competitive endeavor means you go about business with a target on your back. In any event, Bailey will pilot only five hand-picked mounts in this afternoon's stakes races, and four of Jerry's rides have characteristically low morning-line odds of 7 to 5, 9 to 5, 2 to 1, and 5 to 2. MassCap entrant Vision and Verse is the lone outsider at 6 to 1, but Bailey is the first-call jock for top trainer Bill Mott, and the chance to ride an improving horse who was runner-up in last year's Belmont and Travers Stakes is the reason Jerry has even bothered to venture to Suffolk Downs for today's $600,000 race.

As a courtesy—and to make sure the losing riders don't slip out the back door without talking to the media—I sweep the locker room midway through the day to introduce myself to each MassCap jockey and to remind them about the post-race press conference. Most top-notch riders who compete in graded races know the drill, but every year there are scheduling difficulties with out-of-town jocks needing to be whisked straight to Logan Airport to catch the last outbound Saturday shuttle. Winners, I've learned, don't mind taking the time to linger after a big race. But when Real Quiet, for example, lost last year's MassCap at 4 to 5, jockey Gary Stevens blew out of the track so fast that two Suffolk Downs valets had to chase him down in the parking lot because the losing rider had forgotten his helmet and expensive Kevlar safety vest.

Aaron Gryder, up from New York to ride 5-to-1 speedster David, informs me that he might have a travel dilemma. His mount is owned by Barry Schwartz, the co-founder of a multi-billion-dollar fashion empire, and when the CEO of Calvin Klein has his private jet waiting for you on the tarmac, you don't diddle around. Gryder anticipates that he might not even be able to shower before rushing off to make his flight, but Aaron, a courteous sort with a wicked sense of humor, asks if I want his post-race quote ahead of time.

Because David is a textbook example of a one-dimensional speed horse, and since trainer Michael Hushion has been saying all week that his colt will be gunned straight to the lead, Aaron knows that he will either wire the MassCap or, more likely, lead the field as far as he can before being reeled in by the closers. Rolling his eyes and adopting a mock-serious tone, the jockey addresses an imaginary reporter in classic also-ran racetrack phraseology: "He's a good horse, he showed speed, and he hung in as well as he could. We'll regroup and go from there.

"But," Gryder adds with a mischievous glint, "if we win, we're staying."

With little fanfare or notice, young Dyn Panell is another emerging Suffolk Downs regular who has picked up a last-minute berth in the MassCap. The trainer of Makeyourselfathome failed to find a veteran rider anywhere on the East Coast capable or willing to tack 107 pounds for the sake of riding the longest shot on the board in a Grade II handicap, so trainer Peter Bazeos turned to the local kid. With a deft score earlier on the card, Panell has now won eleven races over the past five racing programs, and Dyn has begun to attract attention as the second-leading New England jockey with his quiet, focused style. Since I know he won't be going anywhere after the MassCap—unlike the others, Panell is scheduled to swing into the saddle atop a 20-to-1 turfer in the nightcap—I forgo trying to explain in fragmented Spanish exactly what a "press conference" entails, and instead just wish the twenty-three-year-old good luck.

On the track, the undercard unfolds in a blur of speed, color, and noise. In the stands, the Suffolk Downs diehards are playing fast and loose with their bankrolls, and every flash of the tote board yields an exponentially dizzying chaos of betting volume. Wagering on individual races begins to eclipse the amount the track would ordinarily handle for an entire *program* on a typical winter afternoon, and by the time the stakes portion of New England's Million Dollar Day of Racing rolls around, the glut of money that begins to slam down on the favorites is staggering.

The formidable tandem of Jerry Bailey and Bill Mott do not disappoint their zealous backers, nailing the Old Ironsides Stakes with Distant Mirage ($2.80), the Miss Indy Anna Stakes with Dream for a Moment ($3.40), and the Drumtop Handicap with Queen of Norway ($4.20). But the parade of low-priced winners is blown to the stratosphere by nine-year-old stalwart King Roller ($76.40) in the $250,000 Moseley Handicap. The local long shot grinds out a 3/4-length upset over top national sprinters under patient handling by Winston Thompson, and when Bailey can manage no better than fourth with 7-to-5 favorite Run Johnny, the out-of-the-money performance triggers an $11,065 trifecta and a chorus of salty epithets from the vocal Eastie railbirds.

TWENTY MINUTES before showtime, the Suffolk Downs paddock is electric. Oblivious to the crush of humanity, the eight Massachusetts Handicap entrants calmly circle the walking ring, heads down, all business, surrounded by camera flashes and the highly charged buzz of boisterous horseplayers. A knot of several hundred dignitaries—

owners, trainers, racing officials, politicians, minor celebrities, and anyone with enough influence to score a coveted pre-race paddock badge—stand stacked on the lawn adjacent to the finish-line gazebo, where a television team completes the final scripted section of its broadcast before focusing on fate itself for the main event.

Sixteen minutes out, the jockeys file up the locker-room stairwell, emerging into the bright chaos wearing multicolored silks and the stoic expressions of gunslingers. Five minutes later, after a brief bit of strategizing with their trainers, the riders are hoisted onto their respective steeds, strutting past the overflowing flower boxes and red, white, and blue bunting for one final turn beneath the box seats before they hit the track. Ahead of the field for the sixty-first edition of the $600,000 showcase race, top-hatted jazz master Joe Kelly strides to the crown of the homestretch, places his shiny brass bugle to his lips, faces the East Boston crowd, and belts out the first few bawdy notes of "Fugue for Tinhorns," his raucously flawless call to post.

On the track, Running Stag is foaming at the mouth while champing at the bit, but the restrained, beefy bay acts more curious than crazed when he passes in front of the jammed grandstand, twitching his ears while prancing past the tote board, on which he commands solid 8-to-5 favoritism. Vision and Verse (3 to 1) is the second choice in the betting, with Out Of Mind (7 to 2) also attracting substantial action. Pleasant Breeze (6 to 1) is getting mild play in the mutuels, despite another inopportune hindrance for Jim Bond: Lost during the commotion of the past few days were his client's prominent burgundy racing silks, which should have shipped from New York along with the horse. The replacement jockey aboard Bond's second-string steed will now have to contest the MassCap in someone else's substitute colors. Although the stand-in outfit is similar in design, one press-box degenerate points out that the new silks belong to a local owner who has gone winless on the season—another untimely omen.

In the grand scheme of things, the most peculiar pre-race portent occurs to 88-to-1 outsider Makeyourselfathome. While warming up around the far turn, the longest shot on the board abruptly jumps a shadow. Jockey Dyn Panell is launched airborne, and when he lands, the spooked steed attempts to flail at the downed reinsman with his hind hooves. Although the embarrassed rookie is able to remount, Suffolk Downs itself manages to get kicked in the teeth over this incident: The shadow on the racetrack was caused by an overhead advertising banner for deep-pocketed gaming rival Foxwoods, which has hired an airplane to fly deliberately low over the heads of East Boston's captive cache of gamblers.

At 5:43 PM, the horses arrive at the starting gate for the MassCap. The loading at the gate is orderly and uneventful, with the exception of brawny Out Of Mind, who is reluctant to step forward into the narrow enclosure. Not to be outdone, the last Thoroughbred in line similarly delays the start—but in the case of Running Stag, you get the distinct impression that the charismatic people's choice *knows* he's the star of the show and is simply hamming it up for the anxious crowd.

At 5:45 PM, three events occur in succession, all within a single second:

The padded steel door in back of Running Stag slams shut.

A Suffolk Downs assistant starter shouts, "Locked up!" from behind the gate.

Sensing that thirty-two Thoroughbred feet are obediently planted in the rich, brown loam, veteran Tom Schwigen instantly flicks his starting switch, releasing the electromagnetic lock holding closed the massive front doors of the barrier.

"THEY'RE OFF and running in MassCap 2000!"

When announcer Larry Collmus utters the first seven words of his most important race call of the season, the opening phrase is drowned out by an enthusiastic wave of sound from the grandstand, an overpowering roar of pandemonium that can only described as the unmistakable, jubilant din of horse racing.

Then, four jumps from the gate, jockey Joe Hampshire runs smack into trouble—and it seems as if everybody but the leading rider realizes it.

Pleasant Breeze breaks inward from post 7 into David, then pinballs outward while Hampshire, shaking the reins, cracks his steed six times on the right shoulder in an effort to straighten the careening, traction-less Thoroughbred. The aggressive handling results in overcorrective steering, and Pleasant Breeze tries to bounce back off his fleet-footed rival before Aaron Gryder cues David to pull away from the perilous pocket of traffic. Gryder's speedster is quick to respond, but Makeyourselfathome, with Dyn Panell sitting chilly, beats the bumped front-runner to the punch, securing both the rail and the lead for the first of two passes under the finish wire.

Running Stag is keen, pulling hard on his steering bit, eager to be involved in the chase. Even while under classic "feet on the dash-board" restraint from jockey John Velazquez, the barrel-chested bay is fourth, widest of all as the field guns into the clubhouse turn. Such a rambunctious expenditure of early effort might compromise most racehorses, but Stag is full of himself and very much on the bridle, so this ground-losing gambit effectively allows Velazquez and Stag to trap Hampshire and Pleasant Breeze into an even more unenviable position: A quarter mile into the MassCap, Joe and his mount are caught three wide, committed to a spot toward the front, hot on the heels of two rail-running speed freaks while a physically imposing favorite bears down ominously, pressuring the pack from outside.

Behind the top quartet, Gander checks back slightly on the rail in fifth.

Vision and Verse is a well-placed sixth.

The Groom Is Red is an even-paced seventh.

Out Of Mind trails, practically cantering along with an unobstruct-ed view of the intensifying speed duel, a distant eighteen lengths off the action.

And we've got four of them battling it out early on . . . The pace looks very fast . . . David is in front . . . Aaron Gryder has David on the lead by a length as they enter the backstretch . . . Pleasant Breeze is second to the outside . . . They went the opening quar-ter in twenty-two and four-fifths seconds, a solid fraction . . .

325

Having roused his steed so early in the race, Hampshire now has little choice but to force the issue, because asking a keyed-up Pleasant Breeze to back off at this juncture will result in a serious slowdown of momentum. Complicating matters, Velazquez has expertly slipped Running Stag into Joe's blind spot on the backstretch, just to the outside and a length behind the dueling duo. By the time the field hits the 4-1/2 furlong pole, Panell has opted to concede the lead without giving up position, skimming the inside rail with Makeyourselfathome. The impossible long shot and the heavy favorite are a joint third, eyeball to eyeball behind David and Pleasant Breeze.

A half mile out, Vision and Verse is roused by Jerry Bailey. But when the nation's top jock smooches at him for more, you can see the four-year-old's bobbing head begin to shy from the spray of sandy kickback. Gander, the gray, is similarly being pushed for run by Shaun Bridgmohan, but not responding. In the back of the pack, Rick Pitino's horse, The Groom Is Red, is living up to all the pre-race jokes about being as bad as the coach's sorry Boston basketball team. Out Of Mind, the copacetic West Coaster, remains content to lope along by his lonesome, still last behind a :46-2/5 opening half mile.

It's David in front, and he heads into the far turn leading Running Stag by a length and a half . . . Makeyourselfathome under heavy pressure . . . Pleasant Breeze is fourth—he's not keeping up right now . . .

With three furlongs left in the sixty-first Massachusetts Handicap, it suddenly dawns on everyone at Suffolk Downs—screaming horseplayers and hard-scrubbing jockeys alike—that unheralded speedster David just might steal this $600,000 showdown in front-running fashion. When Pleasant Breeze is unable to match the attack under the duress of such a demanding pace, freewheeling jockey Gryder glances once, quickly, to his left to be sure the rail is secure. But the cagey rider has enough horse sense not to even bother looking over his right shoulder, because he can both feel and hear the relentless, pummeling hoofbeats of Running Stag rapidly gathering steam on the far outside.

Hurtling forward with long, fluid strides, Velazquez sits motionless, his back so flat and straight you could serve a formal British tea upon it. The twenty-eight-year-old jockey has a handful of horse in reserve, and as Stag's unruly black mane whips furiously against his face, Johnny V. has little difficulty keeping the Thoroughbred's head sleek, straight, and focused—the epitome of an aggressive, athletic partnership of racehorse and rider relishing both the pursuit and subsequent reeling in of prey.

And David is still there at the quarter pole . . . Running Stag on the outside is second . . .

After six furlongs in 1:10-3/5, Aaron Gryder looks like a marked man on the lead. But the 113-pound reinsman remains cool under pressure, and when Running Stag finally hooks his target at the top of the lane, David gamely digs in and finds another gear.

They're into the stretch . . . It's David! . . . but here comes Goliath!

Makeyourselfathome, left in the leaders' wake, is still running respectably, well within himself but not nearly as fast as the graded-stakes stars flying by to his outside. Joe Hampshire is all over his mount—cajoling, whipping, pleading—yet Pleasant Breeze backpedals laboriously with each and every stride. Vision and Verse is being punched on but can't find any kick. Gander and The Groom Is Red are spent. The only entrant sneaking up on the excitement from way, way back is the lumbering mass known as Out Of Mind, who effortlessly loops the entire group. Six wide at the top of the homestretch, jockey Eddie Delahoussaye hasn't even cocked his stick, and the late-striding steed is picking apart the pack with extraordinary ease, trying to go from last to first with 1-1/2 furlongs left in the race.

Running Stag on the outside to the front! . . . David all out to stick with him!

David and Running Stag extend themselves in lockstep through the homestretch. But by the eighth pole, the body language of the two even-termed combatants tells a different story: Without a wasted motion, Velazquez finally collars a fading David 200 yards from the wire, and this time the surging Stag knows he's put away his adversary for good.

Out Of Mind is gaining in the center of the track!

The big Brazilian is truly rolling. When a leg-weary Pleasant Breeze veers in and out of his path through the final sixteenth, Delahoussaye practically runs his equine locomotive right over the top of the punch-drunk rival. This jaw-dropping move is visually impressive, but it's also a tad too late for Out Of Mind: The leader is leveling out beautifully, eyes wide and black nostrils flaring, and as Stag sails untouched through the final sixteenth, his jockey's only task is to keep him on a straight course the final few jumps to the wire.

It's Running Stag! . . . Close to home! . . . Running Stag and Out Of Mind!

John Velazquez pumps his right fist as his tangerine and white silks flash first under the Suffolk Downs finish line, precisely 1:49-2/5 after the starting gate ripped open.

RUNNING STAG WINS THE MASSCAP!

Out Of Mind cruises home barely a fifth of a second later, officially 1-1/4 lengths behind the British victor. David—very fast but unable to last—is third, followed by Vision and Verse, Gander, Makeyourselfathome, Pleasant Breeze, and The Groom Is Red. In the front row of clubhouse box seats, trainer Phil Mitchell shouts into a cell phone, gleefully attempting a rundown for Richard Cohen, the overseas client who owns Running Stag.

Cohen, suffering from cardiac complications, had badly wanted to make the trek from London to see his horse at Suffolk Downs, but a recent angioplasty grounded all travel aspirations. On the phone, the lusty roar of the masses drowns out the exact words of his trainer, but the vocal explosion unmistakably conveys what has happened. An ocean, a continent, and a cosmic crapshoot away from East Boston, the man who just won the MassCap with Blackwater's brother is so overcome with joy that he breaks down and cries.

FROM THE STANDS, the aftermath of a major stakes event appears orderly, polite, and scripted.

On the racetrack itself, it rarely is.

Moments after the MassCap, press photographers, reporters, grooms, valets, trainers, owners, track officials, and security guards all rush the Suffolk Downs racing strip, crowding the entrance to the winner's circle, sinking to the shins in deep, sandy loam that claims countless pairs of dress shoes and finely tailored pants cuffs.

The solitary unsaddling of the also-rans precedes the ceremonial crowning of the champ, who gallops back last. Yet while the swarming media lavishes attention upon the winner—Running Stag's every returning step is framed by popping flashbulbs—valuable insight can be gleaned from the attitudes and actions of those who finished behind him. In horse racing, defeat is a far cry from failure.

Richard Mandella is so enthused upon greeting his jockey when Eddie Delahoussaye guides his steed through the chaos that one might mistakenly think Out Of Mind won the MassCap. The West Coast trainer's widely acknowledged strength is patience, and Mandella views each race as an educational opportunity for both himself and his horses.

"The horse ran a terrific race," Mandella says into my tape recorder when asked for his initial MassCap assessment. "He made a hell of a run. He's kind of learning, and I think he's turned himself into one of the best right now."

Delahoussaye concurs, similarly pleased. "He was farther back than I thought, but they were going pretty fast early. This is the first time he's hooked real quality horses, and he proved that he belongs with them. Next time we'll turn the tables."

Not far away, the tack is being removed from a laboring David, who ran as hard as he could for as long as he could. Trainer Michael

Hushion, huddling with his jockey, laments the sizzling fractions that he believes cost his horse the MassCap. Aaron Gryder, a horsebacking realist, attempts a diplomatic spin, explaining that David didn't necessarily lose the race—he simply got beat by faster animals.

"He ran great," Gryder says, offering no apologies for his run-and-gun tactics, which, after all, were his trainer's exact instructions. "I don't think the fast pace was the problem. He just got outrun. They were just better than him today."

In the center of the homestretch, a stern Jim Bond allows Joe Hampshire to make a brief account of his seventh-place trip aboard Pleasant Breeze. The jockey shrugs his shoulders before offering a handshake of gratitude for the MassCap mount. Even from a distance, it is clear that the beleaguered trainer is not pleased with the way his replacement jockey rode such an important race.

"He told me to stay within striking distance but to keep the dirt out of the horse's face," a humble Hampshire details to a media relations staffer immediately after weighing in. "When we went around into the first turn, I was feeling pretty good. I said, 'Man, I'm right where I'm supposed to be.' But when we got to the second turn, I pushed the button and he wasn't there for me. He didn't have much finish in him today."

Bond, hands on hips, glares away when I ask for his version of what happened in the MassCap.

"Strike one was losing Behrens," he says tersely after a moment of stony silence. "Strike two was not getting Jorge [Chavez]. And this . . . "—the trainer trails off and flips his arm in dismissive vexation, indicating the general direction of the racetrack and what has just transpired over it—"This was strike three."

A few feet away, assistant Roger Teal is high-fiving rider John Velazquez, who is perched atop the valiant winner. Phil Mitchell strides purposefully through the MassCap throng, affectionately slaps Running Stag's sweaty left shoulder, embraces his jockey with a firm, two-handed clasp, then whirls on his heels and pumps his fist in the direction of the Suffolk Downs grandstand, eliciting a spirited eruption from the Eastie faithful.

"The reception that we got from the Boston crowd last year made it all the more important that we come back," Mitchell gushes to anyone who will listen. "Because there's nothing like coming back to the scene of a defeat and putting it right."

A blanket of white carnations is draped over Running Stag's glistening neck as onlookers press in from all sides. Accustomed to attention but unused to the feeling of refrigerated foliage on his back immediately after a strenuous workout, the MassCap champ first attempts to shrug off his glitzy victory bouquet, then unleashes a fully torqued kick with both back legs, proudly scattering both crowd and carnations in every direction.

Mission accomplished, a satisfied Stag begins to nip intently at the floral arrangement, brazenly asserting his equine supremacy as if imparting an unspoken bit of racehorse wisdom: "Why take the time to stop and smell the flowers when you can ravenously devour them instead?"

CHAPTER EIGHT

GOING LEGIT

Too much hope is perhaps the worst sin in horse racing.
—SIMON BARNES, *The Times* (London)

THE DAY AFTER a major horse race can be the most relaxing afternoon of the season. Strangely enough, it can also be the most depressing.

If the race itself was exciting and without injury, and the weather was decent, and a sizable crush of customers genuinely left the joint in high spirits, then track management is allowed to bask in the afterglow. The headlines in the papers will be jaunty, congratulations will abound from appreciative fans, and even hard-edged union tellers and exhausted food-service staffers will return to work smiling, flush with fat pockets thanks to an afternoon of robust tipping. Skeptical backstretch workers will adopt a jovial mood, fueled by the contagious buzz of a big day, and even though it sounds corny, a positive spirit of "Yes, we can do this!" will ripple through the racetrack.

For Suffolk Downs, yesterday's MassCap was by far the year's best day of business, both in terms of attendance and betting volume: The $4,943,148 wagered by 17,847 fans produced the second-largest wagering handle in track history.

"Just like the good old days, kid," booms legendary announcer Big Jim Hannon, who still makes a daily visit to the press box before heading downstairs to work his shift behind the betting lines. "God, do we miss those good old days."

Under the Barn 6 shed row, the MassCap champ appears in fine fettle, although Running Stag's stablemate, sprinter Mister Tricky, exited his last-place try in the Moseley Handicap with a slight muscle strain. Some might consider it unconventional, but trainer Phil Mitchell reveals that he plans to race Stag right back one week from today in the Brooklyn Handicap at Belmont Park, primarily because of those aforementioned concerns that his star steed will otherwise get bored.

"Yesterday was something that we planned over a year ago and it's just so nice that it all came to fruition," Mitchell reflects. "It was just such a wonderful day and the horse had a great trip through the race and everything worked out. I mean, it's a plan that was hatched twelve months ago and it's all come good. He's come out of the race great, he licked his pot clean, and he looks in great shape this morning, ready to ship back out and start another war."

I shake hands with Phil and his two assistants, wishing them well in their travels. I try to give Running Stag a parting stroke on the nose, hoping his good luck will rub off on me. Instead, the dynamic animal attempts to rip my arm out of its socket, a sure sign that the hot-blooded horse is his usual frisky self.

It is not until the actual Sunday races start that a case of post-MassCap blues starts to settle in. Exactly zero reporters show up to work today, and the "auxiliary press box" that was used all last week to handle media overflow has quietly reverted to its regular usage as a linen storage area for the now-vacant Terrace Dining Room. Race-caller Larry Collmus and the two college interns have left for Monmouth Park to begin summer gigs on the Jersey shore, so Bish and I are the only degenerates skulking around the empty office for the final week of the season. Outdoors, only a smattering of customers dot the grandstand apron, decidedly downscaled from yesterday's shoulder-to-shoulder throng. Every year after the showcase race, you can tell by looking down from the press box that a few of the younger members of yesterday's crowd actually had such a great time attending New England's Million Dollar Day of Racing that they decided to come back for more on Sunday, which in and of itself is a good sign. But the newcomers sport a collective look of bewilderment, wondering

"Where the hell is everybody?" upon realizing that the everyday fare at Suffolk Downs grinds on without boisterous beer tents, rockin' bands, and hip college girls in halter tops soaking up the conspicuously absent MassCap atmosphere.

"Everything back to normal?" a bleary, hungover press-box denizen asks as I peruse the Sunday papers. The place is so empty you can almost hear an echo when I sardonically reply, "That depends on your definition of *normal*."

Most of the morning-after news stories on this June 4 are rife with feel-good recaps of the main event. But *Boston Globe* columnist Michael Madden—an insightful regular who admirably eschews the press box in favor of blending in with hardcore horseplayers downstairs—delivers some unflinching post-race scrutiny, keying on the unavoidable irony of how the most talented everyday Suffolk Downs jockey ended up being the unlikely aggressor in the MassCap pace meltdown, sealing his own fate by gunning too fast too soon in the most important two minutes of the meet.

> . . . [A]nd while Hampshire was "excited and very pleased," the same could not be said for Bond . . . Hampshire chose to use his mount hard at the start on Pleasant Breeze and said that was per orders of Bond . . . Bond, though, was visibly displeased and said he didn't want his horse used so hard so early. Pleasant Breeze finished a most disappointing seventh . . . The New York trainer said he learned his lesson: "Don't leave home without Jorge [Chavez]."

Apparently, Joe Hampshire's skein of bad luck is intent on following him straight into Sunday, making no distinction between $600,000 Grade II stakes competition and bottom-barrel maidens. In the opener, it's back to everyday reality aboard Show Me Mary, a heavily favored Texas shipper who figures to have a weak field at her mercy. But when the pack turns for home, Hampshire is forced to pull up his filly after she bobbles in distress. Eliciting a weak chorus of boos from the sparse crowd, Joe dismounts as the rescue crew arrives, removes his tack, and trudges alone with his head down the entire length of the grandstand back to the paddock.

Hampshire's horses then run second, fifth, and seventh until mid-way through the afternoon, at which time the routine stewards' rulings are released. Word spreads through the locker room that both Hampshire and Dyn Panell have been issued five-day suspensions for "careless riding," thanks to their respective actions in a roughly ridden race last Wednesday, a unique double disqualification all but forgotten amid the MassCap hoopla.

Upon receiving news that their penalty periods will commence tomorrow, both Joe and Dyn take out their frustrations on horseback, dueling headlong around the track in Race 6. The result is a tenacious photo-finish between Negotiator and Play Bill, and when the numbers are posted, the bitter veteran ends up barely edging the passionate rookie. Hampshire's 120th victory of the meet means he has won almost as many races as his second- and third-place rivals combined, and the purse from this minor score is just enough to loft his seasonal earnings above the seven-figure mark.

Despite these accomplishments, Joe opts for an early exit, calling it quits immediately after the winner's circle ceremony. Discouraged with the way things transpired over the last twenty-four hours, unenthused about his remaining three mounts on the card, and apparently indifferent to the trainers who secured his services and the bettors who have backed him with advance wagers, the standings-topping jockey will end his Suffolk Downs season the same way he started it: on vacation.

With a commanding forty-seven-win cushion and a meet-leading bankroll of $1,004,038, the thirty-six-year-old reinsman can rest assured that the unexpected holiday will hardly dent his wallet, because choice mounts aboard the fastest Thoroughbreds in New England will be waiting when he returns to the saddle next week at Rockingham Park. The circuit will pack up and migrate north for the summer, and the top jock will shift with it, leaving behind a complex season of uncertainty. The last six months at Suffolk Downs have tested

Joe Hampshire in ways that are difficult to document, yet those intangible trials are highly revealing when it comes to the caustically honest distinction between being a leading jockey, and being a leader.

ON THE FINAL MONDAY of the racing season, Suffolk Downs is the focal point of a surprising flurry of media requests. Before I can set the morning coffee down on my desk, the way-too-cheery automated phone attendant chirps "You have nineteen new voice messages!" Upon hearing that the bulk of urgent calls are from staffers on practically every TV news desk in the city, my first two thoughts, in succession, are (1) *This can't possibly be good*; (2) *I'll bet whatever it is they're calling about has absolutely nothing to do with horse racing.*

Right on both counts.

Apparently, someone in the chain of command in Boston's beloved Red Sox Nation let it slip over the weekend that Suffolk Downs is being considered as one of many possible locations for a new Fenway Park, which the team wants taxpayers to pay for by ponying up $625 million. Although the latest version of this build-a-ballpark brain scheme is news to us, it's technically an old story recycled with fresh financial details. For decades, the Eastie oval has been the rumored site for a myriad of state-of-the-art football, basketball, hockey, baseball, and entertainment complexes. Eventually, each and every grandiose plan ends up unceremoniously dumped, usually because the racetrack idea is little more than a highly leveraged bluff to scare local leaders into believing that Boston's pro sports teams would actually consider the unthinkable abandonment of their traditional homes within the heart of the city.

Still, each time this topic percolates freshly to the top of the news cycle, politicians from Revere and East Boston fall all over themselves in a tragically comic ploy to roll out the red carpet. Sure, they say, a horse track is a nice enough sporting venue to have in one's backyard. But the mere thought of the Olde Town Team relocating its famous Green Monster to the intersection of Route 1A and Revere Beach Parkway is enough to launch the locals into an apoplectic fit of fervent civic pride, presumably driven by visions of behind-the-scenes dollar signs and the copious patronage pirating such a large-scale, high-profile project would pocket.

Already, the mayor's office in Revere is floating a story that the city has brokered a meeting between the team and track owners to bring the two sides together. Yet when I run this critical bit of info past Bob O'Malley, it is the first time the Suffolk Downs chief operating officer has even heard of the nonexistent powwow. Having worked his way through various versions of this tale many times before, Bob's reaction is one of courteous resignation: We have to be polite, say the property owners are willing to listen to any and all development proposals, but repeatedly emphasize that Suffolk Downs intends to be in the primary business of Thoroughbred racing for a long time to come. And although the key is to not risk offending the same local leaders allegedly elected to go to bat for *our* interests, you have to wonder where all these eager officials were several months back when the sixty-five-year-old track begged for political clout to help preserve a sporting venue that also happens to be the largest and longest-running jobs source for North Shore constituents.

Half a year has elapsed since special-session legislation mandated the emergency appointment of a blue-ribbon committee to refine and revamp the state's archaic racing legislation. To date, the thirteen-member committee of politicians and regulators has yet to release even a preliminary plan, let alone a single finding, suggestion, pitch, or proposal for the betterment of the Commonwealth's sagging $622-million pari-mutuel industry. This week, the Suffolk Downs race meet will limp to a close without any of the sweeping statutory changes promised at the start of the season, and no proactive legislation looms on the horizon to allow the sport to move forward—or at least keep pace with—ravenously expanding competition from rival gambling establishments.

Recently, I asked one highly regarded industry consultant why Massachusetts continually lags behind other states in legislative progress. After a pensive pause, the specialist candidly cited the Commonwealth's insidious reputation for ruthless backroom wheeling and dealing. "In most states, there's a basic assumption that when you get money to the right connections, they'll deliver what you paid for," the legislative expert offered, choosing his words gingerly. "Yet in Massachusetts, it's pretty well known that's not always the case."

This year, Sterling Suffolk Racecourse will fork out $65,750 in documented lobbying expenses, nearly doubling the money the track disclosed spending last year. A sizable chunk of that cash will be paid to newly hired lobbyist Charles Flaherty, the former House Speaker whose services as an influence broker became available after he resigned amid ethics violations and a guilty plea to felony tax-fraud charges. Another $23,750 has been earmarked for curiously ambiguous "additional expenditures" that must be reported to the state. Yet despite spending twice as much for the privilege of playing politics, Suffolk Downs has so far gained nothing of discernible value from this exasperating, state-sanctioned shakedown, which from a historical perspective appears to have changed little since maverick racetrack operator Bill Veeck bluntly summed up his aggravating haggles with Beacon Hill insiders in *Thirty Tons a Day*, in a chapter cynically titled "The Great and Glorious Commonwealth":

> When you're operating a racetrack, you find the politicians coming around, eyes agleam. They don't want their pictures taken and they expect you to sign every tab . . . You're looked upon as a little bank to shake something out of. It is impossible to get involved in something as closely tied to politics as horse racing without coming out with the distinct impression that politics is the principal industry of Boston, and quite probably, the whole of the Great Commonwealth. The politicians come at you like a swarm of locusts . . . The one thing the politicians have succeeded in doing has been to create an atmosphere in which it is felt that nothing can be done without paying somebody off . . . As long as you're going to have a corrupt political system, you might as well swelter under the most politically corrupt one around . . . Everybody was wallowing happily inside the status quo because everybody had come to regard the status quo as the best insur-

ance for continued fun and profit . . . Suffolk Downs, which should have been the dominant track in New England, had been locked into the status quo. (pp. 99–106)

Written more than thirty years ago, Veeck's frustrations ring true today, perhaps explaining why one of the century's most forward-thinking sports entrepreneurs fled Beantown after only two tumultuous seasons manning the helm at Sufferin' Downs.

Call it wishful desperation, but even at this late point in the legislative session, there is some sentiment in the battered and fragmented New England racing community that no news is good news, that the political machinery will come through to reward its horsebacking cavalry of good soldiers. Bullied by the process, industry leaders have been openly suggesting that everyone should just pipe down, be good sports, play along without bothering anybody, and—well—simply hope for the best. The November elections are still five months away, but anyone with a stake in the game is aware that a number of key gambling issues will be decided by regional voters, including one Massachusetts initiative to ban greyhound racing and a New Hampshire ballot question to legalize video slot machines. Additionally, several local Indian tribes are close to attaining federal recognition status, which could pave the way for reservation casinos built on land trusts close to Boston. As a result, some track executives and a number of horsemen now believe that Suffolk Downs is better off waiting to see if any of these events come to pass before embracing any impending action that the blue-ribbon panel might take, because word from the wiseguys is that the legislature will not look kindly upon another request for pari-mutuel reform so soon after this current crisis. Once again, Thoroughbred racing in New England is relegated to playing the political waiting game, a crooked, rigged endeavor in which hope functions not so much as a beacon of inspiration as a cruel sentence whose repeated imposition only prolongs the inevitable.

After dutifully returning all my media phone messages, I finally whittle the call-back list to someone who isn't a reporter, someone I'd actually enjoy speaking with. At the family horse farm in New Hampshire, recently retired jockey Abby Fuller has segued fluidly into her new role as a stay-at-home mom, and she and husband Mike Catalano have been spending time with their new baby while mulling plans for the future. Last year at this time, life was decidedly different for the couple: Team Catalano had a hot horse in the MassCap, the stable was the subject of lots of good press, and the outfit was hitting the winner's circle consistently. Mike didn't have to adhere to a haggard travel schedule, and their phone wasn't ringing off the hook with a megalomaniac power boss calling to impose grand plans of equine management upon his hardworking trainer. Catalano's road record this season is absolutely baffling—the Maryland-Delaware foray ended up a disheartening 4-for-79—while back on the home front, Mike has very quietly and without complaint lost stock belonging to several smaller clients, including Galloping Gael, his MassCap starter from last season. In just a few short months, Catalano has gone from a position of power to being demoted to also-ran status in Michael Gill's number-crunching power stable, and since second string doesn't mesh well with Mike's pride, he's graciously told the Suffolk Downs leading owner he'd prefer not to accept that opportunity.

Abby and Mike aren't panicking, though. With the New England circuit shifting close to their home near Rockingham for the summer, this might be a good time for their racing outfit to regroup. Then again, Fuller tells me, considering the uncertainty of the industry, it could also be a good time to think about other career options. Catalano and Gill have managed to part on good terms, even to the point where Gill has offered his former conditioner a fresh start learning his mortgage business. After having spent most of his youth and all his adult years on the backstretch, Mike Catalano has never known any trade other than caring for racehorses, and now, at age thirty-two, the somber economic realities of his profession have left him seriously contemplating the abandonment of Thoroughbred training altogether.

Under the shed row, there is a term for this life-altering choice, a succinct, two-word phrase spoken when one comes to the difficult decision of voluntarily yet regretfully allowing the demanding, rewarding way of racetrack life slip away in hopes of finding greener pastures on the other side of the stable gate. Although no one outside the race-horse realm would ever understand it, this brief bit of backstretch slang is laced with irony, because anyone who has ever bet their soul on the sport knows that saying good-bye to the game to work a "nor-mal job" is never a trade-up, no matter how much money you make. Sure, you can leave horse racing. But if you've ever laid hands on a Thoroughbred out of sheer love, horse racing for certain is never going to leave you. That's why racetrack lifers always believe you'll be back—no matter how earnest and serious you seem—when you suck up the courage and tell them that you've finally had it, that you're giv-ing it all up, moving on, leaving the game, and *going legit*.

THE PACK flies into the final turn of the nightcap on the next-to-last day of the racing season, a cool June afternoon whose eerily bright sky suffuses the salt marsh, arriving late on the scene after a stinging cas-cade of morning rain. Half An Hour, a track record holder now rele-gated to $8,000 claiming sprints, forces a three-way duel from the outside, skimming atop the mud while bearing down upon a pair of neck-and-neck rivals. Between horses, Tilly's Boy is driven hard by Jose Delgado, who has won the previous four races and is now three furlongs from becoming the eighth jockey in sixty-five years to win five on a single Suffolk Downs program. To attain that elusive slice of history, Delgado must first overpower even-money stalwart Saratoga Ridge, who cruises determinedly along the rail, ears relaxed, darting stride fluid and nimble. The hard-hitting gelding's teeth clamp firmly into the steering bit, his lithe, white head a furious pendulum, and it is clear that the Ridge is a racehorse who wants more rein from his rider: back legs churning, front hooves extending, an equine machine of rhythm, muscle, and impulse about to seize the lead at the midway mark of lifetime start number 129.

At $299,521 in cumulative winnings, just about any piece of today's purse puts Saratoga Ridge over the distinguished three-hundred-grand earnings mark. And when the eleven-year-old glides off the turn, making the first start for his new barn after a May 24 claim, it is evident the wily Eastie warrior is engaging in his customary cat-and-mouse antics, waiting for competition to catch up before pouncing into overdrive. Responding when roused, the Ridge dives through a narrow passage adjacent to the inner fence, and when headed by a resurgent Tilly's Boy, the tenacious gray kicks again to commandeer the lead at the five-sixteenths pole. Crouched forward in the irons, a slop-smeared Ender Jimenez flips down a fresh set of goggles and moves his fists higher up his mount's neck to gain leverage for the stretch drive, and when he smooches and clucks to his partner to pick up the pace, what the jock is *really* doing is calling upon 55 million years of equine evolution and centuries of refined, selective breeding to draw forth the visceral fight-or-flight Thoroughbred instinct that never fails to unleash a forceful burst of acceleration from such a delicate, agile creature.

Saratoga Ridge blasts past the quarter pole, and the microsecond that his left front foot hits the homestretch, his ankle shatters, disintegrating to fine shards and fragments.

It is impossible to see the actual fracture from the grandstand. But when the front-runner's bobbing head lunges unnaturally low and the rider is practically catapulted forward over his withers, it is dreadfully evident that something has gone wrong. Jimenez recovers instantly, bolting upright in the saddle to snatch back his stampeding steed, slamming on the brakes to halt Saratoga Ridge before the injured animal can further damage his forelimb. The remaining jockeys swerve wildly—they probably heard the sickening snap of bone before Ender could even holler out for racing room—all six reflexively clearing a wide berth for the stricken pacemaker. But the stubborn old roan will have none of this: The Ridge wants to run, resisting the unexpected tug of the reins. Never before has he been asked to come to a dead stop from full flight, so the bullish gray lowers his head and muscles Jimenez with all his might as if there is something unnaturally wrong with the rider and it is the Thoroughbred who is compelled to take the initiative and force things forward.

At top speed, a half-ton horse will bear the equivalent of 100 times the force of gravity on each hoof with every stride, and pain—if there is any in the immediate aftermath of serious trauma—is often little more than a twinge of annoyance for an adrenaline-fueled pack animal. Saratoga Ridge obstinately strains onward for a full furlong before his gait slows enough for the jock to bail out of the irons, and by the time the gelding finally slows to a clumsy walk just inside the eighth pole, his cadence is no longer fluid; he is bouncing and hobbling, not in obvious distress, but glaring around irritably with a heightened, throbbing, ears-up sense of self-awareness that makes the Ridge realize there just might be a damn good reason his race suddenly ended so far before the finish wire.

Jimenez supports as much weight of the animal as he can until help arrives, leaning shoulder to shoulder against his mount in the middle of the muddy homestretch. The wizened white horse just stands there snorting, looking more pissed off than in pain, flicking his tail from side to side in aggravation. The track veterinarians descend upon the scene immediately, and a small knot of gawkers gathers on the grandstand apron to watch them fit a protective brace to the gelding's left front foot. Trainer Ron Dandy, who has only had Saratoga Ridge under his care for two weeks, paces off to the side by himself, binoculars dangling distractedly, looking at his hurt horse but trying not to. Talking intently into a cell phone, the meet's leading conditioner is presumably detailing to his owner what just happened, but at this point neither Dandy nor his client are aware that another outfit had submitted an irrevocable $8,000 claim for the Ridge just prior to post time. Technically, this well-respected workhorse is no longer Ron's property. But until the new purchaser steps forward to assume full responsibility for the gelding's medical care, the veteran horseman will stand by to do the right thing for the battle-scarred Thoroughbred, who is quietly starting to slip into shock.

Saratoga Ridge is none too happy about being the awkward center of attention, and he stamps a back leg up and down while one of the vets injects a sedative into his neck to ease the discomfort and keep him calm. The back-and-forth chatter between doctors on the in-house walkie-talkie channel does not yield a promising prognosis: At least one—and quite likely both—sesamoid bones are broken, shearing the crucial impact-bearing bones at the ankle joint. In addition, a nearby artery and vein have ruptured, resulting in soft-tissue damage that has caused considerable swelling around the sensitive suspensory ligament. The vets will try their best to save him, but when the equine ambulance rolls up to return the Ridge to his stall for X-rays, the venerable gray balks and refuses to enter. It's as if he's seen enough in his eleven years as a racehorse to know that once he steps gingerly out of the Suffolk Downs mud and into this padded van for an uninvited ride home, he stands no chance of ever again getting back on track.

GETAWAY DAY means different things to different racetrackers. The old-timers reminisce fondly of an era when New England racing packed up and moved from track to track like a circus, and at each stop on the circuit, the insiders skimmed a bit of "traveling money" from the wagering public by tying up a closing-day race before the show hit the road. Back then, when Thoroughbred racing left town for the season, the final day was bound to be heavily attended and the betting pools were sure to be large. The fix was in not so much because the jockeys wanted to fleece the fans but because the performers who risked a meet's worth of horsebacking hazards felt a proud twinge of entitlement after putting their necks on the line so everyone else could enjoy America's number-one spectator sport. Despite the wistful deception, it wasn't like the illicit orchestration was a total scam, either: Often, the rigged race would be scripted to be won by some down-on-his-luck horseman everyone knew *really* needed the purse money, so the traditional getaway day betting bonanza carried a sense of racetrack nobility: robbing the unknown clubhouse rich to take care of one's own backstretch poor.

Nowadays, a twelve-month racing season and the advent of nonstop simulcasting means fewer fans care whether the betting product takes the form of living, breathing animals or two-inch television images composed of pixels, so the social immediacy of getaway day has little bearing upon the race-going public. Today's turnout at the East Boston oval is uninspiring, and tomorrow at Rockingham Park, essentially the same horses ridden by the same jockeys and trained by the same conditioners will gallop their circles thirty-five miles to the north in New Hampshire. The only true Closing Day collusion in the jocks' room this afternoon involves paying off the valets well enough to endure the getaway-day drudge work, which basically means humping everyone's tack box and riding equipment from one locker room to the other so the circuit can continue its two-stop tour in monotonous, unbroken continuity.

Upstairs, once the final horse crosses the finish wire, large portions of the concrete facility will be closed off to the public, and Suffolk Downs will transform overnight from a historic coastal racecourse into a cost-efficient betting bunker. The mechanical chirp of self-service wagering machines and the muted broadcast feeds from far-flung simulcasts will replace the pounding hooves and cheers of a live stretch drive, and the serene greenery of the infield will soon be overwhelmed by industrial soundstaging and a fleet of portable toilets for a series of heavy metal concerts that bring in a few extra bucks during the three-month off-season. The dirt course will bake rock-solid in the relentless summer sun; trash and racetrack residue will collect in unused, sealed-off stairwells, and scattered *Racing Form*s will quickly fade to brittle sheets of yellowed parchment, making it seem like ancient times since those past performances represented real Thoroughbreds. In essence, once the horses split, the backstretch characters are gone, and the endless tiers of orange grandstand seats have been claimed by flocks of brazen shore birds, Suffolk Downs reverts to a shell of a racetrack, a broken-down sporting palace on the cutting edge of urban decay.

When I was a budding young degenerate just starting out in the press box, one of the friendliest and most helpful guys I met was a former New England jockey named Jimmy Davern. I didn't know much about his background, partly because Jimmy was tight-lipped about why he retired from riding, but mostly because I was too busy being captivated by his raucous racetrack tales about the good old days. It was evident that Davern really liked to live it up in his heyday, and after hanging around a bit, I gradually pieced together his story: Jimmy began riding in 1950, and he excelled at all the now-defunct New England tracks. In 1973, a mount flipped on top of him in the starting gate at 'Gansett, crushing his spine. Doctors inserted a pair of steel rods and told Jimmy he would never walk again. Davern essentially told the doctors they could go fuck themselves, and within a year he was back on his feet. The feisty jock ambled around with a limp and could do everything he once did, except ride.

A self-described fool with money, legend has it that Jimmy took his insurance settlement and bet it all on some far-out stock tip, which he was fond of doing when not chasing riches at the wagering windows. But this time, Davern beat the odds, and his long-shot investment soared sky-high, leaving him set for life. Yet instead of retiring comfortably, Jimmy couldn't stay away from the races. He accepted work as a minor racing official wherever they'd have him, and when he went away on vacation, Davern simply visited other tracks. He came back to the sport not because he *had* to or *wanted* to, but because he *needed* to. He missed the camaraderie. He missed his friends. And when Jimmy died of cancer late last year just before the start of this Suffolk Downs season (he'd told hardly anyone he was sick), his wake was packed with backstretch lifers who did nothing but swap great stories and laugh about the golden age of the game. Several times that night I overheard my all-time favorite Davern anecdote, and a composite version follows, much like Jimmy often told it himself, eyes bright with mischief:

> It's getaway day in Rhode Island, so of course we tie up a race. Now I'm the ringleader, so I've got all the money, see? We make a huge score, like maybe fifteen thousand, and I've got all this cash stuffed inside a shoe box so we can divide it up the next day when racing starts again at Suffolk. Except I'm in a good mood and I want to go out. So I meet up with a couple of lady friends

and we live it up, dancing the night away. The last thing I remember is shoving that damn shoe box underneath the front seat of my Caddy for safekeeping, and then the next thing I know it's just before dawn and I have no idea where I am. I see lots of tall buildings, so I figure I'm in Boston, and I have to be at work pretty soon to gallop horses. By blind luck, I see some guy on the street who just happens to be a horseplayer, and he gives me a lift out to the track. All the while I'm thinking the other jocks are going to kill me for losing all that money, and on top of that, I don't even know where I left my brand-new car, so I've written that off too. Then we pull into the parking lot—the sun is just starting to come up over the grandstand, it's a beautiful morning—and there, sitting all by itself in the middle of the empty lot, is my Caddy. The doors are wide open, the windows are all down, and the keys are in the ignition. I have no idea how it got there. I look under the front seat and there's the box, untouched and overflowing with money. Best of all, I just pulled on my riding boots over my street clothes, got my whip and helmet out of the trunk, and walked inside that stable gate to go work horses, grinning and thinking "What a life!"

At face value, this devil-may-care fable has nothing at all in common with the modern version of getaway day at Suffolk Downs. This afternoon, the final few races of the meet will tick into history with little fanfare, and no major wagering coup will be orchestrated at the betting windows. Even if some local jockey does end up wandering the streets in a disoriented funk at daybreak, his chances of being recognized by a racetrack enthusiast are about as remote as getting hit by lightning. If you play the game in New England, not only do you have few options once a race meet comes to a close, you most likely don't have a brand-new Cadillac to worry about misplacing, either. A whirlwind of change has blown the industry upside down since the days when likable rogues like Jimmy Davern lived a life of nostalgic hijinks. Yet one essential track trait remains, fully intact and unbroken, shared

just as fervently by free spirits from a bygone era as by today's dedicated lifers who've chosen to ride out recent hard times: a raw, visceral
love and profoundly deep respect for horse racing.

The allure of the sport has always been about overcoming disap-
pointment, defeat, and frustration. That's the seductiveness of the
gamble in this game, whatever the actual terms of the bet. There has
always been an unspoken willingness by racing's participants to endure
the lowest of lows for the remote possibility of latching onto the highest of highs, and it doesn't matter if your stake in the wager is financial, emotional, or physical: This form of gambling goes beyond cash-
ing tickets. Whether they're fans in the grandstand or laborers on the
backstretch, those who invest in horse racing with time, love, courage,
and determination have a lot more to lose than money. The payoff
comes when some sort of jubilant windfall finally *does* occur, because
those rare moments of Thoroughbred glory are euphoric, unequaled
and so powerfully high that they're nearly narcotic.

There is a cruel radiance to the racetrack: You can be so disappointed by failing to get what you aspire to that you never even realize that
obscurity can fuel a potent current of quiet dignity. Battered but not
beaten, the hard-luck horses and people of New England embody this
better than anyone else in the industry. The way the game is played at
the East Boston oval might not be the cleanest, the prettiest, or the
most aesthetically appealing, but the fact that it's still alive at all has to
count for *something*. A season at Suffolk Downs is about as honest as
it gets in this slickly marketed realm of modern racing, and the 2000
meet has been hallmarked by many difficult and gritty "low points"
that could easily have been stripped from this story to sanitize it. But
feel-good highlights selectively edited to guarantee a polite, upbeat
ending don't do justice to the reality of the racetrack and those who
embrace it. The hands-on horse workers, grind-it-out grandstanders,
bush-league jockeys, and lifelong losers at this downtrodden betting
factory aren't all shining testaments to the splendor of the game. But
that's not the point.

Splendor ain't all there is.

Two hours after the getaway day finale goes to a maiden named

Hoss'n Around, I find myself wandering the backstretch on a late spring night that badly wants to be summer, one of those pleasant, ephemeral New England evenings when the pavement still shimmers June heat after 8:00 PM and empty stables cast long, textured shadows in the dirt beneath searing pink twilight. Out beyond the gigantic Route 1A oil tanks, the sunset itself is a fierce orange smear refusing to yield, while simultaneously, hovering above Revere Beach, the thin, luminescent moon waits patiently for its turn to ascend. After a hot, sticky day, the wind has shifted direction and now wafts in off the Atlantic, and the balmy breeze offers a whiff of sea salt tinged with the organic backstretch aroma of decaying manure and fresh hay. Lines of heavy trucks rumble off the racetrack property, and from the rear of each and every horse van, curious Thoroughbred heads calmly peer at the receding surroundings, taking everything in with stoic equine anticipation, facing backward while looking forward to the next stop on the circuit.

Directly across from the eighth pole, a relaxed group of gate-crew workers and maintenance laborers mill about in front of a work shed adjacent to the barn area. Tom Schwigen—the longtime Suffolk Downs gate boss whose rough charm, rebel drawl, and cowboy swagger prevent him from being mistaken for anything other than a starter of horse races—holds out a cold beer and I gladly accept his offer. Some of the guys lounge around on neatly stacked piles of lumber (first thing tomorrow, the grandstand paddock will be demolished to make way for a bigger and better saddling enclosure), and the gang of assistant starters is actively engaged in topping each other's all-time war stories about the professional perils of working the gate. They trade harrowing tales of being locked inside steel cages with thrashing and bashing half-ton beasts and can rattle off the names of unruly gate horses from decades back, the way some Thoroughbred aficionados recall famous Kentucky Derby winners. The assistants brag and laugh about things like busted knuckles, crushed toes, and broken teeth, but for the most part, their audacious bravado is just a battle-weary way to blow off steam at the end of a long season. Off to the side, Schwigen modestly tells me his boys made it through 798 races from January through June without a serious gate mishap, a fact that starter Tom imparts quietly but with obvious pride, ranking the meet among the safest he's started in four decades of locking and loading 'em at tracks all throughout the East.

"Did you see Race 14 today?" Schwigen asks me, knowing full well that I did, nodding in the direction of one of his assistants. "Did you see the great work my man did to keep that filly calm?"

Tom is referring to an incident in which Ginkris became entangled in her starting stall. Although that mare ended up being freed without injury, her violent thrashing caused the skittish filly to her inside, Shahbella, to become frenzied with panic. The stewards scratched Ginkris as a veterinary precaution, but Shahbella, thanks to the crew member's calm but decisive action, ended up recovering well enough from her scare to win the race.

"Ah, that was nothin'," the assistant says, embarrassed at being singled out for praise. "I just grabbed her by the tail. Now from the grandstand, that looks mean. But that keeps her head straight and her feet on the ground. She wasn't going nowhere," he says, taking a strong pull off his longneck Bud before pointing it at his boss. "If it wasn't for that guy right there, I wouldn't know anything about handling horses the right way. He taught me all I know."

As the others drift off one by one, the gate guy and I banter back and forth until darkness softly asserts itself atop the backstretch barns. I don't know his name and he's never met me, but introductions aren't necessary when Thoroughbreds provide a common bond. We've seen each other coming and going at Suffolk Downs, but we both acknowledge that neither of us has a clue what the other one's racetrack work is like.

"Yeah, that's true," the assistant starter says, well aware that being good at his job requires not getting noticed. "No one ever knows what we actually *do* in there until we fuck up. Then, all of a sudden, everyone comes out of the woodwork with a better way of doing it."

Imploring me to stay for one more round, the gate crewman explains how he ended up on the front lines of the racing industry.

Many years ago, his grandfather owned the old binocular rental stand at Suffolk Downs ("back when people wanted to watch races in person instead of on jumbo TV screens"), and like any good granddad of the era, the old man took the curious kid with him everywhere he went, including—and most especially—to the racetrack and the bookie joint.

"Back then, the bookie always operated out of a cobbler's shop, in the back of some shoe repair store," he tells me. "*Always.* Now think about that for a minute. How many cobblers do you see around today, if that tells you anything? All the bookies and shoe repairmen have been forced out of business by changing times. And now, horse racing almost has too."

The kid grew up and tried his hand at various odd jobs, some of them at the track, but never one steady line of work that kept him gainfully employed around Thoroughbreds. He met a girl, got married, and bought a house. Last year, they invested in a cheap horse who had a myriad of nagging problems, with the hope of rehabbing and eventually racing the injured animal. On the Fourth of July, he cautioned his wife against taking the highly strung steed out of its stall for a pleasure jaunt, and his wife shattered her pelvis while trying to ride the unwilling racehorse against her husband's warnings.

"First thing I told her, lying crumpled on the ground, was 'I told you so.' So now, she's my ex-wife—no more house, no more horse, no more wife. For me at least, handling horses has always been a hell of a lot easier than handling people."

After nearly a year of being down on his luck and sleeping in cars on the East Boston backstretch, the horseless horseman finally caught a break when he heard Tom Schwigen had an opening on his crew. Landing on the gate team turned his life around, and the assistant starter credits his new gig with allowing him to save a little bit of money, finally obtain health insurance, move into a new apartment, and even begin dating a new girlfriend. Life is good right now, and to top it off, after the races today his boss told him he can use a guy like him on the gate this summer at Rockingham. The man's self-respect is evident when he beams and flashes the crisp hundred-dollar-bill starter Tom tipped him for a season's worth of work well done.

"But what I *really* want to do," the assistant says, getting ahead of himself, allowing his mind the luxury of reeling off a dream in the backstretch blackness, "is to raise my own Thoroughbred: train him, feed him, care for him, and someday watch him race. He doesn't even have to win. I don't care if he ever earns a cent. Just as long as I get him to the gate."

There is one of those long, unpredictable pauses in a conversation between two beer-buzzed strangers, but the moment does not feel at all awkward against the backdrop of a blissful New England evening.

"You know, I can't figure it," he says, breaking the silence with a broad sweep of his arm across the darkened Suffolk Downs home-stretch. "Why would anyone ever want to be anyplace else?"

EPILOGUE

SEVEN YEARS have elapsed between the time I first chronicled the 2000 Suffolk Downs season in a journal and this book's publication.

In December 2000, I resigned from my job as media relations director. I now work various freelance gigs, and I still return to Suffolk Downs to fill in as the track's backup announcer.

A number of executives also left Suffolk Downs roughly around the same time. The most notable departure was that of Lou Raffetto, now president and chief operating officer of the Maryland Jockey Club, which hosts the famous Preakness Stakes.

Suffolk Downs itself continues to struggle. Portions of the property have been sold for retail development to department stores, supermarkets, and fast-food chains. The local industry remains beset by political woes. Even the region's historic Thoroughbred calling card, the MassCap, has fallen victim to financial troubles: The showcase race was canceled in 2003, 2005, and 2006 because of the track's lack of money.

Horse owner Michael Gill branched out from coast to coast. As his enormous stable grew, so did the heat from the national spotlight, which focused on the way he treated horses and ran his business. Gill was passed over for the prestigious Eclipse Award for foremost owner in 2003 and 2004, despite leading North America in wins and purse earnings. When his stable again led the continent in 2005, he was voted outstanding owner. During his acceptance speech, Gill spoke bitterly and vowed to quit the sport.

Mike Catalano and Abby Fuller took a brief break from Thoroughbred racing. They later relocated to Florida and now train horses on the Gulfstream Park and Calder Race Course circuit.

Joe Hampshire won every riding title at Suffolk Downs between 2000 and 2003. He finished second in the 2004 standings, then left town to compete on the mid-Atlantic circuit. He currently rides at Philadelphia Park.

Then-rookie Dyn Panell is now the dominant rider in New England. Howard Lanci is still the clown prince of the locker room.

Rudy Baez is a racing official at Suffolk Downs, supervising the jockeys as clerk of scales.

Although they were mentioned only briefly in this book, I would like to pay respects to two jockeys who rode regularly at Suffolk Downs during the 2000 season: Gary Birzer fell from his mount at Mountaineer Park in July 2004 and crushed two vertebrae, paralyzing him from the waist down. Michel Lapensee died from severe neurological trauma at Suffolk Downs when he was trampled by trailing horses after his own mount broke a leg in October 2005.

My father and stepmother, Paul and Joyce Thornton, were each diagnosed with cancer in the autumn of 2001. Joyce fought with dignity, but she died in May 2002. After surgery and months of chemotherapy, my dad pulled through. During his recovery, he vowed to return to the track and work hands-on with horses, using the sport as his incentive. Cancer-free for the last four years, Paul Thornton trained award-winning New England horses in both 2005 and 2006, and was voted the region's outstanding trainer after his stable earned the highest Suffolk Downs winning percentage in 2006.

ACKNOWLEDGMENTS

THIS BOOK is based on my own personal observances, opinions, and research. In instances where another person's words or ideas explained something better than I could, those sources have been gratefully attributed.

Numerous racetrack media guides, news clippings, and press releases from the Suffolk Downs archives helped solidify the book. Some biographies and interviews (i.e., post-race quotes and stable notes) were compiled by other press-box staffers.

A number of periodicals provided a wealth of documentation: *Daily Racing Form*, the *Blood-Horse*, *Thoroughbred Times*, *American Turf Monthly*, *Turf and Sport Digest*, *Sports Illustrated*, and *New England Sport*.

Regional newspapers were valuable sources for details: the *Boston Globe*, *Boston Herald*, *Lawrence Eagle-Tribune*, *Lowell Sun*, *Providence Journal*, *New Hampshire Union Leader*, and *Revere Independent*.

I relied on a network of Thoroughbred organizations for specialized statistics: Equibase, The Jockey Club, Bloodstock Research Information Services, Association of Racing Commissioners International, Keeneland Library, and the Massachusetts State Racing Commission.

Two books especially shaped my thoughts on the manuscript: *Thirty*

Tons a Day, by Bill Veeck with Ed Linn; and *Racing Days,* with photographs by Henry Horenstein and text by Brendan Boyd. In addition, epigraphs at the start of several chapters came from *Twist the Axe,* by Maj Ragain; and *The Quotable Horse Lover,* edited by Steven D. Price.

A big thanks to the entire New England racing community, especially its press-box degenerates, past and present.

I am indebted to the entire PublicAffairs staff for taking a flier on a long-shot manuscript, and especially to Lisa Kaufman, who not only made this book happen, but made it better thanks to her meticulous editing.

Deep appreciation to my parents, Sandra and Paul, who probably never dreamed it would be a winning bet to introduce their son to the exhilarating world of the racetrack.

And much love and gratitude to my wife, Dena.

PUBLICAFFAIRS is a publishing house founded in 1997. It is a tribute to the standards, values, and flair of three persons who have served as mentors to countless reporters, writers, editors, and book people of all kinds, including me.

I. F. STONE, proprietor of *I. F. Stone's Weekly*, combined a commitment to the First Amendment with entrepreneurial zeal and reporting skill and became one of the great independent journalists in American history. At the age of eighty, Izzy published *The Trial of Socrates*, which was a national bestseller. He wrote the book after he taught himself ancient Greek.

BENJAMIN C. BRADLEE was for nearly thirty years the charismatic editorial leader of *The Washington Post*. It was Ben who gave the *Post* the range and courage to pursue such historic issues as Watergate. He supported his reporters with a tenacity that made them fearless, and it is no accident that so many became authors of influential, best-selling books.

ROBERT L. BERNSTEIN, the chief executive of Random House for more than a quarter century, guided one of the nation's premier publishing houses. Bob was personally responsible for many books of political dissent and argument that challenged tyranny around the globe. He is also the founder and was the longtime chair of Human Rights Watch, one of the most respected human rights organizations in the world.

· · ·

For fifty years, the banner of Public Affairs Press was carried by its owner Morris B. Schnapper, who published Gandhi, Nasser, Toynbee, Truman, and about 1,500 other authors. In 1983 Schnapper was described by *The Washington Post* as "a redoubtable gadfly." His legacy will endure in the books to come.

Peter Osnos, *Founder and Editor-at-Large*